NomosStudium

Prof. Dr. Gerhard Robbers
University of Trier

An Introduction to German Law

Seventh edition

 Nomos

Die Deutsche Nationalbibliothek verzeichnet diese Publikation in der Deutschen Nationalbibliografie; detaillierte bibliografische Daten sind im Internet über http://dnb.d-nb.de abrufbar.

Die Deutsche Nationalbibliothek lists this publication in the Deutsche Nationalbibliografie; detailed bibliographic data is available in the Internet at http://dnb.d-nb.de.

ISBN 978-3-8487-5834-0 (Print)
ISBN 978-3-8452-9968-6 (ePDF)

7. Auflage 2019
© Nomos Verlagsgesellschaft, Baden-Baden 2019. Gedruckt in Deutschland. Alle Rechte, auch die des Nachdrucks von Auszügen, der fotomechanischen Wiedergabe und der Übersetzung, vorbehalten.

Foreword to the seventh edition

The law is a topic for ongoing discussion. Its development, formation and application are constantly debated in the interests of attaining agreement and acceptance. This debate is open to an international audience, and it is part of the general democratic process. Such debate can only be fruitful if it does not lose itself in the details, if it preserves the wider perspective. This general introduction aims to contribute to the attainment of that wider perspective and does not claim to provide an exhaustive and penetrating analysis of the intricacies of the law. This aim is perhaps also sufficient justification for my boldness in going beyond the limits of my own area of specialisation. The diverse help and intensive advice of colleagues and co-workers has made this project possible. The translation into English is originally the work of Michael Jewell, revisions and updates for the previous edition had been translated by Nina and Oliver Windgätter, those for this edition have been inserted by the author.

Trier, May 2019 *Gerhard Robbers*

Translator's Note

Accurate translation of a legal text is a difficult task. On the one hand terminology must be chosen which makes it easy for the reader to relate the topic under discussion to similar ideas in his or her own legal system. On the other hand the danger of ignoring subtle differences in meaning must be avoided. In addition, a translator into English has to consider the fact that there are many countries in which legal business is conducted in English and that in the various countries different terms may be used to describe the same concept.

My approach has been to attempt to use the terminology of England wherever this is compatible with German thinking. I have done so for two reasons. The first is that England, as a country of the European Union, will presumably be the main market for this translation. The second is that the English system, being the original source of the common law, will hopefully be the most commonly accessible of the English language systems for other English speaking lawyers, whether in the Commonwealth, the United States or in countries where English is the main foreign language.

I have included key German terms in brackets for the benefit of those who already have some knowledge of German legal terminology or wish to acquire it.

Michael Jewell

Table of contents

A. General Structures

I. The Legal Tradition, Areas of Law and Sources of Law

1. The Legal Tradition

The German legal system is closely connected to the overall development of the European and Anglo-American legal systems. Situated in the centre of Europe, Germany has, from the earliest times, experienced a constant exchange of legal ideas. Common roots and historical experiences are the reasons for the structural similarities of the legal systems; their differences are answers to the special circumstances of each country's political development. In particular, the unification of Europe in the European Union is today playing a part in the strengthening of common features. There is hardly an area of the law today which is not at least touched, if not moulded, by the law of the European Union. This development is new in terms of institutional structures, but not in the substance of generally common development. 1

The idea of codifying the law, which grew out of the European Enlightenment of the 17th and 18th centuries, together with 19th century political efforts to achieve unification, led to the creation of comprehensive statutes for a series of important areas of the law. These give German law the characteristics of a codified legal system, in other words, one whose rules are laid down in legislation which covers all aspects of the law. This characteristic is not the least of the factors which identify German law as Continental European. Nevertheless, the decisions of the courts play a considerable role in the further development and concretisation of the law, so that the contrast to the Anglo-American tradition is less sharp than it is often said to be. 2

Like most other Continental European legal systems, German law is to this day profoundly shaped by the reception of the Roman law. Gathered together in late antiquity, many Roman legal rules were disseminated throughout Europe between the 12th and 16th centuries, starting in Upper Italy. This dogmatically perfected, written legal system was accepted alongside, and often in the place of, the various Germanic tribal customs. Particularly in the 19th century, these inherited texts were systematised and form the basis for the law in force in Germany today. 3

The current shape of German law cannot be understood without bearing in mind the catastrophe of the National Socialist dictatorship from 1933 to 1945. Up to the present day, the formulation and application of laws is influenced in significant ways by the desire to avoid a repetition of such injustice. In particular, this is the justification for the fact that the German Basic Law, as the constitution of a social, democratic, constitutional state under the rule of law, permeates all other areas of the law. Today, the key characteristics of the German legal system are the central role of the Bill of Fundamental Rights (*Grundrechte*) and the principle that Germany is a constitutional state under the rule of law (*Rechtsstaatsprinzip*). They give the entire legal system, down into its smallest details, structure and direction. This and the considerable influence of constitutional review are powerful forces for the constitutionalisation of politics. The various elements of this development, with further characteristics of a constitutional democracy such as democratic government, the social state and federalism, are rooted in older traditions which have often taken centuries to develop and which, to a lesser or greater extent, are common to all countries of the European-North Atlantic legal family. 4

5   The catastrophe of National Socialism also runs through the ongoing debate between legal Positivism and anti-positivist legal thinking. This discussion is about the question from whence the law receives its binding force. Typical of legal Positivism is the currently dominant view that positively given law and morality are strictly separate issues. In this view, even extremely immoral laws can claim to be legally binding, although not morally binding. The only prerequisite is that the provisions in question should have been declared to be law by the appropriate authorities. The positive effects of this view are that it leads to dependability, constancy and certainty of legal orientation; negative effects can be that it leads to unacceptable contents of the legal order. Anti-positivist theories, on the other hand, insist that it is an essential requirement for a valid law that it should be in accordance with ethical principles. In this view, law loses its binding force whenever it comes into conflict with fundamental moral principles. The standards against which the law is measured are derived from various sources: from historical experience; as natural law from human nature or from nature as a whole; from practical reason; as fundamental structural principles derived from cultural or historical development in the sense of a cultural or natural law with variable content; from divine revelation or creation; or, lastly, from the common body of international thinking on human rights. Both the positivist and the anti-positivist schools of thought are of approximately equal strength, although in practice a cautious positivism is perhaps the predominant view again. Its possible excesses are moderated by the social force of the Basic Law and its inherent legitimacy. However, it is not very fruitful to view these two approaches in sharp opposition. Rather, one should seek the common ground.

2. Areas of Law

a) Private Law – Public Law – Criminal Law

6   Traditionally, the law is subdivided into the three great fields of private law, public law and criminal law. This division is also universally followed in academic teaching. The position accorded to certain legal principles depends on it, as does the structure of the legal system. Based on historical developments, these distinctions are in part objectively well justified. However, there are numerous areas of overlapping, and with the development of new areas of law and shifts in legal and constitutional theory, this classification is increasingly questionable.

7   Many theories have been developed to distinguish private law from public law. The dominant theory today is the theory of specialised law. It describes public law as the embodiment of those rules which confer powers and impose obligations exclusively on the holders of public office. This means in particular the state, but also supranational organisations such as the European Communities. Private law, on the other hand, is directed at all legal subjects. According to an interpretation typical of 19th century thinking, this theory has as its background the right of the state in the public sphere to command its citizens and to expect obedience, while equality and freedom of the individual were considered to be characteristic of the private sphere. Today, the point of distinction is rather that the state is more strictly limited by public law, for example, by the Fundamental Rights, and that its powers need special justification.

8   However, in practice both areas of the law are converging increasingly. In private law, inequalities of bargaining power, for example between large companies and consumers, are increasingly regulated according to standards which were developed for

the curbing of state power. On the other hand the state may not avoid its constitutional duties even if it makes use of the rules of private law.

Public law includes the following: The Constitution, which at the Federal level means   9
the *Grundgesetz*, and at the level of the *Länder* also the constitution of each *Land*. It also includes amongst many others the law on voting rights, citizenship, political parties, the regulation of the functioning of the various organs of state such as the *Bundestag* and *Bundesrat*, the rules of court and procedural law. The general principles of administrative law as well as its various specialised fields, such as the law regulating the police, foreign nationals, local government, state officials, the environment, public building operations and taxation are also considered to be part of public law.

Despite the fact that it is traditionally classified into a category of its own and treated   10
separately, criminal law is in effect also part of public law, because only the state has the authority to inflict punishment. Nevertheless, it traditionally viewed as an independent area of law. It includes the law on lesser offences (*Ordnungswidrigkeiten*) which reacts to lesser wrongs with warnings and fines.

Private law, with its fundamental concept of private autonomy, takes as its starting   11
point the individual as a free legal subject and provides legal institutions to facilitate the free development of the personality such as contract, ownership and possession, the company or the institution of marriage. This area too is regulated in numerous individual laws, with its centre in the Civil Code (*Bürgerliches Gesetzbuch*, abbreviated *BGB*). However, it is often the case that public law provisions are contained in statutory instruments which must essentially be regarded as part of the civil law, and vice versa.

b) Substantive and Adjective Law

A further, widely used distinction concerns the difference between substantive and ad-   12
jective law. This distinction, too, is fluid and often the one category blurs into the other. The substantive law includes the rights and duties of legal subjects as well as the basis of legal institutions such as contract, public office, or marriage. Adjective law on the other hand is a term to describe the ways in which rights are enforced: procedural law, the rules for the conduct of litigation (evidence) and the division of powers.

c) Relationship to European and International Law

The law of the European Union is an independent legal system which is tightly inter-   13
woven with the legal systems of the member states. Insofar as these categories have any relevance, it can be said to include public law, private law and even the beginnings of criminal law. Article 23 paragraph 1 of the *Grundgesetz* imposes on the Federal Republic an obligation to integrate itself into the European Union.

The *Grundgesetz* also shows a very positive attitude to public international law. Public   14
international law consists primarily of the law which governs the relations of one state to another. The – few – generally accepted rules of public international law form part of German law and take precedence over ordinary statutes.[1]

---

1 Article 25 GG.

3. Sources of Law

a) Statutory Instruments

15   The central function of statute law in the German legal system is immediately obvious. Statute is an expression and prerequisite of the general application of the law, and thus of the essentially equal applicability of the law to every person. At the same time it is an expression and prerequisite of the public nature of the law, a necessary condition for its democratically justified force. Statute is considered to be an essential basis for reliable justice whose task it is to provide a secure point of reference. It must be admitted that this function is increasingly called into question by the frequency of amendments, to which the statutes are almost entirely subject. The complexity of the language used, and the great number of laws and their labyrinthine structure also impede to an ever increasing extent their function of making the law available to the public – for an ordinary citizen a statute often is hardly comprehensible any more. On the other hand, the technical complexity of many problems makes detailed regulation necessary. All in all, the idea of codification seems to have reached a crisis point. Nevertheless, statute is still decisive for wide fields of the law.

16   In the material sense, every abstract general legal rule is a statute (*Gesetz*). In principle they are applicable in an unlimited number of cases, i.e. they are abstract, and the are applicable to every person, i.e. they are general. It can take the form of a constitution; a parliamentary statute; an ordinance, regulation or executive order made by the government or an administrative body on the authority of a parliamentary statute; or a by-law of the sort which self-administrating bodies such as a commune (the smallest unit of local government) are authorised to make. A statute in the formal sense on the other hand, includes only those rules which are passed into law by parliament irrespective of their content. Such a statute could therefore regulate a single specific situation.

b) Decisions of the Courts

17   Despite the significance of the codification concept it would be incorrect to regard the German legal system one-sidedly as being determined by statute and thus to see it in strict contrast to the Anglo-American and other systems who place emphasis on judge-made law. Judge-made law, that is, the legal principles developed and concretised in court decisions, carry considerable weight in the German system too. This is primarily so because of the unavoidable need to interpret and concretise statutes – a statute can never anticipate all the possible situations which might arise in practice. The legislator often deliberately avoids overly specific regulation of specialist problems and leaves the development of the law to the courts.

18   On the other hand the overwhelming consensus in Germany is that the decisions of the courts are not a source of law. They are merely an indication of what those, whose job it is to apply the law, understand the law to be. But even from this starting point the courts have often played a dominant role in the development of the law. In doing so, they have at the very least supplanted the academic writings which, from the 19th century right up to the middle of the 20th century, often exercised a decisive influence over German law. Nevertheless, even today academic writings are of some importance in the development of legal theory, i.e., in the presentation of the internal logic of legal rules.

The idea of binding the courts by the decisions of the courts above them in the sense of a strict doctrine of precedent is unknown in German doctrine. This would mean that the decisions of higher courts on a particular point of law would bind all subsequent judicial decisions, and could only be overcome under observation of strict limits. Instead, in German law it is generally the case that court decisions only have the force of law between the parties to that particular dispute. The courts are bound to observe the requirements of statute law and justice[2] not the previous decisions of courts. Thus, even for a lower court, the decisions of the highest courts are not binding. An *Amtsgericht*, the lowest German court, can reach a different conclusion and decision from that which the *Bundesgerichtshof*, the highest civil court in Germany, has reached previously on the very same point of law. Only when a higher court in deciding a case on review has set aside the decision of the lower court and referred the case back for a new decision is the decision of the higher court binding, and then only in that specific case.   19

To nevertheless attain the necessary measure of consistency in the decisions of the courts the second-highest level of courts (*e.g. Oberlandesgericht*) must, generally speaking, refer the matter to a higher court for a decision on the point of law if they wish to depart from the reasoning previously followed by an *Oberlandesgericht* or higher court. Such a referral is known as a "divergence referral" (*Divergenzvorlage*). For that specific case, the court making the referral is then bound by the legal opinion of the higher court. Similar provision is made for the situation where one senate of one of the highest courts wishes to diverge from the jurisprudence of another senate of the same court. In this situation a so-called "Grand Senate", consisting of individual judges from various senates, is called together to make a binding decision on the point of law.   20

An exception is also made in the case of the Federal Constitutional Court (*Bundesverfassungsgericht*, abbreviated *BVerfG*). In terms of section 31 para. 1 of the Federal Constitutional Court Act (*Bundesverfassungsgerichtsgesetz*, abbreviated *BVerfGG*) its decisions bind the constitutional organs of the Federal Government and the various States as well as all courts of law and administrative structures. In some cases its decisions have the force of statute law.   21

However, it would be a distortion of the practical reality to look at things solely from the formal, legal point of view given above. The decisions of the superior courts have a decisive influence on all court decisions which goes far beyond what has already been said. In the great majority of cases the lower courts follow the decisions of the higher courts. The power of the higher courts to restructure the law can hardly be emphasised enough. The superior courts often formulate a type of headnote containing the *ratio decidendi* of the case (*Leitsatz*), which is printed at the head of the published version of the decision. These, by now, have achieved a quasi-normative force.   22

Finally, it is not entirely unheard of for the courts to go beyond a mere interpretative, concretising, gap-filling approach. Sometimes they also reach conclusions which are in conflict with the wording of the statute. Such development of the law is not totally impermissible. If circumstances or the convictions of the legal community change it can become the duty of the courts to decide against the literal meaning of the statute (*contra legem*). The basis and extent of this exception are, however, extremely contentious.   23

---

2   Article 20 para. 3; article 97 GG.

Whatever the extent of this power may be, the courts are always bound by the value judgements of the constitution.[3]

c) Custom

24 Related to the law created by the courts, but nevertheless to be strictly distinguished from it, is customary law. Custom is recognised as a source of law. It is a consequence of the legal force of factual situations, specifically custom, tradition, and values handed down over time. One speaks of customary law when a practice of long standing exists and the persons affected by the practice are convinced that it is legal. Such customary law is binding on the courts if they are making a decision on the point in question. Some critics argue that before a custom can become binding on the courts it must first have been recognised by the courts. Sometimes the requirement that the practice be of long standing is also called into question. In view of the fact that on most points the legal system has been worked out in detail by statutes or decisions of the courts, only a very limited place remains for the customary law. Customary law on the local level does, however, have some relevance. Here, one speaks of an observance. For example, in deciding whether a path or road is a public way in actual use by the general public, reference is made to the fact that there is a long tradition of actual use by the public which has always been considered to be legal.

d) The Hierarchy of Norms

25 The traditional view is that various types of legal rule stand one below the other in a clear and strictly hierarchical relationship, the so-called ladder structure of the legal system. There is an order of priority between legal rules. In each case the rule one step below must be consistent with the rule one step above it. If that is not the case, then the lower, inconsistent rule is null and void, and indeed this usually applies from the moment the two rules are in collision, i.e., *ex tunc*.

26 The highest written norm in the German system is the constitution. On the federal level this is the Basic Law (*Grundgesetz,* abbreviated *GG*). In terms of article 1 para. 3 GG the Fundamental Rights are binding on legislation, judicial decisions and the executive as law with immediate effect. In terms of article 20 para. 3 GG the legislature is bound by the constitutional order, and executive authority and the courts are bound by law and justice. In this way the constitution lays down its primacy over all other laws of the state. It binds all other laws of the state to the sovereignty of the People, who, as the giver of the constitution, have created the binding basis of all law.

27 An extremely contentious question is whether an unwritten natural law of binding force stands above the constitution. The Federal Constitutional Court reached a cautious conclusion on this point, which reaches into the most fundamental questions of belief, at an early stage. It said that it was not feasible to make a constitutional ruling on the basis of theories of natural law because of the large number of conflicting theories which compete with one another as soon as one leaves the sphere of fundamental

---

3   See BVerfGE 34, 269/280; 96, 375/398.
    BVerfGE: *Entscheidungen des Bundesverfassungsgerichts* – decisions of the Federal Constitutional Court. The following is an example of how these law reports are cited: BVerfGE 65, 182/190; 34, 269/280. This citation refers to two cases. It means that the first case cited can be found in volume 65 of the reports. The case starts at page 182 of the report and the passage cited is at page 190. The second case is in volume 34 and starts at page 269, the passage cited being at page 280.

legal rules. For the decision of specific questions the only possible guide is the Basic Law.[4] However, according to an earlier decision of the court even a provision of the constitution can be void if it disregards to a completely intolerable extent fundamental principles of justice, which belong to the basic values embodied in the constitution.[5] These principles have been confirmed by the Federal Constitutional Court in its judgements on the subject of unjust laws in the former East Germany (German Democratic Republic, *Deutsche Demokratische Republik, DDR*), and in which it has especially pointed at the fundamental principles laid down in the international human rights treaties.

Next in rank to the constitution is the formal statute passed by parliament. Thereafter come statutory instrument and by-laws. Administrative regulations are also of considerable importance. They are initially promulgated by the executive as internal administrative guidelines and are thus intended to be binding only on the administrative authority to which they are directed. They aim at producing the greatest possible consistency in the interpretation, concretisation and application of the law. Due to the duty to treat like cases alike, which arises from article 3 para. 1 GG, they can also have force outside of the administration. In addition the Federal Administrative Court (*Bundesverwaltungsgericht*, abbreviated *BVerwG*) has recognised that the administrative organs of state have their own competence to concretise statute law in terms of which administrative regulations can also have binding effect for the courts.[6] 28

Decisions of the executive and courts are bound by all of these higher norms insofar as these norms are themselves valid. 29

A further complication arises from the structure of Germany as a federal state. The basic principle is that the fulfilment of the functions of the state is a matter for the various States of the federation. The – numerous – areas of competence of the structures at federal level are expressly listed.[7] A further principle, however, is that federal law "breaks" (takes precedence over) State law.[8] This means that if the law of a particular State collides with a law made by the Federation, then the federal legislation takes precedence. No further distinction is made according to the rank of the law in question. Subordinate legislation at federal level will take precedence even over the constitution of a State, insofar as the Federation has the competence to make a law on the matter in question. 30

Public international law (law of nations) in principle takes its place beside Germany's national law. In terms of article 59 para. 2 GG, international treaties require incorporation by statute to have any force within Germany. This applies insofar as they regulate the political relations of the Federation or relate to subjects of federal legislation. They then have the status of an ordinary, formal, federal statute. This is, for example, the position regarding the *European Convention for the Protection of Human Rights and Fundamental Freedoms*. A further detail is contained in article 25 GG: The general rules of international law are part of federal law. They take precedence over statute and create rights and duties for the inhabitants of the Federal Republic without more. This is a particularly clear instance of the open and friendly attitude which the Basic 31

---

4 BVerfGE 10, 59/81.
5 BVerfGE 3, 225/232 ff.; 95, 96/132 ff.
6 BVerwGE 72, 300/320.
7 Articles 30, 70 ff., 83 ff. GG.
8 Article 31 GG.

Law takes towards international law. Such general rules of international law require no act of incorporation to have binding force within Germany. On the other hand, up to the present only a few fundamental principles have been recognised as general rules of international law. Nevertheless, the minimum standards set by international law do have some relevance in the law relating to aliens: Foreigners must be treated as legal subjects, they have a right of access to independent courts, they may not be treated in an inhuman manner and may not be arrested without legal ground. Such general rules of international law form a step of their own in the ladder of the legal system: below the constitution, but above parliamentary statutes.

32   The law of the European Union exists as an independent legal system. As far as the Federal Republic of Germany is concerned, the sovereign powers which have been transferred to the EU have formerly been transferred by way of article 24 para. 1 GG. In terms of this provision the federation is entitled to transfer sovereign powers to international organisations by statute. As far as the European Union is concerned, article 23 GG now contains very detailed corresponding provisions. Article 24 GG remains of importance for the transfer of sovereign powers to other interstate authorities. An example is Eurocontrol, the European-wide air traffic control system which exercises sovereign powers in the performing of its functions in ensuring safety.

33   It is the general view that the law of the European Union takes precedence over German law in a concrete case, including the constitution. Primary Union law, in other words the founding treaties of the Union as well as the various complementary and amending agreements, can, however, be scrutinised by the Federal Constitutional Court for compatibility with the Basic Law (*Normenkontrolle*). This can be done, because in terms of article 59 para. 2 GG the Constitutional Court is entitled to test the constitutionality of the parliamentary statutes which approve the various treaties. With respect to secondary Union law, in other words the laws promulgated by the various organs of the Union, a particular problem arises as to whether they are subject to being tested for compatibility with the Fundamental Rights guaranteed in the German Constitution. On this point the Federal Constitutional Court has ruled that in principle such testing is possible, and that the secondary community law is thus subordinate to the German Fundamental Rights, insofar as German cases are concerned. It adds that the necessary enforcement of rights is undertaken by the Federal Constitutional Court in co-operation with the Court of Justice of the European Union in Luxembourg. The Federal Constitutional Court will concern itself with the general protection of a certain absolute minimum standard, while the Court of Justice of the European Union will guarantee the protection of Fundamental Rights in specific cases.[9] The Federal Constitutional Court thus claims a sort of reserve jurisdiction in cases in which the protection of fundamental rights by the Court of Justice of the European Union no longer seems to be generally guaranteed due to failures in many individual cases or where in a particular case fundamental rights have suffered an intolerable violation. This is a far-reaching proposition, but it is justified by peculiarities of a gradual transfer of ever more sovereign rights and thus public responsibility to the European institutions.

---

9   BVerfGE 89, 155 ff.

e) Interpretation

Law lives in the medium of language. Legal rules are fixed in language, usually in writ-   34
ing. They require interpretation to be understood. Such legal interpretation is one of
the main tasks of lawyers. A highly sophisticated methodology has been developed for
this purpose. In the past a series of different interpretative methods were distinguished.
The literal approach to interpretation asks what the current possible meaning of the
words of the rule may be. The grammatical approach looks carefully at the grammatical structure, and often the position of a single comma can change the entire meaning
of a sentence. The systematic approach considers the rule in the system of the statute
as a whole, which produces, for example, indications of the character of the provision
– whether it is a rule or an exception, or what its scope in a particular sphere of life is.
"Genetic" interpretation looks for indications of how a provision should be interpreted in the events immediately surrounding its creation, for example, in the records of
parliamentary debates and the reasons given for the passing of the law. This is usually
done with the intention of discovering the subjective will of the legislator. The broader
historical approach to interpretation puts the rule in the context of wider historical developments and sees it as a part of political and social development, as part of the history of law and of ideas. Finally, teleological interpretation asks what the meaning and
purpose (Greek: *telos*) of the rule is. Various other approaches to interpretation are often listed alongside these classical approaches, for example the comparative law approach to interpretation, the application of rules with reference to their likely results,
their acceptability, and, in the context of European integration, EU-friendly integra-
tion-oriented interpretation.

Up to the present no particular order in which the approaches should be applied or   35
hierarchy importance of approaches has established itself. Each of the approaches has
its place in interpreting a provision, and only when all are applied together does one
gain an accurate idea of what the provision is to achieve. One must also always bear
in mind the circumstances which the rule was designed to regulate. Today the teleological approach is to a certain extent dominant while the words of the text serve to limit
the number of possible interpretations. A particularly significant question is whether
the subjective will of the historical legislator as determined by interpretation is binding, or rather the objective meaning of the statute. The courts often accord the subjective will of the legislature only secondary importance, because it is often difficult to
establish, and particularly because it can often be outdated: What the legislature had
in mind in 1896 when it set up "*boni mores*" as a standard for determining the validity of contracts in section 138 of the Civil Code (§ 138 BGB) would often not be appropriate in the modern situations which the Civil Code is required to regulate. It is
rather the objective, modern will of the statute which is binding. No doubt in the case
of new statutes the views of the legislator will be of greater relevance in determining
this objective will than would be the case for older laws. Teleological interpretation,
which asks what the purpose of the law is, is more the very aim of interpretation than
a method of interpretation among others. If there is a gap in a statute, i.e., if no express statutory provision is made for a particular set of circumstances, then reasoning
by analogy is often helpful. This involves the application of a legal rule to a different,
but similar, set of facts.

Because of the pre-eminent status of the constitution, the so-called constitutional con-   36
formity approach to interpretation (*verfassungskonforme Auslegung*) which has been

developed by the Federal Constitutional Court is of particular importance. If a law is amenable to several different interpretations, of which one would bring the law into conflict with the constitution and another would be compatible with the constitution, then that interpretation is to be preferred which would make the law compatible with the constitution. In this way the right of the legislature to lead is respected.

II. Structure and Functioning of the Court System

1. General Structures and Principles

37 The basic rules on the structure and functioning of the courts are contained in article 20 para. 3 and article 92 ff. GG. Provisions, which apply to the court system in general, can also be found in the Law on the Constitution of Courts (*Gerichtsverfassungsgesetz*, abbreviated *GVG*). The provisions of the various procedural acts regulate further details for particular branches of the court system. The most important of these are the Civil Procedure Act (*Zivilprozessordnung,* abbreviated *ZPO*); the Criminal Procedure Act (*Strafprozessordnung,* abbreviated *StPO*); the Administrative Courts Act (*Verwaltungsgerichtsordnung,* abbreviated *VwGO*); the Labour Courts Act (*Arbeitsgerichtsgesetz*); the Finance Courts Act (*Finanzgerichtsordnung*); the Social Courts Act (*Sozialgerichtsgesetz*); and the Federal Constitutional Court Act (*Bundesverfassungsgerichtsgesetz* abbreviated *BVerfGG*). In addition there is the procedural law of the European courts.

38 Legal disputes are decided exclusively by judges. The judges are subject to nothing other than the requirements of the law and justice. This principle of the independence of the judiciary is one of the central achievements of the modern constitutional state under the rule of law (*Rechtsstaat*). The judge is independent in a double sense in terms of article 97 GG. Firstly, nobody, particularly not the government or the administrative apparatus, can dictate to the judge what the decision on the case should be. Secondly, the exercise of his or her judicial function can and may not have personal consequences for the judge. For this reason judges are essentially appointed for life. Against their will they can only be dismissed prematurely, sent into compulsory retirement, suspended from office or transferred to a different court if this is ordered by a court decision in accordance with the law.

39 Generally speaking, cases are decided by professional judges. However, the German system also has lay judges. These are citizens who take up an honorary position as judge in addition to their normal jobs for a specified period of time. They are chosen for this position by an extremely complex procedure. They always sit as part of a panel of judges, but their vote is of equal weight to that of the professional judge. The original aim of this institution was to bring into the legal system expert knowledge, a popular element and democratic transparency, although it is questionable whether this has really been achieved.

40 All court cases, insofar as the proceedings are oral, are public. Only in special circumstances, for example, where the spectators are guilty of gross misconduct, or where it is necessary for the protection of the parties to the proceedings, or for reasons of state, can the public be excluded. The original aim of holding hearings in public was to ensure the observance of due process by allowing the public to observe proceedings and thus protect those affected against arbitrary state action. On the other hand, in modern times the need to protect the parties, the accused, or witnesses from publicity has

become an increasingly important factor, because exposure in the media can often have more severe consequences than the penalty imposed by the court. Even a finding of not guilty can often not make good the damage caused to the parties by the public discussion of the case. Especially for this reason, but also for the purpose of avoiding a threat to the independence of the judges' decision, a ban is imposed on radio and television transmissions. The taking of pictures or the making of films or tape recordings for publication is also in principle not allowed during proceedings.[10]

2. The Structure of the Court System

The courts are essentially divided into five big groups which correspond to the main divisions of the law: the regular courts (*ordentliche Gerichtsbarkeit*), the Labour Courts, the General Administrative Courts, the Social Courts, and the Financial Courts. In addition to these there are the Constitutional Courts, and finally the European jurisdiction. There is no supreme court with jurisdiction over all aspects of the law equivalent to the Supreme Court of the United Kingdom, or the US Supreme Court or the Swiss *Bundesgericht*. This separation of jurisdictions leads, not infrequently, to different approaches to specific questions and often to difficult problems of distinguishing fields of jurisdiction and separating legal issues. A logical justification for maintaining this division, which owes its development to historical factors, lies in the special expertise which is made possible by the specialisation of the courts. Because the various fields of law are often based on different fundamental principles and have different procedural rules, it may be that this approach leads to better decisions in specific cases. The separation of jurisdiction certainly is not conducive to achieving unity in the legal system. 41

Apart from the vertical division of different fields of jurisdiction one beside the other, there is also a horizontal, hierarchical division into various instances. As a general rule a case begins in one of the lower courts, and can often end up in one of the higher courts by way of a series of legal remedies. The most important of these legal remedies are appeal on questions of fact or law (*Berufung*), proceedings in error similar to the English order of certiorari (*Revision*), and the request for relief from an administrative or court order (*Beschwerde*). In an appeal (*Berufung*) the appellate court re-hears the entire matter, in other words it also re-tries material issues of fact and hears witnesses. In proceedings in error (*Revision*) the court only deals with disputes on points of law. In contrast to this the request for relief (*Beschwerde*) generally only relates to one or two specific issues arising out of the whole trial. The various instances also each have jurisdiction for a specific geographical area. Court decisions are delivered by single judges, or panels of judges referred to as a chamber (*Kammer*) or senate (*Senat*). Whatever the composition of the court it is referred to as a *Spruchkörper*. 42

A decision as to which panel will hear a case and which judges will be part of the panel must always be taken before the matter is pending so as to rule out all possibility of manipulation. For this purpose every court draws up a plan allocating duties to the various panels. 43

Without going into detail, the situation can thus be described as follows: The jurisdiction of the regular courts (*ordentliche Gerichtsbarkeit*) includes the civil and the criminal jurisdictions. These were the only fields which had been entrusted to independent 44

---

10 § 169 GVG.

courts at the start of the 19th century, thus the description "regular courts" which originates from this period. Civil jurisdiction essentially covers disputes at private law. Criminal jurisdiction includes criminal matters and cases arising from the law on lesser offences.

45   The lowest court of regular jurisdiction is the *Amtsgericht*, which corresponds roughly to the English Magistrates' Court or County Court. One step up is the *Landgericht*. Above it is the *Oberlandesgericht* and finally there is the highest of the regular courts, the *Bundesgerichtshof* which has its seat in Karlsruhe and Leipzig. The territorial jurisdiction of the *Bundesgerichtshof* covers the whole of the Federal Republic of Germany and it is one of the supreme federal courts. The *Oberlandesgericht* is in each case the highest court of a particular State (*Land*) and each is responsible for normally several *Landgerichte*. These in turn are each responsible for usually several *Amtsgerichte*.

46   Alongside the regular courts stand the Labour Courts (*Arbeitsgerichte*). They decide labour disputes, such as whether the dismissal of a worker was permissible. The various instances in the hierarchy, in ascending order, are the *Arbeitsgericht*, the *Landesarbeitsgericht* and the *Bundesarbeitsgericht* whose seat is in Erfurt.

47   The general administrative courts decide administrative disputes insofar as these do not fall within the jurisdiction of one of the special administrative courts, namely the Social Courts or the Finance Courts. In certain specific cases jurisdiction over administrative disputes has been given to the regular courts for historical or practical reasons. Thus, the decision as to the amount of compensation to be paid where property is expropriated in terms of article 14 para. 3 GG must be made by the regular courts. The general administrative courts are arranged in the hierarchy *Verwaltungsgericht*, *Oberverwaltungsgericht* (in some States this level is referred to as the *Verwaltungsgerichtshof*) and the *Bundesverwaltungsgericht* which sits in Leipzig.

48   The social courts decide matters arising from social legislation, for example, whether someone has a claim to an old-age pension. The hierarchy consists of the *Sozialgericht*, the *Landessozialgericht* and the *Bundessozialgericht* in Kassel.

49   The finance courts deal with matters arising from the law of taxation. Here there are only two levels: the *Finanzgericht* at the *Land* level, and the *Bundesfinanzhof* in Munich.

50   The division of the courts according to various areas of law can lead to inconsistencies on particular points of law. To solve such problems a common senate of the highest courts of the Federation is provided for in article 95 para. 3 GG. This admittedly has very limited jurisdiction. It consists of judges drawn from the highest federal court in each field.

51   Federal courts are only empowered to decide issues of federal law. On questions of state law the courts of the State have the final say. In addition these courts serve as the lower instances in matters relating to federal law. There is thus not a complete institutional separation of jurisdictions according to whether state law or federal law is applicable. However, some areas of federal law may only be dealt with by federal courts. For example, for disciplinary measures against soldiers the first instance is the Armed Services Court with the possibility of an appeal to the Federal Administrative Court (*Bundesverwaltungsgericht*). For public servants in the service of the federal government (*Bundesbeamte*) disciplinary matters are dealt with by the Federal Disciplinary Court at first instance and appeals go to specialised senates – the disciplinary senates –

of the Federal Administrative Court. In addition there are the judicial service courts for disciplinary matters relating to federal judges. Lastly, the Federal Patents Court is the first instance for matters relating to patents, with appeals going to the *Bundesgerichtshof*, the highest of the "regular" courts. In terms of article 96 para. 2 of the Basic Law the special military courts only come into existence if war breaks out.

Constitutional courts have an exceptional position in the system. Each State has set up a constitutional court (*Verfassungsgerichtshof*, sometimes known as the *Staatsgerichtshof*). They decide disputes arising from the constitution of each State according to procedures laid down in state law.   52

Of exceptional importance is the Federal Constitutional Court (*Bundesverfassungsgericht*) in Karlsruhe.[11] It is the highest German court and is one of the most powerful and highly respected institutions in Germany. The Federal Constitutional Court deals exclusively with questions relating to the Basic Law which come to it by way of one of several specifically listed procedures.[12] However, since the Basic Law – of course notwithstanding the validity of the European Union law – is the highest norm in the entire German legal system, and influences all areas of the law, the entire legal system is shaped by the jurisprudence of the Federal Constitutional Court. Separating constitutional law from ordinary law is often difficult. Even although the Federal Constitutional Court often has to decide highly politicised issues, its decisions nevertheless remain legal decisions. It does not have the option of refusing to decide a point of law on the basis that it has particularly intensive political implications.   53

Finally, the growing significance of the jurisprudence of the Courts of the European Union for Germany must be noted. These courts are the General Court (*Gericht der Europäischen Union,* abbreviated *EuG*) and the European Court of Justice (*Europäischer Gerichtshof,* abbreviated *EuGH*), both of which sit in Luxembourg. Their influence is exerted through the procedures which are provided for in European Union law, particularly in the procedure for giving a preliminary ruling on points of law. In terms of this procedure, courts of the member states which are in doubt as to the correct interpretation of a point of Union law relevant to the case before them refer the point to the Courts of the European Union for decision. The decision is then binding for the court which referred the matter (article 267 TFEU). Neither the material law nor the interaction of state institutions can be understood today without constantly bearing in mind the role of Union law.   54

III. Legal Education and Careers

In Germany the concept of a lawyer is determined by the idea of the all-round lawyer. A qualified lawyer is expected in principle to be competent to deal with every aspect of the law, with due allowance for an initial period of familiarisation with the details of a special area. Every law graduate is in principle able to take up any type of legal career. Legal education thus aims primarily at the teaching of legal methods, not of detailed rules. Law is studied in the law faculties of the universities. It stands alongside other fields of study – a general first degree in another subject is not a prerequisite for studying law. The period of study at university lasts about 8 semesters, in other words, four years, but there is no upper limit. It culminates in the First Judicial Examination (*Erste*   55

---

11 Articles 92 ff. GG.
12 See, for example, articles 93 and 100 GG.

Juristische Prüfung), after which the student has the status of a *Referendar*. This is the equivalent of having completed a law degree but not yet having been admitted to practice. The examination is administered in part by the state justice ministries in co-operation with professors and practitioners, as well as in part by the universities themselves.

56   This is followed by a two-year period of practical training called the *Referendariat*. The *Referendar* spends several months working respectively in the courts, in government departments, in law firms and in other positions so as to become familiar with the way in which the law is applied in practice. These two years are followed by the Second Judicial State Examination, the *Assessorexamen*. Once this examination is passed the candidate is a fully qualified lawyer (*Volljurist*) and in principle capable of doing legal work of any kind. To a very limited extent it is also possible to study law at technical colleges (polytechnics). These courses, in contrast to those offered at universities, are supposed to be exclusively devoted to teaching practical work skills. However, they only deal with selected aspects of the law and, at least for the present, do not enable their graduates to take up ordinary legal careers. One type of legal qualification which is offered at the polytechnics is that of legal executive (*Rechtspfleger*). A legal executive works independently in the legal field (§§ 1, 2 of the Law on Legal Executives). The type of work covered includes land registration, the business of associations, putting debtors on notice and certain types of insolvency proceedings.

57   Most lawyers go into private practice (Germany does not have a split bar as in Britain) or take up employment as a legal adviser. They are empowered to give clients legal advice and to represent them in court. To represent clients in the courts one must be admitted to practice by a Legal Practitioner's Chamber, bodies of self-administration for legal practitioners comparable to the Bar Associations in the United States or the Law Societies in the United Kingdom. Only a very small number of lawyers are admitted to the bar of the *Bundesgerichtshof*. Apart from this requirement, lawyers can appear before any court. Legal practitioners are officially recognised by the Federal Legal Practitioners Ordinance (*Bundesrechtsanwaltsordnung*, abbreviated BRAO) as an independent organ of the legal system (§ 1 BRAO). However, this does not mean that they are part of the state bureaucracy – they are free professionals.

58   Many young lawyers also take up careers in the commercial field. They may then work in organisations, primarily in a legal capacity, and become employees in the legal departments of large firms or work as in-house counsel. However, they often leave a purely legal career so as to become active in general business management. Here they are in competition with people with a commercial education.

59   A fully qualified lawyer is automatically eligible for appointment as a judge. The profession of judge is a career which is regularly taken up by the *Assessor* directly after the Second Judicial State Examination if he or she wishes to follow this career. It must be said, however, that usually only lawyers with good results in the State Examinations are successful in applying for such a post. This decision is taken by the ministerial officials responsible for the particular court. The judges in the higher courts are chosen by special committees for the election of judges.

60   Closely connected to the career of a judge is the career of a state legal representative. His or her job is the prosecution of criminal matters. In some of the States there is a regular exchange of personnel between the courts and the state prosecutor's office.

There is considerable demand for lawyers in state administration. These lawyers are regularly given the status of *Beamte*, which implies life-long employment. This too is a career which is often taken up by the better graduates directly after the Second State Examination. It leads to administrative duties in the offices of municipal, state and federal government departments with the possibility of promotion up to the rank of Permanent Under-Secretary of State (*beamteter Staatssekretär*). Furthermore, there is a significant demand for lawyers in international organisations such as the United Nations and the European Union, where the duties are once again primarily administrative. 61

The notaries' profession is regulated differently in the various States. A notary's main business is the execution of notarial deeds, but he or she is also involved in the drafting of agreements involving land, deeds of partnership, and inheritance and marriage agreements, for example. The southern German States have the office of official notary. This is someone who is either in the employ of the state or is in private practice but works exclusively as a notary. The northern German States assign the duties of a notary to lawyers in private practice. 62

Only a small number of lawyers take up an academic career. It is usually necessary not only to have a doctorate, but also to have completed a second, more demanding thesis called a *Habilitation*. These degrees require both a written component, which usually takes the form of a monograph, and an oral examination. Generally speaking, a candidate for a professorship does not stay at the university where he or she completed the *Habilitation*, but must hope to be offered a chair at some other university. 63

Legal education is a topic for constant discussion. The structures of German legal education, as well as the methods taught and specific issues dealt with, are still directed towards the training of candidates for judicial office. The result is that too little attention is given to matters such as the drafting of contracts or statutes, administrative skills and the ability to advise clients. Strong arguments are made for the shortening and often also for the division and specialisation of legal studies. The graduates of such a reformed system would be able to start working earlier, and education and labour costs would decrease. It is indeed questionable whether there is a need for so many lawyers with a global command of all aspects of the law. On the other hand reforms should not damage the important economic and cultural role played by the legal profession. This consists of the organisation of society according to legal principles and presupposes an understanding of other fields of law and of other areas of human activity. One of the cardinal juristic virtues is expressed in the maxim *audiatur et altera pars* – one should listen to and tolerantly consider contrary opinions, not least in the interests of persuading others of one's own opinion. 64

IV. Sources of Legal Information and Research Tools

The law, which tends to become an unmanageable mass due to its breadth and complexity, is formally very accessible. Federal laws are published in the Federal Gazette (*Bundesgesetzblatt*, abbreviated *BGBl.*). It appears in two parts. The first part (*BGBl. I*) contains the parliamentary statutes and other statutory instruments of the federal government as well as other important public notices. The international agreements entered by Germany are published in part two (*BGBl. II*) along with the laws ratifying or implementing them and related notices. Part two also contains provisions on customs duties. A third part of the Federal Gazette (*BGBl. III*) contains a collection 65 of Federal Laws in Force which were collected together in the late 1950's but which have not been updated.

66 The Federal Taxation Gazette is the official publication for statutes and regulations, particularly of the Federation and of the States, on the subject of taxation. The federal ministries also have official publications in which publications relevant to the particular department are reproduced.

67 The same applies to each of the States. There are gazettes for the publication of parliamentary statutes and other statutory instruments as well as official publications produced by one or several ministries. The local levels of government, in other words the districts (*Kreise*) and, at the most basic level of local government, the communes (*Gemeinden*) also often have their own official publications in which matters relating to local government are made public.

68 Draft bills can be obtained from the printing offices of the *Bundestag* and *Bundesrat* (the two houses of the federal legislature) and also from the state legislatures (*Landtage*).

69 Most States publish updated collections of statutes in force in that State. Here all the statutes of the State involved are collected, together with the latest amendments, whereas the official gazettes of the federal and state governments generally publish only the latest amendments to the laws. Nowadays, most statutes are accessible in their current version via the internet (for federal laws: www.gesetze-im-internet.de).

70 Beck publishers issue loose-leaf collections of the most important statutes and regulations relating to specific fields of law. For example, *Schönfelder: Deutsche Gesetze* covers civil and criminal law, *Satorius I: Verfassungs- und Verwaltungsgesetze* covers public law and *Sartorius II: Internationale Verträge, Europarecht* covers international and European law. In addition, there are similar collections covering various state laws and certain specialised areas. Nomos publishers issue a three-volume work on German law annually. The texts of the most important statutes appear in very modestly priced paperback editions from various publishers.

71 The most important decisions of the highest courts are contained in law reports which are published by the judges of the respective courts. The most important in practice are the Decisions of the Federal Constitutional Court (*Entscheidungen des Bundesverfassungsgerichts*, abbreviated *BVerfGE*); Decisions of the *Bundesgerichtshof* in Civil Matters (*Entscheidungen des Bundesgerichtshofs in Zivilsachen*, abbreviated *BGHZ*); Decisions of the *Bundesgerichtshof* in Criminal Matters (*Entscheidungen des Bundesgerichtshofs in Strafsachen*, abbreviated *BGHSt*); Decisions of the Federal Labour Court (*Entscheidungen des Bundesarbeitsgerichts*, abbreviated *BAGE*); the Federal Administrative Court (*Bundesverwaltungsgericht*, abbreviated *BVerwGE*); the Federal Social Court (*Bundessozialgericht*, abbreviated *BSGE*) and the Federal Fiscal Court (*Bundesfinanzhof*, abbreviated *BFHE*). Generally speaking, the highest courts of the various States also have similar reports. Many decisions are reported in specialist publications. Important decisions usually are freely accessible in the internet.

72 The number of books published on legal subjects has become almost unmanageable. Textbooks usually present a specific area of the law, or part of an area of the law in the case of the bigger fields. They make the most important structures, key issues and problems of application comprehensible for students and not infrequently for practitioners too. Some are simply a first introduction to a subject, or are content to merely

state and summarise the law, others are academic studies at the most profound level. Certain issues are regularly dealt with very intensively in monographs of a high academic standard.

Commentaries are very important from a practitioner's point of view. They arrange   73
the law, particularly the relevant court decisions, in accordance with the arrangement of the statute being commentated, paragraph by paragraph. Each of the more important statutes is the subject of several, sometimes very substantial, commentaries.

The range of periodicals on offer is also characterised by great variety. A few journals   74
which deal essentially with all areas of the law stand alongside a great number of publications devoted to a more or less specialised aspect of the law. These generally contain essays on specific points of law as well as publishing and commentating new court decisions and reviewing newly published books.

A helpful starting point in dealing with legal literature is the Karlsruhe Legal Bibliog-   75
raphy (*Karlsruher Juristische Bibliographie, KJB*). It appears on a monthly basis and provides an evaluation of all newly published legal essays and monographs in Germany as well as selected foreign publications. The numerous abbreviations used by lawyers are listed and explained by *Hildebert Kirchner/Dietrich Pannier* "Catalogue of Legal Abbreviations" (*Abkürzungsverzeichnis der Rechtssprache*), 6th edition 2008.

Legal computer databases are of essential importance. JURIS contains references and   76
also some complete texts to statutory instruments, court decisions and academic publications. Beck-online is an equivalent to JURIS and contains the large programme of this publishing house in a data-base. Various legal publications such as the *Neue Juristische Wochenschrift* (NJW) and the *Neue Zeitschrift für Verwaltungsrecht* (NVwZ) as well as databases for specific areas of the law and collections of court decisions and legal texts are available on CD-ROM.

Literature:

Johann Braun, Einführung in die Rechtswissenschaft, 4. ed. 2011
Kristian Kühl/Hermann Reichhold/Michael Ronellenfitsch, Einführung in die Rechtswissenschaft, 3. ed. 2019
Thomas M. J. Möllers, Juristische Arbeitstechnik und wissenschaftliches Arbeiten. Klausur, Hausarbeit, Seminararbeit, Studienarbeit, Staatsexamen, Dissertation, 9. ed. 2018

B. Public Law

I. History of Constitutional and Administrative Law

77 After the Frankish Empire had been divided into three parts the German Empire gradually developed out of its Eastern part in a process which took place mainly in the 10th century. Its leaders understood it to be the successor to the Roman Empire, and its kings were crowned as Roman Emperor. The empire thus called itself the "Holy Roman Empire". From the late 15th century onwards the name "Holy Roman Empire of the German Nation" became current, thus giving recognition to the formation of a national identity which had become apparent in the intervening period.

78 Formally speaking the Empire was an elective monarchy. The German kings were elected by the Elector Princes. Nevertheless, dynasties were able to establish themselves in certain periods, some of considerable duration. The most important of these were the Habsburgs. The elective king was generally crowned emperor. Sovereign power was in the hands of the Emperor and Parliament (*Reichstag*) who had to work together in certain important matters. The *Reichstag* was formed of the most important bearers of authority, the estates. These were the electoral princes who formed the College of Electoral Princes who elected the king; the Princes of the Empire, and lastly the imperial cities, although the membership and powers of the latter were a subject of disagreement. Some of the great princes of the church who were also territorial rulers were part of the electoral college. These were the Archbishops and Elector Princes of Trier, Mainz and Cologne. The others were part of the College of Princes of the Empire.

79 Already in the time of the Holy Roman Empire there were certain fundamental principles, the so-called *leges fundamentales,* which today would be described as constitutional law. These included the Golden Bull of 1356, in which the procedure for the election of the king was laid down. It also specified which princes were members of the electoral college. There were originally seven of them, but this was later repeatedly amended. Also regarded as *leges fundamentales* were the Decree of Augsburg of 1555 and the Peace of Westphalia of 1648 which ended the Thirty Years War of 1618-1648. Typical of the whole history of this empire was the constant conflict between the central imperial authority and the princes in their territories who were asserting claims to independence. With the Thirty Years War and the Peace of Westphalia, the central authority was permanently weakened. The formation of modern, absolutist states took place at the level of the territories, the predecessors of the modern federal states. The courts of the Empire, particularly the *Reichskammergericht*, did, however, continue to be of some importance.

80 The Reformation, which is especially attributed to *Martin Luther* and is often regarded to have started in 1517, was probably the most significant event for the constitutional development up to the present day in many respects. It led to a series of armed conflicts culminating in the Thirty Years War. Parallel events and developments can be observed particularly in England and France. In Germany the Catholic and Protestant confessions ended up equally strong and equally exhausted by the conflict. The constitutional consequences were multi-faceted. The final collapse of religious unity left a political and ideological vacuum which was filled by the development of the modern, centralised, sovereign and, essentially, secular and thus not religiously founded state. State neutrality, philosophical enlightenment and a reliance on reason as opposed to

theological arguments developed against this background. Too much emphasis was placed on the idea of the state. The consequence was a secularisation of the whole of the law relating to the state. The results of the military conflict favoured and accelerated the development of the national state. The destruction of property and social bonds created conditions in which the idea of equality could grow. The equilibrium of the confessions in Germany led to a specifically institutional and group-oriented concept of equality.

The absolutist state, which had been developed during the religious wars, particularly in France, was able to establish itself in Germany, especially in Prussia and in Austria, which at that stage was still one of the states of the Empire. In this form of government the territorial ruler, in his or her capacities as supreme legislator, supreme judge, and supreme executive authority, united all sovereign power in his or her person. The ruler was not subject to the law of the land (*legibus solutus*) and was answerable only to God. For the administration, which had previously been the business of the various noblemen and estates, this meant a largely centralised, essentially hierarchical restructuring aimed at complete rationalisation and efficiency. It also meant that all fields of life were subject to the power of the monarch. The demand for division of powers and the recognition of human rights was the obvious, if not inevitable, reaction to this situation. 81

The French Revolution at first also encouraged further demands for reform and ideas about rights in Germany. The military successes of France against the German Empire led to a last great reform of its structure in the resolution (*Reichsdeputation-shauptschluß*) of 1803 compensating various princes for the territories which they had lost to the French. Many of the smaller independent territories were absorbed by the bigger states. The principalities ruled by the church were almost completely dissolved and, in a continuation of this process, most of the lands of the Catholic Church were secularised, in other words, expropriated. 82

The creation of the Federation of the Rhine, a union of west and south German territories, by *Napoleon* led to the dissolution of the Empire. In 1806 Emperor *Franz II* abdicated as emperor and discharged the estates from their duties to the Empire. This step was technically unconstitutional, but it led to the factual end of imperial authority and thus ended the Holy Roman Empire of the German Nation. 83

Only after the defeat of *Napoleon* was an attempt made to re-organise Germany at the Congress of Vienna in 1815. The place of the Holy Roman Empire of the German Nation was taken by the German Confederation (*Deutscher Bund*), an association of sovereign princes in Germany. Constitutional development now took place predominantly at the state level. The various states received constitutions, starting in 1818, with a second wave in 1830, and finally in the aftermath of 1848 (for example, in Prussia). 84

These were generally seen as having been conferred on the people by the ruler, and were generally imposed from above. Not the sovereignty of the people, but the sovereignty of the prince, the monarchic principle, lay at their root. Most of these constitutions entrusted the power to make laws to the monarch in co-operation with parliament. Voting rights were limited. Most of the constitutions guaranteed certain rights, but these were seen as the rights of the subject (as opposed to human rights), and were confined to the citizens of the particular state in question. 85

86   The middle-class revolution of 1848 with its ideas about Fundamental Rights was a failure, and was unsuccessful in its attempt to unite Germany in a new empire, which now was to exclude Austria. However, to this day its democratic constitution, the *Paulskirchenverfassung*, which played a foundational role for the Fundamental Rights, remains a crystallisation point for positive constitutional developments in Germany.

87   The German Confederation lasted until 1866, when Prussia, under its Prime Minister *Bismarck*, founded the North German Confederation (*Norddeutscher Bund*), a strong empire with a centralist structure. After the Franco-German war of 1870/71 the South German States, with the exception of Austria, acceded to the North German Federation, thus creating the German Empire (*Deutsches Reich*) of 1870/71 – Bismarck's Empire. Its constitution was based in essence on that of the North German Federation, with a relatively strong central government and the King of Prussia as the hereditary German Emperor. A feature of this constitution is that it contained no express provisions on Fundamental Rights, largely for reasons relating to competence. However, significant aspects of Fundamental Rights were incorporated in the ordinary statutory law of the Empire. For example, due process (procedural fairness) was guaranteed in the Imperial statutes on the administration of justice, i.e., the Criminal Procedure Act (*Strafprozessordnung*), the Civil Procedure Act (*Zivilprozessordnung*); and the Law on the Constitution of Courts (*Gerichtsverfassungsgesetz*). Economic freedom was provided for in the Civil Code (*Bürgerliches Gesetzbuch*), another law of this period. From the point of view of international law the German Empire of 1870/71 is the same entity as today's Federal Republic of Germany.

88   Defeat in the First World War (1914-1918) led to revolution. The monarchy was toppled and the Weimar Republic was established. It was based on the recognition of the sovereignty of the people and guaranteed numerous Fundamental Rights; these were, however, partly comprehended as mere guidelines for the legislature and not as law to be directly in force. The President, who was directly elected by the people, played the key role in any political conflict. He appointed the Chancellor (*Reichskanzler*) entirely at his own discretion and was empowered to rule without reference to parliament by means of emergency decrees.

89   The lack of co-operation between the democratic parties who at first dominated the scene, and particularly the Great Depression after 1930, led to the seizure of power by the National-Socialists (Nazis) who were organised in the National-Socialist German Worker's Party (*Nationalsozialistische Deutsche Arbeiterpartei*, abbreviated *NSDAP*). In the brown-shirted stormtroopers (*Sturmabteilung, SA*), the *SS* (*Schutzstaffel*) and later the *Gestapo* (*Geheime Staatspolizei*, secret police) they possessed the machinery to terrorise their opponents, and made every use of it. The National-Socialists, who at least initially had the support of a substantial part of the German population, disregarded, abused and destroyed the legal principles and constitutional structures which had gained binding force over a long period of time. They brought upon the world the disaster of the Second World War and, in a perfidiously systematic way, set about murdering the Jewish and other elements of the population which they considered to be "non-Aryan".

90   Only the complete victory of the Allies and the unconditional surrender of Germany in 1945 put an end to their appalling destruction of law, justice and culture. The experience of National Socialism and the determination to prevent anything like it from happening again is the strongest influence on the law of the Federal Republic of Germany

to this day. The Basic Law, which came into force in 1949, is thoroughly pervaded by this desire. These experiences are, however, also fundamental to the internal self-understanding of Germany. Its political debates, their high points and weaknesses cannot be understood without bearing this background in mind.

The victorious powers at first divided Germany into four zones of occupation, after first giving the various eastern parts of the country to Poland and the northern part of East Prussia to the Soviet Union. As the tensions between the West and the Soviet Union increased, the zones of occupation of the three Western powers (Britain, France and the USA) drew closer together. In 1949 they were consolidated as the Federal Republic of Germany (*Bundesrepublik Deutschland*) and in the same year the "German Democratic Republic" (*Deutsche Demokratische Republik*, abbreviated *DDR*) was created in the Russian zone. **91**

On 8 May 1949 the Parliamentary Council (*Parlamentarischer Rat*), consisting of members of the newly elected State parliaments, passed a constitution, which was called the "Basic Law" because it was hoped that the division of Germany would soon end, allowing a permanent constitution for the whole country to be created. After adoption by the State parliaments and approval by the Western occupation powers it came into force at midnight on 23 May 1949. Although it was originally conceived as a short-term temporary measure, it was soon accepted by the people, and today it can fairly be described as a centre of identification for the German people. **92**

The socialistic constitution of the DDR of 1949 was replaced by a new constitution in 1968 which in turn was fundamentally revised in 1974 by the removal of all references to a possible reunification of Germany. **93**

Only with the end of the confrontation between West and East was it possible to achieve German unification on the 3 October 1990. The details are contained in the Two-plus-four treaty between the victorious powers (Britain, France, the Soviet Union and the USA) on the one hand, and the Federal Republic of Germany and the German Democratic Republic on the other hand. A number of additional international treaties, for example, with the Republic of Poland, complete the arrangement. In terms of the treaty the responsibility of the victorious powers for Germany is ended. The two German states agreed on the terms of unification in the unification treaty of 31 August 1990. With this treaty an era had ended. The confrontation between East and West, the Cold War and the division of Germany had deeply influenced the legal thinking. After some uncertainties in the beginning, Germany today has grown together again; certain and sometimes important differences remain. New challenges arise also for the legal system, especially the preservation and development of the European unification and the integration of new, especially Muslim parts of the population. **94**

Literature:
Hans Boldt, Deutsche Verfassungsgeschichte, vol. I, 3. ed. 1994, vol. II, 2. ed. 1993
Manfred Botzenhart, Deutsche Verfassungsgeschichte, 1806-1949, 1993
Heinz Duchhardt, Deutsche Verfassungsgeschichte 1495-1806, 1991
Hans Fenske, Deutsche Verfassungsgeschichte, 4. ed. 1993
Ernst Forsthoff, Deutsche Verfassungsgeschichte der Neuzeit, 4. ed. 1997
Werner Frotscher/Bodo Pieroth, Verfassungsgeschichte, 17. ed. 2018
Axel Gotthard, Das Alte Reich 1495–1806, 5. ed. 2013
Dieter Grimm, Deutsche Verfassungsgeschichte, 1776-1866, 3. ed. 1995
Ernst Rudolf Huber, Deutsche Verfassungsgeschichte seit 1789, 8 vols., 2./3. ed. since 1984

Jörn Ipsen, Der Staat der Mitte: Verfassungsgeschichte der Bundesrepublik Deutschland, 2009

Kurt G. A. Jeserich/Hans Pohl/Georg-Christoph von Unruh (eds.), Deutsche Verwaltungs-geschichte, 6 vols., since 1983

Michael Kotulla, Deutsche Verfassungsgeschichte, 2008

Klaus Kröger, Einführung in die jüngere deutsche Verfassungsgeschichte (1806-1933), 1988

Adolf Laufs, Rechtsentwicklungen in Deutschland, 6. ed. 2006

Christian-Friedrich Menger, Deutsche Verfassungsgeschichte der Neuzeit, 9. ed. 2003

Dietmar Willoweit, Deutsche Verfassungsgeschichte, 8. ed. 2019

Dietmar Willoweit, Reich und Staat, 2013

Reinhold Zippelius, Kleine deutsche Verfassungsgeschichte, 7. ed. 2006

II. Constitutional Law

1. General

a) Concept, Nature and Function of the Constitution

95   The Basic Law is the constitution of the Federal Republic of Germany. This means that Germany has a written constitution, codified in a single document. This is the constitution in the formal sense. Each of the States also has a State constitution which is in part closely modelled on the Basic Law, and in part establishes an identity of its own. The Principle of Homogeneity, which is laid down in article 28 para. 1 GG obliges the state constitutions, like all other state law, to comply with the fundamental principles of the Basic Law. In addition, there are important rules of federal constitutional law which have a direct effect on the constitutions of the States and which thus form part of the constitutional law of the States themselves.

96   The Basic Law (*Grundgesetz*) has been designed so as to be particularly difficult to change. The aim is to ensure that there is a broad consensus supporting any change, and to remove the constitution as far as possible from the influence of short-term political tendencies. It can only be changed if two thirds of the members of the parliament (*Bundestag*) and two thirds of the members of the Federal Council (*Bundesrat*), which together make up the core of the legislature, vote in favour. A change can only be made by express alteration of the text of the Basic Law.

97   Certain fundamental positions are not subject to change at all. Article 79 para. 3 GG says: "An alteration of this basic law which would affect the division of the Federation into states, the basic principle that the States should play a part in the legislative process, or the fundamental principles set out in articles 1 and 20, is not permissible." This so-called "guarantee of eternity" (*Ewigkeitsgarantie*) applies to the federal structure of Germany, the protection of and respect for human dignity as well as certain central structural principles such as constitutional government under the rule of law, democracy and the sovereignty of the people, the social state and the principle that it must take a republican form. Through the principles contained in article 1 of the Basic Law the essence of other Fundamental Rights is protected against abolition by way of constitutional amendments as far as this essence is an expression of human dignity. By the internal logic of the provision, article 79 para. 3 itself also cannot be abolished. Isolated modifications of the basic principles named in this provision are, however, allowed if they are "immanent to the system". What this means, in sum, is that the essential identity of the constitution may not be changed. This does not prevent the replacement of the constitution by a new constitution, a possibility expressly provided

for in article 146 GG, but it does prevent the deformation of the fundamental structures of the constitution by a process of creeping subversion.

Apart from the constitution in the formal sense, i.e., the constitutional document which is the Basic Law, a great deal of constitutional law in the material sense is contained in ordinary statutes which directly implement and concretise the Basic Law and provide detailed rules for the functioning of the organs of the constitution. To name but a few, these include the Citizenship Act (*Staatsangehörigkeitsgesetz*), the electoral laws, the Deputies Act (*Abgeordnetengesetz*), the Federal Ministers Act (*Bundesministergesetz*), the Political Parties Act (*Parteiengesetz*), The Federal Constitutional Court Act (*Gesetz über das Bundesverfassungsgericht*), and the standing rules of the various constitutional organs. From the point of view of legislative procedure these laws do not differ in any way from ordinary parliamentary statutes. The only difference is that the standing rules of the various constitutional organs are generally made by these bodies themselves and can be changed more easily, which is justified by the fact that they merely regulate the internal functioning and organisation of these bodies and do not have any direct effect outside of the body in question. In particular it should be noted that Germany no longer uses the otherwise common idea of entrenched legislation (*organisches Gesetz*), i.e. legislation of particular significance which can only be passed or amended by a qualified majority.

98

A most important issue, which has effects reaching right down to the level of finding solutions to individual factual problems, is the general understanding of the essential nature and function of the constitution. Here there are two, essentially opposite, views. One school understands the constitution essentially as a choice, as a line of demarcation between those who form the constituted community on the one hand, and those who stand outside of it on the other hand. This view was first propounded by the constitutional scholar *Carl Schmitt* (1888-1985) in the period of the Weimar Republic. Constitution is in this sense a part of the fundamental difference between friend and foe. In terms of this theory certain norms which are of particular importance for the drawing of the line of demarcation possess a greater weight than other provisions of the constitution. The fact of a fundamental decision which cannot be substantiated any further is of central importance to this theory. Under the current constitutional circumstances, the tendency and general result of this theory is to lead its supporters to view democracy as the value-neutral legal and constitution-making authority of the people. It also leads to an emphasis on the sovereign power of parliament, in effect to a type of social Positivism.

99

Another approximately equally strong school of thought, which, however, was for a long time the dominant view in jurisprudence of the Federal Constitutional Court, was first put forward by *Rudolph Smend* (1882-1975) who also developed his theory in the Weimar period. This theory sees the constitution as a legal medium for integration. Particularly the Fundamental Rights are an expression of a community of culture and values. Such integration in principle takes in all people living within the area in which the constitution is in force. In this view the constitution is not a line of demarcation, but a basis for unity, and must itself be understood and interpreted as a unified whole. It must therefore also be understood as imposing an obligation to realise its postulates. Here the tendency is rather towards the preservation of general principles of law which precede the constitution and take the form of constitutional government under

100

the rule of law. It also tends to bind the constitution-making power of the people to cultural values which have developed over time.

101 Initially the Federal Constitutional Court viewed the constitution in general and the Fundamental Rights in particular as a complete value system. This provided the basis for arguments in favour of a comprehensive protection of individual freedoms. Later, without abandoning its emphasis on the protection of individual freedom, the idea of a closed system was broken open and the court spoke of Fundamental Rights merely as fundamental principles determining the values of the system (*wertentscheidende Grundsatznormen*).

b) Territorial Applicability

102 The Basic Law applies in the area of the Federal Republic of Germany and other areas of equivalent status, for example, on German ships on the high seas. All state officials are bound by the Basic Law, even if they are acting in or on behalf of foreign countries. After the unification of 1990 all further territorial claims are completely excluded. Agreement on this point was the basis for numerous alterations to the constitution (Preamble, article 23, article 146 GG).

103 From a personal point of view the decisive factor is not citizenship, which is regulated by the Citizenship Act (*Staatsangehörigkeitsgesetz*). Rather, the concept of a "German" is of prime importance. This applies both to entitlement to Fundamental Rights, which to some extent applies only to Germans, as well as to the right to vote. The concept of a "German" is defined in article 116 GG and is wider than the concept of German citizenship. A German, in terms of the Basic Law, is any person who has German citizenship or who is of German origin and, as a refugee or expellee, had taken refuge in the area of the German Empire as defined by the borders of 31.12.1937. It further includes the spouse or descendant of any such person. More detailed provisions are contained in the Federal Act on Expellees (*Bundesvertriebenengesetz*) which defines what constitutes German nationality as well as what is meant by a refugee or expellee. In practice these terms cover German emigrants to certain areas of Eastern Europe and China and their descendants who are returning to the Federal Republic. The fact that someone falls within these definitions in itself does not give them a claim to anything. Legal consequences only arise when such a person comes to Germany.

104 German citizenship is primarily acquired by birth. The principle of *ius sanguinis* is applied. This means that a child acquires German citizenship if one of his or her parents is a German citizen. German citizenship can also be acquired by adoption. A child of foreign parents acquires German citizenship by being born in Germany if one parent has been a legal permanent resident for eight years and has a consolidated resident status (§ 4 StAG).

105 A foreigner can also acquire German citizenship. In principle, this requires that the foreigner pledges allegiance to the free democratic basic order, is legally resident in Germany, has a clean record, has been able to find accommodation, and is in a position to support his or her dependants. It is easier for the spouse of a German citizen to acquire citizenship. In addition, the Citizenship Act (*Staatsangehörigkeitsgesetz*) provides for a claim for naturalization under certain conditions (§§ 10 ff. StAG). An effort is still made to prevent dual nationality from arising wherever possible, although additional exceptions to this rule have been created in the last few years. This is espe-

cially true for European Union citizens, who can obtain dual citizenship without any impediments (§ 12 StAG).

2. Fundamental Rights

a) General Principles

The Basic Law puts the Fundamental Rights in the first chapter, right at the start of the constitution. In doing so it is emphasising the fundamental importance of the rights of the individual, which are of foundational importance for the state and constitution. This is in deliberate contrast to the dominant constitutional tradition in the period preceding the Basic Law and is a reaction to the contempt for these rights which was shown by the National Socialists.   106

Taking human dignity as its starting point (article 1 para. 1 GG), the Basic Law guarantees numerous specific rights. This positions it in the European-North American tradition of human rights thinking. In so far as specific rights are guaranteed in the first chapter of the constitution, they are referred to as Fundamental Rights (*Grundrechte*). Other rights, which are scattered throughout the constitution, are called Quasi-Fundamental Rights (*grundrechtsgleiche Rechte*).   107

The rights can be classified either as freedom rights or as equality rights. Article 2 para. 1 GG protects the free development of the personality. This Fundamental Right functions as a general freedom right. To some extent it is a catch-all right which operates whenever the numerous individual freedom rights are not applicable.   108

The general equality guarantee is contained in article 3 para. 1 GG, which guarantees that all people are equal before the law. This Fundamental Right is once again a catch-all behind a number of specific equality provisions such as the guarantee of equality of men and women (article 3 para. 2 GG), or the equality of voting rights (article 28 para. 1, article 38 para. 1 GG). Thus, article 2 para. 1 GG and article 3 para. 1 GG together provide for the comprehensive protection of freedom and equality.   109

In German thinking the Fundamental Rights are of considerable importance. They are indeed the centre and axis on which all legal thinking turns. The functions which are ascribed to them are correspondingly numerous. Fundamental Rights are first of all defensive rights. Particular emphasis has been placed on this function since the 19th century. This means that the state may not interfere with the legal position of the individual unless there is special reason to do so. Unjustified infringements can be blocked by the individual. This means that he or she has legal remedies against unjustified detention, against the confiscation of his or her property, or against the banning of a particular point of view.   110

Apart from their defensive function, the Fundamental Rights also traditionally involve the right to participate in the democratic political process. Particularly in the case of rights such as freedom of assembly, freedom of the press and of opinion and the right to vote this aspect is prominent.   111

To a very carefully limited extent a certain positive dimension entitling to services from the state (*Leistungsfunktion*) is also recognised. In so far as this is practical, the state has a duty to ensure that circumstances conducive to the exercise of the Fundamental Rights are created. For example, the right to freely choose one's career and the associated course of education obliges the state to make available a reasonable   112 (*angemessene*) number of places in educational institutions insofar as such a course of studies is a legal requirement for the exercise of the profession or trade in question.

113   Closely related to this positive dimension entitling to services are the Fundamental Rights as a protective duty of the state to act. Thus, the state is not only required to respect the right to life and physical integrity in its negative defensive sense by not infringing on this right itself. It is also obliged by article 2 para. 2 sentence 1 GG to actively intervene to protect these rights against infringements by third parties or other sources of danger. Thus, for example, the state is responsible for ensuring a healthy natural environment insofar as this is practical.

114   Lastly, the Fundamental Rights are also a guarantee of organisation and procedure. The state must provide appropriate (*angemessene*) organisational and procedural structures to ensure the prompt and effective protection of Fundamental Rights. Thus, administrative officials planning a road-building operation must accord reasonable (*angemessene*) consideration to the rights of owners of neighbouring property by informing them properly and giving them an opportunity to give their views on the subject.

115   These five functions, which the Fundamental Rights are recognised as having, make clear the two dimensions of these rights. Firstly, they are the subjective rights of the individual and of legal persons. However, they simultaneously form a sphere of the objective law. Thus, for example, the free, democratic political process as such is protected. Fundamental Rights also often guarantee specific legal institutions: Marriage (article 6 para. 1 GG), property (article 14 GG), contract (article 2 para. 1 GG), a free press (article 5 para. 1 GG) the structures for regulating industrial disputes (article 9 para. 3 GG). This objective dimension of the Fundamental Rights serves to reinforce the rights of individuals, but is independent of any attempt by a specific individual to enforce rights in a specific instance. Particularly here the state appears in its role as the guarantor of freedom.

116   The Basic Law distinguishes between Human Rights (*Menschenrechte*), which apply to every human being, and Fundamental Rights which are reserved for Germans only, the so-called "Germans' Rights" (*Deutschenrechte*). Examples of general Human Rights are freedom of belief or freedom of opinion. Examples of Germans' Rights are freedom of assembly and association and the freedom to choose one's career. This by no means leaves foreigners entirely without protection as far as these aspects are concerned. In connection with such situations of life they can instead rely on the general Fundamental Right to the free development of the personality laid down in article 2 para. 1 GG. This right can, however, be limited more easily than the more specific rights. The question whether or not the validity of "Germans' Rights" should be extended in certain situations which are characterised by European Union law to citizens of the European Union's member states is controversial, but should be answered in the affirmative. This holds true especially where the freedom to choose one's career is concerned.

117   It is private persons, bearers of Fundamental Rights, who derive rights from the Fundamental Rights. Private persons are first and foremost individuals. Legal persons, i.e., entities such as associations or companies which are constituted as bearers of legal rights by the legal system are also bearers of Fundamental Rights, insofar as the particular right in question is of such a nature that it can be applicable to them (article 19 para. 3 GG). A legal person can have property and is thus entitled to the protection of

article 14 para. 1 GG. It cannot, however, have a conscience, and therefore cannot make any claims based on the freedom of conscience guaranteed in article 4 para. 1 GG. The applicability of Fundamental Rights to foreign legal persons is anachronistically limited by article 19 para. 3 GG. However, they are entitled to base a claim on the procedural rights such as the right to a hearing before a court (article 103 para. 1 GG) and the right to have a case tried by a judge whose identity is established before the trial (article 101 para. 1 sentence 2 GG).

State institutions are essentially not bearers of Fundamental Rights. The main aim of Fundamental Rights is to protect against impermissible acts on the part of the state, not to strengthen the position of public institutions. Only isolated procedural guarantees like article 103 para. 1, article 101 para. 1 sentence 2 GG and the general prohibition of arbitrary action (*Willkürverbot*) are also applicable in favour of the state. However, in many fields of life there are state institutions which are designed precisely to make the exercise of the freedom rights organisationally possible. The most important of these are the state universities and the state-run radio and television corporations. These may rely on the particular fundamental right on which they are based. For the public radio and television corporations this is the right to freely transmit programmes derived from article 5 para. 1 GG and for the universities the freedom of research and teaching, academic pursuits and the arts guaranteed in article 5 para. 3 GG.   118

The state in all its forms is bound to uphold the Fundamental Rights. The Fundamental Rights bind the legislature, the executive and the judiciary as law which is automatically in force without the need for any implementing legislation (article 1 para. 3 GG). Private persons, on the other hand, are essentially not bound by the Fundamental Rights – they are intended to create rights for the individual, not duties. The only situation in which private persons are directly bound by Fundamental Rights (so-called direct horizontal effect, in German *unmittelbare Drittwirkung*) is set out in article 9 para. 3 GG which guarantees the freedom to form coalitions. (The term "horizontal application" is in contrast to the "vertical application" between state and individual). The right to form associations for the protection and promotion of working and economic conditions is guaranteed for every person and for all trades and professions. Agreements which attempt to limit or hamper the exercise of this right are void, and measures with such an object are illegal. This right is particularly relevant to the formation of trade unions and employers associations, the organisation of industrial action and the conclusion of agreements regulating wages and working conditions. Article 9 para. 3 GG thus directly forbids an employer from making it a condition for employment of a worker that the worker should belong to a particular union or that the worker should not belong to a union. Otherwise there is no direct horizontal application of the Fundamental Rights. At very most the prohibition of any action to hamper an attempt to gain election to the federal or state legislatures contained in article 48 GG can also be considered to fall within this category.   119

On the other hand, the idea of indirect horizontal application (*mittelbare Drittwirkung*) has been accepted. The Fundamental Rights permeate all areas of the law because they represent a constitutional decision in favour of certain values. In the interpretation and application of the ordinary law, in other words all laws inferior in status to the constitution, the value judgements contained in the Fundamental Rights must be given effect. Human dignity may also not be injured, freedom and equality   120 must be respected, and this also applies to relations between private individuals. However, in this situation different Fundamental Rights which are in principle of equal status usually stand in conflict with one another: For example, the right of the landlord to the protection of his or her property (article 14 para. 1 GG) and the right of the tenant to artistic freedom (article 5 para. 3 GG) when the tenant wishes to practise his or her trumpet late at night and disturbs the other tenants. Here the law must find a solution which gives reasonable regard to the rights of all the parties with reference to the basic value decisions contained in the constitution.

121   Fundamental Rights are not absolute. Their main task is to guarantee freedom and dignity. This is achieved by means of the so-called sphere of protection (*Schutzbereich*) of the various Fundamental Rights, for example, the right to peaceful and unarmed assembly without prior registration or permission (article 8 para. 1 GG). Armed or non-peaceful assembly is, however, not protected by article 8 para. 1 GG and therefore does not fall within its sphere of protection. An infringement on the sphere of protection by the state that is not entirely unsubstantial is termed *Eingriff*. Infringements on the sphere of protection are not prohibited *per se*, but they always need a justification.

122   For a satisfactory communal life it is necessary to limit certain freedoms and reconcile them with one another. There are thus limitations (*Schranken*) on the Fundamental Rights. The first limits are implicit in the sphere of protection itself. A non-peaceful assembly is not protected. These are the so-called right-immanent limitations (*grundrechtsimmanente Schranken*). In addition, certain rights include a special limitation clause (*Gesetzesvorbehalt*) making the right subject to statute. Thus, on the subject of freedom of assembly, article 8 para. 2 GG says: "With respect to assemblies out of doors this right can be limited by statute or in terms of a statute." The legislature can thus make any interest which it considers to be legitimate and which is in accordance with the constitution the basis for limiting this right. In the case of some rights this can also be done by subordinate legislation or administrative regulations. In some cases the specific limitation clauses contain further limiting considerations (for example in the case of the protection of freedom of movement, article 11 GG, or the inviolability of the home, article 13 GG).

123   Even rights which do not have a specific limitation clause are not absolute. However, they cannot be limited to the same extent. Here the so-called constitution-immanent limitations (*verfassungsimmanente Schranken*) are relevant. These rights may only be limited for the protection of an interest which is set out in the constitution itself. Such limitation is legitimised by the concept of the constitution as an internally consistent whole. The starting position is that all provisions of the Basic Law are of equal rank and equal dignity. Therefore, if two legal goods are in conflict they act as limitations on one another and a compromise must be found which accords the greatest possible respect to both of them. An example: Freedom of belief (article 4 para. 1 and 2 GG) also protects the right to act in accordance with one's beliefs. This right does not have a limitation clause. Thus, one may follow religious tradition and ring bells when a religious service is held. However, when this interferes with the need of other people for peace and quiet (article 2 para. 1 GG) or has a negative effect on their health (article 2 para. 2 sentence 1 GG) some compromise must be reached, usually by limiting the volume of the sound and the times of day at which the bells may be rung.

124   Because of the great importance of protecting Fundamental Rights the limitation provisions must in their turn always be interpreted in the light of the protective object of

the Fundamental Rights. This leads to a limitation of the reach of limitations. In this context the term "limitation limits" (*Schranken-Schranken*) is used, often in a rather over-generalised way which tends to conceal the finer distinctions. The steps in testing a Fundamental Rights provision are thus the following: Sphere of protection (*Schutzbereich*), infringement (*Eingriff*), limitations (*Schranken*), limitation limits (*Schranken-Schranken*).

One of the most important of the "limitation-limits" is the Principle of Proportionality (*Verhältnismäßigkeitsgrundsatz*). It gives expression to the idea that all law must be reasonable (*angemessen*). The Principle of Proportionality permeates the entire legal order. It is one of the central principles of German law. It is generally seen as having three elements which must be tested in succession when deciding whether a measure satisfies its requirements. These are objective suitability (*Geeignetheit*), necessity (*Erforderlichkeit*) and reasonableness or proportionality in the narrower sense (*Angemessenheit*). This progression takes account of the nature of the Principle of Proportionality as a weighing up of ends and means. Every measure must be a proportional (reasonable) means of reaching a proportional (reasonable) goal. In conducting this enquiry the requirement of objective suitability (*Geeignetheit*) means that the means chosen must be capable of producing at least some progress towards the desired end. Necessity (*Erforderlichkeit*) demands that of several objectively suitable means that one must be chosen which imposes the least possible burden on the affected parties. Reasonableness (*Angemessenheit*), often called "proportionality in the narrower sense" (*Verhältnismäßigkeit im engeren Sinne*, also *Zumutbarkeit*, or *Proportionalität*), involves a more complex question. It demands that the disadvantages which the affected parties suffer as a result of the measure must be in proportion to the advantages which the general population will gain from the measure. In other words, it must be a reasonable burden to impose on the affected parties. This means that the advantages and disadvantages must be weighed up against one another. In this process all the legal interests which are involved must be drawn into a reasonable (*angemessene*) balance and preserved as far as this is at all possible.

125

Another important concept which once again draws the bounds for the limitations on Fundamental Rights is the requirement of legal certainty (*Bestimmtheitsgebot*). Laws which limit the Fundamental Rights must be sufficiently clear and certain so that the affected persons can orientate themselves and adapt to the legal situation. The essential content (*Wesensgehalt*) of a right may also not be interfered with (article 19 para. 2 GG). Limiting laws must as a general rule expressly state which Fundamental Rights they purport to limit (article 19 para. 1 sentence 2 GG).

126

The Basic Law contains various provisions which aim to prevent the abuse of the Fundamental Rights. Article 18 GG provides that someone who uses rights such as freedom of opinion, assembly and association to undermine the free democratic constitutional order can be found to be abusing these rights. This provision is based on the experience of the Weimar period and National Socialism when the freedom rights were abused and used to destroy freedom. The decision as to whether rights have been abused may only be made by the Federal Constitutional Court. Up to now this provision has not had any practical significance.

127

b) The Various Fundamental Rights

128 The protection of human dignity in article 1 GG has become the central fundamental right in German law. It is the basis and the essence of all other fundamental rights. Article 1 para. 1 GG states: "Human dignity shall be inviolable. To respect and protect it shall be the duty of all state authority." Following several and in fact often differing secular and religious traditions this guarantee means above all that no single human being may be viewed merely as a means to an end outside of the human being itself. Thus, each individual must be respected because of him- or herself. His or her characteristics, achievements or qualifications do not matter for this; human dignity rather is innate to each individual. Since human dignity is inviolable, it cannot be lost or be forfeited. Only the right to respect which follows from human dignity can be violated. The state must not violate this right itself, and it must actively protect human dignity against assaults from others.

129 The Federal Constitutional Court has held it incompatible with the human dignity of the passengers and staff of a kidnapped aeroplane to shoot down this plane, even when this is done immediately before it crashes into a skyscraper in order to rescue the people inside that house[1]. Since human dignity is inviolable, it cannot, according to the Federal Constitutional Court, be balanced with other protected values.

130 The general right to freedom is contained in article 2 para. 1 GG. It says: "Every person has the right to freely develop his personality insofar as in doing so he or she does not infringe the rights of others or come into conflict with the constitutional order or moral principles." This provision guarantees two main rights. Firstly it protects the general freedom to do as one pleases (*allgemeine Handlungsfreiheit*) in the classical sense which was already formulated in the French Declaration of the Rights of Man of 1789: Every person is free to do or not do whatever he or she pleases. Secondly, it also protects the individuals' inner sphere, his or her general rights of personality (*allgemeines Persönlichkeitsrecht*). This is generally read together with the protection of human dignity in article 1 para. 1 GG. This means, for example, that intimate, highly personal diary entries may not be published against the will of the author. Another example is that every person has the right to control access to information about him- or herself (*Recht auf informationelle Selbstbestimmung*) and decide who should know what about him or her. This provides a constitutional basis for data protection (*Datenschutz*). The overwhelming majority of writers take the view that the right to free development of the personality is to be very widely interpreted. As a backup to the individual rights to freedom such as freedom of belief, opinion and assembly, it protects the entire sphere of freedom of the individual.

131 The limitation clause of article 2 para. 1 GG is equally broad. The rights of others, the constitutional order and the law on morality form the so-called "limitations triad". The only one of these which is of practical significance is the constitutional order. It includes the "rights of others" which can only exist within the constitutional order, and the law on morality is only relevant in the interests of general, legally structured freedom insofar as the Basic Law gives moral rules legal force. The "constitutional order" limitation is interpreted very widely: it means all legal rules, which are compatible with the constitution in form and substance. The free development of the personal-

---

1 BVerfGE 115, 118.

ity can thus be limited by any legal rule which is not unconstitutional in terms of some other provision of the Constitution.

The general right to equality is contained in article 3 para. 1 GG: "All people are equal before the law". The issues raised by the requirement of equal treatment are particularly visible as far as the obligations of legislators are concerned. An older view was that the right to equality amounted to no more than a prohibition of arbitrariness (*Willkürverbot*): the legislative exercises political discretion as long as it does not act arbitrarily. The basic sense of the equality provision is that like things must be treated alike, and unlike must be treated unlike, with due regard to their nature. Any departure from this principle must be justified on objectively reasonable grounds. Today the Federal Constitutional Court tends to take a narrower view of the equality clause: Indeed, it is essentially for the legislator to decide on what basis things are to be considered like or unlike. However, the legislature exceeds the constitutional limits of its competence to make this determination if it treats one group of legal subjects differently from another group of legal subjects although there are no differences of such a nature and such gravity between the groups as to justify the unequal treatment.[2] In this way the application of the general provision on equality is linked to the idea of proportionality (*Verhältnismäßigkeit*) and allows the Federal Constitutional Court much greater scope for testing the validity of laws than the mere prohibition of arbitrariness would. The Constitution's general equality clause is complemented by numerous special equality clauses which structure and modify it for various specific spheres. Thus, article 3 para. 2 provides: "Men and women have equal rights". This means that the legislature may not make the differences between men and woman the basis for drawing distinctions. However, differentiation is allowed if it is based on objective functional and biological differences which play such a decisive role in the sphere of life which a law is to regulate that possible similarities are insignificant in comparison.[3] It is also permissible to compensate disadvantages which have been suffered.[4] Positive measures to create equality between men and women and to overcome existing factual inequalities which have earlier also been declared to be constitutional by the Federal Constitutional Court[5] are expressly exacted by article 3 para. 2 s. 2 GG.

132

All in all the protection of Fundamental Rights is extremely comprehensive and detailed. The provisions of the Catalogue of Fundamental Rights (articles 1-19 GG) and the various quasi-Fundamental Rights which are scattered throughout the Basic Law (articles 20 para. 4; 28; 33; 38; 101-104 GG) follow the classical, liberal tradition of thinking on human rights. Attempts to get additional, usually social, Fundamental Rights included were rejected by the original constitution-making assembly and have also not achieved a breakthrough in the ongoing debate which continues to this day. These attempts relate particularly to a right to employment and a right to accommodation. The most urgent needs in this respect are taken account of in the principle that the Federal Republic of Germany is a social state (article 20 para. 1 GG) and by the function of the Fundamental Rights as positive rights to state assistance. Nevertheless, the extension of the Catalogue of Fundamental Rights to the order of actively and in

133

---

2 BVerfGE 55, 72/88; 85, 238/244; 96, 315/325.
3 BVerfGE 68, 384/390; 84, 9/17.
4 BVerfGE 74, 163/180; 92, 91/109.
5 BVerfGE 85, 191/206.

fact creating equality between men and women and the prohibition of discrimination against the disabled is a step in the direction of social Fundamental Rights.

134 Considering other specialised Fundamental Rights, one can see their current significance for central questions of common life in German society. The law concerning abortion, which is generally prohibited in terms of § 218 of the Criminal Code (StGB) and made subject to punishment, has up to now twice been the subject of important decisions by the Federal Constitutional Court. The basic starting point is the right to life, which is guaranteed in article 2 para. 2 sentence 1 GG. The unborn child also has this right. The state has an obligation to protect its life. The function of the Fundamental Rights as protective duties of the state here come into operation on behalf of those who are in particular need of protection. Thus, the court has always taken the view that an abortion can only be allowed in especially difficult cases of conflicting rights. This is, for example, the case where the pregnancy has resulted from rape, or where it poses a threat to the life of the mother, or where the unborn child (*nasciturus*) suffers from particularly severe physical or mental defects. Mere social disadvantages, for example, where the pregnancy will disrupt the woman's plans for her life, are not sufficient. A solution based on a cut-off date, which allows the woman a free choice within certain time limits as to whether to have an abortion or not, is unconstitutional.

135 However, the Federal Constitutional Court also did accept that the constitution does not demand that all illegal abortions should be punished by the criminal law.[6] Instead it took the view that the protection of the *nasciturus* can only be undertaken together with the mother, not against her. This is particularly the case in the first trimester (12 weeks). Thus, a so-called counselling provision is permissible. Termination of pregnancy in the first trimester remain in principle illegal, but need not be subjected to punishment so long as the pregnant woman submits to intensive counselling, which is to be regulated in detail, and which is to be undertaken with the goal of protecting the life of the unborn child.

136 Article 5 para. 1 GG has repeatedly proved to be of considerable importance. It guarantees freedom of opinion, of information, of the press and of electronic communication. Every person has the right to freely express his or her opinion in words, writing or images. Particularly in the political context, the right to express the most severe criticism has thus repeatedly been protected. In a leading decision, which has maintained its significance to this day, the Federal Constitutional Court on this basis declared that a call to boycott showings of a film made by a director who had previously worked for the National Socialists was legitimate.[7]

137 On several occasions the Federal Constitutional Court has had the opportunity to develop the guarantee of press freedom. This right means that the legal system must see to it that a free press exists. Here the right functions as an institutional guarantee (objective dimension). Thus, the evidentiary privilege of journalists, which entitles them to refuse to give evidence, is constitutionally protected and it is a basic principle that the police may not search the offices of members of the press. In addition the state has a duty to prevent monopolistic tendencies in the business of forming public opinion and

---

6 BVerfGE 88, 203 ff..; contrast the position taken by the court in BVerfGE 39, 1 ff.
7 BVerfGE 7, 198 ff.

must also protect the position of journalists and editors within the various media companies.

The objective aspect of article 5 para. 1 GG has also proved to be relevant with respect to the freedom of the electronic media. In numerous decisions the Federal Constitutional Court has developed broad principles and specific rules on media law from this right. Thus, in light of the numerous different technical means of transmission, there is a right to run radio and television companies as private businesses. However, there must also be public broadcasters to ensure that alternative views also get a hearing and to provide the population with a certain basic measure of information. The legal regulation of this area must ensure that in end effect all relevant social groups and opinions are represented. 138

The limitation provision of article 5 para. 2 GG has also proved to be important on numerous occasions, not only for the practical definition of legal rules, but also for the pervasive influence of the Fundamental Rights. In terms of this norm, freedom of opinion, of the press and of the electronic media are limited by "the provisions of the general laws". Since article 19 para. 1 GG already provides that statutes limiting Fundamental Rights are only permissible if they are of general application and are not directed at specific cases, the concept of "general laws" must mean something additional in the context of article 5 para. 2 GG. The phrase "general laws" here means those provisions which are not directed against the expression of a specific opinion, but which rather aim to protect a legal good which is worthy of protection, without reference to any particular opinion on the matter, that is a common value which takes precedence over the exercise of freedom of opinion. Such laws are in turn to be interpreted so as to give due regard to the importance in a free and democratic state of the rights protected in article 5 para. 1 GG and must therefore be interpreted narrowly insofar as they limit these rights.[8] 139

Apart from the rights in article 5 GG and the voting rights contained in articles 38 and 28 GG, freedom of assembly has been particularly important in giving structure to the democratic development of Germany. This right is guaranteed in article 8 GG and it is regulated in detail in the states' Assemblies Acts, and, as long as the states have not used their legislative power, in the federal *Assemblies Act* (*Versammlungsgesetz*, abbreviated *VersG*). Most importantly, political demonstrations are protected by this provision. No permission from the authorities is required to hold an assembly. Only gatherings within a narrow radius of the buildings of three constitutional organs – such as the Bundestag and the Bundesrat as well as the Federal Constitutional Court – are regulated, primarily by the Law on Regulated Areas (*Gesetz über befriedete Bezirke,* abbreviated *BefBezG*) so that these bodies can exercise their functions unintimidated. Although no permission is required, assemblies in the open must be reported to the authorities 48 hours beforehand, otherwise they may be dispersed by the police. In the case of spontaneous demonstrations (*Spontanversammlung*), in which the participants take part without preparation, it is not necessary to report the assembly to the police. Urgent demonstrations (*Eilversammlung*), where less than 48 hours lie between preparation and demonstration, have to be reported as soon as possible. However, political debate has led to the so-called masking prohibition (§ 17 a VersG) which provides that participants in assemblies may not clothe themselves in a manner which conceals their 140

---

8   BVerfGE 7, 198/208 ff., which has been followed in all subsequent cases.

identity, for example, by wearing masks. This is a rather petty rule and is also difficult to enforce.

141   The law on asylum has been the subject of intensive debate due to the at times considerable numbers of people attempting to enter Germany. The right to asylum is guaranteed in article 16 a para. 1 GG: "The politically persecuted have a right to asylum."

142   The constitution (article 16 a para. 2-5 GG) itself limits the right to asylum to such an extent that this right cannot be invoked by persons entering Germany from a Member-State of the European Union or from some other "safe state" (*sicherer Drittstaat*) as defined by statute. A list of states in which political persecution is presumed not to take place is also defined by statute. Anyone coming from such a state who nevertheless claims to have been politically persecuted must show evidence rebutting the presumption in his or her particular case; otherwise he or she can be deported without further ado. The European Commission coordinates the asylum law within the European Union. In particular, a basis has been established for recognising as binding the decisions of other European states on matters of asylum.

3. Fundamental Constitutional Principles

143   The constitutional system of the Federal Republic of Germany is conventionally particularly characterised by five fundamental constitutional principles: it is a democracy (*Demokratie*), a constitutional state under the rule of law (*Rechtsstaat*), a federal state (*Bundesstaat*), a social state (*Sozialstaat*), and a republic (*Republik*). Article 20 para. 1 GG says: "The Federal Republic of Germany is a democratic and social federation." In article 28 GG the Basic Law also binds the States to observe these principles: "The constitutional order in the States must conform to the principles of republican, democratic and social constitutional government under the rule of law as described in this Basic Law." Further structural choices are to a large extent implicitly contained in the constitution, such as the commitment to the idea of the cultural state (*Kulturstaat*) or to neutrality of world view (*weltanschauliche Neutralität*). Protection of the environment and animal protection are explicitly listed in the constitution (article 20 a GG). The openness of the constitution to European integration is gaining outstanding importance.

a) Democracy

144   Germany is not one of those states which made major contributions to the development of democracy in the modern period (after 1789). Only in 1919 was a democratic system for all Germany created by the Weimar constitution (*Weimarer Reichsverfassung*). This, in turn, was destroyed by the National Socialists after a mere 14 years. The Basic Law takes this first German democracy as its starting point. Of course there are traces of democracy in Germany much further back than that. Communal thinking, with the essentially equal participation of all members of the community in decision making, has always played some part in the whole course of developments. The city constitutions of the Middle Ages provide roots for the idea of democratic rule. The idea of different estates, which had wide currency and which conveyed the participation in the decision making process by the estates which were ordered according to social classes, had primitive democratic elements. However, neither the estates nor the city constitutions necessarily accepted the fundamental equality of all persons, which is the basic premise of modern democracy. This concept, which was established by the

Reformation in the period following 1517, adopted the idea of equality for theological reasons and organised the church on a synodal basis which includes parliamentarism in a seminal state. The idea goes even further back to the religious conviction that all human beings were made in the image of God.

The Basic Law adopts representative democracy. Article 20 para. 2 GG formulates the following principle: "All state authority comes from the people. It is exercised by the people in elections and votes and by special organs of the legislature, the executive and the judiciary." All state authority must therefore be justifiable as the will of elected representatives of the people and thus, ultimately, of the people as sovereign. This end is served by the hierarchical structure of government administration, with the responsibility of the government to parliament at the top of the pyramid. The courts give judgement "in the name of the people". Legislation is essentially made by the elected parliament. Government ministers and the civil service have authority to make subordinate legislation only to the extent that there is statutory authority for doing so. The statute must determine the content, purpose and extent of the authority to make subordinate legislation.[9]   **145**

The central instrument of democratic participation in the power of the state are the elections to the legislatures of the Federation and of the States. These are the *Bundestag* of the Federation and the *Landtag* of each of the States. Democratic participation also takes place through the elections to the communal organs: to the district council (*Kreistag*) for districts (*Kreise*) and commune councils (*Gemeinderäte*) and town councils (*Stadträte)*. In many of the States the mayor of the commune (*Gemeinde*) is also elected directly by the people of the commune. Since the mayor is often also the local police authority, there is indeed also a direct election of police organs, although people are often not aware of this fact. Some special organs of state such as the Prime Ministers of the States (*Ministerpräsidenten*), the Chancellor of the Federation (*Bundeskanzler*) or the President (*Bundespräsident*) are not elected directly by the people, but are, however, always chosen by a democratically legitimated electoral body. Direct democracy (referendums, plebiscites), however, have a very limited role in the Basic Law. This is a constant topic of constitutional debate in Germany. Only for the practically insignificant case of a re-organisation of the federal territory in terms of article 29 GG is a referendum in the form of a *Volksbegehren* or *Volksentscheid* expressly provided for. A *Volksbegehren* is a vote by all members of the population who have the right to vote and relates particularly to the question of whether a *Volksentscheid* vote should be carried out. In the *Volksentscheid* the electorate then decides the specific material question itself.   **146**

At a federal level questions put to the people in the form of a vote or a *Volksentscheid* are not allowed, because they are capable of impeding the decision of the state organ responsible for the particular subject and undermining its independence. In contrast, elements of direct democracy are more strongly developed in the constitutions of most of the States and in local government (*Gemeinden*).   **147**

It is disputed whether a referendum is possible on the basis of article 146 GG, but the better view is that it is. It seems now that the prevailing opinion deems a referendum necessary and not just possible. This subject was of some importance for a certain time due to the accession of the DDR (East Germany) to the Federal Republic of Germany.   **148**

---

9 Article 80 para. 1 GG.

However, the revision of the Basic Law after the unification of Germany proved to be less dramatic than some had expected. There was therefore no occasion for a referendum.

b) Constitutional state under the rule of law

149 One of the central structural elements which give the Federal Republic of Germany its identity is the principle of constitutional government under the rule of law (*Rechtsstaatsprinzip*). This principle stands in contrast to the complete perversion of the law in National Socialism. Together with the comprehensive protection of Fundamental Rights, this principle expresses the ideal self-image of the Federal Republic of Germany to an even greater extent than the principle of democracy. The principle of constitutional government under the rule of law has been concretised into numerous sub-principles and specific rules, particularly in the practice of the Federal Constitutional Court. The basic idea of this principle is to guarantee justice and legal certainty. The guarantee of human rights is the content of the principle itself. Some of its most important individual aspects are mentioned here.

150 The supremacy of the law (*Vorrang des Gesetzes*) demands that all judicial and executive authority should be bound by statute. This excludes the possibility of executive prerogative or innate powers of the courts. The necessity of law (*Vorbehalt des Gesetzes*) means that any intrusion into the sphere of the individual's rights and all important administrative decisions are only permissible if they have a statutory basis. Both principles are at the same time an expression of the principle of democracy since they emphasise the primacy of the elected parliament.

151 The principle of constitutional government under the rule of law also guarantees a general entitlement to have rights enforced. While the Fundamental Right contained in article 19 para. 4 GG guarantees the protection of rights against infringements by the state, the general entitlement to protection of rights which is contained in this principle goes further, and contains a right to be protected by independent state courts against illegal behaviour of all types, including illegal behaviour by other private persons.

152 Also related to the principle of constitutional government under the rule of law is the idea of separation of powers: to ensure freedom, state power must be divided between various different organs which are essentially independent of one another and may not be concentrated in a single centre.

153 The principle of legal certainty (*Bestimmtheitsgrundsatz*) is also considered to fall under the principle of constitutional government under the rule of law: All state action must be sufficiently defined so as to remain predictable. However, this does not exclude the possibility of using general clauses and indefinite legal concepts such as "good faith" or "boni mores" (*Treu und Glauben; gute Sitten*) insofar as these can be given a sufficiently certain meaning by means of legal interpretation. Leaving certain decisions up to the discretion of civil servants is also not excluded by this principle.

154 A further aspect is the protection of legitimate expectations (*Vertrauensschutz*), which can lead not only to procedural, but also to substantive remedies. If the state has created a situation and the complainant has taken steps on the reasonable assumption that the situation will remain unchanged, then he or she generally has a legitimate expectation that the situation will not be changed. An aspect of this idea is the problem of

retrospective legislation. Article 103 para. 2 GG forbids absolutely the retrospective creation of criminal offences. In other cases retrospective legislation is not entirely impermissible, but must be justified by exceptionally important considerations of the common good if new legal disadvantages are to be attached to past events. Such situations are classified as cases of "genuine retrospectivity" (*echte Rückwirkung*). This is in contrast to intervention in an ongoing train of events, so-called "quasi-retrospective" measures (*unechte Rückwirkung*), which is more likely to be permissible; an example for this is the amendment of the law on divorce and its consequences which effected also already existing marriages contracted before the amendment. The absolute prohibition on retrospective criminal laws does not prevent a retrospective extension of periods of limitation so long as any such extension complies with the principles mentioned above. According to the Federal Constitutional Court the provisions of the criminal law relating to limitation of actions are not in themselves the basis for punishment – they are merely the basis for enforcing penalties, and as such are not subject to the total prohibition of article 103 para. 2 GG. On this reasoning it was possible to repeatedly extend the limitations period for National Socialist crimes, and finally to totally abolish the possibility of escaping liability for murder or genocide on the basis of time limitations.

Finally the principle of proportionality (*Verhältnismäßigkeitsgrundsatz*) with its subconcepts of objective suitability, necessity and reasonableness (proportionality in the narrower sense) was also developed out of the principle of constitutional government under the rule of law.   155

It can be seen that most of these legal principles can also be derived from various provisions of the Basic Law, particularly the Fundamental Rights. There they are generally more concretely formulated and, most of all, they are more clearly formulated from a constitutional point of view. On the other hand, the additional possible basis for these principles provided by the principle of constitutional government under the rule of law (*Rechtsstaatsprinzip*) does have the advantage that it sees the constitution as a single whole and avoids the fragmentation of its logic into various narrow special cases.   156

c) Social State

Dogmatically less refined, but by no means to be discounted is the principle that Germany is a social state. The constitution defines the Federal Republic of Germany as a social federation (*sozialer Bundesstaat*, article 20 para. 1 GG) and as a social constitutional state under the rule of law (*sozialer Rechtsstaat*, article 28 para. 1 GG). Together with the order to respect and protect human dignity, the principle of the social state obliges all state organs to provide for social conditions which are compatible with human dignity. Above all the word social means a duty to care for the weak, for example, by providing the material minimum for an acceptable standard of living. For this reason the principle of the social state has repeatedly been drawn on to establish the positive aspect of Fundamental Rights as an entitlement to benefits. In addition, the principle of the social state is also understood as imposing an obligation on the state to work towards the common good. This means that it provides an appropriate doctrinal basis for the limitation of individual interests.   157

d) Republic

158 The Federal Republic of Germany has a republican structure. This is generally understood as being in contrast to monarchy, which is the form of government which was abolished in the revolution of 1918. A second, and today more important, dimension of the concept is that it obliges the community of the state to serve the common good and justice. It thus also forms a link to the old understanding of republic as the embodiment of the *res publica*.

e) Federation

159 The fact that Germany is structured as a federation (*Bundesstaat*) is of central importance, both from the point of view of its theoretical constitutional structure and from a practical political perspective. The historical origins of the federal structure reach right back to the beginnings of the Holy Roman Empire in the 9th century. The central imperial authority and the individual territorial governments have always coexisted, sometimes co-operating, sometimes in conflict with one another. Federal structures have always dominated the political life of this Central European territory. Today Germany consists of 16 federal States (*Bundesländer*): Baden-Württemberg, Bavaria (*Bayern*), Berlin, Brandenburg, Bremen, Hamburg, Hesse (*Hessen*), Mecklenburg-Western Pomerania (*Mecklenburg-Vorpommern*), Lower Saxony (*Niedersachsen*), North Rhine-Westphalia (*Nordrhein-Westfalen*), Rhineland Palatinate (*Rheinland-Pfalz*), Saarland, Saxony (*Sachsen*), Saxony-Anhalt (*Sachsen-Anhalt*), Schleswig-Holstein and Thuringia (*Thüringen*).

160 The States (*Länder*) of the Federal Republic of Germany have sovereign status, as does the Federation itself. Their constitutional position is rather strong, although the Federal Government has had far greater political weight up to now. The exercise of state powers and the fulfilment of state duties is the business of the States except insofar as the constitution does not stipulate otherwise or allows for federal regulation (article 30 GG). It must, however, be said that the latter alternatives often apply.

161 The starting assumption is that legislation is the task of the States (article 70 GG). However, numerous particularly important issues are subjected to the legislative authority of the Federation (articles 71 ff. GG). For some issues the Federation has exclusive authority. Examples are international relations, defence, citizenship of the Federation, and the currency. The States cannot legislate in these fields. Then there are many fields where the Federation has concurrent legislative authority (article 74 GG). These are *inter alia* civil law, criminal law, procedure and the constitution of the courts, the law relating to foreigners, commercial and labour law, law relating to nuclear facilities, competition and cartels. The States are allowed to make laws on these subjects. However, if the Federation exercises its power to legislate on a particular subject, which has happened in most fields, then the competence of the States to legislate on that subject is ended.

162 The States may enact differing legislation in certain regulatory areas (article 72 para. 3 GG) as well as regarding particular federal statutes (article 84 GG).

163 In certain areas of the law regulating the relationship between state and church (often still called *Staatskirchenrecht or rather Religionsrecht*), the laws on the financial system (*Finanzverfassungsrecht*), the Federation has the power to legislate on basic principles (*Grundsatzgesetzgebung*) to ensure consistency on points of basic principle.

In some areas special unwritten authority becomes relevant. This includes the so-called "annex competence" and competence by reason of factual interdependence. These arise when an issue which formally lies in the sphere of state legislation can only be sensibly regulated in conjunction with a subject which lies within the sphere of federal legislation. An example of this is the legal regulation of armed forces universities (*Bundeswehruniversitäten*), which is seen as an annex to the authority of the Federation to legislate on matters relating to defence. Then there is also a competence arising from the nature of the matter, such as deciding what the national anthem should be, matters which, logically, can only be decided at federal level.

164

In accordance with the basic division of functions between the Federation and the States, the administration is also in principle the business of the individual States (articles 30 and 83 GG). However, the Basic Law once again to a significant extent assigns administrative functions to the Federal Government. This applies, for example, to the administration of the armed forces, the administration of the foreign service (state department), and numerous other areas. On the other hand, it is of great practical importance that the States generally provide the administrative apparatus for the execution of federal legislation. Thus, even in fields which are within the exclusive legislative competence of the Federation, the citizen is generally dealing with the administrative officials of the States. Legislation on matters which are within the legislative competence of the States is, of course, also administered for the States by their own administrative officials.

165

For most matters which are within the federal legislative competence, but which are administered by the States, the Federation can do no more than issue general administrative guidelines. Generally, the only sort of supervision which the Federation can exercise over how the law is being applied in specific cases consists of checking whether administrative action is legal. Decisions as to the appropriateness of a particular measure for the implementation are entirely at the discretion of the State's officials. Generally speaking the Federation may not issue directives on specific points to the state administrations. If it concludes that a State is not applying the law properly, and the State refuses to change its position, then the federal government must refer the matter to the *Bundesrat*, which consists of representatives of each of the States (article 84 GG).

166

In some specially designated cases the States perform administrative acts on a commission basis (*Auftragsverwaltung*). They then act as agents of the Federation. In these cases the Federation can give directives to the top levels of the state administration as to how to go about their duties legally and appropriately, and in emergency this power to give directives can also extend to the lower levels of the administration. An example of where this situation arises is the administration of federal roads, particularly the federal autobahns (articles 85 and 90 GG).

167

The sovereignty of the States is also of significance in the regulation of international relations. International relations are indeed a classic example of a matter which is to be legislated on by the Federation (article 32 GG). However, insofar as the States are responsible for legislating on a particular point, they can also enter international treaties with foreign states on that subject with the consent of the federal government. They thus possess partial legal personality for the purposes of public international law (article 32 para. 3 GG). In addition to this, they have the power to create international

168

institutions for the purpose of co-operation with neighbouring countries and transfer some of their sovereign powers to such bodies (article 24 para. 1 a GG).

169 The importance of the States in day-to-day politics is considerable. They exercise their weighty influence over federal policies via their voting rights in the upper house of parliament, the *Bundesrat*. The big political parties are also structured along federal lines. Politics at a state level act as a testing ground and reservoir of future leaders and policies for federal government. There are inefficiencies and frictions between the Federation and the States and between the States themselves which often become obvious. For example, a family moving from one State to another will get a direct experience of these disadvantages due to the change of school systems. Nevertheless, these disadvantages can and must be accepted. They are outweighed by the advantages of preserving the cultural identity of the various regions, the diversity of smaller areas and the opportunities for political experimentation. Political stability is improved by the increased opportunities to participate in the exercise of state power which are created, thus allowing political parties and forces which find themselves in opposition on the federal level to play a part in government on the state level. Finally, federalism is supported by the idea of separation of powers. The division of spheres of activity, powers and duties between state and federal governments and the self-administration at the level of local government help to prevent overly strong concentrations of power. The delegation of power to the States also does not necessarily lead to a splintering of the law or excessive diversity. Rather, for a long time a tendency towards a unitary approach, towards a certain uniformity of the different States, has become noticeable. Many state laws are drafted in a uniform way, in accordance with non-binding model texts which are worked out together by the Federation and the various States. Thus, the statutes of the Federation and of the various States for the regulation of the police do not differ significantly on important issues; laws on schools and municipal regulations regularly correspond in most respects. Indeed, most statutes regulating administrative procedures go so far as to often use the same wording.

f) European Integration

170 The openness of the *Grundgesetz* to European integration is increasingly gaining outstanding importance as an additional fundamental constitutional principle. The fact that conventional constitutional theory has not yet clearly acknowledged this principle does not detract from its importance. Already in the preamble the Basic Law includes a fundamental decision for a unified Europe. This fundamental decision is put into concrete form by article 23. This states that there is a constitutional obligation to further European integration: in order to realise a unified Europe the Federal Republic of Germany participates in the development of the European Union. This is on the assumption that the Union is bound by the principles of democracy, a constitutional government under the rule of law, federalism and the principle of subsidiarity, and must furthermore guarantee the protection of Fundamental Rights at a standard which is essentially comparable to that of the Basic Law. For the purpose of such an integration the Federal Republic of Germany may confer sovereign rights upon European Institutions. However, it may not give up its own existence as a state. It must retain substantial sovereign powers.

171 The law of the European Union and politics on a European scale are of decisive importance for the development of the law in Germany today. Union law is directly applica-

ble, in most cases through so-called regulations (*Verordnungen*) which are binding in all member states after having been enacted by means of one of the numerous legislative procedures of the Union. From the point of view of German legal theory, EU regulations are most closely comparable to a statute. Additionally, there are the far more numerous directives (*Richtlinien*) which must be implemented through the legislation of the member states. Thus, they are at first only binding upon the member states to whom they are addressed. Under certain conditions they apply also directly to citizens. Citizens may rely directly on the directive if the member state does not enact it in due time, if it is sufficiently certain, and if it is intended to confer a legal right upon the citizen.

It is certainly no longer possible to understand German law without taking into account Union law. The gradual process of transfer of sovereignty and the necessary cooperation between national and European authorities is one of the most dynamic areas of law.   172

4. Constitutional Organs

The following are the most important constitutional organs of the Federal Republic of Germany: the President of the Federation (*Bundespräsident*) as Head of State; the *Bundestag* as parliament with central powers of legislation, review and election; the *Bundesrat* as the organ through which the States participate in legislation and administration at a federal level; the Federal Government (*Bundesregierung*) with the Chancellor (*Bundeskanzler*) as Head of Government and the central political figure of the system and the federal ministers (*Bundesminister*) who are the political heads of the various government departments, and finally the Federal Constitutional Court (*Bundesverfassungsgericht*) which exercises considerable judicial powers in the political decision-making process.   173

a) The President of the Federation

The President of the Federation is the Head of State of the Federal Republic of Germany. He or she signs into law the statutes which have been passed by the *Bundestag* and *Bundesrat* (article 82 para. 1 sentence 1 GG). He or she appoints and dismisses the Chancellor (*Bundeskanzler*) after the Chancellor has been elected or deposed by the *Bundestag* and also appoints the federal ministers proposed by the Chancellor. He or she appoints and dismisses the federal judges, federal civil servants and the officers and non-commissioned officers of the armed forces (article 60 para. 1 GG). There are occasional exceptions from these powers: thus, the power to appoint the officials working for the *Bundestag* is exercised by the President of the *Bundestag* and the power to appoint the officials of the Federal Constitutional Court is exercised by the President of the Federal Constitutional Court. The President of the Federation exercises the power to pardon criminals on behalf of the Federation (article 60 para. 2 GG). The President of the Federation represents Germany in international affairs: he or she signs treaties with foreign countries in the name of the Federal Republic of Germany and accredits and receives their diplomatic representatives (article 59 para. 1 GG).   174

The term of office for the President of the Federation is five years. This means that the elections for this office take place in a different rhythm from the legislature periods of the *Bundestag* and the term of office of the Federal Government, which is dependent on the *Bundestag*. The President of the Federation can only be re-elected once. In con-   175 trast to the President of the Weimar Republic, he or she is not elected directly by the people. Instead, the election of the President of the Federation is the task of the Federal Assembly or Federal Convention (*Bundesversammlung,* article 54 GG). The election of the President of the Federation is the only purpose of this assembly. Half of its members are drawn from the members of the Bundestag and the other half are elected by the representatives of the Federal States on the basis of proportional representation (*Verhältniswahl*). The members of this second category are thus not necessarily members of the legislature.

176 The President of the Federation may not be any of the following while in office: A member of the government; a member of a federal or state legislature; a holder of any other office to which a salary is attached or a member of the board of directors of any commercial enterprise. The President may also not practise any trade or profession during his or her period of office (article 55 GG).

177 The political position of the President of the Federation is generally seen as being relatively weak, and, indeed, his or her office consists largely of representative functions. The impact of the federal president depends largely on the personal charisma of the particular individual in office. The limited nature of his or her power can also be seen in the fact that most proclamations and orders of the President of the Republic are not effective unless countersigned by the Chancellor or the minister responsible (article 58 GG). On the other hand, this relative lack of political power is the very characteristic which up to now has made it possible for the bearers of this office to often be seen as the representative of the whole German nation, in other words, to play an integrative role. The legal structure of the office avoids confrontation and division, because it is not designed for the assertion of specific political goals.

178 The President of the Federation is also not the head of the armed forces, in contrast to Germany's past constitutional traditions. In times of peace this position is filled by the Federal Minister of Defence (*Bundesverteidigungsminister,* article 65 a GG). In times of armed conflict the power to command the armed forces passes to the Chancellor (article 115 b GG).

179 The President of the Federation can also play a key role in the legislative process. Since he or she must assent to and promulgate statutes, but only insofar as they have been passed in accordance with the Basic Law, the president has the power to test legislation. According to the predominant view the president is entitled to examine the formal constitutionality of legislation, in other words, whether the correct procedure has been followed in passing it. In addition the president can also examine the material constitutionality of legislation, which means that he or she can test whether the content of the legislation is constitutional. If the president is of the opinion that a statute is unconstitutional he or she can refuse to assent to and promulgate it even although it has been passed by parliament. The statute then does not come into force. This has happened several times in the history of the Federal Republic of Germany.

b) The German Bundestag (Parliament)

180 The German Bundestag (articles 38 ff. GG) is the central political representative organ of the people at the federal level. As a legislative body it co-operates with a number of other constitutional organs. It also elects the Chancellor and monitors the government and civil service.

The *Bundestag* consists of 598 delegates, although slight variations for the duration of one legislative period are possible due to the sometimes rather complicated electoral procedures. Its period of office, the legislative term, is four years, assuming that it is not dissolved at some stage within that period. However, its period of office does not end until the newly elected *Bundestag* assembles for the first time (article 39 para. 1 GG).   181

The delegates are elected in a general, direct, free, equal and secret balloting process (article 38 para. 1 GG). All Germans over the age of 18 have both the right to stand for election (*passives Wahlrecht*) and the right to vote in the election (*aktives Wahlrecht*; article 38 para. 2 GG). Only in very closely defined circumstances, for example, where someone has been convicted of a criminal offence, can these rights be taken away.   182

That an election is general means that in principle the entire nation has the right to vote. Direct means that the imposition of any sort of electoral college or other intermediary which in turn decides on the composition of the parliament is not permissible. The election must be *free*, which means that no pressure or force may be exerted to make the electorate vote in a certain way. There is no duty to vote. Equality means that each vote must have the same value and the same chance of success. This means that each voter must have the same number of votes and that each vote must be of equal weight to the vote of any other voter in determining the result. The act of voting itself must be secret – an open ballot is never permissible.   183

The procedure for electing *Bundestag* delegates is set out in detail in the Federal Elections Act (*Bundeswahlgesetz*) and the Federal Elections Ordinance (*Bundeswahlordnung*). Half of the number of delegates prescribed by this legislation, i.e., 299 are elected according to a winner-takes-all majority vote (*Mehrheitswahl*). The remaining delegates are elected on the basis of proportional representation (*Verhältniswahl*). Every voter thus has two votes.   184

The whole of Germany is divided into constituencies (*Wahlkreise*), each of which includes approximately the same number of voters. In each constituency candidates stand for election and each voter casts his or her first vote for the preferred candidate. The person who wins the most votes in the constituency wins the election. This is the direct mandate which is decided on the winner-takes-all basis by counting each voter's first vote.   185

The other Bundestag delegates are elected according to the system of proportional representation by voting for lists of candidates in each State. Here the second vote of each voter is counted towards one of the state lists. The state lists contain the names of candidates in a fixed order. Such lists can only be submitted by political parties. Which candidates are on the list is determined by internal party elections. In each State the numbers of votes cast for a particular party's list are added up. The proportion of the total vote won by each list determines how many of the candidates on a particular list are elected.   186

For the state lists the five per cent rule applies. This says that if a party's lists receives less than 5 % of the total number of second votes cast in the whole of Germany then the second votes cast for it are to be disregarded. This means that, subject to certain exceptions (for example, to provide for national minorities) a party must win at least 5 % of all second votes if it is to gain seats in the *Bundestag* by means of the state lists.   187

The aim of this rule is to prevent splinter groups from obstructing the work of the *Bundestag* and gaining disproportionate influence in the event that a coalition government must be formed because no party has a majority.

188   The delegates in the *Bundestag* are not legally bound to follow instructions from their party leadership. They are the representatives of the whole nation, and are bound only by their own consciences. However, the numerous causes of actual dependence on the party in everyday life are not amenable to legal regulation. Delegates have a duty to disclose to the President of the *Bundestag* any activities they undertake on behalf of groups or organisations and any financial contributions which they receive from such sources. An important right of the delegates which helps to ensure their independence is parliamentary privilege (immunity). This protects them against legal action or other negative consequences arising from how they vote or statements which they make in parliament. The only exception is in the case of defamation (article 46 para. 1 GG). Parliamentary privilege, on the other hand, serves to protect the delegate in his or her personal freedom. Only with the permission of the *Bundestag* may a delegate be subjected to criminal prosecution, arrested or limited in his or her personal freedom. The only exception is if the delegate is arrested in the course of committing a crime or during the next day (article 46 para. 2 GG).

189   The parliamentary rules which the *Bundestag* gives itself contain the rules concerning the formation and powers of groupings in the *Bundestag*. Such a grouping is called a *Fraktion (Fraktionen* in the plural*)*. A *Fraktion* is defined as a group consisting of at least 5 % of the members of the *Bundestag* (§ 10 *Geschäftsordnung des Deutschen Bundestages,* abbreviated *GOBT*; i.e. Rules of Procedure of the German Bundestag). A basic rule is that only delegates who belong to the same party or delegates who belong to parties which, because of their political objectives, do not compete with one another in any one of the States may form a *Fraktion*. This second alternative is applicable to the CDU, which does not put up candidates in Bavaria, and the CSU, which puts up candidates nowhere but in Bavaria. These two parties form a single *Fraktion* in the *Bundestag*. The *Fraktionen* determine which delegates are to be members of the various committees (*Ausschüsse*) which the *Bundestag* forms to discuss specialised issues. These *Fraktionen* can introduce legislation and, all in all, they play a central political role in parliamentary life.

190   The Bundestag monitors the government and the civil service. Its delegates have the right to put questions to the government: any government minister can be cited to appear before parliament. A means of control which is particularly effective from a political perspective is the investigative committees (*Untersuchungsausschüsse*) provided for by article 44 GG. An investigative committee must be set up as soon as it is demanded by one quarter of the delegates and has wide powers of investigation within the limits of the *Bundestag's* authority. In conducting such an investigation, the rules of criminal procedure must be respected, particularly the rules on examination of witnesses, search and seizure, and the administration of oaths.

191   One of the main duties of the Bundestag is the passing of legislation. This is done in co-operation with various other constitutional organs (article 76 ff. GG). The right to introduce a bill is possessed by the Federal Government, by a group of delegates representing not less than 5 % of the total number of delegates and acting as a *Fraktion*, and by the *Bundesrat*. If the *Bundestag* passes a bill, it then goes to the *Bundesrat*. This is a type of second chamber of parliament. Certain bills can only become law if

the *Bundesrat* assents. The closed list of laws requiring the assent of the *Bundesrat* is specially enumerated in the Basic Law. The list refers mainly to types of legislation which would have a significant impact on matters of particular interest to the States. As far as laws not mentioned in the list are concerned, the *Bundesrat* may raise objections, but if these are rejected by the *Bundestag* the bill can pass into law without the consent of the *Bundesrat*.

The Mediation Committee (*Vermittlungsausschuss*) plays an important role in the relationship between *Bundestag* and *Bundesrat* (article 77 para. 2 GG). This constitutional organ is made up of sixteen members of the *Bundestag* and sixteen members of the *Bundesrat*. The *Bundesrat* can call a sitting of the Mediation Committee in response to a bill passed by the *Bundestag*. In the case of laws requiring the consent of the *Bundesrat* the *Bundestag* and the Federal Government can also call in the Mediation Committee. An attempt is then made in the Mediation Committee to work out a text for a compromise bill, which is usually done by agreeing on changes to the proposed bill. The amended version is then once again put through the legislative process. 192

Once the bill has been passed by the *Bundestag* and, if necessary, by the *Bundesrat* too, it must in the first instance still be countersigned by the Chancellor and the competent Federal Minister and then be assented to and promulgated by the President of the Federation (*Bundespräsident*; articles 82 para. 1, 58 GG). Assent consists of signing the statute after checking its text. Promulgation consists of publishing the statute in the Federal Gazette (*BGBl.*) If the statute does not expressly state when it is to come into force, then it comes into force on the fourteenth day after the day on which the particular edition of the Federal Gazette in which it is contained was published. 193

Decisions in the *Bundestag* and *Bundesrat* can generally be taken by a simple majority of the members present, so long as the minimum number required to form a quorum is present. Some decisions can only be made by an absolute majority, that is, more than half of the total number of members of the house. Particularly important decisions, in particular amendments to the constitution, require a two thirds majority. 194

The *Bundestag* elects from among its members the President of the German *Bundestag* (*Präsident des Deutschen Bundestags,* article 40 para. 1 sentence 1 GG) who maintains order and directs the sittings. The President of the Bundestag is also an organ of the constitution. 195

c) The Bundesrat

The *Bundesrat* provides an opportunity for the States (*Länder*) to participate in administration and legislation at the federal level (article 50 ff. GG). It consists of members of the state governments. Depending on the size of its population, each State has a minimum of three and a maximum of six votes. These must always be cast *en bloc*. The members of the *Bundesrat* are appointed and dismissed by the government of the State which they represent and they are bound to vote in accordance with the directions given to them by their state government. There are some exceptions to this rule, for example, it does not apply to votes in the Mediation Committee. The main business of the *Bundesrat* is to play a role in the passing of federal legislation. Certain important ordinances promulgated by the Federal Government which are specifically listed in the Basic Law also need the consent of the *Bundesrat*. By way of article 23 GG the Bundesrat also has significant influence on the formulation of federal policy relating to the European Union. Political parties regularly make use of the *Bundesrat* as an 196 instrument of opposition on the federal level at times when they are in opposition in the *Bundestag*, but have a majority of the votes in the *Bundesrat*.

d) The Federal Government

197   The Federal Government is the political nerve-centre of Germany (article 62 ff. GG). It consists of the Chancellor (*Bundeskanzler*) and the Federal Ministers. Each minister directs his or her department independently and is responsible for its actions. This is the principle of ministerial responsibility (*Ressortprinzip*). However, the Chancellor has the authority to set government policy. All ministers are bound by the Chancellor's decisions on broad, fundamental issues of policy and the Chancellor can also decide specific questions of particular importance. In the case of differences of opinion between ministers on points which do not fall within the Chancellor's general policy-setting powers, a decision on the matter is made by the government as a whole (article 65 GG). The Basic Law also provides for such collegial decision-making when the more important specific issues are decided, for example, when an important ordinance (executive order) is to be issued.

198   The Federal Government essentially has an open discretion in defining each minister's portfolio – the government has organisational authority (*Organisationskompetenz*). However, some ministries are specifically mentioned by the Basic Law and are sometimes automatically bound to include certain functions. An example of a ministry expressly provided for in the Constitution is the Federal Finance Minister, whose consent is required for extraordinary or additional expenditure, or the Federal Defence Minister who is Commander in Chief of the armed forces in times of peace.

199   From a legal point of view the political parties have no power to exercise influence over the Federal Government. However, in reality their political influence is considerable. If, as is usually the case, the government is a coalition made up of various different parliamentary *Fraktion* groupings, its functioning is often based on a written coalition agreement between the parties making up the governing *Fraktionen*. Such a coalition agreement does not have any legal force, but is of considerable practical importance.

200   The federal ministers are appointed and dismissed by the President of the Federation (*Bundespräsident*) on the advice of the Chancellor (article 64 para. 1 GG). The Chancellor is proposed by the President of the Federation and elected by the *Bundestag* (article 63 GG). Generally speaking the President of the Federation will propose the leading politician of the strongest party in the *Bundestag* for the position of Chancellor, but he or she is not obliged to do so. If the proposed candidate is not elected, then the *Bundestag* can choose a Chancellor itself. If the candidate for Chancellor is voted for by an absolute majority, in other words by more than half the total number of *Bundestag* delegates, then the President of the Federation must appoint him or her. If the candidate has achieved only a simple majority, then the President of the Federation has a choice between appointing the candidate and dissolving the *Bundestag*. Up to now this situation has never arisen. These rules are aimed at producing the most stable government majority possible. Here the Basic Law is once again reacting to the experience of the Weimar Republic whose government was permanently crippled by instability and the difficulty of finding a majority.

201   The same purpose is served by the provisions on the dismissal of the Chancellor. The Basic Law provides for a constructive no confidence vote. This means that the *Bun-*

destag can only express its lack of confidence in a Chancellor by a majority of delegates electing a new Chancellor and requesting the President of the Federation to dismiss the old Chancellor. The President of the Federation must then comply and appoint the newly elected Chancellor (article 67 para. 1 GG).

The Chancellor him- or herself can also call for a vote of confidence. If the government then does not receive an absolute majority, the Chancellor can, if he or she chooses, request the President of the Federation to dissolve the *Bundestag*. The *Bundestag* can, however, prevent its dissolution by choosing a new Chancellor by an absolute majority (article 68 para. 1 GG). 202

The period of office of the Chancellor and the Federal Ministers is bound to the legislative period of the *Bundestag*. Each newly-elected *Bundestag* must go through the process of electing a Chancellor. The period of office of each Federal Minister ends with that of the Chancellor, assuming that the minister is not dismissed before then. There is no provision for a vote of no confidence by the *Bundestag* directed against individual ministers. 203

The constitutional powers of the Chancellor are largely responsible for the fact that the Chancellor is generally the dominant figure in German politics. Germany has proved to be a "Chancellor democracy". Powerful political personalities have found a stable legal basis for their power in the office of Chancellor for a number of reasons. The Chancellor is chosen initially by a majority of the *Bundestag*, and once chosen he or she has a strong position in dealing with the parliament because of the requirement that the Chancellor can only be toppled by a constructive vote of no confidence. The Federal Government presents a united front due to the Chancellor's power to set policy guidelines, the fact that the Chancellor has the ministers of his or her choice, and that it is not possible to direct a vote of no-confidence against a specific minister. The counterpart of this is that the parliament itself is somewhat weakened and its independence is further limited by the dominant position of the political parties. 204

e) The Federal Constitutional Court

The highest German court, the Federal Constitutional Court (*Bundesverfassungsgericht*), is also a constitutional organ. It deals exclusively with constitutional disputes (see especially article 93 and 100 GG). The details of its jurisdiction are regulated in the Federal Constitutional Court Act (*Bundesverfassungsgerichtsgesetz* abbreviated BVerfGG). The court sits in Karlsruhe and consists of two senates of eight judges each. Some specially designated cases can be decided by the court sitting in chambers (*Kammern*) of three judges. Half of the candidates for appointment to the Federal Constitutional Court are chosen by the *Bundesrat*, and half are chosen by the *Bundestag*. The big political parties propose candidates according to their political leanings whenever a position becomes vacant. In practice it is necessary to reach a consensus on the candidates before putting the matter to the vote, because the election of a judge requires a two-thirds majority. 205

The importance of the court arises from the fact that all exercise of state power must be in compliance with the Constitution, and decisions of the Federal Constitutional Court are binding not only in the particular case before it, but also for the future. It can declare acts of parliament void on the basis that they are unconstitutional. The court has often managed to bridge deep political divisions with its decisions. Of all institutions it enjoys one of the highest levels of public esteem. 206

207 The Constitutional Complaint (*Verfassungsbeschwerde*), the Internal Dispute Procedure (*Organstreitverfahren*), Abstract Constitutional Review (*abstrakte Normenkontrolle*) and Specific Constitutional Review (*konkrete Normenkontrolle*) are in practice the most important types of proceedings before the Federal Constitutional Court (article 93 and 100 GG).

208 A Constitutional Complaint can be brought by any person on the basis of an allegation that the state has infringed one of his or her Fundamental or quasi-Fundamental Rights (article 93 para. 1 number 4 a GG). Generally speaking the petitioner is required to exhaust his or her remedies before the lower courts before the Federal Constitutional Court will hear the matter. Constitutional Complaints form by far the greatest part of the court's workload.

209 In the Internal Dispute Procedure (article 93 para. 1 number 1 GG) the court decides disputes between different constitutional organs where the applicant organ alleges that the respondent organ has infringed on its rights or duties. Such a dispute can, for example, arise between the Bundestag and its delegates, between the Bundestag and the President of the Federation, or between the Bundesrat and the Federal Government. Political parties can also make use of this procedure by virtue of their status as quasi-constitutional organs (*verfassungsorganähnliche Stellung*; article 21 GG) if their rights as such have been infringed by a constitutional organ.

210 Abstract Constitutional Review (article 93 para. 1 number 2 GG) can be initiated by the Federal Government, by individual State governments, and by request of one quarter of the delegates of the Bundestag. The aim of such review is to give the Federal Constitutional Court the opportunity to pronounce on a statute whose constitutionality is in doubt.

211 Specific Constitutional Review (article 100 para. 1 GG) also serves to pronounce directly on the constitutionality of a statute. When a lower court in the course of proceedings comes to the conclusion that a statute, which is relevant to the decision of the matter before it, is unconstitutional, it must, generally speaking, refer this law to the Federal Constitutional Court for a decision on its constitutionality. The Federal Constitutional Court's decision on the constitutionality of the statute is binding.

5. Political Parties

212 The political parties are a fundamental element of public life in the Federal Republic of Germany. The Basic Law acknowledges their role in article 21 and also prescribes certain organisational requirements to which they must conform. The parties play a role in forming the political will of the people. Their internal structure must be in accordance with democratic principles. As social groupings they must be primarily self-financing, relying on membership fees and donations. Additional financing from public funds is possible to a limited extent. This is regulated in terms of principles which have repeatedly been called into question and in accordance with complicated rules.

213 The Parties Act (*Parteiengesetz* abbreviated *PartG*), which contains the more detailed rules on this particular subject, gives a rather complicated definition of the concept "political party" in § 2 paragraph 1 *PartG*. The aim of the definition is to promote constancy and stability in political life. It defines a party as an association of citizens who, within the Federation or one or more of its States, wish to influence the political views of the public and participate in the representation of the German people in the

Bundestag or in a state legislature for a long or indefinite period of time. In addition, to be recognised as a party, such an association must offer sufficient indication of the seriousness of its intentions. This requirement is considered in the light of the overall factual situation in general, and specifically refers to the extent and solidity of the group's organisation, the number of its members, and their public behaviour.

The Social-Democratic Party of Germany (*Sozialdemokratische Partei Deutschlands, SPD*), the more conservative Christian Democratic Union (*Christlich-Demokratische Union, CDU*), its Bavarian sister-party the Christian Social Union (*Christlich-Soziale Union, CSU*) and the upper-middle-class, liberally inclined Free Democratic Party (*Freie Demokratische Partei, FDP*) have found support for their views since the founding of the Federal Republic. The ecologically-minded Alliance 90/The Greens (*Bündnis 90/Die Grünen*) has taken its place in the political spectrum since the mid-1980s. After reunification, the Party of Democratic Socialism *(Partei des Demokratischen Sozialismus, PDS)* emerged as the successor of the Socialist Unity Party of Germany (*Sozialistische Einheitspartei Deutschlands, SED*), which had ruled the *DDR* (East Germany), and joined the political arena. It eventually merged with several smaller groups and now calls itself The Left (*Die Linke*). Various nationalist groups have also made an appearance from time to time; recently, the so called Alternative für Deutschland has been able to establish itself.   214

Parties which, in terms of their goals or the behaviour of their supporters, are directed towards the impairment or destruction of the basic system of freedom and democracy or which endanger the existence of the Federal Republic of Germany are unconstitutional and may be banned. Only the Federal Constitutional Court has a say in determining whether a party is unconstitutional. The aim of this rule is to prevent the government of the day from banning opposition parties for opportunistic political reasons. This is the so-called party privilege (article 21 para. 2 GG). At a very early stage in the history of the Federal Republic of Germany two political parties were banned. These were the Socialist Reich Party, a National Socialist party, and the German Communist Party (*Kommunistische Partei Deutschlands*, abbreviated *KPD*).   215

Public life in Germany is determined to a large extent by the political parties. This is often cause for complaint. Not only the parliament, but also appointments to the higher positions in the judiciary, civil service, cultural institutions and some branches of the media are subject to their far-reaching influence. However, since adequate checks and balances are built into the system, the positive aspects of stability and competition which large parties with a broad popular base provide should not be overlooked.   216

6. The Financial Constitution

Germany's constitutional law relating to financial matters (article 104 a ff. GG) is very complicated. The basic principle is that the federal and state governments are each responsible for the costs arising from their respective duties. This means that insofar as the States are responsible for performing administrative functions on their own behalf they bear the costs of doing so, even if the laws which they are administering are federal statutes (articles 104 a and 83 GG). On the other hand, where the States are performing administrative duties on a commission basis for the Federation (*Bundesauftragsverwaltung*) the Federation is responsible for the costs. The Federation can provide the States with financial assistance for particularly important investments.   217

218   The division of responsibility for expenses runs parallel to the right to collect revenue. Certain taxes and revenues, such as customs duties and the tax on insurance policies (article 106 para. 1 GG), belong to the Federation. Others, such as the inheritance tax (article 106 para. 2 GG), belong to the States. Still other taxes, such as income tax on wages, salaries and the income of self-employed people as well as turnover tax (i.e. value added tax, VAT) are shared between the federal, state and local levels of government (article 106 para. 3 ff. GG). The basic principle with respect to these taxes is that each State receives a share of the taxes which were collected in its area. To compensate for the fact that some States are able to generate more revenue than others, a redistribution of revenue between the States (*Länderfinanzausgleich*) takes place. This means that the poorer States receive a share of the revenue of the richer States, and the Federal Government also makes supplementary transfers (article 107 GG).

219   Taxation is administered in part by the finance departments of the States (*Länder*) and in part by the financial bureaucracy of the Federation. These two administrations are to some extent linked in their organisation and duties. Taxes are not merely a means for raising revenue for the government. They are also a legitimate instrument of economic and social policy.

220   All revenue and expenditure of the Federation must be provided for in the budget for each year. The budget is regulated by parliament by means of a Budget Act. The same applies to the *Länder*. Control over the budget thus lies in the hands of parliament. However, statutes which will have financial implications, i.e., which will reduce revenue or increase expenditure require the consent of the Federal Government and the same applies to changes made via the Budget Act (articles 110, 113 GG). Further details concerning the budget and budgetary regulation are contained in various federal and state statutes. The most important of these are the Budgetary Principles Act (*Haushaltsgrundsätzegesetz, HGrG*) and the Federal Budget Ordinance (*Bundeshaushaltsordnung, BHO*).

221   The Federal Court of Auditors (*Bundesrechnungshof*) has the job of checking on the propriety and economic efficiency with which public bodies are drawing up their budgets and conducting their business. The state equivalents are the State Audit Courts. The members of these courts have judicial independence and report to the *Bundestag* on a regular basis (article 114 GG).

222   The *Bundesbank*, officially *Deutsche Bundesbank* (German Federal Bank), plays an important role for the whole economy (article 88 GG). It is independent of the Federal Government. It is part of the European System of Central Banks, which is composed of the European Central Bank (*Europäische Zentralbank*, abbreviated *EZB*) and the central banks of the Member States of the European Union, and which is responsible for monetary policy in the euro area.

7. Military Defence

223   Military defence is in the hands of the Federal Government. It is responsible for creating armed forces for purposes of defence (article 87 a para. 1 GG). The German armed forces are called the Federal Defence Force (*Bundeswehr*). Apart from defending the national territory, the armed forces may only be used for special purposes which are specifically listed in the constitution, for example, in the case of a natural disaster or a major accident. Activities not involving the use of weapons, for example, helping with the harvest, distributing food to the needy or working in development aid projects, are

not regarded as military operations (*Einsatz*) and therefore do not raise questions of permissibility.

The Federal Defence Force is integrated into the structures of NATO (*Nordat-lantischer Verteidigungspakt*), of which Germany is a member. Increasingly, multi-national units which are orientated towards Europe are organised. The Federal Republic of Germany has obliged itself by international treaties not to produce atomic, biological or chemical weapons. The treaty on German unification which was concluded with the victorious powers (Two-Plus-Four Treaty) provides that the Federal Defence Force may not exceed a troop – strength of 370 000.

224

Federal Defence Force troops may be committed to operations under United Nations auspices, whether as "blue beret" peacekeeping troops or in armed conflict aimed at restoring peace and order. The constitutional basis for such operations is set out in article 24 para. 2 GG. This permits the integration of the armed forces into organisations for mutual collective security. However, because of the gravity of such a decision, a special resolution of the *Bundestag* authorising it is necessary. Up to now the duties of the Federal Defence Force and its constitutional regulation have been designed strictly for defence purposes and the avoidance of armed conflict insofar as this is at all possible.

225

Article 12 a GG stipulates that all men over the age of 18 can be conscripted for basic military training. Statutory law provided for this general conscription until 31 June 2011. Since then, general conscription has been suspended and therefore no longer exists in Germany.

226

The Constitution also provides for the important exception that armed military service may be refused on grounds of conscience (articles 4 para. 3 and 12 a GG). Conscientious objectors may be conscripted for alternative service of a civil nature (*Zivildienst*).

227

The Basic Law regulates in great detail what may be done in time of military emergency (*Verteidigungsfall*, articles 115 a – 115 l GG). A military emergency exists if the Federal Republic of Germany is attacked with armed force. The most notable feature of this situation is that there is no martial law in the classical sense. A series of laws aimed at ensuring the ability to mount an effective defence come into operation in the event of a military emergency. The powers of the civil authorities remain essentially intact – there is no significant increase in the powers of the military. The Fundamental Rights may also not be limited. The only exceptions are that a few minor special rules become applicable to the right to property, and the period for which a person may be detained without being brought before a court is extended to a maximum of four days. The main relevance of the rules in the Basic Law applying to military emergencies relates to the redistribution of powers between the organs of the constitution.

228

Some of the bitterest internal conflicts which the Federal Republic of Germany has experienced related to the question of re-armament after the Second World War in the early 1950's and to the emergency laws of 1968, which include the rules for military emergencies mentioned above. Both these debates were overshadowed by the memory of the two world wars which were unleashed by Germany. This is not the least of the reasons why the rules formulated to regulate this issue are modest in scope, being sometimes very strict and complicated, and at other times vague on important issues. Over all they reveal more about the internal condition of Germany in times of peace than about how a war would be legally regulated.

229

8. Religious Communities

230 Freedom of belief, which is guaranteed by article 4 GG, also involves rights for the religious communities. In addition, the Basic Law recognises their special status in that article 140 GG brings into the text of the Basic Law provisions of the law regulating the relations between state and church which had previously been part of the Constitution of the Weimar Republic (*Weimarer Reichsverfassung*, abbreviated *WRV*). Many areas of the law concerning the relationship between the state and the various churches are regulated in concordats and treaties which the state has concluded with the churches. There are two main religious confessions in Germany, namely, the Catholic Church and the Evangelical Churches. The latter are organised at a regional level as State Churches (*Landeskirchen*) and at a national level as the Evangelical Church in Germany (*Evangelische Kirche in Deutschland*, abbreviated *EKD*). Both main churches have approximately the same number of members, with a grand total of about 49 million. There are also many smaller religious communities. Islam has about 4 million adherents in Germany. Many Germans do not belong to any religious community.

231 There is no established church or state church (article 137 para. 1 WRV, article 140 GG). The state must remain strictly neutral in its relations with religious communities. Non-religious philosophies of life are accorded the same status as religious views. The big churches and a series of smaller religious communities are corporations at public law (*Körperschaften des öffentlichen Rechts*). However, this does not imply that they are incorporated into the structures of the state. It is merely an expression of the importance of the religious communities as a factor in public life. A number of specific powers are attached to this status.

232 Despite the essential separation of church and state there are many areas in which they co-operate. Thus, religious communities which are incorporated at public law are empowered to collect taxes. These taxes consist exclusively of contributions of the members of the respective religious community. They usually amount to eight or nine per cent of the tax obligation and are collected as an additional levy along with the income tax or PAYE. The church tax is collected by the state revenue authorities on behalf of the church in exchange for a fee. Every taxpayer can free him- or herself from this church tax by formally leaving the church. Another area of co-operation is religious education in public schools. Religious education is a regular school subject and is taught in accordance with the principles of the particular religious community involved. In addition provision is made for military chaplains.

233 The independence of the religious communities is of central importance. They regulate and administer their own affairs within the limits of the laws which apply to the population as a whole (article 137 para. 3 WRV, article 140 GG). The same applies to church institutions which have only loose legal ties with the official church such as church-run hospitals, old-age homes or kindergartens. Such institutions, run by the (Catholic) *Caritas* or the (Protestant) *Diakonie*, are of considerable social significance. The right of self-determination of the religious communities means that, irrespective of their legal status, they have considerable scope to make their own rules, and the big churches make use of this freedom. It goes without saying that they are free to make their own rules on questions of faith, but their power of self-regulation goes even further to include those fields of their activity which are moulded by their beliefs. Thus, they generally have their own rules on staff representation and protection of informa-

tion. They have their own courts, and in the field of labour law they have a wide discretion in deciding what duties of loyalty are owed to them by their employees.

Literature:

Peter Badura, Staatsrecht, 7. ed. 2018

Bonner Kommentar, 17 vols., since 1952

Christoph Degenhart, Staatsrecht I. Staatszielbestimmungen, Staatsorgane, Staatsfunktionen, 34. ed. 2018

Horst Dreier (Hrsg.), Grundgesetz. Kommentar, 3 vols. 3. ed. 2013-2018

Volker Epping, Grundrechte, 8. ed. 2019

Volker Epping/Christian Hillgruber (eds.), Grundgesetz. Kommentar, 2. ed. 2013

Christoph Gröpl, Staatsrecht I. Staatsgrundlagen, Staatsorganisation, 10. ed. 2018

Konrad Hesse, Grundzüge des Verfassungsrechts der Bundesrepublik Deutschland, reprint of the 20. ed. 1999

Friedhelm Hufen, Staatsrecht II. Grundrechte, 7. ed. 2018

Jörn Ipsen, Staatsrecht I. Staatsorganisationsrecht, 30. ed. 2018

Jörn Ipsen, Staatsrecht II. Grundrechte, 21. ed. 2018

Josef Isensee/Paul Kirchhof (eds.), Handbuch des Staatsrechts der Bundesrepublik Deutschland, 13 vols., 3. ed. 2003-2013

Hans D. Jarass/Bodo Pieroth, Grundgesetz. Kommentar, 15. ed. 2018

Hermann von Mangoldt/Friedrich Klein/Christian Starck, Das Bonner Grundgesetz. Kommentar, 3 Bde., 7. ed. 2018

Gerrit Manssen, Staatsrecht II. Grundrechte, 13. ed. 2016

Theodor Maunz/Günter Dürig (Hrsg.), Grundgesetz. Kommentar, 7 vols. since 1958

Hartmut Maurer, Staatsrecht I, 7. ed. 2016

Lothar Michael/Martin Morlok, Grundrechte, 6. ed. 2017

Ingo von Münch/Philip Kunig (Hrsg.), Grundgesetz. Kommentar, 2 vols., 6. ed. 2012

Thorsten Kingreen/Ralf Poscher, Staatsrecht II. Die Grundrechte, 34. ed. 2018

Michael Sachs, Grundgesetz. Kommentar, 8. ed. 2018

Klaus Schlaich/Stefan Korioth, Das Bundesverfassungsgericht, 11. ed. 2018

Bruno Schmidt-Bleibtreu/Franz Klein (eds.), Grundgesetz. Kommentar, 14. ed. 2018

Michael Schweitzer/Hans-Georg Dederer, Staatsrecht III. Staatsrecht, Völkerrecht, Europarecht, 11. ed. 2016

Ekkehart Stein/Götz Frank, Staatsrecht, 21. ed. 2010

Klaus Stern, Das Staatsrecht der Bundesrepublik Deutschland, 5 vols., since 1980

Reinhold Zippelius/Thomas Würtenberger, Deutsches Staatsrecht, 33. ed. 2018

III. Administrative Law

1. General Principles of Administrative Law

a) Duties and Organisation of the Public Administration

The public administration (*Verwaltung*) fulfils individual, specific state obligations on its own initiative, and subject to legally regulated guidelines. It has long outgrown its earlier role as a mere guarantor of the citizen's safety, and fears that it could operate as an instrument of oppression are also largely groundless today. Rather, the image of the administration today is determined by its comprehensive welfare activities on behalf of the population. The state provides the basic necessities of life (*Daseinsvorsorge*); to a large extent it has become a service industry. The concepts and categories of administrative law are only gradually adapting to this reality. With the far reaching privatisation of the state's activities the structure of administrative law is also changing. Whereas administrative law was previously concerned to ensure that the state itself

234

carried out the activity in an appropriate manner, it is now increasingly focussed on ensuring that the state adequately supervises the provision of services by private service providers.

235   The organisation of the public administration is primarily characterised by the federal structure of Germany and also by the autonomy of the communes. The structure of the public administration follows the structure of the state. The federation (*Bund*) has its own public administration, as do the states (*Länder*), which are generally divided into districts (*Bezirke*), sub-districts (*Kreise*), and communes (*Gemeinde*). Each of these is an administrative authority in its own right. Each institutional unit within the public administration is described as a public authority (*Behörde*). This includes every structure which performs tasks of public administration, for example, The Public Order Office, the State Bureau for the Preservation of Public Monuments, or the Federal Ministry for Labour and Social Affairs.

236   The typical structure of direct public administration (when the state performs its duties through its own administration) can be seen most clearly in the administrative structures of the bigger federal states (*Länder*). Basically, there are three levels of administration: supreme state authorities (*oberste Landesbehörden*) include, amongst others, the state government (*Landesregierung*), the prime minister of that state and the state ministries. They are responsible for the entire state within their particular spheres of activity. Intermediate administrative authorities (*mittlere Verwaltungsbehörden*) operate at the level of the district (*Bezirk*) in about one third of the States. The government at this level (*Regierungspräsidium*) goes by various different names[10] in different *Länder*. Except for the smaller *Länder* and the city-states (Bremen, Hamburg and Berlin) each *Land* is divided into several districts (*Bezirke*), each of which has its own local government (*Regierungspräsidium*). The duties and competences of the levels of government above are gathered together in the government of the particular *Bezirk*. Thus, this level of government acts not only for the Ministry of Agriculture but also for the Interior Ministry, the Social Ministry and so forth. The head of this intermediate level of government is the *Regierungspräsident*. This official is appointed by the government of the *Land*.

237   The lowest level of state (as opposed to communal) administration is the sub-district (*Kreis*). Each district (*Bezirk*) is divided into several sub-districts. Each sub-district in turn consists of several communes (*Gemeinde*). Cities and large towns often form separate sub-districts in themselves and then exercise the various functions of a sub-district. These "sub-district independent" (*kreisfreie*) towns are then themselves part of the lowest level of state administration. Somewhat smaller towns which form part of a normal sub-district may be accorded the status of a "large sub-district town" (*große Kreisstadt*). Such towns are then allowed to exercise some – but not all – of the powers of the sub-district.

238   In a departure from this typical structure various special administrative bodies have become detached from the ordinary structures for historical or practical reasons. These bodies have their own intermediate and low-level administrative structures. Examples of such bodies are the revenue authorities and the forestry authorities, whose jurisdiction with respect to area cannot conveniently be coterminous with the limits of the ordinary administrative districts and sub-districts.

---

10 *Regierung, Regierungspräsident, Bezirksregierung.*

It is fairly common practice to create independent government agencies (*Landesober-behörden*) at the level of the *Land*. They remain answerable to a particular minister, but they are organisationally independent of the relevant ministry. Their area of jurisdiction includes the whole *Land*. Examples are the state statistical offices or the State Criminal Investigation offices. 239

There are also various quasi-administrative, or indirectly administrative, bodies (*mittelbare Staatsverwaltung*) which enjoy a greater degree of autonomy and are legally independent from the state. These bodies take various forms. The first is the *Körperschaft*. This is characterised by the fact that it has members. Typical examples of the *Körperschaft* are the various self-regulatory professional bodies. An example is the Legal Practitioners' Association (*Rechtsanwaltskammer*), of which all legal practitioners with residence in Germany must be members. The chambers of industry and commerce play a similar role for businesspeople. These bodies regulate the activities of their members who in turn have the right to vote and have a say in the formation of policies. The aim is to promote accountability, democratic participation and the sensible utilisation of expert knowledge. 240

An *Anstalt* has both material resources and personnel for the fulfilment of a particular objective. Examples are the various public broadcasters, which are to a large extent independent of government control. 241

Finally there is the public foundation (*Stiftung*) which is an independent fund dedicated to carrying out specific, long term tasks. An example is the Prussian Cultural Heritage Foundation, which is dedicated to the administration of the cultural treasures of the former Prussian state. 242

For some time, there has been a strong general tendency to take administrative activities entirely out of the public sphere and to perform them within the limits of private law. Numerous privatisations have taken place in pursuit of this goal, although privatisation does not necessarily mean that shares in the affected organisations have been sold to the public. Examples are the restructuring of the former federal rail and postal services. 243

The higher levels of public administration have the power to issue directions to the levels of public administration below them and to review their acts. In determining the extent of these powers a distinction is made between procedural and substantive supervision. The power to issue procedural directions (*Rechtsaufsicht*) is more limited than the power to issue substantive directions (*Fachaufsicht*). Procedural directions are concerned only with the formal legality of administrative acts. Substantive directions go further: this power is comprehensive, including not only the power to review the formal legality of an act but also to consider whether the decision in question was appropriate (*zweckmäßig*). The more limited procedural powers of supervision apply in particular to administrative units which have a right to autonomy such as the communes, universities and the governing bodies of the self-regulating professions. 244

The internal structure of each of the administrative bodies is also hierarchical. At the head of each administrative unit is a head of department who is empowered to issue instructions to the other members of the unit. Traces of the old Prussian collegial system, in which decisions were taken by committees of several persons with collective responsibility, are rare. This collegial principle is, however, applied in the decision making with collective responsibility of the government in cabinet. 245

246   In the last few decades, following the Scandinavian example, various types of ombuds-man have become firmly established as protectors of the interests of citizens. Examples are the armed forces ombudsman who responds to complaints from members of the armed forces; the ombudsman for data protection, who deals with illegitimate use of personal information; and the ombudsman for equal rights, who enforces equal oppor-tunities and rights for both women and men. They receive complaints from citizens and in some cases have far-reaching powers to review activities and to raise objections, although they usually have no direct power to issue directions. However, they are of-ten able to exercise considerable influence via their public reports.

b) The Legal Forms of Administrative Action

247   Public administrative action can take numerous, very diverse forms. For example, ad-ministrative activities range from making a formal decision determining the amount to be paid to a person in need by way of social security payments to publishing guidelines of general application dealing with specific details of the procedures followed in decid-ing whether to approve building plans. The rubbish removal services dispose of house-hold waste, and the city council may rent the city hall out for a dance. Legal structures have formed to correspond to these various types of administrative activity.

248   The classical form of administration is the *Verwaltungsakt*. This is defined in § 35 sen-tence 1 of the federal Administrative Procedure Act (*Verwaltungsverfahrensgesetz*, ab-breviated *VwVfG*). In terms of this provision an administrative action (*Verwal-tungsakt)* is any direction (*Verfügung*), decision (*Entscheidung*) or other sovereign act *(hoheitliche Maßnahme)* on the part of an administrative body which is directed at dealing with a specific factual situation in the field of public law. The administrative action in question must, in addition, have immediate legal force for third parties. A "sovereign act" is a 19th century concept. Today it means administrative action in gen-eral in the field of public law with all its relevant powers and limits. A *Verwaltungsakt* thus regulates with immediate effect the legal position of the specific citizen affected. It includes, for example, a decision as to what claims to social security benefits a needy person has in terms of the relevant statute. A direction from a traffic policeman is a *Verwaltungsakt*, as is the approval of building plans, the appointment of an official or the transfer of a child to next-highest class in a government-run school. The traffic signs alongside the road such as a no-stopping sign or a red traffic light also fall into this category. Since such signs are directed at an indeterminate number of road users they are described as a "general direction" (*Allgemeinverfügung*, § 35 sentence 2 VwVfG).

249   The original significance of the classification as a *Verwaltungsakt* was that the admin-istrative courts could only grant a remedy in cases where the complaint concerned a *Verwaltungsakt*. Today article 19 para. 4 GG ensures that a person who is personally affected by an illegal act on the part of public authorities will always have a remedy. In modern law the significance of the *Verwaltungsakt* is rather that it provides the ad-ministration with a means of directly enforcing its decisions against the person affect-ed. In contrast to a private citizen, who can only enforce a claim which is disputed by obtaining a judgement, the administration has to take no further steps at all for a *Ver-waltungsakt* to be enforceable. The *Verwaltungsakt* is, by itself, an independent basis for execution. This applies even if the *Verwaltungsakt* in question is illegal so long as it has not been voided due to a challenge by the affected party. Only a *Verwaltungsakt*

which is void has no effect at all (§ 43 para. 2, 3 VwVfG). A *Verwaltungsakt* will be void if it suffers from a particularly grave defect which, on due consideration of all the relevant facts, is indisputable (§ 44 VwVfG).

Instead of proceeding by way of *Verwaltungsakt* a public authority can often make a public contract (*verwaltungsrechtlicher Vertrag*) with the affected person (§§ 54 ff. VwVfG). This is a particularly appropriate way of proceeding in cases in which mutual rights and duties are to be created. An example would be the situation where a large construction firm is to provide roads and public facilities for an entire suburb. Here the various plans, the granting of permission to proceed, and the various services to be provided by the contractor will often be regulated in the form of a contract.   250

Public administrative bodies can create rules of general application if they are empowered by statute to do so. Such a rule is called a *Rechtsverordnung* (see article 80 GG). The internal business of self-regulating bodies is governed by a set of rules called a *Satzung*. In both cases these are laws, although not acts of parliament (law in the material sense as opposed to law in the formal sense). Public authorities regulate their internal business by means of general directions for the conduct of business (*Verwaltungsvorschriften*), and, for specific cases, by means of directives (*Anweisungen*) and decrees (*Erlasse*). The plan is also a significant instrument of administrative action. Plans, which are formulated in many different circumstances and in various legal forms, influence the future development and behaviour of the citizen, whether because they are legally binding, or because of their factual influence.   251

Apart from situations in which public bodies act to affect the legal position, there are also situations in which they simply perform some act: the municipal gardener mows the grass in the park, the security guard patrols with his or her dog. Such activities are referred to as *schlichtes Verwaltungshandeln* or as factual activities (*Realakte*) of the public body.   252

Unless a statute provides otherwise, public bodies can also make use of private-law forms to achieve their objectives. When office material is bought or a hall is rented to a sport club the transaction usually takes the form of an ordinary private law contract. A public body can thus generally choose in what form it wishes to run a public service. However, it cannot organise its business so as to free itself from the obligation to respect the Fundamental Rights, by which it is always bound. It is, at very least, always bound to respect the principle that public bodies may not act in an arbitrary manner (*Willkürverbot*). At present there is a clear tendency towards the far-reaching privatisation of administrative functions. The aim is to provide more scope for market-oriented thinking. In particular, privatisation means that the restrictions on dealing with personnel which are imposed by the law relating to permanent civil servants (*Beamtenrecht*) are loosened.   253

However, the current trend goes beyond mere privatisation to a de-legalisation of administrative activity as a whole. New ways of dealing with problems are being discovered or are becoming more prominent. Informal gentlemen's agreements are replacing to some extent the use of the *Verwaltungsakt, Rechtsverordnung* and formal contracts. Such agreements between public bodies and private persons are expressly not intended to create legal obligations. For example, the beverages industry undertakes to package its products in recyclable containers and in exchange the responsible public authority refrains from imposing such an obligation by creating binding regulations. The agreement is expressly intended not to be enforceable before a court of law. Instead a party   254 who fails to observe the agreement is faced only by the prospect of countermeasures by the other side. Tolerance of a state of affairs has also become an instrument of administrative action. The relevant public authority is aware of a particular state of affairs or activity which, strictly speaking, is illegal, but does not take action against it because of other considerations and makes its intention not to act known to the affected parties. It is disputed, but should be answered in the negative, whether such failure to act can give rise to a relationship of trust which can effectively amount to authorisation of the activity in question. The problem is that such an informal approach can in effect both deprive the public of information concerning the activity in question and of a say in its regulation, as well as lead to a general erosion of a law's validity. Indeed, this is sometimes the illegitimate motive of the public body in adopting such an approach.

c) Public Property

255 Public property (*öffentliche Sachen*) means things which are specifically for public use. This classification includes such diverse things as streets and parks, the office furniture of public authorities, public buildings, exhibits in public museums, and the service weapons of the police and the armed forces. Such things are generally owned by the responsible public authority, such as the Federal Government, or a *Land, Kreis* or *Gemeinde*. However, it is also perfectly possible for such things to be privately owned. For example, a piece of land over which a public way runs may be private property. The important point is the classification of the property as public property. This characteristic is primarily conferred by allocation (*Widmung*) in modern law. *Widmung* is a *Verwaltungsakt* (see above). The consequence of allocation is that public use then takes precedence over private use of the thing in question. Thus, a road may be allocated for use by public traffic, or a book may be allocated to the collection of a public library. The terms of the allocation also provide more detailed indications of how the thing may be used. For example, a patrol boat may be allocated specifically for the use of the coastguard, or the square before the city hall may be allocated specifically to a particular type of public traffic, namely pedestrian traffic.

256 In this context a distinction is drawn between common use (*Gemeingebrauch*) and special use (*Sondernutzung*). This distinction is of practical importance particularly for public ways and public waters. If a thing is allocated for common use then every person has a right to use it to the extent set out in the allocation. It is then not necessary to obtain additional special permission. Special use goes beyond the ordinary common use and serves particular, specialised needs. Such use requires special permission and usually involves the payment of a fee. For example, a shopping area which has been allocated as a pedestrian zone may be used by any pedestrian. If a café wishes to use the pedestrian zone to provide outdoor tables and chairs for its clients then it requires specific permission for this special use. It will then generally be required to pay a fee for this additional right of use.

d) Administrative Procedure

257 Important provisions concerning the procedures to be followed by the federal bureaucracy in administrative matters are contained in the federal Administrative Procedure Act (*VwVfG*). The various *Länder* have either passed essentially similar laws or simply declared the VwVfG to be governing the activities of their respective bureaucracies. In

addition, there are numerous statutes dealing with special issues which regulate specialised administrative procedures. If there is such a provision it will then take precedence over the general provisions of administrative law. For example, the Nuclear Energy Act (*Atomgesetz*) contains specialised rules for the procedure to be followed in deciding whether to approve a plant for the disposal of nuclear waste.

It is a basic principle that before an administrative act (*Verwaltungsakt*) is issued the affected person must be given a hearing (§ 28 VwVfG). Officials who might have a personal interest in the matter, such as officials who are related to an applicant, may not be involved in dealing with the matter (§§ 20, 21 VwVfG). As a general rule an administrative act only takes effect once it has been communicated to the affected parties (§§ 41, 43 VwVfG). The provisions concerning the annulment of an administrative act once it has been issued are also of importance (§§ 48-50 VwVfG). Administrative acts which are legal and which are favourable to the person concerned may only be annulled under very strict conditions, and such an annulment must generally be accompanied by compensation. Here the principle that legitimate expectations are to be protected (*Vertrauensschutz*) operates particularly strongly. It is easier to reverse a favourable administrative act if it is illegal, but here too there is protection of legitimate expectations. If an administrative decision is unfavourable, then it can be withdrawn far more easily. This applies in the case of both legal and illegal rulings. The reason is that in such circumstances the need to protect the legitimate expectations of the individual affected is less strong.

The decision-making process itself is also specially regulated. Sometimes a public authority has no discretion: If certain prerequisites are met it must make a particular decision. Often, however, it has a discretion (*Ermessen*). If this is the case and certain prerequisites are met then the authority may make whichever decision seems appropriate to it. If the discretion extends to deciding whether the authority should act at all it is said to have an *Entschließungsermessen*. If the authority must act, and merely has a discretion as to what sort of action to take, it is said to have an *Auswahlermessen*. Generally speaking the point of a discretion is to reach the most appropriate decision in a specific situation which the legislature could not provide for in advance. The discretion must always be exercised with reference to the aims of the statute which grants the discretion (§ 40 VwVfG). A discretion is generally created when a statute uses the words "can" (*kann*) or "may" (*darf*) in setting out the legal consequences of a particular situation. For example, § 15 para. 1 of the federal Assemblies Act (*Versammlungsgesetz*) provides that a public assembly outdoors "can" be prohibited if it poses a threat to public order or safety. The discretion is more limited when the statute uses the word "shall" (*soll*). In cases where a public body "shall" do something it is generally obliged to attach a particular legal consequence to the situation described. However, in exceptional cases, where good reasons for doing so exist, it can depart from this rule. For example, the spouse or life partner (i.e. partner in a state registered homosexual relationship, *Lebenspartner*) of a German "shall" obtain German citizenship when specific requirements are met (§ 9 para. 1 StAG).

The conferment of a discretion is never a licence to act in an arbitrary manner. Discretion must always be exercised properly. The following are some of the very detailed limits on the exercise of discretion: The authority must consciously exercise its discretion (*Ermessensnichtgebrauch*); the authority must make full use of the discretion which has been granted to it (*Ermessensunterschreitung*); the authority may not ex-

258

259

260

ceed the limits of its discretion (*Ermessensüberschreitung*); the authority may not base its decision on irrelevant considerations (*Ermessensfehlgebrauch*); and, finally, the authority may not infringe on the Fundamental Rights in exercising its discretion.

261 In certain rare cases, although the authority in principle has a discretion, the particular facts of the case are such that there is only one proper result. In this situation there is said to be a reduction of discretion to zero (*Ermessensreduzierung auf Null*). For example, this would be the case if the fire brigade, due to limited capacity, has to choose between pumping water out of a flooded cellar and fighting a major fire at a chemicals factory which has broken out at the same time. In this case there is only one proper decision – the fire brigade must choose to fight the fire first.

262 It is generally accepted that a discretion only relates to the drawing of a legal conclusion from a given set of facts (*Rechtsfolgeermessen*). If, instead, the dispute relates to whether the prerequisites for the exercise of the discretion have been met then the deciding authority generally has no discretion since it is assumed that this is an issue of recognising general, objective facts where there is no room for the exercise of a subjective discretion.

263 In many instances, the law uses open terms that need to be further interpreted, e.g. when a speed limit for vehicles only applies "when wet". This is referred to as an undefined legal term (*unbestimmter Rechtsbegriff*). The courts exert full judicial review over an administrative body's interpretation of such terms.

264 However, there are situations in which there is uncertainty as to issues of fact, in other words, uncertainty as to whether the prerequisites for the exercise of legal power have been fulfilled, and in such situations the deciding authority must make a decision itself. This is the case in examinations, or where the performance of a subordinate must be evaluated. Whether a candidate for the school-leaving certificate has written a sufficiently good essay in German to pass is to a large extent a matter for the particular person evaluating the essay to decide. This type of discretion as to questions of fact is called *Beurteilungsspielraum*.

265 Another important issue is the making of predictions about the future: Whether, for example, the safety measures at a chemicals factory are satisfactory so that the factory poses no danger. In such situations it is not possible for the legislature to make provision for all relevant factors. Similarly, it is often not possible for the administrative courts to accurately reconstruct the situation in which a decision was made, for example the situation in an oral examination with its moods and impressions.

266 The power of administrative bodies to exercise discretion on such non-legal issues (*Beurteilungsspielraum*) is also subject to limits and rules which to a large extent correspond to those governing the exercise of discretion in applying the law to facts (*Rechtsfolgeermessen*). The intensity of judicial scrutiny of the procedure followed in making a decision will increase with the increasing importance of the affected legal interest and the extent of the potential damage to it.

e) State Liability and Rights to Compensation

267 The law regarding remedies against the state for infringements of the rights of private persons is, at first sight, rather confusing. There are numerous different written and unwritten causes of action for claiming compensation from the state. This complexity can only be justified on historical grounds, but so far attempts to reform the law in

this respect have failed due to disputes as to who has legislative authority to undertake such a reform. Today state liability is subject to the concurrent legislative powers of the Federation (article 74 para. 1 number 25 GG). However, the Federation has not yet made comprehensive use of this power.

One of the most important bases for claims against the state is § 839 BGB which deals with official liability (*Amtshaftung*). This provision states: If a civil servant deliberately or negligently breaches his official duties to a third party then he or she is liable to compensate the third party for any harm which results. This provision is applicable not only to career civil servants in the strict sense (*Beamte*) but also to any person who acts in the exercise of a public office. According to the literal sense of this rule the official is personally liable to the third party. This provision, which reflects earlier views on the subject, is unsatisfactory both from the point of view of the official and from the point of view of the third party. Firstly, it is unfair to the official to place on him or her the whole risk of harm resulting from the exercise of his or her duties on behalf of the state. Secondly, it is unfair to the person who has suffered harm, because a government official will generally not have large amounts of money at his or her disposal and will therefore not be able to provide adequate compensation in situations where considerable damage has been suffered. For this reason article 34 GG transfers the liability of the official to the public authority for which the civil servant was acting. If, in the exercise of official duties which have been entrusted to the civil servant, the official breaches his or her duties to a third party, then as a general rule liability is to be borne by the state or the public body in whose service the official stands. The affected party thus has a claim to have his or her entire loss made good by the public administration. However, this liability only exists if the office bearer has acted wrongfully and culpably (in breach of a duty).

268

There are, however, other cases in which the infringement of property rights is perfectly in accordance with the law but where there is nevertheless a need to provide some compensation for the person affected. This thought is the basis of the rule which provides for compensation to be paid in cases of expropriation. The provision of compensation constitutes a core element of the constitutional right to property. Expropriation is only permissible in the public interest. It may only take place on the basis of a statute which sets out the nature and extent of the compensation to be provided. The compensation is to be determined by reaching a just balance between the interests of the public and the affected party. If a dispute as to the extent of the compensation arises the person affected has a right to bring the case before the regular courts (article 14 para. 3 GG).

269

The guarantee of property can be transmuted into a guarantee of the value of property when the public good requires the expropriation of a particular piece of property. An example would be where a particular piece of land is required for the building of a road and the owner does not wish to sell. The compensation must be just. As a general rule the market value of the property is taken as a basis, but a lesser amount in compensation might be just in some circumstances.

270

The right to compensation for expropriation has a long tradition. In Germany it crystallised around the concept of "sacrifice" (*Aufopferung*). Already in 1794 the Prussian General Code (*Preußisches Allgemeines Landrecht*) stated "The state is obliged to compensate those persons who are compelled to sacrifice their special rights and privileges for the common good". Even today this idea forms the basis for various addi-

271

tional claims to compensation which are not included in article 14 GG, the provision relating to formal expropriation. The reason is that otherwise legal activity by the state can sometimes impose a disproportionate burden (*Sonderopfer*) on certain individuals. An example would be the hindrance of commercial activity by drawn-out construction works or unusual levels of noise from traffic in a particular street. This sort of interference is referred to as an expropriatory infringement (*enteignender Eingriff*) and, according to a firm line of court decisions, the person suffering such an infringement has a right to compensation.

272   Additional protection is provided in the case of a quasi-expropriatory infringement (*enteignungsgleicher Eingriff*). The requirements for such an infringement are generally met when the state causes damage of a pecuniary nature to property. The act in question must be wrongful, although it need not be culpable, i.e., it need not involve negligence or intentional causing of harm. An example would be if the state were to illegally quarter a homeless person in a dwelling with the result that the owner of the dwelling suffers some pecuniary loss.

273   The remedies for expropriatory and quasi-confiscatory infringements only apply when there has been damage of a pecuniary nature to property (*Verletzung vermögenswerter Güter*). In the case of infringements against non-pecuniary interests, such as a person's health or reputation, the resulting gap is closed by the claim based on "sacrifice" (*Aufopferung*). This claim arises in cases where the action of the office bearer causing the harm was not culpable. This is relevant, for example, where a policeman shoots at a fleeing criminal and, without having acted negligently or deliberately, hits an innocent bystander in the leg. Here the bystander can claim his or her medical expenses from the state on the basis of "sacrifice". It is necessary to provide for such a cause of action because the other possible basis for an action in such a situation, namely § 839 BGB and article 34 GG, only applies if the official acted culpably in causing the harm.

274   However, a replacement or compensation in money is often not adequate. Instead the injured party will often want some other sort of remedy. For example, this would be the case if the illegally quartered tenant is still in possession of the house. Here another invention of the courts comes to the assistance of the injured party. This is the claim to remedial action (*Folgenbeseitigungsanspruch*). The claim to remedial action aims at reversing the consequences of illegal administrative action. Various justifications have been suggested for it. One is that it is a necessary conclusion from the relevant Fundamental Rights. It is also sometimes explained by analogy with corresponding causes of action in the private law sphere (§§ 1004, 906, 853 BGB).

275   The claim to restoration of the proper position (*Herstellungsanspruch*) can be seen as a special case of the claim to remedial action. This specialised claim has developed as a result of the peculiarities of social security law (*Sozialrecht*). Social security benefits provided by public bodies are regularly dependent on making applications in good time, paying personal contributions by the due date and making the right choice between various alternative services. Since the relevant rules are often very complicated the public service has a special duty to guide and advise the affected person. If this duty is not complied with a claim for damages is often not an adequate remedy or is simply not allowed by the system. The solution in such cases is the claim to restoration of the proper position. The claim is not dependent on proof of fault. It gives the citizen who has suffered a disadvantage a claim to have the position restored to what it would have been had the bureaucracy fulfilled its duties to him or her properly.

Literature:

Hans Peter Bull/Veith Mehde, Allgemeines Verwaltungsrecht, 9. ed. 2015
Wilfried Erbguth/Annette Guckelberger, Allgemeines Verwaltungsrecht, 9. ed. 2018
Jörn Ipsen, Allgemeines Verwaltungsrecht, 11. ed. 2019
Hartmut Maurer/Christian Waldhoff, Allgemeines Verwaltungsrecht, 19. ed. 2017
Franz-Joseph Peine/Thorsten Siegel, Allgemeines Verwaltungsrecht, 12. ed. 2018

2. Special Administrative Law

Special administrative law includes numerous different areas of law which are distin-   276
guished from one another according to the various different aspects of life which they
affect and the various different contexts in which they appear. Examples are the law
relating to aliens, environmental law, the law governing career civil servants and tax
law insofar as these various fields are the object of state administrative activities.
These divisions and classifications are subject to constant change. Together they give
an impression of the diversity of the constantly shifting administrative activities of the
state. A number of the particularly important special areas will be dealt with below.

Literature:

Dirk Ehlers/Michael Fehling/Hermann Pünder (eds.), Besonderes Verwaltungsrecht, 4. ed. 2019
Wilfried Erbguth/Thomas Mann/Mathias Schubert, Besonderes Verwaltungsrecht, 12. ed. 2015
Friedrich Schoch, Besonderes Verwaltungsrecht, 2018

a) Police Law

Due to changes in the activities of the state, indeed, in the very concept of the state,   277
the whole of administrative law is undergoing rapid change. Police law (*Polizeirecht*)
is perhaps still the classical example of special administrative law. But even within this
field a great deal is in flux. The concept of "police" is itself a matter of contention. In
the past almost all aspects of administration which were regulatory and potentially involved intervention by the state were classified as police activity. This explains old-
fashioned concepts such as "building police", "aliens police" and "trade police". Today the approach is rather to define police in a formal way. According to the formal
approach, "police" includes all public authorities which are referred to as such in the
relevant legislation.

Policing is, as a rule, a matter for the states (*Ländersache*). Each state has its own po-   278
lice force. As a matter of internal organisation a distinction is then made between different areas of policing activity. The ordinary uniformed police forces (called *Vol-
lzugspolizei* or *Schutzpolizei*) are responsible for maintaining public safety and order
insofar as this is not the business of other specialised bodies. The traffic police
(*Verkehrspolizei*) are responsible for regulating and monitoring road traffic. The water
police (*Wasserpolizei*) do the same for the waterways. The criminal investigation unit
(*Kriminalpolizei*) is dedicated to investigating crimes. Apart from this there is the general police bureaucracy which supervises the various specialised fields and which is
generally responsible for ensuring that public safety and order are maintained. The
emergency reserve force (*Bereitschaftspolizei*) is a uniformed force in barracks which
stands ready for emergencies. Generally speaking it consists of young police officers
who are still undergoing training.

The Federal Government also has various police forces. The first of these is the Federal   279
Police (*Bundespolizei*). In terms of the Federal Police Act (*Bundespolizeigesetz*) this

force is responsible for securing the external borders of the Federation in the non-military context as well as for the protection of railways, airports, and air traffic. It is also responsible, together with the Federal Criminal Police Office (*Bundeskriminalamt*), for the protection of the property and personnel of the Federal Government. The Federal Criminal Police is another federal police force. Its primary duty is to combat serious crime and to co-ordinate the efforts of the Criminal Investigation Units of the various *Länder*. It also serves as the German contact for international police co-operation through Interpol.

280   Europol operates Europe-wide. Europol is an organisation which has been created by the member states of the European Union. Its object is to improve the effectiveness of and co-operation between the national police forces. In pursuit of this objective Europol collects, evaluates and disseminates information and specialist skills to member states.

281   The secret services are not to be regarded as police forces. To avoid the development of uncontrollable power concentrations there are various different secret services. The Federal Intelligence Service (*Bundesnachrichtendienst*) has as its objective the collection of information in other countries. Military Counter-Intelligence aims to prevent spying and sabotage in the armed forces. The Federal Office for the Protection of the Constitution (*Bundesverfassungsschutz*) collects and evaluates information about movements with the potential to undermine the free democratic social order or to endanger the existence or security of the Federal Republic. It also monitors the activities of foreign secret services within Germany and activities by foreign governments which endanger the security of the state. Each of the *Länder* also has an Office for the Protection of the Constitution. These organisations are created and regulated by the Federal Act for the Protection of the Constitution (*Bundesverfassungsschutzgesetz*) and the various acts for the protection of the constitution of each *Land*. The Office for the Protection of the Constitution thus serves generally to protect the constitution and to conduct counter-espionage work. To these ends political forces within Germany which are considered to be hostile to the constitutional order are also monitored. The secret services do not have police powers such as the power to arrest persons or seize property. If such action is necessary they must call on the police to carry it out. There have been repeated political attempts to end this strict separation of functions in the interests of more effective action, particularly against organised crime and terrorism. Accordingly, the federation and the Länder have set up the Joint Counter-Terrorism Centre (GTAZ) and the Joint Centre for Countering Extremism and Terrorism (GETZ) for a more effective coordination of the combat against terrorism, in which various institutions cooperate on the basis of already existing laws.

282   Although the *Länder* and the Federation have each exercised their power to pass police acts, there is in practice considerable uniformity in police law, so that one can say generally that there is a common police law throughout Germany.

283   The police forces have a double function. On the one hand it is their duty to avert dangers to legal interests. From this point of view it is their duty to prevent the law from being broken in the first place were possible. This preventive policing function is regulated by the Police Acts of the Federation and the *Länder*. On the other hand, the police have a reactive function. In this context they become active in investigating crime and pursuing criminals. This aspect of their duties is regulated in the Criminal

Procedure Act (*Strafprozeßordnung*, abbreviated *StPO*). The reactive function is largely the task of the Criminal Investigation Units (*Kriminalpolizei*).

The key to understanding the preventive role in police law is the general clause in the various Police Acts (for example, § 9 POG Rh-Pf, § 8 PolG NRW, § 10 BbgPolG). It is the duty of the police to avert dangers to public safety or public order. The police are authorised to take the necessary steps to avert a danger to public safety or order in a particular factual situation. Furthermore, the police may promulgate statutory instruments for the prevention of such dangers.

284

The dominant view is that public safety (*öffentliche Sicherheit*) means two things. Firstly it means the protection from harm of the life, health, honour, freedom and property of the citizen. Secondly it means the protection of the legal order, subjective rights and legal interests and of state and state like institutions from harm (e.g. § 2 number 2 BremPolG).[11] Public safety thus has an individual and a community-oriented aspect. Strictly speaking, all the interests entitled to protection under the head of public safety can be subsumed under the heading of protecting the legal order from harm. It should be noted that the police force is only empowered to act to protect private rights such as a claim for rent or a maintenance claim if it is not possible to obtain a court order speedily enough to protect the right and if, without the assistance of the police, the enforcement of the right would become impossible or significantly more difficult.

285

The concept of public order has lost almost all meaning as a means of defining the protective duties of the police. It means the total of all the (mostly unwritten) rules whose observation is considered to be essential for a fruitful co-existence in terms of dominant social and ethical views. In a pluralistic society it is therefore difficult to define "public order" and from a practical point of view it is largely irrelevant.

286

The police may only take steps interfering with the rights of a specific individual on the basis of the general clause if the interest which is to be protected by their action is in immediate danger. It is not sufficient if there is merely a general danger. An abstract possibility of danger, in other words, a danger which would typically threaten the protected interest in such a situation but which has not yet materialised, is also not sufficient justification for specific action. A fortiori, taking action against individuals because of the possibility that a danger might arise in the future is also not allowed. The concept of danger (*Gefahrenbegriff*) is thus of central importance in police law. Danger, in terms of police law, is a situation which will with sufficient probability result in harm to the protected interest if there is no intervention. It therefore involves forming a judgement as to the future train of events.

287

If the requirements of the general clause are satisfied then the police may act. However, they are, generally speaking, not obliged to act. Instead it is a matter for their professional judgement exercised in good faith whether and how they should act (see e.g. § 3 PolG NRW, § 4 BbgPolG, § 3 POG Rh-Pf). In certain circumstances where important legal interests are threatened this discretion may be reduced to zero. In such cases the citizen has a right to police intervention if his or her own legal interests are endangered. The action which is taken by the police must always be reasonable (*verhältnismäßig*, see e.g. § 2 PolG NRW, § 3 BbgPolG, § 2 POG Rh-Pf).

288

---

11   *Schoch*, Polizei- und Ordnungsrecht, in: *Schmidt-Aßmann* (ed.), Besonderes Verwaltungsrecht, p. 165.

289   Often it is only possible to put an end to a danger by taking steps against a particular person. For example, where a motor vehicle has been parked in a way which poses a risk to traffic then it must be removed, or it may be necessary for the police to take an aggressive drunk into custody until that person is sober again.

290   Against whom the police can act is determined by the provisions on responsibilities to the police (*polizeiliche Verantwortung*). The responsible person, in other words, the person who owes a duty to the police (often called "*Störer*" in German), must tolerate the action of the police and is generally also liable for any costs which arise from the police action.

291   Firstly, there is a responsibility to the police for acts (*Verhaltensverantwortlichkeit*). If the acts of a person constitute a threat to public safety or order then this person is to be the object of police action (see e.g. § 4 PolG NRW, § 5 BbgPolG, § 4 POG Rh-Pf). Here the doctrine of proximate causes (*Lehre der unmittelbaren Verursachung*) is relevant. This requires an evaluative judgement: Generally speaking, if there is a series of causal events leading to the danger, the last person in the temporal sequence who by his or her own free will set in motion one of these events will be the one who is responsible to the police.

292   In exceptional cases the doctrine of proximate causes can make a person liable to the police when he or she deliberately set in motion an earlier, initially neutral, causal event which then led others to behave in a certain dangerous manner (so-called *Zweckveranlasser*). This will depend on a value judgement as to what forms the social core of the train of events. A shop owner who places a particularly fascinating advertisement in his or her window will be the one who is responsible to the police if as a result a crowd of people gather in front of the window and obstruct the traffic. This is so even although the last element in the causal sequence was contributed by the people forming the crowd.

293   Secondly, responsibility to the police may arise from a state of affairs (*Zustandsverantwortlichkeit,* see e.g. § 5 PolG NRW, § 6 BbgPolG, § 5 POG Rh-Pf). If a thing is a source of danger then the action taken by the police is to be directed against the person having actual control over the thing. Generally it is also permissible to take action against the owner or other persons having rights in the thing in question such as the tenant. For example, if there is a danger due to high winds that flower pots will be blown from a balcony and injure passers-by in the street below, then the police may oblige the owner of the dwelling to put an end to the danger.

294   If the responsible persons do not act in good time or do not take sufficient steps, then the police may take the necessary steps themselves and charge any resulting expenses to the person responsible. In exceptional cases where there is no other way to avert a serious danger the police may take action against persons who are not responsible for the danger (see e.g. § 6 PolG NRW, § 7 BbgPolG, § 7 POG Rh-Pf).

295   Apart from the general clause, police law also provides special rules for certain situations which are particularly serious or which occur particularly frequently. The procedures to be followed in these situations are referred to as the "standard measures" and are sometimes very strictly regulated (see e.g. §§ 9 a ff. POG Rh-Pf, §§ 9 ff. PolG NRW, §§ 11 ff. BbgPolG). Examples are the procedure to be followed when arresting a person, the entry and search of rooms, ascertainment of identity, or the instruction to a person to move on from a particular place (*Platzverweisung*). The methods used by

the police in obtaining information have been subjected to very strict rules in the last few years in reaction to the debate about protection of personal information.

Literature:
Volkmar Götz/Max-Emanuel Geis, Allgemeines Polizei- und Ordnungsrecht, 16. ed. 2017
Christoph Gusy, Polizei- und Ordnungsrecht, 10. ed. 2017
Erhard Denninger/Kurt Graulich (eds.), Handbuch des Polizeirechts, 6. ed. 2018
Thorsten Kingreen/Ralf Poscher, Polizei- und Ordnungsrecht, 8. ed. 2014
Wolf-Rüdiger Schenke, Polizei- und Ordnungsrecht, 10. ed. 2018

b) The Law of Communal Administration

The law of communal administration (*Kommunalrecht*) has as its constitutional basis article 28 GG. The term commune (*Kommune*) refers, firstly, to the communes proper (*Gemeinde*). Larger communities of this sort are referred to as towns or cities. Secondly, "*Kommune*" is also used to refer to the sub-districts (*Kreise*) which generally consist of several *Gemeinden*. The states have passed Communal Ordinances (*Gemeindeordnungen*) and Sub-district Ordinances (*Kreisordnungen*) to regulate communal administrative law in detail and there are also numerous statutes dealing with specific issues.

296

The communes and, to a lesser extent the sub-districts and other communal groupings have a right to communal self-administration (*kommunale Selbstverwaltung*, article 28 para. 2 GG). In terms of a rule of thumb developed by the Federal Constitutional Court this means that they are entitled to regulate local matters on their own authority. Matters are regarded as local if they are rooted in the local community or if they are of particular relevance for the local community and if they can be managed satisfactorily by the local community acting alone.[12] The law of communal self-administration also gives the communal groupings a right to have a say in trans-communal planning insofar as this will have a significant impact on their area or their development.

297

The right of communal self-administration was developed in the course of the 19th century. The idea was to draw on the local knowledge of citizens and make them feel that they had a stake in the state as a whole. Today it is an expression of the decentralised organisation of the state. It also allows room for local and regional diversity and makes a useful contribution to ensuring the division of state powers and the freedom of the citizen. On the other hand, communal self-administration is in danger of being overstretched by the numerous tasks and social burdens which the state is inclined to off-load on the communes, particularly in the field of social security. For example, they are expected to bear the financial burden of social security assistance to poor elements of the local population themselves. Money allocated to them by the *Land* often proves to be a "golden bridle" because it is generally only granted for a specific purpose.

298

Subject to any relevant statutes, the communes have the power to regulate the powers, structure and workings of their own organs, installations and businesses. This is the so-called organisational sovereignty. They also have sovereignty in personnel matters, which means that they can select and maintain their own personnel – the commune itself is the employer. They have sovereignty over planning in communal matters, particularly in respect of determining how land is used. Lastly, they have the important

299

---

12 BVerfGE 52, 95/120.

right of financial sovereignty, which allows them to determine independently how revenue is to be collected and expended. For the purpose of regulating their own affairs they have regulatory autonomy, which means that they have the power to create local regulations (*Satzungen*), that is, rules of general application. Insofar as a matter is subject to communal self-administration the public authorities at higher levels of government may only review the formal legality of communal actions. They may not override decisions merely because they would have chosen a different course of action.

300 Matters of general importance which fall outside the sphere of local matters cannot be regulated by the communes. Communes have repeatedly attempted to take a hand in the defence policy of the Federation, for example by declaring themselves a nuclear-weapons-free zone. The predominant view is that they do not have the authority to make such decisions.

301 The matters to which the powers of self-administration apply include duties which the communes have voluntarily taken upon themselves. Examples might be an undertaking to build a swimming pool or to maintain a museum. Furthermore, there are various obligations imposed by statute which they must fulfil. Examples are responsibility for school facilities, the construction and maintenance of public roads, or zoning. In addition there are various tasks which the communes perform as agents of the higher levels of government. In respect of such tasks the higher levels of government have comprehensive supervisory powers. Generally speaking these are matters in which individual communes are active as the lowest of the three levels in the administrative structures of the *Land*.

302 The Communal Ordinances (*Gemeindeordnungen*) of each of the *Länder* follow different models in structuring the internal constitution of the communes. These models are rooted in different historical traditions. Nevertheless, in this respect too there is a general tendency to increasing uniformity. The primary organ of the commune is the communal council (*Gemeinderat*). If the commune is big enough to be entitled to call itself a town or city it is called the town council or city council. This council consists of counsellors (*Gemeinderäte*) elected to terms which usually last for four or five years. They are elected by all citizens of the commune with the right to vote. In some *Länder* the mayor also sits in the council. The communal council decides on all matters of importance within its sphere of self-administrative authority. It therefore to some extent resembles a local representative body. Nevertheless, it would be going too far to call it a parliament. Its functions are too limited and the legal position of a council member is not comparable to that of a member of the *Bundestag*. Indeed, the activities of the commune and therefore of the communal council are more administrative than legislative. Overall administration at the local level therefore has a strong democratic streak because it takes this form.

303 The head of the communal administration is the mayor (*Bürgermeister*), or, in some states, a collective decision-making body consisting of the mayor and councillors. The latter model is found in Hesse, Baden-Württemberg, Rhineland-Palatinate, Lower Saxony, North Rhine Westphalia and Brandenburg (see § 65 HGO, § 50 GO Rh-Pf, §§ 68, 70 ff. GO NRW, §§ 69 ff. BbgGO, §§ 59 ff. BbgKVerf.). Except for the city states (Berlin, Bremen and Hamburg), the mayor is directly elected by the citizens of the commune. He or she is a temporary civil servant (*Beamte*) and is elected for a period of six to twelve years. In the bigger cities the mayor is called the chief mayor (*Oberbürgermeister*) and the councillors, i.e., the people responsible for the various

sub-divisions of the local administration, are called "mayors". Smaller communes have unpaid, honorary mayors. The mayor is the head of local government administration and represents the commune in its dealings with the outside world. He or she conducts the business of day-to-day administration, in other words, the business which recurs on a regular basis and which, measured against the scope of the administrative activities and the financial resources of the specific commune, is of relatively small importance. The mayor prepares the meetings of the local council. As a general rule he or she chairs its meetings and carries out its decisions. If the council makes an ultra vires decision the mayor must raise an objection and, if necessary, get the communal supervisory authority to intervene. Finally, the mayor also fulfils the state functions of the lower administrative structures.

The sub-districts (*Kreise*) have a similar structure. They are self-administering corpora-   304
tions and are at the same time the smallest units in the administrative structures of the *Land*. The organs of the sub-district are the sub-district committee (*Kreistag*), which is an assembly representative of the citizens of the sub-district, and the chief executive (*Landrat*), who is the main administrative official of the sub-district. The chief executive is directly elected, in Baden-Württemberg, however, he or she is generally elected by the sub-district committee (§ 39 LKrO BW). The sub-district committee exists as a collegial administrative authority. The relationship of the organs to each other is different in each *Land*. It is based essentially on the communal constitutional model of each *Land* but there are many variations.

Literature:

Martin Burgi, Deutsches Kommunalrecht, 6. ed. 2019
Thorsten I. Schmidt, Kommunalrecht, 2. ed. 2014

c) Public Construction Law

As a subject in the field of special administrative law, public construction law (*Bau-*   305
recht) is to be distinguished from private construction law, which is dealt with as an aspect of private law. Private construction law is concerned with the relationships between the person commissioning a building project, the architect and the building contractor and the private law relationships with the owners of neighbouring properties. Public construction law, on the other hand, is concerned with the relationship between the person commissioning the project and the authorities responsible for regulating construction (*Baubehörde*) as well as the question of whether construction is allowed at all. There are two different aspects to this subject, namely, zoning law (*Baupla-nungsrecht*) and building regulations law (*Bauordnungsrecht*). Zoning law is concerned specifically with the permissibility of certain types of construction in a particular area. This subject is mainly regulated at the federal level in the Construction Code (*Baugesetzbuch*, abbreviated *BauGB*). Building regulations law is concerned with the permissibility of a specific individual construction plan and the powers of the authorities responsible for regulating construction. This is regulated at the state level by the State Building Regulations (*Landesbauordnungen*, abbreviated *LBauO*).

A person intending to undertake a construction project generally needs approval from   306
the building regulation authorities. Smaller building projects such as small garages often do not need official approval in order to simplify the administrative procedure altogether. Since building operations generally also have an impact on the neighbours of the person who is building, the idea of an administrative act with impact on third par-

ties (*Verwaltungsakt mit Drittwirkung*) is of particular relevance in building law. Public regulations on construction may provide a secured position for the neighbour so as to ensure that his or her interests are taken into consideration when permission is granted. The neighbour can take court action against the public authority if it grants permission to build without due regard for his or her rights. The neighbour can then get the permission to build declared void.

307   Zoning law is part of the trans-regional planning and allotment of land. It involves numerous plans and decisions on how regions should develop. For example, an area might be classified for use as industrial land, a high-density settlement area, urban centre, agricultural land, recreational area, nature conservation area or park for the preservation of exceptional natural landscape. Finally, it is necessary to decide where traffic routes of all sorts should run. Building planning deals with this task using two main tools. Firstly, every commune, acting in its capacity as a self-administrating body, draws up a zoning plan (*Flächennutzungsplan*). This determines how the entire territorial area of the commune is to be used, for example, for residential areas, green spots or commercial use. Taking this zoning plan as a starting point, building plans are then drawn up for individual, exactly delineated areas. The building plan (*Bebauungsplan*) is then passed as a communal regulation. It determines the permissible uses for every single piece of land. Regional planning by the federal and state governments, which determines the overall planning of large areas, is regulated in the Federal Regional Planning Act (*Raumordnungsgesetz*).

308   In determining to what uses specific pieces of land may be put the commune is bound by the Building Purposes Act (*Baunutzungsverordnung*, BauNVO). This lays down in the abstract for what purposes land may be used. It distinguishes inter alia residential, industrial, commercial, and mixed areas as well as villages. Certain building operations may also be permissible in areas in which no building plan has been passed. The Federal Construction Code (*Baugesetzbuch*) regulates this possibility in some detail and distinguishes three different types of area, each of which has different permissible uses. Firstly, there are outlying areas (*Aussenbereich*) in which only very limited building activity is allowed. In such areas only certain privileged types of activity are allowed. Examples are farms or waste disposal sites which, due to their nature, cannot conveniently be constructed in the vicinity of other buildings (§ 35 BauGB). Secondly, there are areas which are subject to communal building plans. In such areas it is only permissible to build in accordance with the provisions of the building plan (§§ 30 ff. BauGB). Finally, the Construction Code provides for coherently developed areas (*im Zusammenhang bebaute Ortsteile*). Here there is no applicable building plan, but any further building activities must be of a similar nature to the buildings which have already been constructed in that area (§ 34 BauGB).

309   Viewed as a whole, public construction law in Germany is relatively strict and rigid. The legitimate interest in safe buildings and community-friendly development should not lead to monotonous development.

Literature:

Ulrich Battis, Öffentliches Baurecht und Raumordnungsrecht, 7. ed. 2017

Klaus Finkenlburg/Karsten M. Ortloff/Martin Kment, Öffentliches Baurecht, vol. I: Bauplanungsrecht, 7. ed. 2017

Klaus Finkelnburg/Karsten M. Ortloff/Christian-W. Otto, Öffentliches Baurecht, vol. II: Bauordnungsrecht, Nachbarschutz, Rechtsschutz, 7. ed. 2018
Frank Stollmann/Guy Beaucamp, Öffentliches Baurecht, 11. ed. 2017

d) The Law Relating to Foreigners and Asylum

The Basic Law is friendly and open to foreigners just as it is friendly and open to inter-   310
national law. Most of the Fundamental Rights and procedural guarantees apply without restrictions to foreigners. However, in line with the international norm, there are
limits on the right to work and political participation. In accordance with European
Union law constitutional provision is made giving citizens of the member states of the
European Union a right to vote in communal elections (article 28 para. 1 sentence 3
GG).

Special rules concerning the legal status of aliens are contained primarily in the Resi-   311
dence Act (*Aufenthaltsgesetz*, abbreviated *AufenthG*). In terms of this act, an alien is
any person who is not a German in terms of article 116 GG, in other words, the term
includes stateless persons (§ 12 para. 1 AufenthG). However, the Residence Act is not
applicable to certain groups of foreigners with special status, for example, those who,
in terms of international law, enjoy consular or diplomatic immunity. The Union citizenship, the right to freedom of movement and other rights established by European
Union law have created a separate set of rules for citizens of the member states of the
European Union which puts them on much the same footing as German citizens (§ 1
para. 2 AufenthG). For them and for the members of their families the special provisions of the Freedom of Movement Act/EU (*Freizügigkeitsgesetz/EU*) apply.

For all others, the rule is that aliens require a permit to enter and spend time in the   312
Federal Republic (§ 4 AufenthG). As a general rule the permit must be obtained in the
form of a visa before attempting to enter Germany. However, citizens of certain countries may be exempted from this requirement, and this has been done to a significant
extent. The same applies to the general rule that anyone entering the country must
have a passport.

The type of permit issued depends on what type of stay is being approved. The possi-   313
bilities are: a visa, a residence permit (*Aufenthaltserlaubnis*), an EU Blue Card, an ICT-
Card, an Mobiler-ICT-Card, a permanent settlement permit (*Niederlassungserlaubnis*)
or an EU long-term residence permit (*Erlaubnis zum Daueraufenthalt EU*, § 4 para. 1
AufenthG). Special provisions apply to someone who wishes to enter the country for
the purpose of taking up work as an employed worker. In such cases a permit may in
general only be granted if the Federal Labour Agency has agreed (§ 18 para. 2 AufenthG). For certain cases the Employment Ordinance provides that such consent is not
necessary.[13] There are special rules applicable to someone who wishes to enter Germany to work as a self-employed person. According to § 21 para. 1 sentence 2 Residence Act such a permit is in general granted if an economic or regional interest exists,
if positive effects on the economy can be expected from the activity, and the financing
of the activity is secured.

The visa can be issued as a European Schengen visa (§ 6 AufenthG) which gives the   314
right of entry and of short term residence in general for up to 90 days. For longer periods of residence a national visa can be issued (§ 6 para. 1 sentence 1 number 1 and

---

13   Beschäftigungsverordnung of 22 November 2004, BGBl. I, p. 2937.

para. 3 AufenthG). The residence permit takes the form of a conditional general permit of residence (*Aufenthaltserlaubnis*, § 7 AufenthG) if an alien is to be allowed to enter subject to a time limit for certain purposes specified in the law. This permit, depending on the purpose of residence, does not always entitle the holder to take up professional activities. The permit giving the right to permanent settlement (*Niederlassungserlaubnis*, § 9 AufenthG) is more far reaching. This permit entitles to work and has no limits as to time or place and may only be limited or curtailed in cases explicitly stated in the law. The same is largely true for the EC long-term residence permit, which – with few exceptions – is equivalent to the establishment permit (§ 9 a para. 1 AufenthG). The EU Blue Card allows high-skilled non-EU citizens to work and live in Germany (§ 19a AufenthG). The ICT-Card allows the temporary transfer of a foreigner within a trans-border company for more than 90 days; if the foreigner already possesses an equivalent permit in another Member State of the European Union, a Mobiler-ICT-Card suffices.

315 The possibility of family members following the permit holder to Germany depends on what type of permit has been granted. In deciding on this issue the protection of marriage and the family demanded by the Fundamental Rights must always be borne in mind (article 6 para. 1 GG, § 27 para. 1 AufenthG). Generally speaking the family will only be allowed to follow if appropriate accommodation is available and resources for their economic existence have been secured (§§ 27 para. 3; 29 para. 1 AufenthG).

316 Foreigners residing in Germany legally and without time limit are entitled to participate in so-called integration programmes to further their integration into economic, cultural, and societal life. This is partly a right and partly an obligation for foreigners. Their primary aim is to obtain sufficient knowledge of the German language and the German legal order, culture, and history (§§ 43 ff. AufenthG).

317 Visa and residence permit can generally be issued with various conditions and directions (§ 12 AufenthG). Limits on freedom of movement once inside Germany are common, and sometimes restrictions on involvement in political activity have been imposed. In principle, aliens do have the right to engage in political activity while in Germany. However, such activity may be restricted or completely prohibited in specific circumstances when in the public interest.

318 As soon as an alien no longer has a valid permit to stay he or she has an obligation to leave the country (§ 50 AufenthG). If his or her presence is a threat to public safety or public order, or if the alien poses some other threat to other substantial interests of the Federal Republic of Germany, he or she can be ordered to leave the country (*Ausweisung*). If the alien is ordered to leave the country his or her permit to stay is voided and the person has an obligation to leave the country. The obligation to leave can be enforced by means of deportation (*Abschiebung*). The person affected must be given written notice that he or she will be deported if he or she does not leave voluntarily by a specified date (§§ 58 ff. AufenthG).

319 An alien may not be deported to a state in which his or her life or freedom is threatened on grounds of his or her race, religion, nationality, membership of a particular social group or political views. The person may also not be deported to a state in which he or she will be subject to a concrete danger of severe damage, especially of being subjected to torture or the death penalty (§ 60 AufenthG). The same principles apply to the extradition (*Auslieferung*) of foreigners who are being pursued for the commission of a crime. It should be noted that the extradition of German citizens to

foreign countries is largely forbidden in terms of article 16 para. 2 GG. The only exceptions are that a German citizen can be extradited to a member state of the European Union or to an international court. The deportation of foreigners who originate from particular states or who are members of certain groups can be delayed on humanitarian grounds. This applies particularly to refugees fleeing from areas affected by war, civil-war or natural disaster.

If it is impossible or undesirable to deport someone who does not fulfil his or her obligation to leave the country, then the alien will be issued with a certificate of toleration (*Duldung*, § 60 a AufenthG). This is subject to a time limit and does not affect the obligation to leave the country. Once the certificate of toleration expires the alien may be deported without further ado unless the certificate is renewed.   320

In preparation for deportation a foreigner can be held in deportation custody by order of court for a period of not more than six weeks (§ 62 AufenthG). Business relating to passports and permits to stay is dealt with by the Foreigners Office (*Ausländerbehörde*).   321

The law on the granting of asylum is regulated not in the Aliens Act, but in the Asylum Procedure Act (*Asylgesetz*, abbreviated *AsylG*). Applicants for asylum receive limited permission to remain insofar as this is necessary to allow time to process their claim to asylum. While the claim is being processed they generally live in collective quarters and are subject to strict limits on their freedom of movement. The right to asylum of people who are politically persecuted is constitutionally guaranteed by article 16 a GG. This article also provides for various restrictions on the right to asylum which were discussed above in the context of the Fundamental Rights. A person is considered to be politically persecuted if he or she is subjected to persecutory measures which pose a danger to life or limb or limits on his or her personal freedom because of his or her race, religion, nationality, membership of a particular social group or political views. This requirement is satisfied if the applicant has reasonable grounds for fearing such persecution. The persecution must be politically motivated and of a certain intensity. If the persecution is not being conducted by the applicant's state of origin then there will only be a right to asylum if the alien's home state is not providing adequate protection. There is no right to asylum if the applicant could have obtained protection somewhere else, particularly by moving to a different area of his or her home state. It is not necessary for the granting of asylum that the applicants views are compatible with the values embodied in the Basic Law (§ 3 AsylG, § 60 para. 1 AufenthG).   322

Literature:
Jan Bergmann/Klaus Dienelt, Ausländerrecht. Kommentar, 12. ed. 2018
Rainer M. Hofmann (ed.), Ausländerrecht. Kommentar, 2. ed. 2016
Reinhard Marx, Ausländer- und Asylrecht, 3. ed. 2017

e) Identity Documents and Residence Registration

The German law on identity documents and residence registration (*Melde- und Passrecht*) is sometimes viewed with scepticism by foreign observers. It is seen as a sign of bondage and the basis for a police state. This view is unjustified. The rules in question, which are subject to numerous provisos, simply serve to ensure maximum administrative efficiency. In terms of the federal General Provisions on Residence Registration Act (Bundesmelde*gesetz*, abbreviated MMG) the inhabitants of a particular place are   323 registered by the registration authorities. This involves recording certain details such as the name, nationality and family circumstances of the person in question. Every person who takes up residence in a new place in Germany has a duty to report within two weeks to the registration authorities.

324 All Germans over the age of sixteen must have an identity document. They must also present it on demand if this is required by any competent authority such as the police. However, there is no obligation to carry the identity document at all times.

f) Data Protection

325 The law on data protection (*Datenschutzrecht*) has expanded to affect wide areas of life. Taking the protection of personality in the Basic Law (article 2 para. 1 GG as read with article 1 para. 1 GG) as their starting point, the Federal Data Protection Act (*Bundesdatenschutzgesetz,* abbreviated *BDSG*) and the Protection of Information Acts of the various *Länder* regulate the ways in which personal information may be dealt with. In addition, numerous statutes, such as the Police Acts, the Federal Registration Act and the Residence Act, contain specialised provisions on this subject for their specific field. The Federal Data Protection Act also regulates the processing (*Datenverarbeitung*) of private data by private persons. The processing of private data is only permissible insofar as it is specifically allowed by statute or the affected person has consented (§ 4 para. 1 BDSG). The affected person has various protective rights, such as the right to information about the details which have been recorded, and the right to have inaccurate or illegally recorded data deleted. These rights cannot be excluded or limited by contract, in other words they remain in existence even if the person affected is willing to renounce them. If data is processed illegally the person processing it will be liable to pay damages for any harm which results (§§ 7, 8 BDSG).

326 Public authorities may only collect, record, alter or use private data for purposes permitted by law, and they may only pass the data on to third parties in a limited set of circumstances (§§ 12 ff. BDSG). A central principle of the protection of data in the state sphere is that individual public authorities may only process such personal data as is essential to the fulfilment of their duties. This means that each department of the administration must be sealed off from the others as far as personal data regarding the population is concerned. This is seen as a separation of informational powers within the administration. The aim is to prevent the danger that modern data technology will make it possible for a state bureaucracy to have full information about each individual in the population at its fingertips and that it could abuse this power. Compliance with these very strict rules for the protection of information is monitored by the data ombudsmen (*Datenschutzbeauftragte*) of the Federation and the *Länder*. This monitoring in no way relieves the various public bodies of the duty to ensure that they are acting legally.

327 There are also strict provisions applicable to private persons (§§ 27 ff. BDSG). Data may only be collected legally and in good faith and may only be processed for legal purposes. It may not be used for purposes other than those for which it was collected without the permission of the person affected and, generally speaking, it may only be passed on to someone else without the permission of the person affected. State supervisory authorities monitor compliance with these provisions and certain types of record must be reported to them.

Literature:
Peter Gola/Dirk Heckmann, Bundesdatenschutzgesetz. Kommentar, 13. ed. 2019
Marie-Theres Tinnefeld/Benedikt Buchner/Thomas Petri, Einführung in das Datenschutzrecht, 6. ed. 2017

g) Public Service Law

The German public service is still moulded by the concept of the *Beamte*, the career civil servant for life, with whom the state has a special reciprocal relationship of loyalty. This remains the case, although the *Beamte* are by now outnumbered by other government employees. As a general rule sovereign powers should be exercised by *Beamten* (article 33 para 4 GG). These officials stand in a special relationship of public service and loyalty. This relationship is structured on the basis of the traditional principles of the professional civil service, which have constitutionally binding character (article 33 para. 5 GG). The fact that these principles have been firmly established at least since the time of the Weimar Republic gives the *Beamten* a sense of rootedness and continuity, but also carries with it the danger of ossification. The details of the law relating to the *Beamten* of the professional civil service are regulated in numerous acts and regulations of the Federation and the *Länder*. Regarding the status of *Länderbeamte*, the federal Act on the Status of Civil Servants (*Beamtenstatusgesetz*, abbreviated BeamtStG) applies.

One of the traditional principles of the professional civil service (*Berufsbeamtentum*) is that of strict party-political and factual neutrality. This does not exclude *Beamte* from being members of a political party. They are, however, required to be actively supportive of the free democratic foundation of the constitution. If they are actively involved in the activities of a radical party this may raise doubts as to their suitability to be *Beamte*. Despite the general duty to be politically neutral and objective, the institution of the political *Beamte* is recognised for specific, high-ranking offices which are specifically listed in the Civil Servants Acts of the Federation and the *Länder*. Examples include under-secretaries of state (*Staatssekretäre*), directors general (*Ministerialdirektoren*), and the Federal Attorney-General (*Generalbundesanwalt*). These officials, who particularly require the political trust of the government of the day, can be sent into early retirement without reasons being given.

Another traditional principle of the professional civil service is the principle of financial support (*Alimentationsgrundsatz*): The state, the master of the *Beamten*, has a duty to provide an adequate salary and to provide equivalent support once a *Beamte* retires. Appointment and promotion must be decided on the basis of performance, ability and suitability. Another principle is that of life-long employment (*Lebenszeitprinzip*): As a general rule the relationship between the *Beamten* and the state is presumed to be for life. However, in exceptional cases it is also possible to have time-limited *Beamten* relationships, as in the case of the elected officials who hold office at the communal level, whose position has a political aspect. Apart from this there are various positions which are subject to time limits for practical reasons such as where someone has been appointed as *Beamte* for a trial period or conditional appointment. Once the age limit is reached *Beamte* go into retirement and are entitled to receive a pension. They are therefore not required to make contributions to pension schemes or unemployment insurance.

328

329

330

331 Because of the principle of life-long employment, *Beamte* can only be dismissed in exceptional circumstances, such as serious misconduct or when dismissal is at the request of the person affected. Dismissal brings with it the loss of all rights arising out of the *Beamten* relationship (*Beamtenverhältnis*), particularly the right to a pension. The aim of the principle of life-long employment is to insulate the professional civil service against party-political pressure, allowing it to remain objective in its decision-making. This objectivity is not affected by the hierarchical principle (*Hierarchieprinzip*) in terms of which *Beamte* have a duty to follow instructions from their superiors. However, the *Beamte* bears full personal liability for the legality of acts performed in the course of duty. If he or she has doubts about the legality of an order given in the course of duty he or she must make these doubts known to a superior at once. This is the so-called "remonstration". If the superior nevertheless confirms the order then the *Beamte* must carry it out, but is no longer personally responsible. However, he or she remains liable and must refuse to carry out the order if it involves the commission of a crime or offence and this was recognisable for him or her or if it constitutes a violation of human dignity.

332 Further duties flow from the duty of loyalty of the *Beamten*. Examples are the duty not to disclose information acquired in the course of duty, the requirement that permission be obtained before the *Beamte* may become involved in additional employment, and not becoming too involved in political activities. On the other hand the state has a duty to care for the *Beamten*, for example, if he or she falls ill. This means that *Beamte* have a right to assistance in paying medical expenses and only have to pay for partial medical insurance themselves.

333 *Beamten* relationships are divided into four groups according to the educational prerequisites and the general demands made on the officials in each career group. It is possible for a *Beamten* to move up the ladder within a particular group during the course of his or her career. To rise into a higher career-group is possible, but is not easy and rarely happens. The four groups are the lower service (for example, an official messenger), the middle service, higher service and high service (*einfacher, mittlerer, gehobener* und *höherer Dienst*). The general requirement for entry into the last group is a university degree.

334 The law applicable to other types of government employees (*Angestellte*) and workers (*Arbeiter*) has gradually become more and more similar to the law regulating the position of *Beamten*. The main remaining differences relate particularly to the fact that other employees and workers can be dismissed more easily, although here too there are notice periods in the interests of the affected employee which reduce the flexibility of the relationship. They may also be required to do work which is not in accordance with their status. In contrast to *Beamten*, public service workers and employees have the right to strike.

Literature:
Sabine Leppek, Beamtenrecht, 13. ed. 2019

h) The Law Relating to Cultural Administration

335 The universities and schools stand at the centre of the law relating to Cultural Administration (*Kulturverwaltungsrecht*). This subject also deals with issues such as the legal position of the mostly state owned communal theatres and opera-houses, which are

usually state owned; adult education centres (*Volkshochschulen*), the Goethe Institutes, which are dedicated to the promotion of the German language and culture, and the public libraries. Common to all of these is a material core of public organisation in the interests of culture. This certainly does not mean that there is no private activity in these fields – private theatres and schools play a significant role. The essential issue here is one of public subsidies and sometimes also of supervision or approval of activities. In this area the state is active in its capacity as the cultural state. As a general rule cultural administration is the business of the *Länder* (articles 70; 73 para. 1 number 5 a; 74 para. 1 number 33 GG).

The school system in Germany is largely state-run. The communes are generally responsible for the schools, while the teachers are generally *Beamte* in the service of the state. The body responsible for the school provides the necessary buildings and equipment, the body responsible for the teachers pays their salaries and determines the syllabus. There are a certain number of private schools which are often run by religious communities, groups representing particular philosophies, or groups with some particular pedagogic or commercial motivation. All schools are subject to state supervision (article 7 para. 1 GG). Private schools can be officially recognised as alternative schools if they in principle are capable of taking the place of similar state schools. If such recognition is granted they may be attended instead of a state school (article 7 para. 4 GG). Viewed as a whole, both the structure of the school system and the content of the material taught are strongly influenced by the state. Since the *Länder* are competent in matters concerning the school system significant differences do exist between the *Länder* in detailed questions. 336

There is a general school-attendance requirement. As a general rule, all children over the age of six (with more specific rules relating to when the school year begins) must attend school. The obligation to attend school ends at the age of 18. The child must attend school full-time for ten years, and thereafter must at least attend school for another three years part-time, or must attend vocational school. The precise content of the rules on this subject depends on which *Land* the child is in. There are no school fees for attendance of state schools. There is no requirement that a child be sent to pre-school. The period prior to reaching the age at which school attendance becomes compulsory is subject to little state regulation. At this stage the services available consist largely of kindergartens run by the church or the communes. 337

There are numerous types and levels of schooling and the diversity is sometimes rather confusing. A primary stage which lasts between four and six years is followed by secondary stage I for pupils aged between about ten and sixteen. This is followed by secondary stage II. This applies both to schools providing a general education and schools providing job-oriented training. 338

The typical school career starts with a primary school (*Grundschule*), which usually lasts four years. In several *Länder,* schooling then takes place in senior primary school (*Hauptschule*) which continues to the 9th grade, or, in *Länder* in which at least ten years of school must be attended, to the 10th grade. This leads to the elementary school leaving certificate (*Hauptschulabschluss*). Instead of attending senior primary school a child may attend technical school (*Realschule*) or combined school (*Gesamtschule*). This leads to a school-leaving certificate after ten years which can form the basis for training in various careers. Many *Länder* abolished the senior primary school (*Hauptschule*). They offer the elementary school leaving certificate in one 339 of the other types of schools. Thirdly, academic high school (*Gymnasium*) can be attended after primary school. This usually starts in the fifth school year and usually leads to the *Abitur*, the equivalent of A-levels in England, after a total of twelve or thirteen years at school according to the relevant *Land*. The *Abitur* gives its holders access to tertiary education. Some *Länder* favour combined schools (*Gesamtschulen*) which are intended to combine all the different types of school into a single school system for everyone.

340   The universities are generally state-run. There are only a few private universities and even these are usually state-subsidised to a significant extent. The state-run tertiary education institutions are generally run by the relevant *Land*, the exception being the two armed forces academies and the German University of Administration Sciences in Speyer.

341   The universities, in contrast to the schools, are protected by the constitutional right to freedom of academic activity, the arts, research and teaching (*Freiheit von Wissenschaft und Kunst, Forschung und Lehre,* article 5 para. 3 sentence 1 GG). Thus, although they are state-run, they in fact enjoy considerable freedom – they are self-administrating bodies.

342   Internally the universities are structured into faculties (*Fachbereiche* or *Fakultäten*). The head of each faculty is the dean, who is responsible for co-ordinating the faculty and taking certain decisions. He or she is chosen from amongst the professors of the faculty by the faculty council for a fixed period of time, usually two years. The faculty council, which is the main decision making body of the faculty, in turn consists of representatives elected by various interested groups, namely students, professors, other academic staff and non-academic staff. In taking decisions relating to certain types of business the professors have the last word.

343   Decisions which are of relevance to the university as a whole are taken by the senate, or sometimes by a special assembly which is elected along similar lines to the faculty councils. The university is represented in its dealings with the outside world by the rector or university president who is also elected by a central university council and is then appointed by the responsible minister. The rector's or president's period of office varies from one *Land* to another and is usually between four and six years.

344   The professors are generally *Beamte* with tenure for life. They are usually appointed by the university, sometimes also by the respective Land minister. The faculty to which the professor is appointed considers various applicants and then draws up a list, usually with three names. The university communicates the list to the minister, who chooses one of the candidates. The minister will generally appoint the person whose name appears first on the list. The professors have a duty to represent their subject appropriately in the fields of research and teaching. Their freedom of teaching, research, academic activity and arts is guaranteed as a fundamental constitutional right.

345   Over the last years technical colleges (*Fachhochschulen*) have gained considerable importance in tertiary education. Their courses are generally somewhat shorter than those offered at universities and have a strong emphasis on practical training. There are also a number of private technical colleges which are often run by the larger religious communities.

Literature:

Michael Hartmer/Hubert Detmer/, Hochschulrecht: Ein Handbuch für die Praxis, 3. ed. 2016

Hermann Avenarius/Felix Hanschmann, Schulrecht: Ein Handbuch für Praxis, Rechtsprechung und Wissenschaft, 9. ed. 2019
Arne Pautsch/Anja Dillenburger, Kompendium zum Hochschul- und Wissenschaftsrecht, 2. ed. 2016

i) Media Law

The basis of media law (*Medienrecht*) in Germany is article 5 para. 1 GG. This guarantees the freedom of the press and the freedom to report in film and in the electronic media. The law relating to printed media, in particular news-papers and periodicals, is contained mainly in the Printed Media Acts (*Landespressegesetze*) of the various *Länder*. For electronic media, namely radio and television, the *Länder* have passed Radio Acts and Media Acts and concluded treaties with one another. With the Tele-Media Act (*Telemediengesetz*), these treaties also regulate tele-media, i.e. electronic information and communication services which are available via the internet. Except for a few specialised issues, media law is once again a matter falling within the competence of the *Länder*, but here too the tendency to seek uniformity is unmistakable.   346

Press activities, including the founding and running of media concerns, are free. The public role of the press in enabling citizens to form an opinion is recognised. For the purpose of fulfilling this role representatives of the press and other media have a right to receive information from public authorities (see e.g. § 9a State Treaty on Radio and Telemedia – *Staatsvertrag für Rundfunk und Telemedien* –, § 41 BDSG). Information may only be refused if providing it would have a detrimental effect on business which is still pending, or if refusal is necessitated by a special duty to maintain secrecy, or if disclosure would be detrimental to an important public interest or to a private interest deserving of protection, or if the effort involved in providing the information would be unreasonable (*unzumutbar*). The press in turn has a duty to take particular care concerning the truth, content and origin of the information which it publishes.   347

Censorship is not allowed. This provision of the constitution (article 5 para. 1 sentence 3 GG), which is of central importance for the freedom of the press and the electronic media, relates to censorship prior to publication. In no circumstances is it necessary to obtain official permission before publishing something. However, this does not free a person from responsibility for the content of the material which they publish. If the content of a publication is criminal or otherwise illegal, for example, if it involves defamation or the betrayal of secrets, it is impermissible and will be subject to the usual penalties. However, seizure of printed material is only allowed in very specific circumstances and only in terms of a court order. Thus, for example, the police cannot simply seize publications on the basis that they pose a threat to national security unless they have a warrant to do so from the appropriate judge.   348

The function of the press in a democratic society is protected by numerous privileges entitling members of the press to refuse to give evidence (see e.g. § 53 para. 1 number 4 StPO). Journalists are not obliged to reveal their sources even if their sources have committed a criminal act.   349

Any person who is affected by allegations in the press has a right of reply irrespective of the truth of the allegations so long as the reply is of reasonable length.   350

An issue which repeatedly comes up for discussion is the extent of the so-called internal press freedom. This debate is concerned with the relationship between the individual journalist on the one hand, and the publisher as owner of the media concern on   351 the other hand. The questions raised by this issue are to be solved according to the principles provided by the theory of the indirect horizontal application (*mittelbare Drittwirkung*) of the Fundamental Rights. The dominant approach is to analyse the situation into a number of different levels of control (*Stufentheorie*). The individual journalist is in principle completely free as against the publisher to write what he or she wishes as far as details in his or her reports are concerned. However, the publisher is entitled to make a binding decision as to the general tone of the publication, particularly its political leanings and the journalist has no right to ignore such general policy.

352   In terms of the law of the *Länder* a number of provisions such as those concerning the public role of the press, rights to information, the right of reply and the right to refuse to give evidence also apply to a lesser or greater extent to the electronic media. The attempt to comply with the goals set by the Fundamental Rights can be seen even more clearly here than in the case of the print media. The goal is to achieve a diverse and balanced media landscape in which all relevant social forces are able to achieve a fair hearing.

353   In earlier times when, for technical reasons, there were only a few channels available all electronic media were therefore state run, although not subject to government interference. This is still the case for some channels today. The television channel *ZDF* (*Zweites Deutsches Fernsehen* which translates as "Channel Two Germany") was set up in terms of an agreement between the *Ländern*. ARD (*Arbeitsgemeinschaft der öffentlich-rechtlichen Rundfunkanstalten der Bundesrepublik Deutschland*, "Channel One") is a union of various different broadcasters financed by the *Ländern*. It covers various regional channels such as the Western Channel (*WDR – Westdeutscher Rundfunk*), Channel Bavaria (*BR – Bayrischer Rundfunk*), and the Northern Channel (*NDR – Norddeutscher Rundfunk*). In terms of the agreement between the *Ländern* these channels are financed by licence fees collected by the state. These must be paid by every person who has a radio or television set. On the other hand these channels are only allowed to spend a limited amount of time broadcasting advertisements. Since these broadcasters are organised as independent public law corporations they are protected against the risk of being forced to serve as the mouthpiece of successive governments. These corporations can invoke the freedom of broadcasting guaranteed in article 5 para. 1 GG. They have an obligation to provide objective reporting.

354   Despite minor differences the public broadcasters are essentially all organised along the same lines. In terms of internal structure they have three organs. The main organ is the radio council or the television council which is made up of representatives of the various socially relevant groups. Its members include representatives of the various political parties, religious communities, trade unions, employers' associations, professional groupings, press and journalists' associations, and independent welfare associations. This council sets general guidelines for broadcasts and checks that these guidelines and the basic principles for programming set by the law are observed. The second organ is the smaller administrative council which is also socially representative but which does include representatives of the government. It is mainly concerned with finances and important personnel decisions. The director of the organisation is elected by the administrative council for a fixed period. He or she is concerned with the day to day management of the organisation and represents it in its dealings with the outside world.

Now that technical developments have made it possible to have numerous radio and television programmes the Media Acts of the *Länder* have opened the market for private broadcasters. Now the market is in a position to provide the diversity of opinion which the Basic Law demands and which the law attempts to achieve. In this way as many social groups and points of view as possible will hopefully be represented. The private media must finance itself entirely out of its own resources. It achieves this primarily by broadcasting advertising. The private media is also subject to the provisions of the Basic Law, which requires that the media must be free and diverse. This is relevant to attempts to create media monopolies. Freedom and diversity can be attained by the implementation of two different principles, namely, the principle of external plurality and the principle of internal plurality. As long as there are sufficient mutually independent private broadcasters to ensure healthy diversity the various broadcasters can be left more or less to their own devices in deciding on their internal structures and programming. However, if this external plurality is threatened, then the private broadcasters would be obliged to ensure internal plurality. This would mean that their internal structures would then have to become representative of various social forces as is the case with the public broadcasters.

355

Private broadcasters require a licence, which is issued by the broadcasting authority (*Landesmedienanstalt*) of each *Land*. These broadcasting authorities are self-administrating bodies, in other words they are not obliged to take instructions from the various governments. The broadcasting authorities generally have two organs, namely, a board and a director. The board consists of representatives of socially relevant groups and of the government of the *Land*. Its task it to monitor, amongst other things, whether the programmes being broadcast are, as a whole, balanced, decides on the priority to be given to the various programmes in cable networks and, where necessary, decides on how broadcasting capacity is to be allocated to particular providers. The director is appointed by the board. He or she represents the broadcasting authority and conducts its business.

356

Literature:

Frank Fechner, Medienrecht. Lehrbuch des gesamten Medienrechts unter besonderer Berücksichtigung von Presse, Rundfunk und Multimedia, 19. ed. 2018

Marian Paschke/Wolfgang Berlit/Claus Meyer, Hamburger Kommentar. Gesamtes Medienrecht, 3. ed. 2016

Jens Petersen, Medienrecht. Ein Studienbuch, 5. ed. 2010

j) Traffic Law

Modern mass transportation has turned road traffic law into an area which has been worked out in fine detail. The basic rules are contained in the Road Traffic Act (*Straßenverkehrsgesetz*, abbreviated *StVG*). Also of considerable importance are the Road Traffic Regulations (*Straßenverkehrsordnung*, abbreviated *StVO*), which contain provisions on the rules of the road and traffic signs, the Vehicle Licensing Regulations (*Straßenverkehrszulassungsordnung*) which set out the conditions for the licensing of motor vehicles, and finally the Driver Licencing Regulations (*Fahrerlaubnis-Verordnung*) which regulate driving licences. Any person who wishes to drive a motor vehicle must have a driving licence (§ 2 para. 1 StVG). Ordinary passenger vehicles may generally only be driven by persons over the age of 18 after the required test has been passed. Driving licences are divided into different classes.

357

358　Every motor vehicle which is used on public roads must be registered with the vehicle registration authorities and must be insured against liability for injuries to third parties (*Haftpflichtversicherung*). This insurance ensures that it will be possible for any third party who suffers injury to obtain compensation. Any person who infringes on the rules of the road to a significant extent can have a driving ban of up to three months imposed on him or her by the authorities or the courts (§ 25 StVG). If a person proves to be unfit to drive a motor vehicle then the administrative authorities must withdraw his or her driving licence completely (§ 3 Abs. 1 StVG). Driving a motor vehicle without the required licence is subject to penalties (§ 21 StVG).

359　Not only the driver (*Fahrzeugführer*) but also the person responsible for the vehicle (*Fahrzeughalter*) is liable for any damage resulting from its use (§ 7 StVG). A person is considered to be responsible for a vehicle if they have it in use for their own purposes and have the necessary power to use the vehicle as they please (*Verfügungsgewalt*). Generally speaking this will be the person in whose name the vehicle is registered.

360　Every user of a public road has a duty to behave in such a way as to avoid harming or endangering other road users, or obstructing or inconveniencing them more than necessary (§ 1 para. 2 StVO). No person having a blood alcohol level of 0.5 per thousand or higher may drive a motor vehicle on a public road. To do so is an offence (§ 24 a para. 1 StVG).

Literature:
Peter Hentschel/Peter König/Peter Dauer, Straßenverkehrsrecht. Kommentar, 45. ed. 2019

k) Social Security Law

361　As an aspect of special administrative law social law is concerned with the law of social services provided by the state. However, in practice this narrow field is complemented by other systems of social security such as private insurance, the pension schemes run by various businesses and the various benefits to which certain civil servants (*Beamte*) are entitled from the state. Social security law in the narrower sense is contained in the Social Security Code (*Sozialgesetzbuch*, which is divided into several volumes and abbreviated *SGB*). Comprehensive as the various existing security nets are, they remain an incomprehensible maze for many people with the result that rights are on the one hand often not enforced due to simple ignorance and on the other hand there are people who take advantage of the system and receive benefits although they are not really in need.

362　Social security law gives concrete expression to the Basic Law's commitment to the principle of the social state (*Sozialstaat*). Although this principle is of only peripheral importance in constitutional theory, it has enormous impact on day-to-day life in Germany. There is hardly another area of the law which is of such direct significance to large parts of the population as social security law. There is constant discussion about what form it should take, how the system is to be financed, and its effects on economic life.

363　Social welfare benefits (*Sozialhilfe*) provide a minimum level of security for the needy elements of the population. The detailed rules on this subject are contained in the Twelfth Book of the Social Security Code (SGB XII). This aims to provide for every person who is not able to provide him- or herself with the material goods needed to lead a life which is compatible with human dignity (§ 1 sentence 1 SGB XII). The reasons for the claimant's neediness are not relevant. A claimant has a legally enforceable right to social welfare benefits. The nature and extent of the benefits appropriate are determined by the authorities in accordance with statutory guidelines and in the proper exercise of their discretion.

One type of social welfare benefit is the payment of basic living expenses (*Lebensunterhalt*, § 27 para. 1 SGB XII). These payments provide for the basic material necessities, including a minimum of social and cultural needs such as radio and cinema (§ 27 a SGB XII). If the claimant has deliberately induced his or her destitution the claimant will receive less, namely only so much as is essential to life. Apart from these benefits there are various types of assistance which are applicable in specific situations, for example old-age and sickness benefits.

364

The amount necessary for basic living expenses is determined according to standard rates which are set by the authorities in each *Land* with reference to the price of a specific basket of goods. At present this on average amounts to € 394.84 per month for single person households (§ 5 para. 2 *Regelbedarfs-Ermittlungsgesetz*, abbreviated *RBEG*). On this basis, single person and single parent households receive from 1.1.2019 onwards in general 424 Euros per month. Additional members of a household each receive a somewhat smaller amount. Apart from these standard welfare payments, special additional payments are possible in a few special cases as are one-off payments in cases of need (§§ 30 ff. SGB XII). Together with additional benefits such as money for rent, the basic amount necessary for daily life is thus covered.

365

The right to social welfare benefits is subsidiary (§ 2 SGB XII). People in need must first apply their own income and savings. Claims such as a claim to maintenance must also be realised as far as possible before claiming social welfare. However, certain capital assets are not affected by this rule. For example, a person claiming social welfare will not be compelled to first sell his or her small family home (§ 90 SGB XII). People receiving assistance must be willing to work. They are expected to take up any sort of work which becomes available without taking into account their earlier social status (§ 11 para. 3 SGB XII).

366

Non-citizens are also in principle able to claim benefits so long as they did not specially come to Germany with the intention of obtaining welfare payments. However, a foreigner who is living off social welfare benefits can generally be ordered to leave the country. Benefits to applicants for asylum can be reduced to that essential for life and can be distributed in the form of goods instead of money (§ 23 SGB XII).

367

Apart from social security benefits there are numerous other types of benefits which can be obtained from the state. Of particular importance and value are the payments made to parents with children under 18 (*Kindergeld*). These payments can continue until the child reaches the age of 25 in exceptional circumstances such as education (§ 2 para. 2 *Bundeskindergeldgesetz*, abbreviated *BKGG*). Child-raising benefits (*Elterngeld*) are paid to a parent to help cover the costs of raising the child (§ 1 *Bundeselterngeld- und Elternzeitgesetz*, abbreviated *BEEG*). Parents who are unable to provide suitable accommodation without assistance will also receive accommodation payments (*Wohngeld*). If necessary, persons in education can be financed by grants as per the Federal Promotion of Education Act (*Bundesausbildungsförderungsgesetz*, abbreviated *BaföG*), which for students, e.g., is given half in the form of a loan and half as a non-repayable grant (§ 17 BaföG).

368

369   All the above types of payment come out of the ordinary tax income of the government. The various payments for the promotion of employment (regulated by book III SGB), on the other hand, come from contributions to unemployment insurance. As a general rule all employees are liable to make contributions to this fund. In addition, the Federal Government also helps to bear the burden, as do employers, who have to pay a special levy for this purpose. The promotion of employment is primarily the task of the Federal Employment Agency (*Bundesagentur für Arbeit*) which has its headquarters in Nürnberg. This is a federal public-law corporation with its own administrative sub-structure throughout Germany in the form of main regional offices as well as numerous sub-offices (*Agenturen für Arbeit*).

370   The Federal Employment Agency is responsible for deciding whether to grant a work permit to foreigners. It also provides information on career choices, promotes the creation of new jobs by means of subsidies and finances courses for training, retraining and further training. An important aspect of its business is to help people to find work. It also provides subsidies (*Kurzarbeitergeld*) to firms which are suffering from a temporary, abnormal loss of demand to prevent short-term problems from resulting in layoffs.

371   After a certain waiting period people who have become unemployed also have a claim to payments from the unemployment insurance fund (§ 136 ff. SGB III). For unemployed persons with one or more children this payment is 67 %, for those without children 60 %, of their last salary after deduction of tax, social security payments and certain other charges which are not payable by unemployed persons (§ 149 SGB III). The person claiming unemployment insurance must be prepared to accept any reasonable offer of employment. What constitutes a reasonable offer depends on the period for which the person has already been unemployed and numerous other factors (§ 140 SGB III). Unemployment insurance payments (*Arbeitslosengeld*) are not need-based. Payments are made to the unemployed person for a maximum of one year, or, in the case of older people who have been contributing to the fund for a long period, for up to 24 months (§ 147 SGB III).

372   After this period has ended there is an alternate claim to unemployment assistance (*Arbeitslosengeld II*, §§ 19 ff. SGB II), but only if a person is in need, and this claim is subsidiary to other possible sources of support. This type of support is also paid in the initial waiting period before an unemployed person becomes eligible for the unemployment insurance payments mentioned above. The payments made are roughly equivalent to social security payments and are paid as long as the person is unemployed.

373   If employees lose their wages due to their employer going bankrupt they have a claim against the Employment Agency for loss of wages due to bankruptcy (*Insolvenzgeld*, §§ 165 ff. SGB III). The agency will then pay the employee's full net salary for up to three months.

374   The social security system also offers a certain amount of security through numerous additional types of assistance dealing with specific problems such as illness, pregnancy, workplace accidents, age, death of a person with a duty of support, and diminution of capacity to work. The services available vary between different population groups such as students, pensioners, employees and workers.

375   The law on health insurance is governed by SGB V. As of 1 January 2019 workers and salaried employees with an income of up to € 60 750 are liable to enrol into health

insurance (*Krankenversicherung*). A person earning more than this amount can choose for him- or herself whether to take out insurance or not. People working only short hours are exempted from the obligation to take out insurance. Spouses and children who are not themselves obliged to take out insurance are automatically insured under the insured spouses name (§ 10 SGB V). Generally speaking, the health insurance fund (*Krankenkasse*) will make payments directly to the doctor, hospital or pharmacy visited by the insured person and pays virtually the entire cost of treatment.

Payments to the state pension system (*Rentenversicherung*), governed by SGB VI, are compulsory for workers and salaried employees with an income of less than € 80 400 (as of 1 January 2019). In the new eastern *Länder* the limit is € 73 800. If a person becomes incapable of working or has reached the required minimum age, the system provides a pension. After a currently ongoing transitional period, the usual minimum age for a pension is 67 (§ 35 SGB V) . Generally speaking, a person will only be able to claim a pension if they have been insured for a certain minimum period. In addition there are pensions for surviving spouses and rehabilitation payments if a person becomes unable to perform their existing job. 376

A person who has been injured by an accident in the workplace or suffers from work-related illness is entitled to accident insurance payments (*Unfallversicherung*) (SGB VII). The main sources of the money in this fund are the various employers' liability insurance associations (*Berufsgenossenschaften*). The members of these associations are the employers. They alone make payments into this fund. 377

Special care insurance (*Pflegeversicherung*) is regulated in SGB XI. It guarantees to the insured the right of out-patient or in-patient care should the necessity arise. Insurance is in principle compulsory even for those who are otherwise exempted from compulsory insurance by law. 378

Care for children and young people is regulated in SGB VIII. It aims to protect young people and promote their development and also to advise and support parents and other guardians in bringing up their children. 379

A special sub-area of social security law is formed by the law on compensation. This involves claims for compensation for, amongst others, victims of war (*Bundesversorgungsgesetz*, abbreviated *BVG*), people injured during the course of military or alternative service (*Soldatenversorgungsgesetz* – *SVG*, *Zivildienstgesetz* – *ZDG*), people who suffer harm as a result of compulsory inoculation (*Infektionsschutzgesetz* – *IfSG*), and victims of crime (*Opferentschädigungsgesetz* – *OEG*). In particular, compensation is paid to victims of the national socialist regime (*Bundesentschädigungsgesetz* – *BEG*). 380

Literature:

Eberhard Eichenhofer, Sozialrecht, 10. ed. 2017
Ralf Kreikebohm/Wolfgang Spellbrink/Raimund Waltermann, Kommentar zum Sozialrecht, 6. ed. 2019
Raimund Waltermann, Sozialrecht, 13. ed. 2018

I) Economic Administrative Law

It is generally accepted that the Basic Law does not mandate any particular type of economic system. The social market economy (*soziale Marktwirtschaft*), as the existing economic system in Germany is called, is not anchored by the constitution, and, 381 equally, the constitution does not create a duty to ensure free-market competition. Instead the constitution leaves the structuring of this area largely up to the legislator. It does, however, provide various binding structures, institutions and rules. Particularly the Fundamental Rights form important fixed points in this particular context. In terms of the Basic Law, whatever economic system is chosen, it must observe the guarantee of private property, the freedom of choice in choosing a career, the freedom to form associations and trade unions, the right to equality and to free development of the personality, which also apply in the economic sphere. On the other hand article 15 GG does make it perfectly possible to nationalise various important means of production so long as just compensation is paid. (This provision has not been applied in practice up to now.) European Union law has gained particular importance especially in the context of economic administration.

382   Economic administrative law is thus not meant as a reference to the steering of the economy by government bureaucracies. It refers instead to the legal rules relating to the numerous and diverse influences exerted by the state in the economy. These may take the form of intervention or of services aimed at promoting a flourishing economy and, above all, at protecting consumers and the general public.

383   This whole area is bound by the guidelines for economic policy laid down in the Stability and Growth Act (*Stabilitäts- und Wachstumsgesetz*). This says that in formulating their economic and financial policies the Federal and State governments must take into account the need for balance in the economy as a whole. They must follow policies which, in the context of the free market system, simultaneously promote stable prices, a high level of employment and balanced trade along with a constant and appropriate level of economic growth.

384   The choice of a career is free (article 12 para. 1 GG). Only for legitimate reasons of the public interest can special prerequisites for the choice and practice of some activity be set up and then only with strict regard for the principle of proportionality (*Grundsatz der Verhältnismäßigkeit*). Most types of economic activity must either be reported to the responsible authority or require permission. Activities which are supposed to be reported to the authorities can be prohibited if this is not done.

385   Economic administrative law is scattered throughout numerous statutes. The classical aspects are regulated particularly in the Trade Regulations (*Gewerbeordnung*, abbreviated *GewO*). They apply to the practice of "business". The statute provides only a negative definition of what constitutes business (§ 6 GewO). The practice of the so-called independent professions of the medical doctor, the legal practitioner, accountant or notary does not constitute a business. Neither does work in primary production such as agriculture, forestry, fishing or mining. Positively, business can be defined as including industrial production and processing, the work of craftsmen, wholesale and retail selling, and the service industry. The Business Regulations contain provisions on the duty to report or obtain a licence for the practice of a business. Detailed regulations concerning the carrying out of business, protection of employees, and rules about business premises, for example, relating to the requirement that the kitchen of a restaurant should meet certain standards of cleanliness, or requirements relating to emergency exits, are now codified in several particular acts (e.g. the Act on Labour Safety – *Arbeitsschutzgesetz*). However, oversight and enforcement are still governed by provisions in the GewO, as long as the relevant act does not contain specific rules

for enforcement (for example rights to obtain information in § 11 GewO or the possibility to fine businesses in § 144 ff. GewO).

In the interests of protecting consumers and business partners one of the now numerous prerequisites for running a business legally is that the person running the business should be considered reliable. Thus, permission to run a restaurant, pub or bar (*Gaststätte*) can be refused if the person applying for permission is considered not to possess the required degree of reliability, for example, if there is reason to believe that he or she will not comply regulations relating to health and food (§ 4 Abs. 1 *Gaststättengesetz*, abbreviated *GastG*). Furthermore, permission can be withdrawn subsequently, for example, if the owner tolerates the buying and selling of illegal intoxicants on his or her premises. The specific requirements which must be met before someone will be considered to satisfy this requirement of reliability cannot be defined in the abstract. Instead it is necessary to consider the particular requirements of the specific activity in each case. Germany's major redesign of its state-federation relations in 2006 (*Förderalismusreform I*) gave the *Länder* power to legislate in this previously federal area of legislation. The federal GastG remains in existence in the states until they exercise their legislative power (article 125 a para. 1 GG). So far, of the nine states that have passed respective laws, the majority (Brandenburg, Bremen, Hesse, Lower Saxony, Saarland, Saxony, Saxony-Anhalt, and Thuringia) have replaced the GastG by passing comprehensive legislation (explicitly e.g. § 13 GastG Brandenburg, § 18 para. 1 GastG Saarland, GastG Saxony). Baden-Württemberg's GastG, however, only regulates parts, and declares the federal GastG to be governing the remaining areas (§ 1 LGastG Baden-Wuerttemberg).

Important duties in the field of economic administration are often carried out by the federal government by means of higher federal authorities (*Bundesoberbehörden*) whose jurisdiction covers the whole country. Examples are the Federal Cartel Office (*Bundeskartellamt*) for the protection of competition, or the Federal Institute for Freight Traffic (*Bundesamt für Güterverkehr*). Occasionally use is also made of federal public-law corporations (*bundesunmittelbare Körperschaften*) and incorporated public-law institutes (*Anstalten des öffentlichen Rechts*), for example the Federal Institute for Financial Services for the control of credit institutions or the Federal Institute for the Regulation of Agriculture and Food. Important functions are also fulfilled by the Federal Office for Export Trading. The production and export of weapons of war requires official permission in terms of the Military Weapons Control Act and the Foreign Trade Act. In the interests of international peace weapons of war and other military materiel may not be exported from Germany to potential flashpoints. Germany is obliged to contribute to international peace in terms of the preamble and article 1 para. 2 of the Basic Law.

Of no small importance is the self-regulation of the economy by means of statutory bodies which represent the interests of their members. Generally speaking, membership of these bodies is compulsory for the persons affected. The affected parties are supposed to regulate their own affairs through these bodies in accordance with the democratic nature of the idea on which such organisations are based. However, their specialised knowledge and dedication is also supposed to serve the public interest. In terms of the Chambers of Commerce and Industry Act (*Industrie- und Handelskammergesetz*) the chambers of commerce and industry are to take into account all the interests of the business people whom they represent. Their specialised knowledge serves

386

387

388

to support the authorities and they act to preserve propriety and good conduct among businesspeople of good reputation. They also promote vocational training. Similar tasks are performed for the trades by the trade and crafts associations in terms of the Trade and Crafts Regulations (*Handwerksordnung,* abbreviated *HandwO*). In some *Länder* there are also agricultural associations. The craft guilds are voluntary associations of independent craftsmen working in the same craft or in related crafts formed to represent the common interests of their members (§§ 52 ff. HandwO).

389   A special aspect of the self-administration of people working in particular fields are the associations of the professions. Examples are the Medical Councils, Law Societies/Bar Associations (*Rechtsanwaltskammern*) and Associations of Accountants (*Wirtschaftsprüferkammern*). In these cases membership is once again usually compulsory for members of the respective professions. They monitor the observance of professional codes of conduct such as the requirement of impartiality and the ban on advertising by legal practitioners. There is also a special court for the legal profession. In cases of breaches of professional conduct this court can impose sentences ranging from a warning to striking the offender off the roll (*Ausschließung aus der Rechtsanwaltschaft*).

390   Subsidies have become a major instrument of economic policy. The term includes a very diverse range of financial assistance provided by the state to promote the economy. They serve as a tool for carrying out large-scale social and economic policies. It is unusual for a subsidy to be directly authorised by statute. Instead they are generally based on some general statement in the budget and are given in accordance with executive directives. The payment of subsidies often has a negative effect on the competitors of the favoured party by distorting the market to their detriment. Insofar as the granting of subsidies may constitute a violation of equal opportunity in economic competition, or of freedom of competition in general (article 3 para. 1 and article 2 para. 1 GG), it is an administrative act with impact on third parties (*Verwaltungsakt mit Drittwirkung*). The affected competitors can take legal action against any illegality in the action of the administration in providing the subsidy. State subsidies can also violate the prohibition of state aid under European Union law (article 107 para. 1 TFEU) and therefore be inadmissible. This prohibition recognises the danger of state subsidies intervening and thereby distorting the European Union's internal market. State aid under this provision means any state support to companies or specific branches of the economy without a market-adequate consideration. State subsidies may, however, be admissible as an exception to this rule for social reasons or to support weak economic regions (article 107 para. 2, 3 TFEU).

Literature:

Werner Frotscher/Urs Kramer, Wirtschaftsverfassungs- und Wirtschaftsverwaltungsrecht, 7. ed. 2019
Winfried Kluth, Öffentliches Wirtschaftsrecht, 2019
Rolf Stober, Allgemeines Wirtschaftsverwaltungsrecht, 18. ed. 2014
Rolf Stober/Sven Eisenmenger, Besonderes Wirtschaftsverwaltungsrecht, 16. ed. 2016
Jan Ziekow, Öffentliches Wirtschaftsrecht, 4. ed. 2016

m) Environmental Law

391   Environmental law (*Umweltrecht*) is, in practice, closely connected to economic administrative law because damage to the environment is to a large extent, if not exclu-

sively, the result of economic activity. Because of the threat to nature and the endangerment of the basis of human life which technical progress potentially poses, environmental law has become an important and highly detailed area of the law. It gathers together the widely scattered legal provisions aimed at preventing use, production and disposal from exceeding the levels at which human health and the natural surroundings will suffer unacceptable damage. The *Grundgesetz* expressly states that protection of the environment is one of the aims of the state (article 20 a GG).[14] It is a subject which arouses a great deal of public interest and is one of the key characteristics of the political landscape as a whole. Not surprisingly, legal developments in the last few years have often stemmed from the requirements of environmental protection.

One of the key ideas of environmental law is the idea of prevention. In other words the purpose of the rules is to avoid dangers which might lead to damage to the environment. In this respect environmental law goes beyond the goals of classical police law, which generally reacts to dangers once they have arisen.   392

Of particular importance in environmental law is the Federal Act for the Prevention of Noxious Emissions (*Bundesimmissionsschutzgesetz*, Emissions Act) and the numerous regulations relating to it. Important preventative and protective measures are contained in the Technical Regulations – Air; and the Technical Regulations – Noise (*TA-Luft und TA-Lärm*). For example, rules as to the quantities of noxious substances which may be emitted into the air are provided by these regulations. The minimum standard to which air must be cleaned before being emitted by large power stations is also prescribed by law. According to the Emissions Act a licence is required for the production facilities which are the most important from the point of view of the production of noxious emissions. Even those facilities which do not require a licence are subject to numerous environmental restrictions.   393

The provisions of the Emissions Act are primarily directed against air pollution and noise. But other environmentally relevant analyses are also taken into account in the process of deciding whether to grant a licence. In terms of § 13 of the act the granting of a licence makes a number of other approval procedures unnecessary. In terms of § 14 the granting of a licence also has various consequences in private law by limiting in certain respects the possible claims against the facility producing the emissions.   394

Measures against water pollution are contained primarily in the Water Resources Act (*Wasserhaushaltsgesetz*) with protective provisions and minimum standards for ground water and surface water. The Waste Water Ordinance (*Abwasserverordnung*) provides minimum standards for industrial and communal effluent which is to be discharged. A tax is imposed on effluent in an attempt to discourage its production. The Water Resources Act, which is framework legislation of the federal government, is complemented by the water legislation of the *Länder*.   395

The numerous and sometimes divergent protective goals formulated in the Federal Nature Protection Act (*Bundesnaturschutzgesetz*) and the Nature Protection and Land Care Acts (*Naturschutz- und Landschaftspflegegesetze*) of the *Länder* serve to promote the general preservation of the natural basis for human life. These acts aim to preserve the resilience of nature, the usefulness of natural resources and the plant and animal kingdoms, and finally the diversity of nature and landscape. These objectives are served by instruments such as landscape planning and by the proclamation of cer-   396

---

14 Article 20 GG.

tain areas as nature or landscape preservation areas, biosphere reservation areas or national parks, thus limiting the purposes for which they may be used. Particular species of plants and animals may be subject to special protection and nothing may be done which might harm them. In addition, nature compensation law has compensatory rules in terms of which any damage inflicted on natural resources must be made good by compensatory or replacement measures so that the balance of natural resources as a whole suffers as little negative impact as possible.

397   Environmental law viewed broadly may also be seen as including the law on the protection of animals. In terms of § 1 of the Animal Protection Act (*Tierschutzgesetz*) human beings have a responsibility to animals as fellow creatures to protect their lives and well-being. This attitude to animals has led to an amendment of the Civil Code (*BGB*) so that, in contrast to the earlier position, they are not viewed simply as things. However, according to § 90 a BGB the provisions for things are to be applied to animals as well insofar as there are no specific provisions to the contrary. From the point of view of criminal law, killing or injuring an animal will at the least be punishable as damage to property. Nobody may cause an animal pain, suffering or harm without reasonable grounds. In the case of animals kept for slaughter there are detailed provisions on appropriate conditions for keeping particular types of animal and for the purpose of ensuring that the slaughter takes place with as little pain as possible. Experiments on animals, particularly for purposes of medical research, may only be conducted for certain specified purposes and only if they are indispensable.

398   The law relating to nuclear energy and protection from radiation is centred on the Nuclear Energy Act (*Atomgesetz,* abbreviated *AtG*) which has strict rules for the licensing and running of nuclear energy facilities. Provision is made for avoiding harm resulting from ionising radiation or providing compensation for it. Emissions of radiation must be kept to the minimum possible as judged by the current state of the art in knowledge and technology. In accordance with Germany's decision in 2011 to abandon nuclear power as a source of energy, § 7 a AtG now provides a closing date for all existing nuclear power plants, the last of which will shut down operations in 2022.

399   In terms of the Chemicals Act (*Chemikaliengesetz*) new chemicals must be tested to establish what effect they have on human health and on the environment. The law on waste is regulated in the Recycling and Waste Products Act (*Kreislaufwirtschaftsgesetz*). It aims to promote recycling by means of provisions for preventing, recycling and disposing of waste. The object is to conserve natural resources and to ensure that waste is disposed of in ways which do not damage the environment.

400   The Federal Act on Soil Conservation aims to protect soil quality, particularly by preventing detrimental changes to the soil and by cleaning up pollution.

401   An important complement to environmental law as a field of special administrative law are the provisions of the criminal law in terms of which causing serious pollution is subject to penalties.

Literature:

Sabine Schlacke, Umweltrecht, 7. ed. 2019
Hans-Joachim Koch/Ekkehard Hofmann/Moritz Reese (eds.), Umweltrecht, 5. ed. 2018
Heinz-Joachim Peters/Thorsten Hesselbarth/Frederike Peters, Umweltrecht, 5. ed. 2015
Reiner Schmidt/Wolfgang Kahl/Klaus Ferdinand Gärditz, Umweltrecht, 10. ed. 2017

n) Law of Taxation

The existing tax law is extremely complicated and scattered throughout many sources. Repeated attempts to simplify the tax system have all failed. At the federal level alone there are about fifty different types of tax and more than one hundred different statutes containing tax law. Tax legislation generally falls within the field of competence of the federation, but the *Länder* also have legislative powers of practical significance in the fields of taxes on consumption (*Verbrauchssteuer*) and luxury goods (*Aufwandsteuer*), taxes on land (*Realsteuer*) and church taxes (*Kirchensteuer*), articles 105; 106 GG; article 140 GG read together with article 137 para. 6 WRV. 402

Taxation provides the main source of income to cover the expenditure of the state. General rules and procedures for the most important types of tax are contained in the Fiscal Ordinance (*Abgabenordnung*, abbreviated *AO*). This defines tax as a payment in money which is not consideration for a particular service provided by the state. The obligation to pay the money is imposed by a public authority on a person who finds him- or herself in factual circumstances to which the duty to pay tax is attached (§ 3 para. 1 first half of the sentence AO). It is perfectly possible that in imposing this obligation the raising of revenue is merely a secondary aim – taxes are often used as an instrument of social or economic policy. The key characteristic of tax is that the obligation to pay it is independent of any specific counter-performance by the state. The person liable for tax can also not specify to what use his or her tax payment is to be put. For example, a pacifist cannot announce that he or she is not prepared to make any contribution to military expenditure and pay the corresponding fraction of his or her tax liability into a blocked account. Only the democratically elected parliament can determine, by way of the Budget Act (*Haushaltsgesetz*), how tax money is to be spent. If the individual taxpayer wishes to influence the way taxes are spent he or she must do so by way of the political process. 403

Apart from taxes there are also other types of obligation to pay money which lead to income for the state and which are governed in part by provisions other than those applicable to taxation. Fees (*Gebühren*) which must be paid for a specific service provided by the state are an important example. For instance, a fee must be paid for the licensing of a motor vehicle or for the issuing of a permit to build. Fees, unlike taxes, are subject to two principles: the equivalence principle (*Äquivalenzprinzip*) and the cost-price principle (*Kostendeckungsprinzip*). This means that the amount charged as a fee may not exceed the value of the service provided by the state, and it may also not exceed the total cost to the state of performing the service. 404

These two principles also apply to contributions (*Beiträge*), by means of which the debtor contributes to the maintenance of a facility in which he or she has an individual interest. An important example is provided by construction law: The owner of a piece of land must make a contribution (*Erschließungsbeitrag*) to the costs of opening the land for use by the creation of roads, and electricity and water connections. 405

Payments which are neither taxes nor fees nor contributions are referred to as a special levy (*Sonderabgaben*). These are only permissible in exceptional circumstances. Their purpose is to make a homogenous group collectively responsible for the costs of some task for which this group bears responsibility. 406

Income tax is a direct tax on the income of natural persons. The types of income which are taxable on this basis are defined in detail. For example, income tax applies 407 to income derived from work either as an employee or self-employed person, from trade, from the renting of property, and from capital assets. In the case of an employee income tax takes the form of PAYE (*Lohnsteuer*), which means that it is retained by the employer and paid directly to the tax authorities.

408 Income tax is regulated by the Income Tax Act (*Einkommensteuergesetz*). In assessing taxable income various sums are subtracted from gross income. These include deductible expenses (*Sonderausgaben*), extraordinary expenses (*außergewöhnliche Belastungen*) and certain tax-exempt amounts (tax free allowances; *Freibeträge*). Operating expenses (*Betriebsausgaben*) and advertising expenses are deducted from income; these are expenses incurred in generating income. Since many individual factors cannot be taken into account when deducting PAYE the taxpayer is compensated for any errors in assessment which go to his or her disadvantage at the end of the year by means of a voluntary assessment which has replaced the former annual PAYE rebate. The taxpayer must submit returns to the revenue authorities by a certain date every year so that tax can be assessed.

409 There are various different tax brackets (*Steuerklassen*) which impose different levels of tax depending on a person's individual circumstances. The income of married persons is generally taxed under a special rule which splits their tax burden. The way this works is that the income of both spouses is added together and then divided so that for tax purposes half the collective income is attributed to each spouse. This can sometimes lead to significant savings for the taxpayer.

410 A single person earning not more than € 9 168 per annum is totally exempted from income tax (1 January 2019 figures). Thereafter the total income is taxed in different progressive zones according to progressive rates. In January 2019 the minimum rate was 14 %. The maximum rate, 45 %, is reached at an annual income of € 265 327 in the case of single persons.

411 The most important type of tax on consumption is the indirect turnover tax (*Umsatzsteuer*) in the form of value added tax (VAT, *Mehrwertsteuer*). It applies to all goods and services provided by a businessperson in the course of business as well as those which the person uses for his or her own consumption. The standard rate is 19 % (§ 12 para. 1 UStG), but there is a special rate for certain favoured goods of 7 %, for example for books, but also for overnight stays in hotels (§ 12 para. 2 UStG). This tax burden is in effect paid by the end consumer of the goods or services and is generally simply included in the final selling price of the goods or services.

412 Acquisition of property by reasons of death (usually by inheritance) and by donation is taxed in terms of the Inheritance and Donations Tax Act (*Erbschaft- und Schenkungsteuergesetz*). In the case of natural persons there are tax-free allowances which depend on the degree of relationship between the parties. Amounts in excess of this are taxed according to a rate which depends on the amount in question and the degree of relationship between the parties.

413 In terms of the Corporate Income Tax Act (*Körperschaftssteuergesetz*) corporate income tax takes the place of income tax in the case of legal persons, certain types of funds (*Vermögensmasse*) and unincorporated associations.

414 All businesses are subject to trade tax in terms of the Trade Tax Act (*Gewerbesteuergesetz*). It is assessed on the basis of the income and the capital assets of the business. Income from this tax flows to the communes who can determine a col-

lection multiplier which in turn determines the actual tax liability in a particular case (article 106 para. 6 GG).

In terms of the Land Acquisition Tax Act (*Grunderwerbsteuergesetz*) all landed prop- 415 erty, including rights in land such as a heritable building lease, are subject to a land tax.

Literature:
Dieter Birk/Marc Desens/Henning Tappe, Steuerrecht, 21. ed. 2018
Thomas Fetzer, Steuerrecht, 5. ed. 2019
Klaus Tipke/Joachim Lang, Steuerrecht, 23. ed. 2018

3. Administrative Procedural Law

As a general rule, a party to an administrative dispute may seek a remedy before the 416 general administrative courts. The procedure to be followed is regulated by the Administrative Courts Act (*Verwaltungsgerichtsordnung*, abbreviated *VwGO*).

In compliance with the guarantee of due process in article 19 para. 4 GG, the Admin- 417 istrative Courts Act provides access to justice in all public law disputes which are not of a constitutional nature and which are not subject to the jurisdiction of other courts in terms of specialised provisions (§ 40 para. 1 sentence 1 VwGO). The exception for disputes of a constitutional nature applies primarily to disputes between organs of the state. These are to be dealt with by the constitutional courts. Specialised courts supersede the general administrative courts *inter alia* for certain areas of special administrative law. For example, disputes relating to social security go to the social courts, tax matters go to the fiscal courts. These courts have their own procedural rules. If these specialised rules prove to have gaps then the Administrative Courts Act serves to supplement them, and the final backup is the Civil Procedure Act (*Zivilprozessordnung*, ZPO). An important provision for special jurisdiction is article 14 para. 3 GG. This provides that in the case of a dispute over the extent of compensation for expropriated property the "ordinary courts", in other words the civil courts, are to decide the matter. The same applies in cases concerning the liability in tort of the state (article 34 GG).

In cases before the administrative courts the inquisitorial maxim, otherwise known as 418 the principle of official investigation (*Amtsermittlungsgrundsatz*), applies. In terms of this principle the court is responsible for investigating the factual background of the case within the bounds set by the relief sought. Whether a fact has been alleged by one of the parties or whether there has been a formal motion to take evidence is not decisive. Because the issues dealt with are issues of public law, with the result that the public interest is always a factor, it is desirable that the truth should be established as objectively as possible.

However, the legal protection provided by the Administrative Courts Act is aimed pri- 419 marily at the protection of individual, subjective rights. Concern about the violation of the general, objective legal order as such is thus generally only relevant insofar as it is relevant to the protection of such subjective rights. The fact that there has been a general violation of the law is therefore not sufficient to give a claimant *locus standi* (*Befugnis zur Klage*) to bring an action, which is one of the prerequisites (*Zulässigkeitsvoraussetzung*) which must be satisfied before the court will hear a matter. The various procedural codes in general avoid the so-called public interest or taxpayer's action (*Popularklage*) in terms of which anybody would have standing to bring an action whenever there has been some sort of irregularity. Instead, for a claimant to have *locus standi* he or she must allege with good reason that he or she has been injured in his or her own rights by state action. This means that such an injury must at least be possible. It also means that the legal provision being relied upon must have been intended to protect the interests of the affected party. As an exception to this rule, actions can be brought by associations in special cases defined by statute (*Verbandsklage*, see § 42 para. 2 VwGO). For example, associations that have been officially recognised as working in the respective field, can start proceedings for violations of federal or state acts against the discrimination of disabled persons (see e.g. § 13 para. 1, 3 *Gesetz zur Gleichstellung behinderter Menschen*, abbreviated *BGG*). Similar provisions exist for recognised environmental associations in the area of environmental protection (see e.g. § 64 *Bundesnaturschutzgesetz*, §§ 2, 3 *Umwelt-Rechtsbehelfsgesetz*, abbreviated *UmwRG*), as well as animal protection associations in Bremen's *Gesetz über das Verbandsklagerecht für Tierschutzvereine*. This trend towards allowing public interest actions, particularly in the field of environmental protection, is furthered by the influence of European Union law.

420   The Administrative Courts Act makes a number of different forms of action (*Klagearten*) available. There is no single, universally applicable form of action. However, there are only slight differences between the various different forms of action, particularly with respect to the limitation periods within which an action must be brought. The differences are also made less significant by the preliminary hearing which is one of the steps which must be gone through before the court will hear the matter in the case of some of these forms of action.

421   The correct form of action if the claimant wants an administrative act (*Verwaltungsakt*) declared invalid is the action to set aside (*Anfechtungsklage*). If the aim is to compel a public authority to issue an administrative act then the correct remedy is the action for the issue of an administrative act (*Verpflichtungsklage*, see for both § 42 VwGO). Before either of these types of action can be brought the so-called objection procedure (*Widerspruchsverfahren*) must usually be complied with (§§ 68 ff. VwGO). The aim of this procedure is to give the administration the opportunity to correct its own mistakes. This means that the party against whom an unfavourable decision has been taken must first raise an objection with the authority which took the decision within one month of notification. The authority which took the decision must then reconsider the matter. If it remains of the opinion that its decision was correct, then it must submit the objection to the authority which rules on objections for it (*Widerspruchsbehörde*), which is usually the next-highest level in the bureaucracy. This authority must then give the final decision of the public authority on the objection (*Widerspruchsbescheid*). Only then can the person affected by the decision bring the matter before an administrative court. Once again, the time period within which the action must be brought is one month from the date of the final decision.

422   For the remaining forms of action before the administrative courts it is not necessary to follow the objection procedure before bringing the matter before a court and there is also no limitation period within which the action must be brought (§ 43 VwGO). The main distinction is between the action for a declaratory order (*Feststellungsklage*) and the general action for relief (*allgemeine Leistungsklage*). The action for a declaratory order provides a declaration as to a legal relationship, for example, whether a

person has German nationality. The general action for relief is aimed at compelling the administration to perform some action, for example, the withdrawal of a defamatory allegation.

A special type of action before the administrative courts is the action for the striking down of a legal rule (*Normenkontrolle*, § 47 VwGO). Local bye-laws (*Satzungen*) and statutory instruments (*Rechtsverordnungen*) in terms of the Construction Code (*Baugesetzbuch*), particularly building plans (which determine to what use all the pieces of land in a particular area may be put) are subject to being struck down by the *Oberlandesgericht* on the application of persons who suffer an infringement of a right by the rule in question. The application may also be brought by public authority. The same applies to the testing of legal provisions which are lower in status than legislation passed by the *Landtag* insofar as such testing is permitted by the law of the relevant *Land*. Thus, for example, it may be possible to test regulations of the *Land* or bye-laws of the communes before the administrative courts. Each *Land* has made provisions for such points in the acts implementing the Administrative Courts Act. 423

Since taking a matter through the administrative courts can be a very laborious process and since a legal remedy must often be granted swiftly to be of any use there is a need for a preliminary short-process procedure. For this purpose the affected party is helped in two ways. Firstly, § 80 VwGO provides that both the submission of an objection to a *Verwaltungsakt* and the bringing of the action to set aside have a suspensive effect on the administrative decision objected to (§ 80 para. 1 VwGO). In other words, if the person affected submits an objection to a *Verwaltungsakt*, or if he or she brings an action to have it set aside then, as a general rule, the administrative decision in question may not be implemented until the dispute has been decided. The affected party is thus provided with temporary protection. The suspensive effect can, however, be prevented by an order for the immediate implementation of the decision on grounds of the public interest or because of some other interest of greater weight than that of the complainant. In the case of certain types of administrative acts whose implementation is urgent the suspensive effect is presumed not to apply (§ 80 para. 2 VwGO). For example, in a situation in which immediate action by the police is necessary, there will be no suspensive effect, and the same would be the case where the payment of public charges and costs is in issue. However, an application to have the suspensive effect restored or imposed in the first place can always be made to the court or to the relevant public authority (§ 80 para. 3, 4 VwGO). 424

In other types of procedure the court can always grant an interlocutory order (*einstweilige Anordnung*) in terms of § 123 VwGO if speedy relief is necessary. Similar provision for speedy relief is made for applications which involve the striking down of legal rules (§ 47 para. 6 VwGO). The interlocutory order is to be used to make preliminary provision for the legal position until a decision can be reached in the main action. Interlocutory orders can, and often must, be made within a very short time. For this reason the procedural requirements are less strict than those for the main action. The court can make an order on the basis of a mere allegation without first hearing oral argument and indeed without giving the opposing party any opportunity to be heard at all. However, the court will consider an application for such an order very carefully before granting it. The decision may only be temporary in effect, in other words, it may not render a decision in the main action pointless. However, it is not infrequently 425 the case that the main action is never heard because the interlocutory order of the court in the preliminary hearing proves to be acceptable to both parties.

Literature:

Friedhelm Hufen, Verwaltungsprozessrecht, 11. ed. 2019

Ferdinand Kopp/Wolf-Rüdiger Schenke, Verwaltungsgerichtsordnung. Kommentar, 24. ed. 2018

Konrad Redeker/Hans Joachim von Oertzen, Verwaltungsgerichtsordnung. Kommentar, 16. ed. 2014

Wolf-Rüdiger Schenke, Verwaltungsprozessrecht, 16. ed. 2019

Thomas Würtenberger/Dirk Heckmann, Verwaltungsprozessrecht. Ein Studienbuch, 4. ed. 2018

C. Criminal Law

I. History and System

1. History

Accounts of German criminal law generally take the time of the Germanic tribes as   426
their starting point. This is the period of the great migration, which ended in the 6th
century. The history of German criminal law is a history of European criminal law. In
situations which today would involve a reaction of the criminal law to illegal behaviour, Germanic law (like all archaic legal systems) required penitentiary payments
by the perpetrator to the victim or to his or her clan, or a blood feud was conducted to
make the perpetrator atone for his or her act. It is possible that already at this time
there were public punishments for the violation of duties to the community such as
treachery in time of war or offences against tribal deities. Generally speaking the success of the attempted crime determined how seriously the deed was regarded. Nevertheless, a distinction was already drawn at an early stage between deliberate acts and
those which had happened by accident.

The Frankish period, from the founding of the Merovingian kingdom to the division   427
of the empire (end of the 5th century to the middle of the 9th century), brought a
strengthening of the central penal authority and the anchoring of criminal law in written sources. The continuing influence of Roman law together with Christianity
favoured the development of public punishment in the place of the private feud. The
laws of some of the tribes were recorded in Latin, for example, the Lex Salica in about
500 A.D.

The Mediaeval period up to about 1500 is characterised by the strengthening of the   428
principalities as against the central authority of the Empire. The power to inflict punishment passed to the territories, towns and petty princes. This strengthened the tendency towards public punishment. However, it also led to the fragmentation of the
criminal law and its increasing harshness, indeed cruelty, with the imposition of corporal forms of punishment and torture. The feudal system bloomed in knighthood, but
outside fortified strongholds physical danger always loomed. Particularly the towns,
with their interest in trade, reacted to these threats with decisive harshness, resorting
to torture and summary procedures.

Private records of regional customary law, such as the "Saxon Mirror" (*Sachsen-*   429
spiegel) written by *Eike von Repgow* in 1230 and the "Swabian Mirror" (*Schwaben-*
spiegel) of 1275, provided a basis for a systematic approach to criminal law. The Empire (*Reich*) and the Church attempted to discourage the custom of conducting feuds
and to create safe periods and areas with the campaigns for the "peace of the lands"
and the "peace of God". However, these attempts only achieved partial success right
at the end of the Mediaeval period with the Eternal Peace of 1495 (*Ewiger Land-*
frieden).

The reception of Roman law starting in the 12th century was of central importance for   430
public criminal law as it was for other aspects of the law. The detailed and systematic
Roman law was conducive to the creation of a class of secular lawyers and was applied in the ecclesiastical courts in Germany from the 13th century onwards. On the
one hand this development was in line with the legitimation of the Empire as the Holy

Roman Empire and successor of ancient Rome, and on the other hand it promoted the creation and administration of the territorial principalities.

431   The attempts to achieve a uniform system of criminal law throughout the Empire culminated in the Constitutio Criminalis Carolina of Emperor Charles V (*Karl V*). This was promulgated in 1532 and was the first criminal code applicable to all Germany. It contained the most important provisions concerning crime and punishment and was concerned mainly with matters of procedure. This code already gives expression to the idea of punishment according to the rule of law. It takes into account the principle that the accused must have a guilty state of mind (*Schuldprinzip*), and deals with grounds of justification (*Rechtfertigungsgründe*), attempt (*Versuch*) and liability as an accessory (*Teilnahme*). It also provides definitions of the acts (actus reus) constituting various offences (*Deliktstatbestände*). As far as the procedural aspect was concerned, the use of torture was limited to certain situations defined by statute and the use of an inquisitorial procedure was mandated, i.e. the court was required to undertake a comprehensive investigation of the facts of the case. Further refinement of the procedural law took place with the coming into force of the Imperial Police Ordinances[1] of 1530, 1548 and 1577. The German-language Constitutio Criminalis Carolina, also known as the *"Peinliche Halsgerichtsordnung"*, was based to a large extent on the Constitutio Criminalis Bambergensis produced by *Johann von Schwarzenberg* (1465-1528). In some German territories it was applicable, at least as a subsidiary source of law, until the 1870 Criminal Code of the North-German Federation came into force.

432   The academic study of criminal law became a significant influence for the creation of a uniform criminal law for all Germany from the 17th century onwards. This academic activity was inspired primarily by Italian and Spanish jurists and the Canon Law. Perhaps the most important writers were *Benedict Carpzov* (1595-1666), *Johann Samuel Friedrich Böhmer* (1704-1772) and *Christian Thomasius* (1655-1728). *Thomasius* was active in opposing the persecution of people accused of being witches and, together with *Samuel Pufendorf* (1632-1694) and *Christian Wolff* (1679-1754) embodies the start of the Enlightenment in Germany.

433   In this period academics began to consider what the purpose of punishment is and attempted to organise criminal law on the basis of reason. In this way the criminal law found a basis in the common good, legality and the right of the individual. Like all state laws, criminal law became secularised to a significant extent in this period, in other words, it largely lost its religious and theological connections. Detention became the standard form of punishment. *Jeremy Bentham* and *Cesare Beccaria* achieved significant influence in Germany. On his accession to the Prussian throne in 1740 *Friedrich II* (Frederick the Great) abolished the use of torture. A systematic approach, the embodiment of the law in statutes, the general applicability of law and its accessibility to everyone as well as especially humaneness and justice were key ideas of the Enlightenment. These ideas became important for criminal law with the codification movement in the 18th century and were embodied in the Prussian General Code of 1794,[2] the Constitutio Criminalis Theresiana of 1768 in the Austrian territories, and the Codex Juris Criminalis Bavarici of 1751 for Bavaria.

---

1   *Reichspolizeiordnungen.*
2   *Preußisches Allgemeines Landrecht (ALR).*

Against this background the French *Code pénal* of 1810 and the Bavarian Criminal   434
Code of 1813, which was created by *Paul Johann Anselm von Feuerbach*
(1755-1833), formed the basis of German criminal law in the 19th century. Its development was typified by codification in many of the German principalities, but at the
same time academic writers kept the idea of a common criminal law throughout the
German-speaking lands alive. The Prussian Criminal Code of 1851 formed the basis
for the Criminal Code of the North-German Federation of 1870. This code became
applicable throughout the newly-founded German Empire as the Imperial Criminal
Code[3] of 1871. Despite numerous amendments and the complete restructuring of the
General Provisions in 1975 this code is still applicable today in its 1998 version. The
impact of European Union law on the criminal law is still relatively small, but it is
growing.

The Weimar Republic initiated numerous reforms in the criminal law. In particular, it   435
reformed the prison system and introduced special rules for dealing with youthful offenders.

The criminal law also suffered from the perverting influence of the National Socialists.   436
The regime introduced the idea of convicting people of new offences by analogy with
existing statutory crimes and introduced castration as a punishment for sexual offences. These innovations were abolished by the allies after the Second World War. Alterations of the law during this period which were not tainted by National Socialist
ideology and which were therefore not abolished after the war were the introduction
in 1943 of special provisions of criminal law for juvenile offenders (*Jugendkriminal-
recht*) and the introduction in 1933 of provisions for securing, reforming and treating
more leniently persons with reduced criminal capacity.

2. System

The starting point for German criminal law is the Criminal Code (*Strafgesetzbuch*, ab-   437
breviated *StGB*). In its Book of General Provisions (*Allgemeiner Teil*) it sets out structural principles applicable to all aspects of criminal law such as the provisions as to
the area of application, the general forms of punishable behaviour such as attempts
(*Versuch*) and completed crimes (*Vollendung*), the requirements of intent (*Vorsatz*) or
negligence (*Fahrlässigkeit*), liability as a principal (*Täterschaft*) or as an accessory
(*Teilnahme*), crimes consisting of acts (*Begehungsdelikte*) or omissions (*Unterlassungs-
delikte*) and the system of sanctions for criminal behaviour.

The section on specific offences (*Besonderer Teil*) sets out the specific requirements of   438
individual crimes. Examples are crimes against life such as murder (*Mord*) and
manslaughter (*Totschlag*), assault and battery (*Körperverletzung*), theft (*Diebstahl*)
and fraudulent misappropriation of property (*Unterschlagung*), fraud (*Betrug*), robbery (*Raub*) and extortion (*Erpressung*), offences against the security of the state
(*Staatsschutzdelikte*) and crimes against the environment.

In addition, many important types of crime are dealt with in other statutes since their   439
subject matter connects them with the general rules for various areas of life. Examples
are offences related to the illegal presence of aliens within the area of the Federal Republic, which are dealt with in the Residence Act (§§ 95-97 AufenthG), or offences relating to drugs which are regulated in the Narcotics Act (§§ 29-31 *Betäubungsmit-*

---

3 *Reichsstrafgesetzbuch.*

telgesetz, abbreviated *BtMG*). The general provisions of the Criminal Code are also applicable to such offences. Criminology (*Kriminologie*) is related to criminal law in terms of subject matter but is to be distinguished from criminal law as the study of the rules governing the treatment of crime. Criminology is an empirical discipline concerned with the causes and varieties of crime and the effects of the sanctions imposed on people who break the law. Criminalistics, on the other hand, is the study of techniques for the investigation of crimes.

440   Criminal law must also be distinguished from the law relating to lesser (summary) offences (*Ordnungswidrigkeiten*). Lesser offences are acts which a statute subjects to a fine, as opposed to acts which are subjected to fines or imprisonment by the criminal law. For the least significant offences the penalty may be no more than the issuing of a warning or the imposition of a minor fine of between € 5 and € 55 (§ 56 para. 1 sentence 1 OWiG). The law on lesser offences has its roots in the punitive administrative law of the 19th century. Its provisions are contained in the Lesser Offences Act (*Ordnungswidrigkeitengesetz,* abbreviated *OwiG*). In addition, the *Länder* have also passed legislation on this subject. Many of the lesser offences are also set out in specialised acts regulating a specific area of activity. These special acts also often impose penalties higher than the € 1 000 which is the usual maximum penalty for lesser offences. The idea is that the fine should be greater than the economic benefit which the wrongdoer obtained by committing the offence. If the usual maximum penalty does not achieve this aim, then it can be exceeded. The minimum penalty is always € 5 (§ 17 para. 1 OWiG). In contrast to criminal law, lesser offences also apply to legal persons. The original idea behind the concept of lesser offences was to decriminalise the ethically neutral disregard for administrative rules. Most traffic offences are accordingly classified as lesser offences. However, in modern times even serious offences in the economic sphere are dealt with under the head of "lesser offences". The significance of the distinction between crimes and lesser offences is that the procedure for the latter is greatly simplified. The administrative authority responsible for the particular matter imposes a fine against which the affected party can appeal to the courts. They then decide the matter following a simple procedure.

441   The imposition of fines as well as the commission of crimes in certain fields is recorded in registers such as the Central Register of Traffic Offences (*Verkehrszentralregister für Verstöße im Straßenverkehr*). If repeated entries are recorded then further steps may be taken, for example, the suspension of the offender's driving licence in the case of traffic offences. These registers are to be distinguished from the Federal Central Register (*Bundeszentralregister*). In this register, various types of decision are recorded, for example, the issuing of an order for an alien to leave the country or the pardoning of someone who has been convicted of a crime. Courts and public authorities are supplied with information from this register where this is necessary for the fulfilment of their duties. The registry also issues certificates of conduct on application by the affected party. Such a certificate gives information on past convictions in strict accordance with rules laid down by statute.

442   Apart from the minor fines and warnings which can be imposed in terms of the law on lesser offences there are also a number of other non-criminal sanctions which are aimed at compelling the person against whom they are directed to behave in a certain way. These too are strictly distinguished from criminal law although they are sometimes referred to as punishments. Examples of this sort are coercive fines (*Zwangs-*

geld) and coercive detention (*Zwangshaft*) which may be imposed to put pressure on a person who is reluctant to carry out certain types of civil obligations (§§ 888, 889 ZPO) or fines and detention as penalties in reaction to acts which are incompatible with such an obligation (§ 890 ZPO). A court may impose penalties (*Ord-nungsstrafen*) for contempt of court for misconduct during a sitting or to compel a witness to speak. The penalties imposed in terms of the law relating to young offend-ers are also not considered to be criminal penalties. Disciplinary proceedings against members of the armed forces and against civil servants (*Beamte*) serve to uphold disci-pline within the service, and schools may impose various forms of punishment for the purposes of maintaining order in schools. Private law also recognises certain penalties aimed at the enforcement of private law rights. Such private law penalties often have much the same effect on the person on whom they are imposed as penalties under criminal law. An example is penalties for breach of contract (*Vertragsstrafe*, §§ 336 ff. BGB). Of great social significance are the penalties which can be imposed by clubs, particularly in the world of sport. The legal situation relating to private penalties im-posed by businesses is unclear. Such penalties are used to counter petty criminality within a business organisation without involving the public authorities in the matter. The sanctions imposed by clubs and businesses are purely private in nature. In the reli-gious sphere there are various types of ecclesiastical punishments which serve to main-tain order in the life of the religious community but which are also intended to protect the spiritual integrity of the person on whom they are imposed. None of these types of punishment involve the social and ethical condemnation by the community as a whole of the person punished. Such condemnation is reserved to the criminal law.

Literature:

Thomas Fischer, Strafgesetzbuch und Nebengesetze, 66. ed. 2019
Urs Kindhäuser (ed.), Strafgesetzbuch, 7. ed. 2017
Karl Lackner/Kristian Kühl, Strafgesetzbuch mit Erläuterungen, 29. ed. 2018
Leipziger Kommentar zum Strafgesetzbuch, *Heinrich Wilhelm Laufhütte, Ruth Rissing-van Saan, Klaus Tiedemann et alt. (eds.)*, 14 vols., 12. ed. since 2006
Hinrich Rüping/Günter Jerouschek, Grundriss der Strafrechtsgeschichte, 6. ed. 2011
Eberhard Schmidt, Einführung in die Geschichte der deutschen Strafrechtspflege, 3. ed. 1983 (reprint 1995)
Adolf Schönke/Horst Schröder, Strafgesetzbuch. Kommentar, 30. ed. 2019
Systematischer Kommentar zum Strafgesetzbuch, *Jürgen Wolter (ed.)*, 9. ed. 2017

II. General Provisions of the Criminal Code

1. Basic Principles

The universally accepted view is that the purpose of the criminal law is to protect legal interests and to influence the willingness of people to behave in certain ways. It is limi-ted to protecting the basic values of the social order. 443

An act can only be punished if provision was made for its punishment by statute be-fore the act was committed. This is called the rule of law (*Gesetzlichkeitsprinzip, nul-lum crimen, nulla poena sine lege*). This fundamental legal principle, which is laid down in article 103 para. 2 GG and in § 1 StGB limits the scope of the criminal law in a number of ways. In the first place, it implies that laws imposing criminal liability may not be retrospective in effect (*Rückwirkungsverbot*). This means that an act which, at the time when it was performed, was not subject to punishment may not 444 subsequently be made punishable. Subsequently increasing the punishment applicable to a particular act is also not permissible (§ 2 StGB). The principle also imposes a duty to formulate rules of criminal law with sufficient certainty. Every person should be able to predict in advance whether and how his or her behaviour is punishable. Closely connected to this aspect of the principle is the prohibition on the ad hoc creation of new offences by analogy with existing crimes (*Analogieverbot*). This means that no act may be punished as a crime unless it is explicitly expressed to be a crime. Finally, every provision imposing criminal liability must be contained in an act of parliament (*formelles Gesetz*). For this reason punishment may not be imposed on the basis of customary law or on the basis of subordinate forms of legislation such as ministerial or local government regulations. However, blanket provisions in a parliamentary statute which make the contravention of other acts, regulations or even administrative decisions punishable are permissible so long as they are sufficiently certain.[4]

445   In terms of geographical scope, the criminal law is applicable to all crimes committed within the country. This is the principle of territoriality (*Territorialitätsprinzip*). This is supplemented by the protective principle (*Schutzprinzip*). In terms of this second principle certain acts which are committed outside Germany but which infringe on legal interests inside Germany are punishable under German law (§ 5 StGB). Crimes such as genocide (*Völkermord*), trading in slaves (*Menschenhandel*) or trading in forbidden drugs (*Drogenhandel*) are punished in Germany according to the principle of universal law (*Weltrechtsprinzip*). This principle says that crimes against certain types of legal interest which are recognised by all civilised states are punishable according to national law irrespective of what legal rules are applied in the country where the crime was committed and irrespective of the nationality of the perpetrator. Crimes committed by or against German citizens outside of Germany are also sometimes punishable in terms of German law (§§ 3-7 and 9 StGB).

446   The accused can only be punished if he or she has committed a crime. In terms of the conventional analysis, this requires the fulfilment of three requirements. Firstly, the accused's behaviour must correspond to the elements of one of the situations disapproved of by the law which are listed in the Book of Specific Offences of the Criminal Code or in some other statute. Secondly, the act or state of affairs in question must be unlawful (*rechtswidrig*) which will not be the case if the accused is able to establish any grounds of justification (*Rechtfertigungsgründe*) such as self-defence (*Notwehr*). Thirdly, the accused's behaviour must be culpable. This means that it must be possible to hold him or her responsible for having fulfilled the elements of the crime, and the accused cannot be held responsible if various grounds of exemption exist (*Entschuldigungsgründe*). Examples are mental illness, conflicting duties (*entschuldigende Pflichtenkollision*) or an error as to the prohibited nature of the act (*Verbotsirrtum*). If any one of these three requirements is not satisfied then the act may not be punished.

2. Commission of an Act Corresponding to the Elements of a Crime[5]

447   The first step to meeting this requirement is that there must be some act or omission. Generally speaking what is required is some act on the part of the accused: For exam-

---

4   See, for example, § 315 a para. 1 No. 2 StGB.
5   *Tatbestandsverwirklichung.*

ple, the accused shoots the victim or takes a thing. However, the accused may also become guilty of a crime by omission (*Unterlassungsdelikt*) if he or she fails to act in a situation in which the law imposes on him or her a duty to do so. The so-called "genuine crimes by omission" impose penalties on the failure to fulfil a duty to act which is expressly imposed by law. This is the case, for example, where a person fails to fulfil his or her duty to help in terms of § 323 c StGB. This "good Samaritan" provision imposes penalties on a person who fails to provide the necessary assistance which can reasonably be expected of him or her in the circumstances of an accident or of general danger or emergency.

There are also so-called pseudo-omissions which constitute crimes. They are present if by an omission an act is committed which generally requires positive action. § 13 StGB provides that not to take steps to prevent an act or situation which fulfils the factual requirements of a crime is in itself a crime if the accused has a legal duty to prevent the act or situation from occurring. The accused must in other words have a form of guarantee obligation (*Garantenpflicht*). If such an obligation exists the accused can be charged with the crime whose factual elements he or she failed to prevent from being satisfied as if he or she had actively committed that crime. The accused is then charged on the basis of the paragraph whose requirements have been fulfilled read together with § 13 StGB. Such an obligation may arise in numerous different ways. Only a few of the most common sources of such obligations will be mentioned here. One possibility is that the obligation may arise directly from statute. An example of this sort would be the obligation of parents to take care of their own children: a mother may not allow her child to starve to death due to her own inactivity. The guarantor position can also arise from an actual assumption of responsibility. This would be the case where someone undertakes an obligation in a contract, for example, to provide all necessary medical treatment. The obligation often arises simply from a factual situation, such as when someone becomes part of the crew of a sailing boat. The guarantor's liability often arises from prior conduct by which a danger is created. For example, there are some cases in which courts have held that a person who at least negligently causes a road accident has a duty to assist those who are injured as a result. Guarantee obligations can also arise from special relationships of trust such as that between members of a family or people sharing a house. **448**

A distinction is also traditionally made between different types of crimes depending on the type of facts which satisfy the requirements of the crime. Result crimes (*Erfolgsdelikte*) focus on the causing of a particular result. For example, manslaughter (*Totschlag*, § 212 StGB) requires the death of a person. State of affairs crimes (*Tätigkeitsdelikte*) focus on a particular act or state of affairs. Here merely doing the forbidden act is criminal irrespective of its consequences. Examples are the crimes involving false statements such as perjury (*Meineid*, § 154 StGB) or the making of false statements to a public authority while not under oath (§ 153 StGB). **449**

Another distinction is based on the intensity of the infringement required for criminal liability. Injury crimes (*Verletzungsdelikte*) require actual damage to a protected object. Risk crimes (*Gefährdungsdelikte*) punish the mere creation of a concrete risk of harm. An example of this sort is endangering road traffic (*Gefährdung des Straßenverkehrs*, §§ 315 b-315 d StGB). Sometimes even the creation of a mere abstract danger is punishable, for example aggravated arson (§ 306 a StGB). **450**

451   The completion of a result crime presupposes a causal connection between the act of the accused and the result in question. Much is contentious in this area. The courts take as their starting point a test of factual causation which is called the condition theory (*Bedingungstheorie*) or the equivalence theory (*Äquivalenztheorie*). In terms of this test an act is a cause of a result if it is a *conditio sine qua non* of its occurrence, in other words, but for the particular act which is being labelled as a cause the result would not have occurred. In terms of this equivalence approach every cause is treated as being of equivalent weight – the mother of the murderer also caused the victim's death, because, but for her giving birth to the murderer, the victim would not have been killed. The courts meet the obvious need to limit liability more strictly than this test would do by requiring the fulfilment of further elements. In particular, the requirements of intention or negligence serve to further limit liability as does the test for whether the causal connection is too remote.

3. Intention and Negligence

452   Most crimes require that the perpetrator should have acted intentionally to be liable (§ 15 StGB). To act intentionally the perpetrator must know that his or her actions fulfil the objective elements of the crime and he or she must have desired this. This second element of intent (*Vorsatz*) causes the most difficulties. It is definitely present where the perpetrator specifically desires the criminal consequence. An example would be where the perpetrator kicks the victim because he or she desires to kill the victim or because at the very least the perpetrator views this possible consequence with approval. If the perpetrator sees the criminal consequence as an inevitable result of his or her acts, then one speaks of direct intent (*direkter Vorsatz*). Some crimes go further and require that the perpetrator must have been motivated by the desire to cause the criminal consequence. This intensified form of direct intention is called *Absicht*.

453   The perpetrator is also regarded as acting intentionally if he or she consciously takes the criminal consequence into the bargain because it is necessary to achieve some other object. The fact that the perpetrator regrets the criminal consequence will not affect his or her liability if the perpetrator deliberately takes it into the bargain (*billigend in Kauf nehmen*). In this situation the perpetrator is said to have contingent intent (*bedingter Vorsatz*).

454   According to statute there are also many offences whose requirements will be satisfied by mere negligence (§ 15 StGB). These crimes are generally punished less severely than intentional crimes. Here the basis of criminal liability is an unlawful lack of due care. A person is already guilty of negligence if the person hopes that he or she will be able to avoid the possibility that his or her act will have a criminal result although the person is aware that he or she is acting in breach of a duty of care. This is called conscious negligence (*bewusste Fahrlässigkeit*). Unconscious negligence (*unbewusste Fahrlässigkeit*) describes the situation where the accused does not foresee the criminal consequence and acts carelessly despite the fact that objectively, from the point of view of a neutral observer, and subjectively, in the perpetrator's own particular circumstances, he or she should have been able to foresee and avoid the result.

4. Liability as a Principal and other Forms of Participation

455   A person is liable as perpetrator (*Täter*) if the person commits a crime alone. The person is then called the sole perpetrator (*Alleintäter*, § 25 para. 1, first alternative StGB).

If several people commit a crime together, then a distinction must be made according to what part each of them played. If several people act to carry out a common purpose (*gemeinsamer Tatentschluss*) then they act as co-perpetrators (*Mittäter*) and each of them is liable as if he or she had committed the crime as a perpetrator (§ 25 para. 2 StGB).

These possibilities must be distinguished from the commission of a crime through the agency of another person (*mittelbare Täterschaft*, § 25 para. 1, second alternative StGB). This includes many possible constellations. A person who commits a crime through the agency of another uses the other person as an instrument by steering that person's will. In other words, he or she is in control of the commission of the act in question. For example, this can take place by the exercise of duress, as when a bank robber forces a bank employee to open the safe and hand over the money by threatening the family of the employee. Another form of crime by agency is where the person who is being used is misled into performing the act. For example, this would be the case where a police officer is induced to arrest an innocent person by the provision of misleading information. In such a case only the person who induces the unjustified arrest is liable for false imprisonment (*Freiheitsberaubung*, § 239 StGB). The person used as an instrument to commit the crime (*Tatmittler*) may, in appropriate circumstances, be liable for the negligent commission of the act if this is a punishable offence.

456

As far as other participants (*Teilnehmer*) in a crime are concerned, a distinction is made between instigators (*Anstifter*, § 26 StGB) and accessories (*Gehilfe*, § 27 StGB), that is, persons guilty of aiding and abetting the crime. While a perpetrator wants to do the act as his or her own act, other participants are, according to the courts, primarily characterised by the fact that they want or approve of the act as the act of another person. These distinctions are, however, much disputed. The instigator gets the perpetrator to do the deed, for example by persuading the perpetrator to do it or promising the perpetrator various benefits if he or she does it. The instigator is liable to be punished as if he or she had committed the crime him- or herself. Accessories, on the other hand, are punished less severely. The accessory's contribution to the crime consists in assisting the perpetrator to commit it. In contrast to a co-perpetrator he or she does not intend the commission of the crime as his or her own act. Examples of this sort of participation are the provision of a weapon which is to be used to commit a robbery. Both in the case of instigators and of accessories a necessary condition for liability is the unlawful and intentional commission of some act which corresponds with the elements of a specific independent crime by the principal. If the main crime consists of some negligent act then there can be no liability for accessories or instigators. The guilt of the perpetrator is not relevant in determining the guilt of the accessory or instigator.

457

5. Completed Crimes and Attempts

Any person who completes an act fulfilling all the elements of a crime is punishable. In the case of many offences the law provides that an attempt is also punishable. This applies to all felonies (serious offences, *Verbrechen*). In contrast, an attempt to commit a misdemeanour (less serious offence, *Vergehen*) is only punishable if express provision to this effect is made (§ 23 StGB). Here the distinction between felonies and misdemeanours, which used to be important with respect to the types of punishment possible, still plays a role. Felonies are defined as any criminal act which is punishable by a

458

term of imprisonment of at least one year. Misdemeanours are defined as all crimes which are not felonies (§ 12 StGB). An attempt may be punished less severely than the completed crime, but need not be. An attempt is punishable although the specific object of the crime has not as yet suffered any harm. The basis for the punishment of attempts is the unlawful intention of the perpetrator insofar as it has had some effect on the legal community. Public trust in the legal system would be shaken if a person who has the intention to commit a significant crime and has begun to carry this intention out were to remain unpunished.[6]

459   The requirements for an attempt are satisfied once the perpetrator subjectively sees him- or herself as having begun to carry out his or her plan to do an act which satisfies the elements of a crime (§ 22 StGB). An outside observer must be able to perceive that the intentions of the perpetrator are serious and that, at least in the mind of the perpetrator, the elements of a crime are about to be satisfied. In contrast to attempt, mere preparations to commit a crime are not punishable. An example would be if the perpetrator buys a train ticket with the intention of creating an opportunity to steal from the intended victim during the journey. However, in certain cases such preparatory steps in themselves constitute a crime. For example, preparing to forge bank notes is in itself punishable (§ 149 StGB).

460   It is not necessary that the planned method of committing a crime should have an objective chance of success before liability for attempt arises. For example, if the perpetrator has forgotten to load his or her pistol, but pulls the trigger with the intention of killing the intended victim he or she will be liable for attempted manslaughter, §§ 212, 22 ff. StGB or attempted murder, §§ 211, 22 ff. StGB. This is a case of a – punishable – attempt to do the impossible. However, the court can reduce the sentence or refrain from imposing any punishment at all if the perpetrator's failure to realise that the attempt could not succeed was due to gross lack of understanding (§ 23 para. 3 StGB). For example, if the perpetrator attempts to poison somebody (who suffers from no allergy) with a glass of apple juice the court can decide not to inflict punishment.

461   Attempts to do the impossible are to be distinguished from attempts to commit an imaginary crime (*Wahndelikt*), although this distinction is sometimes difficult to draw. In this situation the perpetrator attempts to commit a crime, but the act is in fact not illegal. In other words, the perpetrator imagines that his or her act is forbidden by a rule of law which in fact does not exist. In the case of a futile attempt (*untauglicher Versuch*) on the other hand the perpetrator believes that he or she is fulfilling the elements of an existing crime when in fact the perpetrator is not. An example of an attempt to commit a non-existent crime is when the accused in criminal trial believes that it is a crime for him or her to give false evidence and nevertheless dishonestly swears that he or she did not do the deed. This is an imaginary crime because giving false evidence is only a punishable offence if done by witnesses other than the accused or by expert witnesses (§ 153 StGB).

462   If the act is still at the stage of an attempt then the perpetrator can free him- or herself from criminal responsibility by reversing his or her intention in good time (§ 24 StGB). For this possibility to be applicable the perpetrator must have voluntarily given up the further commitment of the crime. If the perpetrator subjectively believes that he or she has already done everything necessary for the completion of the crime the perpetrator

---

6   *Kindhäuser*, Strafrecht. Allgemeiner Teil, § 30 side note. 9 f.

must voluntarily prevent the completion of the crime. For example, if the perpetrator has administered poison to his or her victim, so that in the absence of intervention the victim will die, then the perpetrator must ensure that the victim is successfully treated if the perpetrator is to avoid liability. If the act will not be completed without effort on his or her part, then the perpetrator must voluntarily make at least a serious effort to prevent the completion of the crime.

6. Illegality and Grounds of Justification

As a general rule, if a person does an act fulfilling the factual elements of the definition of a crime the perpetrator is acting illegally. The illegality (*Rechtswidrigkeit*) of an act or omission is suggested by the fact that it fits the definition of a particular crime. This is a logical conclusion because the definition of any specific crime describes a situation of which the legal order disapproves. Illegality is a contradiction of the law.   463

In exceptional cases such an act may nevertheless be lawful due to some ground of justification (*Rechtfertigungsgrund*). In these exceptional cases the legal order tolerates the act because, exceptionally, it is in accordance with the values of the legal system. Because the legal order is considered to be a harmonious whole the predominant view is that grounds of justification are always applicable in criminal law irrespective of where in the legal system they are derived from.   464

A particularly important ground of justification is self-defence (*Notwehr*). A person who does an act which is necessary for self-defence does not act illegally (§ 32 para. 1 StGB). Self-defence is defined as defensive measures which are necessary to avert an immediate (*gegenwärtig*) and illegal attack on oneself or another person. The legal order essentially does not require any person to tolerate an attack on his or her legal interests if the attack is one of which the legal order itself disapproves. The defender is thus protecting not only his or her own interests but also the integrity of the legal system as a whole. If the defender acts to protect the interests of another person the situation is described as one of "emergency assistance" (*Nothilfe*). Self-defence may provide a ground of justification even if the attacker is not acting culpably. Self-defence can thus be invoked when warding off attacks from children who lack criminal capacity as well as people in a state of intoxication or suffering from mental illness. However, a general limitation of the right to self-defence is assumed in such cases. Self-defence can also be invoked in the protection of any sort of legal interest. A requirement for self-defence is the intention to defend oneself or others. It can thus only be applicable so long as the attack continues. For example, if the thief has succeeded in securing the booty in his or her den before the victim discovers where it is, then the victim cannot invoke self-defence as a ground of justification if he or she in turn forcibly enters the house of the thief to recover his or her property. On the other hand, if the victim is in hot pursuit of the thief and the criminal has not yet had an opportunity to secure his or her booty, then the illegal attack on the victim's legal interests is regarded as still continuing and the owner will have the justification of self-defence if the victim uses force to recover his or her property.   465

Defensive force is only justified insofar as it is necessary (*notwendig*). If the defender uses force in excess of what is necessary then the defender is guilty of using excessive force (*Notwehrexzess*). The defender will then be criminally liable unless he or she was acting in confusion, fear or shock in the heat of the moment (§ 33 StGB). Furthermore, the principle of proportionality (*Verhältnismäßigkeitsgrundsatz*), which is an-   466 chored in the constitution, has permeated the law relating to self-defence with the result that even if the amount of force used was necessary to defend the legal interest threatened it will not be justified if it was disproportional (*unverhältnismäßig*). A disproportional use of force cannot be a ground of justification. Thus, if the legal interest to be defended and the legal interest of the attacker which must be infringed for the purpose of the defence are out of proportion to one another, then the potential defender must tolerate the infringement of his or her legal interests by the attacker. For example, if a fifteen year old boy is sitting in the next-door neighbour's cherry tree stealing cherries the lame owner of the cherries may not shoot the thief because, although this use of force is necessary to protect his or her property, it is disproportional. If the neighbour were to shoot the defensive action would not be justified in terms of § 32 para. 1 StGB.

467　Another ground of justification is necessity (*rechtfertigender Notstand*, § 34 StGB). In this defence the criminal law takes account of situations in which the infringement of a legal interest is permissible even although the person whose interest is to be infringed is not attacking the person acting out of necessity. This is in contrast to self-defence, which is only applicable in the case of an illegal attack. If a person does an act to avert a current danger to his or her legal interests or those of some other person he or she will be able to rely on this defence if two requirements are satisfied: Firstly, it must not have been possible to avert the danger in any other way, and, secondly, the balance of the conflicting interests must indicate that the protected interest is significantly more important than the interest infringed on. It may, for example, be permissible for a doctor to drive in the wrong direction in a one-way street in order to arrive at an injured person on time.

468　In this balancing of interests the rank of the affected interests and the degree of danger to which they are exposed are the main factors to be considered. The act must always be a reasonable (proportional) means of averting the danger. All interests meriting protection, both on the side of the right infringed on, and on the side of the right protected, must be taken into account even if they are only indirectly affected. Of particular importance in making this judgement are the nature and origin of the danger as well as its intensity and immediacy. However, attention must also be given to the nature and extent of the infringements threatened by the defensive action, the rank and value of the colliding legal interests and the likelihood that the intervention will be successful in protecting the more important interest which is threatened. Special obligations to accept certain risks, as in the case of police officials, firemen or soldiers must also be taken into account. The same applies to special protective duties arising from the status of guarantor (§ 13 StGB).

469　Apart from self-defence and necessity the criminal law also recognises a number of other grounds of justification. Thus, the consent of the injured party may justify assault and battery. For example, this is the case where someone participates in a sport such as boxing or football which is known to be dangerous and in which injuries of the sort inflicted are known to occur regularly. However, consent will not always be a ground of justification. It might already be relevant at the stage of examining whether the factual elements of the crime have been satisfied. For example, if someone orders his or her old furniture to be chopped up for firewood then not even the elements of the definition of unlawful damage to property (*Sachbeschädigung*, § 303 StGB) will be satisfied. Above all, consent is not a ground of justification if the person giving consent cannot dispense with the protection of the law or cannot dispense with it to the necessary extent. This may be the case if the legal order considers the protection of the law not to be something which is subject to his or her discretion. Thus, it is no ground of justification that the victim has consented to his or her own death. Killing a person with his or her consent is a special crime in terms of § 216 StGB (*Tötung auf Verlangen*).

Further grounds of justification may arise from official powers of intervention, particularly the powers granted to the police. Official authority granted to a third person may also be a justification. Yet another possibility is the right of every person to arrest a criminal who is caught in the act (§ 127 para. 1 sentence 1 StPO).   470

7. Culpability (Mens Rea) and Factors Excluding a Culpable State of Mind

The accused is only liable to be punished if his or her act fulfils the elements of the crime, was unlawful, and was done with a culpable state of mind (*schuldhaft*). Culpability means that the accused can be held personally responsible for the relevant act. More precisely, it must be possible to reproach him or her for forming the intention which led to the act. It is the accused, in other words, the subject, who must be reproachworthy. The reproach expresses a disapproval of the accused's behaviour. A prerequisite for this is that the accused must have had the ability and the opportunity to act in conformity with the law. The criminal law as it stands thus presupposes the free will of the accused. This approach is challenged by some critics who support a deterministic view and therefore do not recognise the concept of culpability in the traditional sense.   471

From the point of view of the criminal law culpability is only possible if a person has criminal capacity (*Schuldfähigkeit*). Children under the age of 14 do not have criminal capacity (§ 19 StGB) and capacity must specifically be proven in accordance with the Juvenile Courts Act in the case of youths (aged 14 to 17, § 3 JGG). If, at the time of doing the act, the accused is incapable of understanding that what he or she is doing is unlawful, or if he or she is incapable of acting in accordance with this insight, then the accused lacks criminal capacity and cannot be punished (§ 20 StGB). This is so in the case of a psychological disease such as a psychosis, but also in the case of severe disturbances of consciousness which may, for example, arise from jealousy or fear. Lack of criminal capacity may also arise from feeble-mindedness or other psychological abnormalities such as neuroses or compulsive urges. The law also recognises the possibility of diminished responsibility arising from any of the above causes. The sentence may then be reduced appropriately (§ 21 StGB). If the accused has deliberately or negligently induced his or her lack of capacity so as to commit a crime while in this state (for example, getting drunk so as to summon up courage for the crime) then the accused will normally remain criminally liable in accordance with the doctrine of "actio libera in causa".[7]   472

The concept of culpability is not defined by the criminal law. The law does, however, describe a series of defences, in terms of which there is no personal guilt due to exceptional circumstances.   473

A particularly important defence excluding culpability is exculpating necessity (*entschuldigender Notstand*, § 35 StGB). This states that a person who does an illegal   474

---

7 See *Krey/Esser*, Deutsches Strafrecht, Allgemeiner Teil, side note 702 ff.

act to ward off immediate danger to life, limb or liberty, which cannot be averted in any other way, and which threatens him or her, or a family member, or some other person to whom the person has a close relationship, does not act culpably. The standard example of this is "*Karneades' spar*" – two survivors of a shipwreck are holding onto a spar to keep afloat, but the spar is only sufficient to keep one of them afloat. The one pushes the other into the sea with the result that the other drowns.

475 For this defence the interest being defended by the accused need not be more important than the interest infringed upon by his or her defensive action. This is what distinguishes exculpatory necessity from necessity as a ground of justification excluding unlawfulness, which was discussed above. The accused must, however, have chosen the least damaging alternative to achieve his or her rescue. A further limitation is that this defence is only applicable if the accused was acting in defence of a limited number of particularly important legal interests and if he or she was acting to protect him- or herself or the interests of someone close to him or her. If the circumstances are such that the law requires the accused to tolerate the danger, then the defence will also not be applicable. Here the principle of proportionality takes effect: if the threatened interest is significantly less important than the interest which the accused has infringed upon in defending his or her interests, then the reduction of injustice which results from the defensive action is also proportionally less. This is particularly the case where the person invoking exculpatory necessity caused the danger him- or herself, or where the person stands in a particular type of relationship as is the case when the person has the status of a guarantor. The penalty may, however, be reduced if the accused would not have been required to tolerate the danger in question but for the fact that he or she occupied a special position. This is often relevant with respect to members of the police force and of the sea and mountain rescue services.

476 A further defence excluding culpability is excessive use of force in self-defence (*Notwehrüberschreitung, Notwehrexzess*, § 33 StGB). If the accused has exceeded the limits of self-defence, particularly the measure of defensive force necessary, due to confusion, fear or shock then his or her act remains unlawful. Nevertheless, the accused is deserving of special sympathy and his or her behaviour is therefore considered not to be culpable.

477 Office bearers and soldiers who perform an act contrary to criminal law in accordance with non-binding instructions from their superiors are acting illegally but may be found not to have acted culpably (§§ 63 para. 3 BBG; § 5 para. 1 WStrG).

478 In special circumstances very cautious recognition is also given to an extra-legislative defence excluding culpability if the accused finds him- or herself confronted by an unusual, almost insoluble collision of duties (*Pflichtenkollision*) and can therefore not be held by the law to have acted culpably. This defence will be recognised if the accused acted in accordance with his or her conscience and his or her actions, which were determined by his or her pursuit of the rescuing purpose, were in the circumstances the only way to avert even greater damage to legal interests of great importance. This defence was accepted in the case of doctors in institutions for people suffering from mental deficiencies who, during the National Socialist period participated in the euthanasia action ordered by Hitler by selecting certain patients for death. The defence was accepted in this situation because their actions in effect led to the saving of other patients – had they not made some show of co-operating they would have been replaced

by other persons who would have been prepared to co-operate fully and then none of the patients would have survived.

A particularly difficult and contentious question is how to deal with crimes of conscience. Generally speaking a person who acts contrary to a provision of the criminal law due to his or her belief (generally arising from religious grounds) in the absolute ethical correctness of the person's behaviour is to be judged differently from a criminal who was motivated by personal gain. Indeed, the dominant view is that even if the accused breaks the law on grounds of conscience he or she is acting both unlawfully and culpably. Otherwise the criminal law would amount to no more than a recommendation. However, the special status of a person who acts on grounds of conscience is given expression in the guarantee of freedom of conscience in article 4 paragraphs 1 and 2 GG. Due regard is paid to this special status by recognising that the culpability of the accused is lessened and that in special cases there may be no culpability at all.[8]However, in view of the intense migration into Germany there seems to be a tendency in court practice to use actions that are based in other cultural traditions rather to intensify punishment.

8. Mistake in the Context of Criminal Law

The consequences of mistakes on the part of the perpetrator are an area of the criminal law which to this day does not have a clear theoretical basis. What is at least clear is that, in contrast to some foreign legal systems, the old principle that "ignorance is no excuse" no longer applies as a general principle in German criminal law today. Because of the principle of culpability it is of crucial importance in determining the legal consequences of a mistake to determine whether it affects the reprehensibility of the crime. The law makes a distinction essentially between mistakes of fact (*Tatbestandsirrtum*, § 16 para. 1 StGB) and mistakes of law (*Verbotsirrtum*, § 17 StGB). In addition there are many other types of mistake which are not regulated by statute.

A mistake of fact describes the situation in which the person committing the act in question is at the time not aware of a circumstance or fact which is one of the elements of the crime in question. The accused does not realise what he or she is doing from the point of view of the elements of the offence, and the accused therefore lacks the state of mind which is necessary if he or she is to have intention with respect to the elements of the crime. For example, the accused takes from the change rooms a tennis racquet which the accused believes to be his or her own but which in fact belongs to someone else. In this case it does not occur to the accused that he or she is taking something which belongs to somebody else and the accused is therefore acting without the intention to steal as defined in § 242 StGB. The mistake of fact absolves the accused of liability for an intentional act. However, in appropriate cases the accused may nevertheless be liable on the basis of negligence if doing the act in question negligently is a punishable offence. A type of mistake which frequently occurs is a mistake as to the person of the victim or the object of the crime. If the situation as imagined by the perpetrator fulfils the elements of the crime just as the actual situation does then the perpetrator remains liable to be punished. There is then no operative mistake of fact. For example, if the perpetrator mistakes the intended victim's brother for the intended

479

480

481

---

8   Compare BGHSt 2, 194/198; BVerfGE 32, 98/106 ff.

victim due to poor light and proceeds to shoot the brother fatally the perpetrator will still be liable for causing the death (*error in persona vel in objecto*).

482 In the case of mistake of law the perpetrator is mistaken as to the illegality of his or her act. At the time of acting the perpetrator is not conscious of doing anything wrong (§ 17 StGB). The perpetrator is often perfectly aware of what he or she is doing, but believes incorrectly that it is permissible. The perpetrator is then acting without culpability and cannot be punished if he or she could not be expected to avoid making this mistake. If, on the other hand, the accused could have avoided making the mistake then he or she is punishable, but the sentence may be reduced in terms of § 49 para. 1 StGB.

483 If the accused has erroneously assumed that there are factors justifying his or her otherwise unlawful behaviour then the predominant view is that the accused is to be treated as if he or she had made a mistake of fact in terms of § 16 StGB. This would apply in the case of putative self-defence. The accused mistakenly believes that he or she is being attacked and injures the imagined attacker in an attempt to defend him- or herself. Here the accused can at most be punished for negligently causing bodily injury (*fahrlässige Körperverletzung*).

484 If the accused is mistaken as to the legal limits of a recognised ground of justification or if the accused acts on the assumption that the law recognises a particular ground of justification which in fact does not exist, then he or she is making a mistake as to the permissibility of the deed (*Erlaubnisirrtum*). An example would be if the person acting in self-defence goes beyond the appropriate defensive measures in the belief that he or she is entitled to use every possible means of defending him- or herself. Since the assessment of the accused here only differs in degree from that of the legal system the accused is treated as if he or she had made a mistake of law in terms of § 17 StGB. This means that the accused can only claim not to have acted culpably if he or she could not reasonably have avoided the mistake. In other cases the best the accused can hope for is the imposition of a lesser sentence.

485 Mistake with respect to a prohibitory rule (*Verbotsirrtum*) describes the situation in which the perpetrator sees his or her behaviour as being legal because the perpetrator is not aware of the rule prohibiting his or her act, or believes that it is invalid. The same applies if the perpetrator comes to a false conclusion as to the scope of the prohibition as a result of a false interpretation. This, too, is a case of mistake of law.

486 Mistake with respect to defences excluding culpability are essentially irrelevant. However, an exception to this is where the accused is mistaken as to the existence of facts which would make a particular defence excluding culpability applicable. This would be the case if, for example, the accused kills a person because the accused mistakenly believes that this is the only way in which he or she can save his or her own life. If the accused could not have avoided the mistake then the accused is not culpable because it is irrelevant to his or her psychological state at the time of committing the crime whether the situation forcing the accused to do so was real or existed only in his or her mind. If the mistake could have been avoided then the predominant view is that the perpetrator is liable to be punished but the sentence is to be reduced in terms of § 35 para. 2 to the extent set out in § 49 para. 1 StGB.

9. The System of Penalties

Why the state imposes penalties is certainly one of the most important basic issues in criminal law. The system of penalties in German criminal law avoids committing itself to a single theory on this point. Today the purposive approach (*Zwecklehre*) which was developed in the 19th century stands in the foreground. This approach emphasises various different purposes of imposing penalties. One important purpose of imposing punishments is general deterrence (*Generalprävention*). The general threat of punishment, its imposition and execution, are all aimed at reminding the world at large of the consequences of crime and thus deterring the general public from committing criminal acts. In addition there are the aims of specific prevention and deterrence (*Spezialprävention*). These aim at preventing or deterring a specific individual from committing crimes. Once a crime is committed the aim is to reform the perpetrator. The main emphasis here is on re-socialisation or, if the perpetrator was not sufficiently integrated in society before, on socialisation. Specific prevention also opens the possibility of permanently isolating perpetrators who are not capable of being reformed. **487**

These so-called relative theories stand in contrast to the absolute theories of punishment. They see the sense of punishment as being retribution for the wrong which has been done and for the guilt of the perpetrator. Here the purpose of the punishment is, on the one hand, to take revenge against the perpetrator, and on the other hand it is to force the perpetrator to atone for the crime. **488**

The existing criminal law combines these ideas. It emphasises the culpability of the perpetrator, to a greater extent than do most foreign legal systems, as the basis for meting out and limiting punishment (§ 46 para. 1 sentence 1 StGB). If prevention were seen as the only purpose of punishment then punishments of unlimited severity could be viewed as being both acceptable and useful. Retribution is therefore seen as a measuring and limiting factor today, not as an issue of revenge as in the past. In Germany today it is generally accepted that the penalties of the criminal law are by nature a public expression of social and ethical disapproval of the perpetrator's behaviour because he or she has broken the law while in a culpable state of mind. At times there has been criticism of the concept of imposing punishment at all and the demand has been made that it should be replaced completely with a mere treatment of the offender. However, for the past few years this view has not been in the foreground of the debate. **489**

In individual cases it is the task of the courts to impose a specific sentence. The law merely determines the type of punishment to be imposed as well as usually setting out maximum and minimum sentences for a particular crime, in other words, it provides a framework for the imposition of punishment. The court must fill in this framework for the specific criminal act with reference to the culpability of the perpetrator in the circumstances and also with reference to the effect which a particular punishment is likely to have on the perpetrator's future interaction with the rest of society (§ 46 para. 1 StGB). The aim of upholding the legal order may also play a role (§§ 47 para. 1 sentence 1; 56 para. 3 StGB). There is thus a unified theory of the purposes of punishment. **490**

In determining the punishment the court must take the culpability of the perpetrator as its starting point, but it must also take numerous other factors into account. The motives (*Beweggründe*) and objectives of the perpetrator, his or her attitude and state of mind as revealed by the perpetrator's behaviour, and the amount of will-power ex- **491** ercised in committing the crime are all significant factors. The sentence will also depend on the seriousness of the offence, the way in which it was carried out, and the consequences of the crime which are due to the perpetrator's fault. The past record of the accused and his or her personal and economic circumstances must be taken into account, as must the accused' behaviour subsequent to the commission of the crime. In this respect attempts to make good the harm done and reach some sort of reconciliation with the victim are of particular importance. An aggravating circumstance which is often relevant is the question of whether the accused is a repeat offender, in other words whether the perpetrator has previous convictions.

492   The primary types of punishment are imprisonment (*Freiheitsstrafe*) and the imposition of fines (*Geldstrafe*). The death penalty (*Todesstrafe*) is completely abolished by article 102 of the Basic Law and may also not be re-introduced. Corporal punishments (*Leibesstrafen*) such as flogging and mutilation are also never allowed.

493   The maximum penalty which can be imposed is life imprisonment. In all other cases imprisonment is for a fixed period of time. The period of imprisonment which may be imposed in cases where life imprisonment is not applicable ranges between a minimum of 1 month and a maximum of 15 years (§ 38 StGB). A period of imprisonment of less than six months may only be imposed if the special circumstances of the crime or the personality of the perpetrator make the imposition of a short period of imprisonment essential for the purposes of having an impact on the personality of the perpetrator or upholding the legal order. This approach is based on the view that, because of the environment in prisons, the imposition of a term of imprisonment often does more harm than good both to the perpetrator and to society as a whole. Sentencing the perpetrator to an indefinite period of imprisonment or to forced labour during imprisonment is not permissible.

494   The carrying out of a sentence of imprisonment and the relevant legislation is up to the Länder. The main aim is to resocialise the offender. The period of imprisonment is served in correctional centres in which prisoners are generally offered vocational training and paid work. Insofar as it is feasible the prisoners are also given tasks outside of the prison and further relaxation of the terms of imprisonment, such as giving the prisoners opportunities to move freely outside the prison as well as "holiday from prison", are possible.

495   Today the normal form of punishment is the imposition of a fine, with imprisonment only being applied in particularly severe cases. Following the Scandinavian example, German law does not measure fines in absolute terms but in daily earning rates (*Tagessätze*). The minimum fine consists of five daily earning rates, the maximum of 360 daily earning rates, unless a special act punishes a particular offence with a higher number of daily earning rates. In determining the cumulative sentence to be imposed for a series of crimes a fine of up to 720 daily earning rates can be imposed. The amount of money represented by a daily earning rate is separately determined by the court in each individual case, having regard to the personal and economic circumstances of the perpetrator in each case. Generally speaking the determination is based on the perpetrator's average net income per day or, if he or she is unwilling to work, on the average net income per day which the perpetrator is capable of earning. The aim of imposing fines in this way is to ensure that when a fine is imposed it affects a wealthy perpetrator at least as severely as it does a poor perpetrator. The amount of a daily earning rate is at least € 1 and at the most € 30 000. This means that in absolute

terms the minimum fine which can be imposed is € 5 and the highest fine which can regularly be imposed is € 10 800 000, or, in the case of cumulative fines, € 21 600 000 (§§ 40, 54 StGB).

In addition to fines and imprisonment the Criminal Code recognises the suspension of a person's driving licence (*Fahrverbot*) as an additional form of penalty (*Nebenstrafe*). This suspension can be imposed for a period of one to three months in the case of offences relating to road traffic. For some perpetrators this is a more severe punishment than the imposition of a fine. The suspension of a person's licence by the court does not exclude the additional possibility that the responsible authorities may withdraw the offender's licence altogether on the basis that he or she is unfit to drive (§ 44 StGB, § 3 StVG).   496

A further consequence (*Nebenfolge*) of being sentenced to a period of imprisonment of one year or more for the commission of a crime is that the convict automatically loses the capacity to hold public office within the next five years. The convict also loses the right to gain or to continue to exercise any rights gained by a public vote (§§ 45-45 b StGB). The possibility of imposing this punishment and of withdrawing the right to vote is also provided for in the case of certain other crimes. In these cases the loss of rights lasts between two and five years at the discretion of the court.   497

A sentence of imprisonment of up to two years can be suspended on probation if there is reason to believe that the mere imposition of the sentence will have a sufficient warning effect on the person convicted to deter him or her from committing any further crimes even without the serving of the sentence (§§ 56-58 StGB). The period for which the sentence is suspended (*Bewährungszeit*) is set by the court at between two and five years. The court can also impose various conditions when suspending a sentence, such as ordering the perpetrator to make good the damage he or she has caused, or ordering the perpetrator to perform various forms of community service. The court can also issue various directions. The most significant of these is that the person convicted may be placed under the supervision of a probation officer who has the duty to help him or her to lead a law-abiding life. However, the court may also impose a duty to report regularly as well as restrictions on movement, and requirements for training, employment, free-time activities and the economic circumstances of the person convicted.   498

If the period of probation is completed successfully then the court will discharge the suspended sentence. However, if the person on probation again commits a crime during the period of probation, thus showing that the expectations on which the suspension of the original sentence were based were false, then the court will withdraw the suspension of the sentence. The perpetrator will then generally have to serve the whole of the original sentence in addition to the sentence imposed for the new offence. The same applies if the person on probation repeatedly disregards the conditions and directions imposed by the court when the sentence was suspended.   499

It is also possible to release a person who has been serving a term of imprisonment on probation for the rest of his or her term of imprisonment. This is generally done once the convict has served two thirds of his or her period of imprisonment. The minimum period already served must be two months. A convict will only be released on probation if there is a reasonable chance that the convict will not commit any further crimes on his or her release. The convict can only be released on probation if he or she consents. If certain strict requirements are fulfilled the prisoner can already be released on   500 probation after having served only half of his or her sentence. In the case of life imprisonment release on probation is not possible until the convict has served at least fifteen years of his or her sentence. There is also the additional possibility of a pardon irrespective of the crime involved. The right to grant a pardon is usually vested in the prime minister of each of the *Länder* (in Berlin it is the Senate) and in the President of the Republic, each acting within his or her own sphere of authority.

501 To avoid inflicting a disproportionate amount of suffering on the perpetrator the court can in suitable cases issue a warning and reserve sentencing (*Verwarnung mit Strafvorbehalt*, §§ 59-59 c StGB). This can be done if the perpetrator is liable for a fine of not more than 180 daily earning rates. The court can then convict the accused and determine the appropriate punishment but refrain from sentencing him or her to undergo this punishment. If the court does this it sets a period of probation of up to three years. The person convicted may then subsequently be sentenced in the same circumstances as those in which a court would withdraw the suspension of a sentence which has already been imposed.

502 Finally, the court can refrain from imposing punishment if the consequences which the crime automatically has for the perpetrator are so severe that the imposition of a punishment would clearly be inappropriate (§ 60 StGB). In such cases the act is deserving of punishment, but not in need of punishment, because the perpetrator has, in a sense, punished him- or herself through the consequences of his or her act. An example would be where a mother has lost her child in a motor accident caused by her own slight negligence.

503 Apart from the forms of punishment, auxiliary punishment and further consequences of crime mentioned above, the Criminal Code also provides for the reformation (*Besserung*) and detention (*Sicherung*) of offenders (§§ 61-72 StGB). This reflects the two-track approach of the criminal law, which was originally derived from the Swiss example. These last two measures are justified on a purely preventative basis. Nevertheless, the imposition of such measures presupposes that the measure is not out of proportion to the significance of the crimes which the perpetrator has committed and is expected to commit and the seriousness of the danger which he or she poses (§ 62 StGB). The forms of detention and reformation which are applicable for all crimes include detention in a psychiatric hospital in the case of mentally ill perpetrators, detention in a rehabilitation centre for drug addicted perpetrators, and detention of repeat offenders for reasons of public safety (*Sicherungsverwahrung*). In addition, ongoing supervision (*Führungsaufsicht*) is a possibility in the case of certain crimes, as are withdrawal of a driving licence in the case of offences relating to the driving of motor vehicles, and a prohibition on the practice of a certain profession or trade if the perpetrator has abused such a position. For these types of measure a lesser degree of danger is sufficient, in contrast to the measures involving restrictions on the perpetrator's freedom, which can only be ordered if the perpetrator is expected to commit serious criminal acts. Detention of repeat offenders for reasons of public safety can be for an indefinite period once it has been imposed and aims to protect society from dangerous habitual criminals. However, such measures are generally viewed by the courts as being unjust and are not often imposed at present. Overall, the question of how to combat recidivism is an unsolved problem.

504 Finally, the Criminal Code provides for the forfeiture of benefits which the perpetrator or his or her accomplices have derived from the crime (§§ 73-73 e StGB). Objects

which were used in a crime or were intended for the preparation or commission of a crime can be confiscated. The same applies to objects created by criminal activities (§§ 74-76 a StGB). Examples are forged bank notes, firearms used in a robbery, or the tools used in a burglary.

Literature:

Urs Kindhäuser, Strafrecht. Allgemeiner Teil, 8. ed. 2017

Volker Krey/Robert Esser, Deutsches Strafrecht. Allgemeiner Teil, 6. ed. 2016

Rudolf Rengier, Strafrecht. Allgemeiner Teil, 10. ed. 2018

Johannes Wessels/Werner Beulke/Helmut Satzger, Strafrecht. Allgemeiner Teil. Die Straftat und ihr Aufbau, 48. ed. 2018

III. Specific Offences

As the constitution in article 103 para. 2 exacts certainty (*Bestimmtheitsgebot*) as far as possible, the elements of the specific offences are defined with great precision and in great detail. As a result the definitions often appear to be of great complexity and lacking in plasticity, perhaps to the extent of damaging the social effectiveness of the criminal law. However, past experience has shown that broad, simple definitions tend to favour arbitrary action on the part of the state. Yet the limitation of the power of the state to inflict punishment is precisely the point of the now generally accepted words of *Franz von Liszt* (1851-1919), who described the criminal law as "the Magna Carta of the criminal".

505

The book of the Criminal Code setting out the specific offences arranges the various crimes according to the interests protected. Here too expression is given to the fact that the primary aim of the criminal law is the protection of legal interests. The book of specific offences (*Besonderer Teil*) begins with the crimes of endangering international peace (*Friedensverrat*, §§ 80 ff. StGB), high treason (*Hochverrat*, § 81 StGB), and endangering democracy and the *Rechtsstaat* (*Gefährdung des demokratischen Rechtsstaates*, §§ 84 ff. StGB). The first two provisions are directed against preparations to wage aggressive war and incitement of the population to wage aggressive war (§§ 80, 80 a StGB). Although these two provisions hardly ever have any practical application because these crimes are in fact hardly ever committed they nevertheless have considerable significance as structural elements of the legal system. They implement in a particularly prominent way the provision in article 26 of the Basic Law, which directs that preparations for the waging of aggressive war are to be subjected to punishment. This is the only provision of the constitution which expressly contains a criminal prohibition. The decision to emphasise pacifism as a basic value is also the rationale for making it a crime to recruit German citizens for foreign armies (§ 109 b StGB). It can be said generally that many of the crimes listed at the start of the Book of Specific Offences are a reaction to the experience of National Socialist barbarism. For example, the crimes of disseminating the propaganda of organisations hostile to the constitution (§ 86 StGB) or of using their symbols (§ 86 a StGB) are aimed especially, if not exclusively, at National Socialist symbols and propaganda. Stirring up hatred against minorities (*Volksverhetzung*), glorification of violence and incitement to racial hatred (*Aufstacheln zum Rassenhass*) are also subjected to criminal penalties on the basis of this experience (§§ 130, 131 StGB). These provisions provide a necessary instrument for dealing with constant challenges.

506

507   Apart from the crimes just mentioned, the first chapters are primarily concerned with crimes which every state makes generally punishable in the interests of securing its own existence. These crimes include vilification of the state or its symbols, defaming the head of state (§§ 90, 90 a StGB), treason (*Landesverrat*), various types of secret service activity, and sabotage against certain facilities. The punishability of crimes (§§ 105 ff. StGB) such as electoral fraud (*Wahlfälschung*), intimidation of constitutional organs (*Nötigung von Verfassungsorganen*), or deceiving, bribing or intimidating voters protects the integrity of the political process as set out in the constitution. Also in this category are crimes against foreign states: Attacking the organs and representatives of foreign states and offences against the flag and other sovereign symbols of foreign states belong in this category (§§ 102-104 a StGB). Like the punishment imposed on crimes against international peace, this last group of crimes is an instance of the objective of keeping Germany in peaceful co-existence with the peoples and states of the international community.

508   While the protection of the state was regarded as an exceptionally important objective of the criminal law in the past, protection from the state is of relatively greater importance today, leaving aside for the moment the central objective of the criminal law, namely, protection by the state. The various final paragraphs (§§ 331-358 StGB) of the Book of Specific Offences are therefore important. These paragraphs subject various forms of illegal activity by public officials acting as such to punishment with the aim of strengthening or restoring public confidence in the incorruptibility of the public administration, but particularly because the victims are vulnerable in a special way in view of governmental powers. The taking of bribes (*Bestechlichkeit*), prosecuting innocent persons, perversion of justice, false certification while acting in an official capacity, betrayal of official secrets or divulging information about an individual's tax position and various other offences are all subjected to significant penalties which are generally more severe than those applicable if similar acts are committed by private persons.

509   A series of provisions are attempts by the legislature to react to special challenges to the public community. The crime of civil disorder (*Landfriedensbruch*) and particularly the crime of forming and supporting criminal and terrorist organisations are aimed in the first place at the threat posed to the democratic constitution by violent opposition and terrorism (§§ 125 ff. StGB). However, some of these provisions are proving to be increasingly important in combating new forms of international organised crime. The imposition of punishment on money laundering (*Geldwäsche*, § 261 StGB) also serves this criminal policy aim of combating organised crime. This provision gives effect to the 1988 United Nations convention against the illegal trafficking in addictive substances. This convention creates an obligation to make money laundering punishable. Any person who conceals an object, hides its origin, or otherwise attempts to prevent the law enforcement authorities from seizing it, is henceforth liable to be punished with a term of imprisonment of up to five years if the thing in question is a product of, amongst other things, felonies or misdemeanours relating to the illegal trade in drugs. Money laundering means introducing wealth derived from organised crime into the legal economy for the purpose of disguising its origins. However, § 261 StGB deals with a broader range of crimes than just money laundering.

510   By now crimes against the environment are firmly established as part of the Criminal Code (§§ 324-330 d StGB). Anyone who runs facilities which pose a threat to the en-

vironment, such as nuclear power stations or chemicals factories, without the necessary permission is liable to have criminal penalties imposed on him or her. The same applies to dealing with nuclear fuel without permission. Water, soil and air, but also nature reserves are specially protected by the criminal law against pollution or other dangers. Impermissible pollution of water, running a facility which pollutes the air to an extent which is dangerous to human health in contravention of duties under administrative law, or causing noise levels which pose a danger to health are also all criminal offences. Waste products may also not be disposed of illegally.[9]

The introduction of crimes against the environment is particularly prone to raise considerable social, political and jurisprudential problems. The prosecuting authorities often lack the necessary specialised knowledge of the complex technical and scientific background. At a more general level it is doubtful whether criminal penalties aimed at specific individuals provide an adequate response to the structures in which large scale manufacturing, mass production and complex social interactions take place today. It is thus arguable that the imposition of criminal penalties tends to affect the small offender and petty crimes, or to arbitrarily single out and punish individuals without regard to the interrelationships of collective responsibility for a particular type of harm. 511

A particularly difficult problem which arises here, but also in the context of offences such as tax evasion (§ 370 AO), is the close connection between administrative acts, in other words acts by the state, and acts by individuals which may attract criminal penalties. For example, if the relevant authority grants permission to run a chemicals facility in contravention of the law, then the question arises whether the facility in question is an unlicensed facility in terms of § 327 StGB. Although the point is contentious, the dominant view is that the accessory role of the administration in such crimes has the effect that the illegal granting of permission may exclude criminal liability. However, this argument does not apply if the administrative act is void. The use of licenses which have been granted illegally can also be illegal, for example in cases where the responsible authority and the perpetrator have knowingly colluded. If the relevant authority knowingly tolerates illegal activities then the conclusion may be drawn that the illegal behaviour is justified by this tolerance. Generally speaking it is presumed in such cases that the behaviour of the perpetrator has been tacitly approved by the authority.[10] 512

The crimes which generally attract the most public interest are offences involving homicide (*Tötungsdelikte*). 589 accomplished cases involving murder (*Mord*) or manslaughter (*Totschlag*) were reported in Germany in 2015.[11] The law provides that murder is to be punished with life imprisonment (§ 211 StGB). Any person who kills another person will be guilty of murder if one of the following requirements are satisfied: The killing must have been motivated by bloodlust, or the satisfaction of sexual urges, or greed or other reprehensible motives, or the killing must have been done in a cruel and brutal or treacherous way, or by using methods which pose a danger to public safety in general, or for the purposes of facilitating or concealing some other crime. Murder is thus characterised either by a set of circumstances which are particularly reprehensible or by particularly reprehensible motives. 513

---

9 See *Fischer*, Strafgesetzbuch, vor § 324 side note 3-4.
10 *Fischer*, Strafgesetzbuch, vor § 324 side note 4 ff.
11 2015 Police Criminal Statistics (*Polizeiliche Kriminalstatistik* 2015), p. 33..

514 Any killing of a human being which does not amount to murder is punishable as manslaughter (§ 212 StGB). The minimum penalty for this crime is five years imprisonment. Manslaughter, like murder, is only applicable if the killing was intentional. In addition to murder and manslaughter there are the crimes of negligent homicide (*fahrlässige Tötung*, § 222 StGB) and battery with fatal consequences (*Körperverletzung mit Todesfolge*, § 227 StGB).

515 Suicide (*Selbstmord*) and attempted suicide are not punishable. However, the involvement of other people in a suicide can expose them to punishment under a number of different heads. The details of this subject are highly contentious. One possibility is that a third party may be found guilty of having committed murder or manslaughter through the agency of another (*mittelbare Täterschaft*) if the third party incited a person lacking criminal capacity to commit suicide or induced the suicide by means of threats or lies. Also highly contentious is whether the third party is liable for causing death by omission if he or she has a duty of care arising from a guarantee obligation (*Garantenstellung, Garantenpflicht*) towards the person committing suicide and does not prevent the suicide from killing him- or herself. An example would be if a husband fails to call a doctor after his wife takes an overdose of sleeping tablets with the intention of committing suicide. Up to now the courts have generally taken the view that the third party becomes responsible at the point when the person attempting suicide is no longer in control of the situation, for example when the suicide loses consciousness.[12]

516 Another extremely contentious subject is the involvement of doctors in ending life.[13] Traditionally a distinction is drawn between active voluntary euthanasia and passive voluntary euthanasia. An example of active voluntary euthanasia is where a doctor shortens the life of a patient by doing something, for example, by providing him or her with a deadly drug. In contrast, passive voluntary euthanasia describes the situation in which the doctor fails to take steps which would prolong life despite the fact that they are technically feasible. It is clear that active voluntary euthanasia and assisted suicide are punishable as the crime of killing at the request of the victim (*Tötung auf Verlangen*, § 216 StGB). Passive voluntary euthanasia (*passive Sterbehilfe*) is particularly contentious. The doctor must respect the will of a mortally ill patient who refuses further life-prolonging treatment . Since 10.12.2015 the businesslike support of suicide is punishable (§ 217 StGB) with imprisonment of up to three years or with a fine. Participants who do not act businesslike, relatives of or persons close to the person committing suicide are not punishable.

517 An alsohotly debated issue of policy in criminal law is the punishability of abortion (§ 218 StGB). Here the Federal Constitutional Court has pointed the way. In terms of its latest ruling the legislature need not subject abortion in the first three months of pregnancy to punishment so long as the unborn child (*nasciturus*) is adequately protected in other ways.[14] Abortions during this period are thus as a general rule not punishable if the pregnant woman has been advised in a specially regulated procedure (§§ 218 ff. StGB). The abortion remains illegal but it is not penalised. According to the conception of the legislature the *nasciturus* is better protected against abortion if the mother is advised in such a way than by the threat of punishment which has widely

---

12 See BGHSt 32, 367/373; BGH NJW 1988, p. 1532.
13 See *Fischer*, Strafgesetzbuch, vor § 211, side note 16 ff.
14 BVerfGE 88, 203 ff.

proven to be ineffective. The position of the criminal law on this subject is a clear example of the fact that its function is not only to protect values accepted by the majority against infringements. Instead its task is to mark the boundaries established by the constitution for the protection of the weak and of minorities even if this is done against the opposition of broadly-based public attitudes.

One of the crimes which occur most frequently is theft (*Diebstahl*). Theft is particularly prevalent in the form of shop-lifting, that is, the theft of goods from self-service shops. In contrast to the criminal law, certain sectors of the population are inclined to view shoplifting as an amusing display of high spirits (*Kavaliersdelikt*) rather than a crime. § 242 StGB provides a definition of theft which is as complicated as it is precise: Anyone who takes a moveable thing, which does not belong to him or her, from another person with the intention of appropriating it for him- or herself or a third party is liable to be punished by means of a fine or by imprisonment for up to five years. The legal interests protected by this provision are ownership (*Eigentum*) and custody of a thing (*Gewahrsam*). Custody of a thing in criminal law does not have precisely the same meaning as possession (*Besitz*) in private law but generally speaking the two concepts will correspond. Custody of a thing describes a factual relationship of control over a thing accompanied by the will to control it.

The act involved in theft is the taking away of a thing. This is the breach of another person's custody of a thing, in other words, the termination of the other person's custody without the will of the person having custody. A further requirement is that some other person must gain custody of the thing. This custody can be established by the perpetrator him- or herself or by a third party, for example, when the thief arranges for some other person to collect the stolen property. The new relationship of custody is established when the perpetrator or the third party is in a position to exercise control over the thing without hindrance by the person who formerly had custody of it. A person also has custody of a thing if they control a general sphere of custody. For example, the shop-keeper has custody of the goods in the supermarket. In such situations the thief may already have broken the original custody when he or she unobtrusively puts the goods into his or her bag while still in the shop. The many different circumstances in which the question arises whether a theft has taken place have been dealt with by the courts in a voluminous body of case law.

The elements of the crime of theft are only fulfilled if the perpetrator has the intention to unlawfully appropriate the property in question for him- or herself or a third person. This means above all that the perpetrator must desire to include the thing in his or her own property to the exclusion of the person having custody and contrary to the rules of property. If the perpetrator lacks the intention to appropriate the property for him- or herself because he or she merely intends to use it briefly and then return it, then one speaks of wrongful use of the thing (*furtum usus*). This is indeed not a case of theft, but in certain cases the deed may nevertheless be punishable. Thus, in § 248 b StGB the legislature has provided that the unauthorised use of motor vehicles and bicycles is a punishable offence.

§ 248 a makes special provision for the theft of items of minor value. A thing is classified as being of minor value if it is worth less than € 25. The theft of such things is only prosecuted on application by an authorised person unless the state prosecution service considers it necessary to act without application because there is a special public interest requiring prosecution. This means that the theft of items of minor value is a

518

519

520

521

offence which is only prosecuted on application (*Antragsdelikt*), as are battery and the negligent infliction of physical injury (§§ 223, 229, 230 StGB). In such cases prosecution depends on the bringing of an application by a person – usually the victim – who is entitled to do so. The application can be made to the police, the state prosecution service or the *Amtsgericht*. The idea behind this approach is to relieve the criminal justice system of the burden of prosecuting petty crime. To protect themselves against shop lifting shopkeepers generally apply for prosecution of even minor thefts.

522 In contrast to theft, where alterations in property relationships take place against, or without, the will of the person entitled to the property, fraud describes the situation in which the perpetrator exploits a mistake on the part of the victim. Fraud requires, firstly, that the perpetrator should damage the wealth of another by conveying false information or distorting or suppressing true facts so as to create or maintain a misconception. Secondly, this must have been done by the perpetrator with the intention of obtaining for him- or herself or a third party some illegal financial benefit. Fraud is punishable by a fine or a term of imprisonment of up to five years (§ 263 para. 1 StGB). In simplified terms, fraud describes the situation in which the perpetrator causes the victim to make a mistake as a result of which the victim voluntarily deals with his or her property in a disadvantageous way.

523 Another particularly common crime is the offence of leaving the scene of an accident illegally (§ 142 StGB), otherwise known as hit-and-run driving (*Fahrerflucht*). In terms of this provision any person who is involved in a road traffic accident is liable to be punished if he or she leaves the scene of the accident before complying with certain duties. For example, the person must make it possible for the other persons involved in the accident and anyone who has suffered harm to establish his or her identity, the details of his or her vehicle, and what part he or she played in the accident by remaining at the scene of the accident and admitting that he or she was involved in the accident. If no-one is willing and able to record this information then the person must remain on the scene of the accident for a reasonable time to see whether anyone does want the information after all. Typical situations in which this provision is relevant are where cars are damaged while parking at night, or where roadside fences alongside infrequently used roads are damaged. Anyone who leaves the scene of an accident legally must subsequently provide the relevant information without delay (*unverzüglich*). In law "without delay" always means without culpable delay. Depending on the circumstances this means that the person involved must drive to the nearest telephone and report the accident to the police or to the person who has suffered harm. In the case of certain, less severe accidents, the court may additionally mitigate the punishment or refrain from punishment altogether, if the person involved in the accident voluntarily makes possible ascertainment within twenty-four hours. This highly complex provision protects the interest of the parties to the accident and the victims in having the facts of the accident recorded in as much detail as possible for the purpose of establishing a claim for damages or providing a defence against such a claim.[15]

524 The crime of unlawful compulsion (*Nötigung*, § 240 StGB) has proved to be of considerable political importance. It belongs to a group of offences such as false imprisonment (*Freiheitsberaubung*), kidnapping (*Menschenraub*), hostage-taking (*Geiselnahme*), or child abduction (*Kinderentziehung*) which are all crimes against personal

---

15 See *Lackner/Kühl*, Strafgesetzbuch, § 142 side note 1.

freedom (§§ 234 ff. StGB). The accused will be guilty of unlawful compulsion if he or she unlawfully compels another person to act, or to tolerate a state of affairs, or to refrain from acting, by means of violence or the threat of some serious disadvantage. The crime may be punished by means of a fine or a period of imprisonment of up to three years. The act in question is illegal if the application of force or the threat of the disadvantage is seen as been reprehensible in relation to the goal at which the compulsion is aimed. The aim of making unlawful compulsion punishable is to protect the right freely to form, and act in accordance with, one's will. Unlawful compulsion means forcing another person to act contrary to his or her will.[16] Violence means in essence physical violence, although the force in question may be psychological accompanied by force. To make a brief generalisation of the different theories it can be said that violence is a physical application of pressure to overcome resistance.[17] Unlawful compulsion plays a significant role in road traffic law. For example, a person who suddenly breaks on the highway for no good reason but simply for the purpose of forcing the following car to break hard may be liable for unlawful compulsion, as may a driver who drives unreasonably close to the car in front in an effort to compel its driver to make way.

Overall, there are many aspects of unlawful compulsion which are contentious, and court rulings on this subject are contradictory. This is particularly the case with respect to the political aspect of this provision. A regular instrument of political protest is the obstruction of public ways (*Straßenblockade*). This often forces other road users to make detours or endure long delays. There are numerous examples of such actions in recent German history. One instance which caused a great deal of debate was the blockading of military bases to prevent the stationing of missiles. Another example is the blocking of roads by angry employees in response to the threatened closure of their workplace. In these situations it must be born in mind that disturbing the flow of traffic may be justified by the fundamental rights to freedom of expression and freedom of assembly. However, this will only be the case if the disturbance is a temporary side-effect of the exercise of these rights and must be tolerated in view of the balancing of interests demanded by the constitution. However, disturbances which aim specifically at attracting public attention by means of the compulsion which they exercise are not protected by these provisions.[18] At present the extent to which the ultimate political or other aims of the perpetrators in such cases are to be taken into consideration when judging the reprehensibility of the act is still hotly debated.[19]

525

Literature:

Urs Kindhäuser, Strafrecht. Besonderer Teil I, 8. ed. 2017, Besonderer Teil II, 9. ed. 2016

Volker Krey/Uwe Hellmann/Manfred Heinrich, Strafrecht. Besonderer Teil, vol. 1, 16. ed. 2015, vol. 2, 17. ed. 2015

Wilfried Küper/Jan Zopfs,, Strafrecht. Besonderer Teil, 10. ed. 2018

Rudolf Rengier, Strafrecht. Besonderer Teil I, 21. ed. 2019

Rudolf Rengier, Strafrecht. Besonderer Teil II, 20. ed. 2019

Johannes Wessels/Michael Hettinger/Armin Engländer, Strafrecht. Besonderer Teil, vol. 1, 42. ed. 2018

---

16 See *Lackner/Kühl*, Strafgesetzbuch § 240 side note 4.
17 *Krey/Heinrich*, Strafrecht Besonderer Teil vol. 1, side note 328 a ff.; *Fischer*, Strafgesetzbuch, § 240 side note 8; BVerfGE 92, 1 ff.
18 BVerfGE 73, 206/250.
19 See on this point BGHSt 35, 270.

Johannes Wessels/Thomas Hillenkamp/Jan Schuhr, Strafrecht. Besonderer Teil, vol. 2, 41. ed. 2018

IV. The Law on Juvenile Offenders (Jugendstrafrecht)

526 Separate rules apply to the criminal responsibility of minors and young people. These rules are supposed to take account of the special circumstances which exist when someone is growing up, and to provide an appropriate reaction to the dangers and opportunities presented by this period of life. The more important provisions are contained in the Juvenile Courts Act (*Jugendgerichtsgesetz,* abbreviated JGG). Insofar as no special provision is made, the general rules of the criminal law apply.

527 In terms of § 19 StGB children under the age of 14 lack criminal capacity and can therefore not be punished. In severe cases, namely where the child's well-being is threatened (*Gefährdung des Kindeswohl,* § 1666 BGB) the state can take action against the parents via the guardianship court (*Vormundschaftsgericht*). The law on young people's welfare provides for numerous types of help and protection in the 8th Book of the Social Security Code (SGB VIII). The possibilities range from counselling to separating the child from his or her parents if necessary.

528 Any person who is at least 14 years old is capable of having criminal capacity. However, a minor will only be held responsible if, at the time of doing the act in question, the minor's moral and intellectual development is sufficiently advanced to allow him or her to comprehend the wrongness of the deed and to act accordingly (§ 3 sentence 1 JGG).

529 Once an offender has turned nineteen the Juvenile Courts Act is no longer applicable. Criminal liability is then determined in accordance with the provisions of the Criminal Code. However, important provisions of the Juvenile Courts Act remain applicable to youths between the ages of 18 and 20 (*Heranwachsende*) if they are still immature in terms of personality or if the way in which the crime was committed indicates that it was more in the nature of a youthful mistake (§ 1 para. 2 JGG).

530 The law on juvenile offenders differs from the ordinary criminal law primarily in terms of the penalties applicable. The dominant idea is correctional education. For this reason a distinction is made between three types of sanction: educational measures for juvenile delinquents, disciplinary measures and juvenile detention. These measures show particularly clearly that the law on juvenile delinquency is by nature a special aspect of a comprehensive body of law on young people's welfare.

531 The range of possible educational measures for juvenile delinquents (*Erziehungs-maßregeln*) includes firstly numerous types of directions (*Weisungen*) which the judge can issue to the youth in question. The judge can, for example, issue directions as to where the youth is to spend his or her time, or direct that the youth is not to go to certain places, or is to take up a job or a training opportunity, or is to do specific pieces of work (§§ 9 ff. JGG). In addition these measures may include the imposition of an obligation to make use of certain types of help (§§ 9, 12 JGG, §§ 30, 34 SGB VIII). Since the emphasis here is on educational measures the judge has considerable discretion in deciding which specific steps should be taken in an individual case. If necessary, the judge can also alter the measures imposed during the time for which they are in force, which is for a maximum of two years.

Disciplinary measures (*Zuchtmittel*) include warnings (*Verwarnungen*), the imposition of conditions (*Auflagen*), and arrest for youthful offenders (*Jugendarrest, §§* 13 ff. JGG). In the scheme of the law on this subject they are more severe sanctions than are the educational measures for juvenile delinquents. Their purpose is to make it clear to the youth in question that he or she must bear the responsibility for the wrong which he or she has done. A warning involves pointing out most emphatically to the youth the wrongness of what he or she has done (§ 14 JGG). Conditions include the obligation to apologise to the victim, to do everything possible to put right the damage caused, or to perform work for, or make payments to, a charitable institution (§ 15 JGG). Arrest for youthful offenders is usually an even more severe penalty. It may consist of "leisure-time arrest", in terms of which the youth is placed under arrest only during his or her free time. A period of short-arrest can be imposed for up to six days, ongoing arrest for up to four weeks. Ongoing arrest can also be imposed on youthful perpetrators who ignore conditions and directions (§ 16 JGG).

532

In contrast to the previous two categories of possible measures, juvenile detention (*Jugendstrafe*) is regarded by the Juvenile Courts Act as being penal in nature (§§ 17 ff. JGG). It is imposed if other disciplinary measures have proved to be insufficient or if the seriousness of the crime demands it. In other words, the idea of retribution assumes a more prominent place here. Juvenile detention means detention for at least six months. The maximum period is ten years. A seventeen year old who commits murder can thus be sentenced to a maximum of ten years juvenile detention. A sentence of juvenile detention is served in special youth detention centres, a period of juvenile arrest is served in facilities set up specifically for this purpose (§§ 90 para. 2; 92 JGG).

533

Special provisions also apply with respect to procedure in the law on juvenile offenders (§§ 33 ff. JGG). Cases involving youthful offenders are tried by special juvenile courts (*Jugendgerichte*) in the first two levels of courts, namely the *Amtsgericht* and the *Landgericht*. They are assisted by juvenile court assistants (*Jugendgerichtshilfe*) in investigating the personality, development and environment of the accused. The juvenile court assistants' task is to ensure that points relating to the upbringing, welfare and social interests of the young offender are given proper emphasis in the course of the trial. The juvenile court assistants are involved during the whole period of implementation of punishments and corrective measures with the aim of promoting the (re)socialisation of the offender. This assistance to the juvenile courts is provided by the Youth Offices (*Jugendämter*) in co-operation with the Associations for Youth Support (*Vereinigungen für Jugendhilfe,* § 38 JGG). Proceedings before the juvenile courts are closed to the public (§ 48 JGG). Remedies against the court's decision are limited in the interests of a rapid application of corrective and punitive measures (§ 55 JGG). On the other hand, the power of the prosecuting authorities to refrain from taking further action is wider: in such cases the state prosecution service can request the court to issue further warnings, directions and conditions (§ 45 JGG).

534

Literature:
Ulrich Eisenberg, Jugendgerichtsgesetz, 20. ed. 2018
Klaus Laubenthal/Helmut Baier/Nina Nestler, Jugendstrafrecht, 3. ed. 2015
Bernd-Dieter Meier/Britta Bannenberg/Katrin Höffler, Jugendstrafrecht, 4. ed. 2019
Heribert Ostendorf/Kirstin Drenkhahn, Jugendstrafrecht, 9. ed. 2017
Friedrich Schaffstein/Werner Beulke/Sabine Swoboda, Jugendstrafrecht, 15. ed. 2015
Franz Streng, Jugendstrafrecht, 4. ed. 2016

V. The Law of Criminal Procedure

535   The law of criminal procedure (*Strafprozessrecht*) contains the rules for the investigation and prosecution of crimes. It is regulated primarily in the Criminal Procedure Act (*Strafprozessordnung,* abbreviated *StPO*). Provisions concerning the institutions of criminal prosecution, particularly the courts and the state prosecution service (*Staatsanwaltschaft*), are contained in the Constitution of Courts Act (*Gerichtsverfassungsgesetz,* abbreviated *GVG*).

536   Only a judge can convict and sentence an accused (article 92 GG). The court of first instance for lesser crimes is the *Amtsgericht.* Appeals can be taken to the *Landgericht,* and to the *Oberlandesgericht* and *Bundesgerichtshof,* depending on the case. The *Landgericht* and *Oberlandesgericht* also serve as court of first instance in some cases. For serious crimes, such as those involving homicide, the court of first instance is the *Landgericht* while certain exceptional crimes, such as those against the security of the state, are tried at first instance before the *Oberlandesgericht.* In contrast to legal systems which follow the Anglo-American tradition there is no jury of laymen. The entire trial, including conviction and sentencing, lies in the hands of the judge. The court in any particular matter will consist of a panel of several judges. In the lower courts the panel will also include lay assessors (*Schöffen*). Thus, at the level of the *Amtsgericht,* the court will consist of a professional judge and two lay assessors (*Schöffengericht*) unless it is a simple matter, in which case it will be dealt with by a single judge. At the level of the *Landgericht* the general practice is to have a court of three professional judges and two lay assessors. The divisions of the *Oberlandesgericht* in each *Land* and of the *Bundesgerichtshof* are called senates and consist exclusively of professional judges.

537   The whole process of investigating criminal activities up to the stage of charging the accused with the crime (*Anklageerhebung*) is the business of the state prosecution service, as is the presentation of the prosecution's case at trial (§§ 141 ff. GVG). The state prosecution service must also see to it that the court's decision is executed (§§ 36, 451, 463 StPO). In investigating the crime and tracking down the perpetrator, the state prosecutor makes use of the services of the police, particularly the criminal police (*Kriminalpolizei*). The police also have an independent duty to investigate if they suspect that a crime has been committed. They then call the state prosecution service in without delay. The police and state prosecution service derive their knowledge of possible crimes from their own information gathering, from charges laid by victims of crime or third parties, and also from information provided by other authorities or the courts.

538   The state prosecution service is in charge of the investigation (§§ 152, 160 StPO). For purposes of investigation it is entitled to issue instructions to its various auxiliaries, in particular the police (§ 152 GVG). Who is an auxiliary of the state prosecution service (*Ermittlungsperson*) is determined by various acts and regulations of the *Länder.* Officials who fall into this category have special powers in terms of the Criminal Procedure Act such as powers of arrest, search and seizure.

539   The state prosecution service is an executive authority, but is also, like the courts, an independent organ administering the law. It can thus not easily be classified as belonging to one or the other branch of government. There are state lawyers attached to every court empowered to deal with criminal matters. These lawyers then carry out the duties of the state prosecution service for that court. In the lower courts the state pros-

ecution service falls within the sphere of authority of the *Land* and is thus part of the civil service of the particular *Land*. The state prosecution service at the level of the *Bundesgerichtshof* and in cases of first instance before the *Oberlandesgericht* falls within the sphere of the federal government. At this level the service is directed by the Federal Attorney General (*Generalbundesanwalt*).

The state prosecution service is independent of the court (§ 150 GVG). As part of the 540
civil service it is answerable to a certain extent to the relevant minister of justice (whether of the *Land* or the Federation, §§ 146, 147 GVG). However, it has a duty to be objective, in other words it must investigate and assess all the facts relevant to the case (§ 160 para. 2 StPO). This also applies to facts which tend to exculpate a suspect or an accused person or even a person who has already been convicted (§ 160 StPO). This means that, in contrast to some other legal systems, the state prosecution service is not a party to the case in a criminal trial. Instead it is a strictly neutral institution. Furthermore the state prosecution service is bound to uphold the rule of law (*Legalitätsprinzip,* § 152 para. 2 StPO). This means that it must prosecute if a crime has been committed. As a general rule, it does not have a discretion to decide whether to prosecute or not. It is particularly these principles of objectivity and of the rule of law which limit the power to issue instructions to the officials (*Beamten*) of the state prosecution service.

Before various measures which involve the use of force against the suspect (such as arrest or searches), or measures such as the monitoring of telephone conversations can 541
be implemented the police and the state prosecutor must bring the matter before a judge. This judge is called the investigation judge (*Ermittlungsrichter*). With the exception of certain special cases he or she will be a judge at the *Amtsgericht* level (§§ 162 para. 1; 169 StPO). Apart from this, judges have no independent function in investigative proceedings until the suspect is charged with the crime.

The criminal investigation authorities have a series of precisely defined statutory powers for the purposes of investigation. One of the central issues of legal policy is how to 542
reach a reasonable balance between the interest of the community in the investigation and prosecution of crime, and the interests of suspects and third parties who are affected by such investigations.

One of the most important steps in the investigation of a crime is the questioning of 543
the suspect (§§ 133 ff. StPO). It is useful in establishing the facts of the case and the likelihood that the perpetrator is guilty, but it also guarantees the right to a fair hearing to which the suspect is entitled in terms of § 163 a para. 1 StPO, article 103 para. 1 GG and article 6 of the European Convention for the Protection of Human Rights and Fundamental Freedoms (ECHR). The suspect is at no stage obliged to make any admissions or a confession. The suspect does not have to assist the authorities in establishing his or her guilt. The suspect also has no obligation to tell the truth. The suspect does not have to appear before the police, but can be summonsed to appear by the judge and the state prosecutor and then force may be used if necessary to compel him or her to do so (§ 134 StPO). At his or her first questioning by the police the suspect must be told what accusation is being made against him or her. The suspect must also be told that he or she is not obliged to make any admissions, that he or she has a right to legal representation, and that he or she can apply for the gathering of evidence which is favourable to his or her case (§ 136 StPO).

544   Certain methods of interrogation are forbidden (§ 136 a StPO). The suspect's freedom to form his or her will and act in accordance with it may not be infringed upon by maltreatment, fatigue, physical attacks, the administration of drugs, torture, deception, hypnosis, or by interfering with his or her ability to remember or understand. This applies even if the accused has consented to any of these methods. A lie-detector may also not be used in criminal matters. It is often difficult to distinguish permissible investigative methods from illegal deception. It is, however, clear that a false assurance that a fellow suspect has already confessed is not a permissible method of extracting information. The investigating officer may also not promise to ensure a milder punishment if the suspect co-operates. Private diary entries of the accused may only be used as evidence against the will of the accused in the case of the most serious crimes. Public officials may only give evidence concerning official business with the permission of their superiors (§ 54 StPO). Blood samples may only be taken by a doctor (§ 81 StPO). The above rules are referred to as prohibitions on the gathering of evidence (*Beweiserhebungsverbote*).

545   In contrast, prohibitions on the use of evidence (*Beweisverwertungsverbote*) provide what may be done in the course of trial with evidence which has been obtained illegally. In this area there is little theoretical clarity. The "legal sphere" theory (*Rechtskreistheorie*) which has been developed by the *Bundesgerichtshof* makes a distinction according to whether the prohibition exists for the purpose of protecting the legal sphere of the accused or not. This means, for example, that a failure to inform some other witness of his or her right to refuse to give evidence does not make his or her testimony inadmissible as against the accused, because the right to refuse to give evidence exists for the purpose of protecting the person who is being questioned, not for the purpose of protecting the accused.

546   Admissions which have been obtained by using illegal methods of interrogation are not admissible evidence. However, in terms of the highly contentious court decisions on this subject, the inadmissibility of such evidence does not affect the admissibility of evidence derived from it. In other words, further evidence which is discovered as a result of evidence obtained by inadmissible means may be used.

547   The rules applicable to the questioning of witnesses are similar to those applying to the questioning of suspects (§§ 48 ff. StPO). They too can only be summoned for questioning and, if necessary, compelled to attend, by the court or by the state prosecutor. However, witnesses are obliged to answer questions and must tell the truth. An exception is made in the case of certain types of witness who have a privilege and who can thus refuse to give evidence. Examples are close relatives of the suspect and certain professionals such as doctors, lawyers and religious advisers, all of whom are not obliged to disclose information which has become known to them in their professional capacities (§§ 52 ff. StPO). As in any court proceedings, any person who has an obligation to answer questions can be forced to do so by a period of imprisonment of up to six months which can be ordered by the court.

548   Other investigative measures which are named in the Criminal Procedure Act include obtaining reports from experts, for example, an assessment of the blood alcohol level of the accused at the time of the crime. Furthermore, corpses may be examined or dissected, suspects may be examined and observed by psychiatrists, and blood samples, photographs and fingerprints may be taken or molecular genetic examinations may be

conducted. The investigating officers may also search for, seize and secure evidence (§§ 81 ff. StPO). DNA tests may also be used to establish identity (§§ 72 ff. StPO)

A particularly extreme measure is pre-trial investigative detention (*Untersuchung-shaft*). This is only allowed if there is a strong suspicion that the person arrested is guilty (*dringender Tatverdacht*), if certain additional requirements are satisfied, and if it is proportionate (§§ 112, 112 a StPO). The requirement that there should be a strong suspicion of guilt is satisfied if it is highly probable that the person to be arrested committed the crime. Pre-trial investigative detention may only be ordered if this is necessary to ensure a proper trial. This requirement is satisfied if the suspect has attempted to escape, or is likely to do so, or if there is a danger that the suspect will cover his or her tracks, for example, by destroying evidence or attempting to interfere with witnesses. In the case of particularly severe crimes, such as murder or manslaughter, pre-trial investigative detention is permissible whenever the possibility of flight or interference with the investigations cannot be excluded. Lastly, pre-trial detention is permissible in the case of serious crimes if there is a danger that the suspect will commit similar crimes again before trial. | 549

A regular occurrence is the preliminary arrest of a suspect by the investigating authorities in terms of § 127 para. 2 StPO. If this is done then the affected person must be brought before a court on the following day at the latest (§ 128 StPO). Pre-trial investigative detention can only be authorised by a judge. The necessity of continued arrest is automatically reviewed at regular intervals (§§ 117, 121, 122 StPO). Other types of investigative activity which also require authorisation by a judge are the seizing of property (§ 98 para. 1 StPO), detention of a suspect for observation (§ 81 para. 2 StPO), or the monitoring of post or telecommunications (§§ 100 para. 1, 100 b para. 1 StPO). This applies in a particularly strict manner to the "bugging" of apartments (*Lauschangriff*, §§ 100 c ff. StPO), which was introduced into the criminal prosecution procedure after article 13 GG had been amended for this purpose. This regulation permits with strict limits the acoustical surveillance of suspects. | 550

One of the most difficult and contentious issues in the field of criminal investigation is the use of informants (*V-Leute*) and undercover agents. Informants are members of the criminal world who provide information to the investigating authorities. Undercover agents are police officers who are introduced into the criminal world. They gather information for the purpose of solving and also preventing crimes (§§ 110 a ff. StPO). Apart from the personal danger to which they are exposed, they are contentious because their powers are ill-defined and the very nature of their activities means that they are making use of deception. They are often even forced to participate in criminal activities themselves to avoid exposing their true identities. | 551

If sufficient evidence is obtained the state prosecutor will charge the accused with the crime before the appropriate court (§ 170 para. 1 StPO). This is the case if there are sufficient reasonable grounds for believing that the suspect is guilty (*hinreichender Tatverdacht*), in other words, when the accused is likely to be convicted on the evidence as it stands. Only the state prosecutor can charge the suspect – this is the principle of official action (*Offizialprinzip*, § 152 para. 1 StPO). In the case of certain less serious offences which do not substantially affect the public interest the victim or some other affected party must make an application for the prosecution of the offender before the state prosecutor will act. There are also certain crimes such as criminal trespass (*Hausfriedensbruch*, § 123 StGB), criminal defamation (*Beleidigung*, §§ 185, 189 | 552

StGB), damage to property (*Sachbeschädigung*, § 303 StGB) or assault and battery (*Körperverletzung*, §§ 223, 223 a StGB) which, as a general rule, are prosecuted privately (see § 374 StPO). In these cases the injured party and certain other people can then bring a charge without first involving the state prosecution service. The state prosecution service will only intervene and charge the accused in such matters if it is in the public interest to do so (§ 376 StPO).

553   If there are not sufficient grounds for charging the accused, then the state prosecution will generally discontinue the proceedings. This will be done if the behaviour in question is not criminal, or if there is insufficient evidence. It will also be done if there is some procedural bar to proceedings, for example, if the charge against the perpetrator has become time-barred, or if the necessary application for prosecution has not been brought. In addition the Criminal Procedure Act also provides for various other possible grounds for discontinuing proceedings which are of great practical importance. The state prosecutor can discontinue proceedings on the grounds that the offence is trivial. The state prosecutor can also do so if directions and conditions have been complied with, or because the crime in question is insignificant in relation to another crime which the perpetrator has also committed (§§ 153-154 StPO). These situations are illustrations of the principle of discretionary prosecution (*Opportunitätsprinzip*) in terms of which the state prosecution service takes only such action as seems appropriate to it. In most cases the exercise of this discretion requires the consent of the court which would be responsible for the main trial, and sometimes the consent of the suspect him- or herself is also required. The court can also take similar steps after the accused has been charged (§ 153 a para. 2 StPO).

554   The charging or indictment of the accused by the state prosecutor is followed by interim proceedings (*Zwischenverfahren*, §§ 199 ff. StPO) in which the court decides whether the accused should be discharged or whether the matter should proceed to trial (§§ 203, 204 StPO). The charge sheet is sent to the accused who then has the opportunity to respond to it. If there are reasonable grounds for thinking that the accused might be guilty (*hinreichender Tatverdacht*), then the court will give permission for the case to proceed and open the main proceedings (*Hauptverfahren*). The court can also order further investigations (§§ 202 ff. StPO). Since the mere fact of being publicly placed on trial on criminal charges brings considerable disadvantages for the accused even if he or she is eventually found not guilty, prominent accused regularly attempt to persuade the court not to allow the matter to proceed to trial.

555   If the case is allowed to proceed the next step is the main trial (§§ 213 ff. StPO). Because a full trial involves a considerable effort, many lesser matters are dealt with in accordance with a simplified summary procedure (*Strafbefehl*) on application by the state prosecutor (§§ 407 ff. StPO). The accused need not be heard by the court before an order for summary punishment is made, but he or she does have the option of objecting to the summary sentence. If the accused does so then the matter must proceed to a full trial.

556   In the interests of the accused the procedure as a whole, including the main trial, is formalised to a significant extent (§§ 226 ff. StPO). This is felt necessary to make it possible for the accused to respond appropriately in what is generally an unfamiliar and threatening environment from his or her point of view. After the presiding judge has established that all parties are present the witnesses leave the courtroom. If the accused fails to appear without sufficient reason, then the court will order that he or she

should be brought before the court. The court may also issue a warrant for the accused's arrest (§ 230 para. 2 StPO). As a general rule proceedings may not be conducted unless the accused is present. However, leaving special exceptions aside, the trial may proceed without the accused if the accused him- or herself has deliberately and culpably induced his or her inability to take part in the proceedings and has thus knowingly prevented the trial from being conducted in the ordinary way. The same applies when the accused disturbs the proceedings by unruly behaviour (§§ 231 a, 231 b StPO).

The next step is for the president of the court to question the accused about his or her personal circumstances. The state prosecutor then reads out the charge. If the accused is prepared to give evidence about the matter he or she is then examined, but only after his or her right to remain silent has been pointed out to the accused. The examination of the accused is carried out primarily by the presiding judge. The other judges, lay assessors, state prosecutor and the defence counsel are also given the opportunity to put questions to the accused.   557

The court then proceeds to gather evidence (§ 244 StPO). Witnesses are examined and expert witnesses testify. The court can also admit real evidence (for example, the weapon with which the deed was done) and inspect the scene of the alleged crime (*Augenscheinseinnahme*, §§ 86 ff. StPO). Documentary evidence (*Urkundenbeweis*) may also be important, for example in a fraud case where a contract of sale has been read out incorrectly (§§ 249 ff. StPO). The court gathers evidence on its own initiative, in other words, the inquisitorial maxim applies. In addition the state prosecutor, the accused, the defence council and any additional person who may be joined as co-prosecutor (§§ 395 ff. StPO; this is often the victim, who is interested in getting the accused convicted) can apply to have evidence admitted.   558

After the court has finished gathering evidence the state prosecutor makes his or her closing speech. Thereafter the accused or his or her representative replies. The accused always has the last word (§ 258 StPO) so that his or her version of events is fresh in the court's mind when the judges begin to consult on how to decide the case. The court then considers its decision and finally the decision is handed down (§ 260 para. 1 StPO).   559

One of the most important principles in criminal law, and a principle which has effect particularly on criminal procedure, is the principle that, if there is a reasonable doubt, the court must make the finding most favourable to the accused (*in dubio pro reo*). In terms of this principle punishment can only be imposed if it has been clearly established that all the factual requirements for conviction and the imposition of punishment have been satisfied (§ 267 para. 1 StPO). If the matter remains in doubt then the accused must be discharged.   560

This principle is limited to some extent by an exception which is motivated by considerations of criminal policy. The exception says that where it is certain that the accused has committed one or the other of two crimes, but it cannot be established which of the two prohibitions has been violated, then, the accused can be convicted of the lesser of the two crimes (*Wahlfeststellung*). However, this rule only applies where both charges are ethically and psychologically comparable. In certain cases the accused may be alternatively convicted of one of two crime (*ungleichartige Wahlfeststellung*), e.g. theft and receiving of stolen goods.   561

562   Another fundamental legal principle is that nobody may be punished twice for the same deed (*ne bis in idem*). This rule is explicitly set out in article 103 para. 3 GG.

563   The accused is entitled to make use of the services of defence counsel at any stage in the proceedings (§ 137 para. 1 sentence 1 StPO). A defence lawyer may not simultaneously represent several persons who stand accused of the same crime and may also not represent several accused in a single trial (§ 146 StPO). The aim of this rule is to avoid conflicts of interest in situations where one accused attempts to place the blame on another. In some cases legal representation is mandatory (*notwendige Verteidigung*, §§ 140 ff. StPO). This is the case, for example, when the accused is charged with a felony (serious crime). The same applies in all cases in which the seriousness of the deed or the complexity of the case makes the services of defence council necessary. Defence counsel will also be required in any case in which the accused is not capable of conducting his or her own defence. The provision of help in such situations in which the accused faces serious dangers arises from the duty of the state to take care of its citizens (*Fürsorgepflicht*). Even someone who is suspected of having committed a wrong – and at this stage the wrong is still only a suspected wrong – cannot be left alone. This is particularly so because each accused is to be presumed innocent until proven guilty (*in dubio pro reo*). If the accused refuses to appoint defence counsel in a case in which legal representation is mandatory, then defence counsel will be appointed by the court. This will also be done if there is reason to fear that the defence counsel chosen by the accused will lay down his or her mandate during the course of proceedings or will cease to be available for some other reason (§§ 141, 142 StPO). In these situations the defence counsel is referred to as court-appointed counsel (*Pflichtverteidiger*).

564   The court will also appoint counsel if the defence counsel chosen by the accused is excluded from the proceedings (§§ 138 a-138 d StPO). This may be the case in special circumstances, for example where the defence lawyer is also implicated in the crime which is the object of the investigation, or if the defence lawyer abuses his or her contact with the accused to conduct criminal activities, or if the lawyer poses a substantial danger to the security of a prison. This could be the case where the lawyer smuggles drugs or weapons into the prison or is acting as a courier between members of a criminal organisation. In very exceptional cases involving special dangers the accused can be fully isolated (*Kontaktsperre*) in terms of the Introductory Provisions to the Constitution of Courts Act (*Einführungsgesetz zum Gerichtsverfassungsgesetz*, §§ 31-38 EGGVG). However, the defence as such is only affected by such isolation to the extent that the contact between defence counsel and the accused is interrupted just as contact to all other persons is interrupted unless they are granted special permission to see the accused.

565   The defence counsel is an independent organ of the legal system since he or she is a legal practitioner (§ 1 BRAO). The defence counsel has an obligation both to his or her client and to the legal system as such. The defence counsel may not commit an illegal act even in the interests of protecting his or her client, and the defence counsel may also not behave in an improper manner. If the defence counsel knows that his or her client is guilty, then the defence counsel may indeed argue that his or her client should be discharged on the basis of insufficient evidence, but the defence counsel may not create the impression that he or she believes the client to be innocent. However, this generally accepted rule is probably of more significance in theory than in practice.

The law of criminal procedure is distinguished from the law relating to the execution   566
of sentences imposed by the court. The law on this latter subject is scattered throughout numerous statutes and subordinate sources of law. Important general provisions
are §§ 449 ff. StPO, §§ 82 ff. JGG for juvenile and immature offenders, and the Execution of Criminal Sentences Act (*Strafvollstreckungsordnung*). The Act on the Serving
of Criminal Sentences (*Strafvollzugsgesetz*) regulates the way in which sentences of imprisonment are served. Special chambers in the various criminal courts concerned with
the execution of sentences ensure that sentences are carried out in accordance with the
principles of the *Rechtsstaat* and decide on questions relating to the enforcement of
sentences.

Literature:

Karlsruher Kommentar zur Strafprozessordnung, ed. by *Rolf Hannich*, 8. ed. 2019
Hans H. Kühne, Strafprozessrecht, 9. ed. 2015
Ewald Löwe/Werner Rosenberg, Die Strafprozessordnung und das Gerichtsverfassungsgesetz, 26. ed. 2012
Lutz Meyer-Goßner/Bertram Schmitt, Strafprozessordnung, 62. ed. 2019
Claus Roxin/Bernd Schünemann, Strafverfahrensrecht, 29. ed. 2017
Klaus Volk/Armin Engländer, Grundkurs StPO, 9. ed. 2018

D. Private Law

I. History and Structure

1. History

567 The history of German private law is intertwined with European legal history as a whole. In the Middle Ages it was still indiscriminately combined with public law in the laws of the various Germanic peoples. To an even greater extent than the other disciplines, the development of a common German private law is linked to the reception of Roman law between the 13th and 16th centuries. It thus takes up the thread where the legal developments of the ancient world left off. Even today important private law concepts are based directly on Roman thinking.

568 The Eastern Roman Emperor *Justinian* (527-565) organised a project to summarise the law as recognised in his time in the *corpus iuris civilis*. It consisted of four parts, the Institutes, the Digests (also known as the Pandects), the Codex of Justinian and the Novellae Constitutiones. The Digests, which historically are the most important part, contain a collection of fragments from the writings of the Roman jurists, particularly from the 1st to the 3rd century A.D. The *corpus iuris civilis* came into force in the Western parts of the Roman Empire in 554 A.D. It attained lasting influence in Italy and Southern France. From the 11th century onwards the Digest was studied systematically, starting in the universities of Upper Italy, with the law faculty of the University of Bologna, which had been founded by Irnerius (1055-1125) in 1119, playing the leading role. Here Irnerius and his followers developed the gloss as a method of presenting the law. The gloss was a series of explanatory notes on the various Latin texts, with an eventual tendency towards systematisation and unification. From the end of the 13th century onwards the formerly dominant Glossators were replaced by the Post-Glossators, also known as the Commentators or, because of their activity as practical legal advisers, as the Consiliators. Bartolus de Saxoferrato (1314-1357) and his pupil Baldus de Ubaldis (1327-1400) were the most important representatives of this school. Their method, the *mos italicus*, is characterised by practically oriented commentaries on the classical texts.

569 The law schools of the upper-Italian cities soon became important centres of academic legal learning for German students too. The Roman law, which had been perfected by the Glossators and Commentators, spread through Germany as it did in most other parts of Europe. Even more importantly, the systematic approach to solving legal problems spread with it. The Roman law, which was the "common law" of the land, served as a backup to the local laws of each territory and city, in other words, it was applicable whenever the local law made no provision for a particular problem.

570 In the course of the Enlightenment a rationalist approach to law (*Vernunftrecht*) was developed. This sought the roots of the law in reason. As this approach became dominant, the Roman law was given a new interpretation in accordance with the spirit of the times (the *usus modernus*). In particular, this meant that it underwent a new rationalisation and systematisation. The increasingly important idea of codification, together with the rise of the nation state in Prussia, led to the promulgation of the Prussian General Code (*Preußisches Allgemeines Landrecht*, abbreviated *ALR*) in 1794. This, in essence, codified all laws in force at the time. In contrast to the French *Code civil* of 1804 with its revolutionary postulate of equality, and freedom of ownership, the Prus-

sian General Code still entrenched traditional privileges. A significant factor for the future development of German private law was that the French *Code civil* remained in force in the territories on the left bank of the Rhine (which at times were under French rule) throughout the 19th century. In 1809 the Grand Duchy of Baden promulgated a slightly modified German translation of the *Code civil*.

The rationalist legal thinking of the Enlightenment had abstracted legal rules from the local and personal peculiarities of human beings to a significant extent. Legal rules were derived from reason and were seen as eternal and of universal application. At the beginning of the 19th century the Historical school of legal thinking, founded by *Gustav Hugo* (1764-1844) and *Friedrich Carl von Savigny* (1779-1861) arose in reaction to the rationalist approach. It saw the law as arising from the quietly developing internal energies of the nation and being rooted in the national character (*Volksgeist*) of a people. These jurists were largely opposed to a further codification of the private law in Germany and concentrated on a renewed role for the Roman law, which was seen as a type of customary law. They attempted to go back to the original sources, and their efforts developed into Pandectism, a word derived from the title of their most important object of study. The Pandectists strove to create a closed system of legal concepts and generally recognised doctrines. These efforts were based on the belief that a legal system can be complete, in the sense of having a solution to every problem. They approved the idea of analytical jurisprudence (*Begriffsjurisprudenz*) which held that legal problems could be solved by logical calculations involving the application of legal rules. Overall this amounted to a form of legal Positivism. 571

Those legal theories, which sought to orientate themselves on the Roman tradition, developed a Romanist body of learning. The creators of this learning, which was the fruit of the Historical school, found themselves in difficulties in trying to explain the received Roman law as the product of the German national spirit. Alongside their theories a Germanist school grew up. This school's leading representatives were *Jacob Grimm* (1785-1863), *Carl Friedrich Eichhorn* (1781-1854) and *Otto von Gierke* (1841-1921). This school was concerned with genuinely Germanic private law. It emphasised legal institutions such as the *Genossenschaft*, a type of co-operative society, and opened the law more enthusiastically to social concepts. 572

Rudolph von Jhering (1818-1892) played the most important role in giving legal studies a new direction in the next generation by emphasising the fact that the law is a means to an end. His formulation of the "struggle for justice" (*Kampf ums Recht*) introduced a new epoch. This phrase already contains the seeds of the development of private law, and indeed of all law, in the direction of the "theory of party interests" (*Interessenjurisprudenz*) of the early 20th century. This school of thought sees law as the expression and enforcement of individual interests. These theories are still influential today, although they are now modified by the so-called value-oriented jurisprudence (*Wertungsjurisprudenz*). This introduces the idea of legal value judgements based on human rights and the common good, thus softening the raw struggle of conflicting interests for legal structure and enforcement. 573

The German Civil Code (*Bürgerliches Gesetzbuch*, abbreviated *BGB*) was a late consequence of the rationalist idea of codification, but its creation was also facilitated by the successful systematisation which was largely the achievement of the Romanist school. The Civil Code, which was promulgated in 1896 after many years of preparatory work and came into force on 1.1.1900, is still in force today. This code, which 574 has been amended many times in the interim, is primarily the fruit of the unification of Germany in the Empire (*Reich*) of 1870/1871. The subsequent development of the Civil Code has taken place mostly through the decisions of the courts. Specific legal institutions which are not expressly mentioned in the Code have been created by the decisions of the courts. Apart from actual amendments to the Civil Code, the legislation of the 20th century has produced numerous special statutes which complement the Civil Code and often also modify it for a specific field of law.

2. Structure

575 The above development still determines the system of private law today. The Civil Code, consisting of five books, stands at the centre of the private law. In accordance with rationalist thinking, it starts with a Book of General Provisions (*Allgemeiner Teil*). This contains those provisions which, in principle, are applicable to all the following books. Next follows the law of obligations (*Schuldrecht*), with provisions regulating legal relations between persons, most importantly contracts and torts (delict). The following book is the law of things (*Sachenrecht*), which regulates the legal relationships between persons and things, for example possession, ownership and other real rights such as lien and mortgage.

576 The fourth book contains the law of the family, with the central provisions on engagement, marriage, divorce and the law relating to children. The Code is completed by the fifth book which contains the law of succession. In contrast to the private law systems of other European states, and in contrast to the Roman legal tradition, the law of marriage and the family is thus not the first division of the Code. Only questions relating to the attainment of legal capacity have been left in the Book of General Provisions.

577 In addition to the great codification of the private law in the Civil Code there are numerous special provisions of the private law contained in individual statutes which take account of specialised problems or which are aimed at complementing the provisions of the Civil Code. Some important laws, to name but a few, include the following: the Commercial Code (*Handelsgesetzbuch*, abbreviated HGB) which regulates commercial transactions; the law of corporations in the Act on Private Limited Companies (*GmbH-Gesetz*) or the German Stock Corporation Act (*Aktiengesetz*); business law, which regulates matters such as the law against unfair competition; and the law on negotiable instruments which is regulated in the Cheques Act and Bills of Exchange Act. Labour law, with all its complexities, has to a large extent become an independent body of law. It is regulated by numerous individual acts such as the Employees' Representation Act (*Betriebsverfassungsgesetz*) and the Co-Determination in Industry Act (*Mitbestimmungsgesetz*). Labour law lacks a statutory basis in many respects, and consists instead of judge-made law which is based on general provisions in the constitution. Apart from the above there are numerous statutes regulating various specific problems, for example the Condominium Act concerning separate ownership of individual apartments in a multi-unit building (*Wohnungseigentumsgesetz*); the Product Safety Act (*Produktsicherheitsgesetz*) and the Product Liability Act *(Produkthaftungsgesetz).*

578 This development has to a large extent overwhelmed the ideal of systematisation which was connected with the idea of codification. Practical legal business today is no longer determined by logical construction and perfection of the law as a unified whole.

Instead rules are created for compartmentalised aspects of life with reference to the specific interests which are affected and which are insisted upon. The more modern descriptions of the private law are also increasingly departing from the system of the Civil Code and are instead divided according to spheres of life, typical problems and groups of cases. On the one hand this makes the law more concrete and vivid; on the other hand it accelerates the loss of inner coherence of the system – a general phenomenon in the modern state. However, the structure of the Civil Code remains of decisive importance for the understanding of the private law, which still has a certain inner logic.

Literature:

Ulrich Eisenhardt, Deutsche Rechtsgeschichte, 7. ed. 2019
Walter Erman, Handkommentar zum Bürgerlichen Gesetzbuch, 15. ed. 2017
Othmar Jauernig, Bürgerliches Gesetzbuch, 17. ed. 2018
Eugen Klunzinger, Einführung in das Bürgerliche Recht, 17. ed. 2019
Karl Kroeschell, Deutsche Rechtsgeschichte, vol. 1, 12. ed. 2008, vol. 2, 9. ed. 2008, vol. 3, 5. ed. 2008
Dieter Medicus/Jens Petersen, Bürgerliches Recht, 26. ed. 2017
Dieter Medicus/Jens Petersen, Grundwissen zum Bürgerlichen Recht, 10. ed. 2014
Heinrich Mitteis/Heinz Lieberich, Deutsche Rechtsgeschichte, 19. ed. 1992
Münchener Kommentar zum Bürgerlichen Gesetzbuch, *Franz J. Säcker/Roland Rixecker/Hartmut Oeker/Bettina Limperg* (eds.), 8. ed. since 2018
Hans J. Musielak/Wolfgang Hau, Grundkurs BGB, 15. ed. 2017
Otto Palandt, Bürgerliches Gesetzbuch, 78. ed. 2019
Hans Schlosser, Grundzüge der Neueren Privatrechtsgeschichte, 10. ed. 2005
Dieter Schwab/Martin Löhnig, Einführung in das Zivilrecht, 20. ed. 2016
Theodor Soergel/Wolfgang Siebert, Bürgerliches Gesetzbuch, 13. ed. since 1999
Julius v. Staudinger, Kommentar zum Bürgerlichen Gesetzbuch, 17. ed. since 2017
Harm P. Westermann, Grundbegriffe des BGB, 17. ed. 2013
Franz Wieacker, Privatrechtsgeschichte der Neuzeit, 3. ed. 2016

II. The Book of General Provisions of the Civil Code

The Book of General Provisions (*Allgemeiner Teil*) of the Civil Code (*Bürgerliches Gesetzbuch* abbreviated *BGB*) consists primarily of fundamental provisions relating to persons and things as the subjects and objects of the law. These are followed by rules concerning legally relevant declarations of will (*Willenserklärungen*) and their validity as the basic elements of legal transactions. In addition this part of the Code contains provisions relating to limitation of actions (*Fristen und Verjährung*).   579

1. Capacity to Have Rights and Duties

A person's capacity to have rights and duties (*Rechtsfähigkeit*) begins with the completion of birth (§ 1 BGB). This means for example, that a person can become the owner of property and sue or be sued. Certain provisions provide that in certain situations the capacity to have rights and duties begins before birth. The *nasciturus* (conceived but unborn child) can inherit, provided that he or she is subsequently born alive (§ 1923 sentence 2 BGB). The same applies when the *nasciturus* is harmed by some act giving rise to liability in tort such as a motor accident. In such a situation the child   580 becomes entitled to claim damages once born.[1] Capacity to have rights and duties ends on death. All human beings, in contrast to animals and things, have this capacity. It is not possible to deprive a person of his or her capacity to have rights and duties.

581   The rules in the Civil Code concerning the capacity to have rights and duties do not determine a person's capacity to have rights and duties in other fields of the law. For example, in constitutional law the *nasciturus* has a constitutionally protected right to life and physical integrity (article 2 para. 2 sentence 1 GG). Since different areas of the law have to take into consideration differing factors, the criminal law also takes a different attitude from the private law. For the purposes of distinguishing the abortion of a foetus (§ 218 StGB) from the killing of a person (§§ 211 ff. StGB) the Criminal Code takes as the dividing line not the completion but the beginning of the birth process, in other words, the onset of labour.

2. Capacity to Perform Legal Acts

582   The capacity to have rights and duties (*Rechtsfähigkeit*) must be distinguished from the capacity to perform legal acts (*Geschäftsfähigkeit*, §§ 104 ff. BGB). This is the capacity to enter valid legal transactions, for example, the ability to conclude a contract. The law also distinguishes the capacity to be liable in tort (*Deliktsfähigkeit*, §§ 827, 828 BGB).

583   Anyone who has attained the age of majority has the capacity to perform juristic acts. According to German law, majority is attained on the completion of the eighteenth year of life (§ 2 BGB). Anyone below that age is referred to as a minor. The day on which a person was born is included in calculating how old they are. Thus, someone who was born on 1 January 1983 at 23:55 is reckoned as having completed his or her 18th year on 31 December 2000 at 24:00 and is thus already considered to be a major and to have full legal capacity for the whole day of 1 January 2001.

584   A person who has not yet completed the seventh year of life has no capacity to perform juristic acts (*Geschäftsunfähigkeit*, § 104 number 1 BGB). A person who is suffering from a pathological mental disturbance of indefinite duration which prevents the free determination of the will also lacks the capacity to perform juristic acts (§ 104 number 2 BGB). A declaration of will purporting to have legal consequences is void if made by such a person, i.e., it has no legal effect (§ 105 para. 2 BGB).

585   If a minor has completed the seventh year of life, then he or she has a limited capacity to perform juristic acts (*beschränkte Geschäftsfähigkeit*, § 106 BGB). This means that a declaration of will on his or her part is not void, but that it requires the prior consent (*Einwilligung*, § 183 BGB) of the minor's legal guardian (usually the parents of the child) to be legally binding. If the guardian does not give consent before the transaction is concluded, then at least not unilateral juristic acts are suspensively invalid (*schwebend unwirksam*). Such a transaction can, however, be ratified subsequently by the guardian, in which case it becomes legally binding (§ 108 BGB).

586   An exception to this rule is that transactions entered into by a person with limited legal capacity are legally binding insofar as they involve only legal benefits (*lediglich rechtlicher Vorteil*) for him or her and no legal obligations (§ 107 BGB). It is thus possible for a person with limited capacity to enter a transaction accepting the gift of a

---

1   BGHZ 58, 48.

piece of land. This is also considered to be the case when the land is burdened by a mortgage (*Hypothek*) or brings with it the duty to pay rates and taxes such as the land tax. The reasoning is that these are merely a diminution of the benefit. The Code also provides that the contracts of minors are legally binding if the minor is able to perform his or her side of the bargain with resources which the minor's guardian has made available for him or her to dispose of freely or which have been put at the minor's disposal with the consent of his or her guardian. This is the so-called "pocket money provision" (*Taschengeldparagraf*, § 110 BGB). A person with limited capacity to perform juristic acts can thus independently buy a bicycle if his or her parents have given him or her € 500 for this purpose; and a seventeen year old student can validly take piano lessons and buy textbooks with the money which her parents give to her every month.

Partial legal capacity (*Teilgeschäftsfähigkeit*) goes even further. The legal guardian of a minor can give consent to enter a contract of employment or, subject to ratification by the Guardianship Court (*Familiengericht*) give permission for the minor to set up as a self-employed businessperson (§§ 112, 113 BGB). This entitles the minor to conclude any legal transaction incidental to the running of the business or which is necessary to enter, perform or terminate the contract of employment. Thus, a sixteen year old working for a construction firm can terminate his or her employment with that firm and take up employment with a different construction company. Only a few, particularly risky, legal transactions, such as taking out a loan or offering to stand surety are excluded. These are transactions which even the guardian cannot authorise – they require the consent of the Guardianship Court (§§ 112 para. 1 sentence 2, 113 para. 1 sentence 2, 1643, 1821 ff. BGB).

587

3. Legal Persons

Under the provisions of the Civil Code it is also possible for groups of persons and other organisations as such to have legal capacity if they are legal persons. One legal form which the German private law recognises is the institution of the foundation (*Stiftung*, §§ 80 ff. BGB). It is a fund of money which has been appropriated to a particular purpose. Of great importance are the association (*Verein*, §§ 21 ff. BGB) and various types of corporation and partnership (*Gesellschaft*). There are numerous statutes dealing specifically with particular types of corporations and other joint undertakings such as the Stock Corporation Act (*Aktiengesetz*), the Act on Private Limited Companies (*GmbH Gesetz*) or the Commercial Code (*Handelsgesetzbuch*) and special provisions in the Civil Code such as §§ 705 ff. concerning the *Gesellschaft bürgerlichen Rechts*, a type of partnership, which does not have legal personality.

588

The association (*Verein*) is the archetype of numerous forms of corporations and other joint undertakings. It is of considerable social relevance, not only in the economic sphere, but also as a form of organisation for non-profit purposes. It has a constitutional basis in article 9 para. 1, 2 GG: All Germans have the right to form associations and societies. Associations whose objects or activities constitute an infringement of the criminal law or which are directed at the abolition of the constitution, or against the promotion of goodwill between nations, are, however, banned.

589

The capacity to have legal rights (*Rechtsfähigkeit*) provides a basis for legal persons to become the owners of property. A legal person can only act through its organs, in other words its executive board, its manager, or its members in general meeting. In terms

590

of § 31 BGB a legal person is liable for torts committed by its office bearers. The personal liability of office bearers, shareholders and members differs from one type of legal person to another depending on their purposes and internal structures.

591   The association (*Verein*) acquires the capacity to have legal rights by being registered in the Register of Associations kept at the relevant *Amtsgericht* or by special grant. Once registered, it has the status of a "registered association" (*eingetragener Verein*, abbreviated *e.V.*). There must be at least seven founding members. In addition there are types of associations which do not have legal personality (§ 54 para. 1 BGB). However, for practical purposes their position is by now much the same as that of a registered association. The original aim of the legislature in making this distinction was to create a mechanism for monitoring associations: Associations which were not registered (and thus not subject to monitoring) were therefore not accorded legal capacity, with the result that members of such an association were jointly and severally liable for the debts of the association. Nevertheless, numerous trade unions, political parties and student organisations were set up as unregistered associations. The resulting disadvantages have largely been avoided by provisions in their articles of association and by now also by means of special statutory provisions (§ 50 para. 2 ZPO, § 3 ParteienG).

592   The peculiarity and independence of the association can also be seen in the extent of its internal autonomy. A cause of considerable controversy and interest is for the most part the power of an association to take disciplinary measures against members who infringe against the associations rules or act in a manner contrary to its interests. This power is derived from the articles of association of the association, to which the members have given their assent in joining the association or in taking part in founding it. Such disciplinary measures are of considerable economic significance in some cases, for example, when imposed by a football club on professional players. A particularly contentious issue is whether the courts of the state are able to review the decision of an association to discipline a member. The position is that the courts will merely consider whether the punishment imposed has a sufficient basis in the rules of the association, whether the prescribed procedure has been followed, whether the rule being applied is illegal or contrary to public policy, and whether the punishment is patently unreasonable. The court may also consider whether the factual findings made in the course of the association's internal proceedings were accurate.[2]

4. Declaration of Will

593   The declaration of will (*Willenserklärung*, §§ 116 ff. BGB) is one of the essential structural characteristics of German private law. Here especially the original liberal spirit of the Code finds expression. Other types of legal obligation, even those arising from tort/delict, take second place, even, however, in practice, they may be of equally great importance. Some important developments have thus taken place outside statute law. Nevertheless, the law relating to declarations of will remains a central anchor point for the understanding of the basic structure of the Civil Code. Declarations of will (*Willenserklärungen*) are distinguished from legal transactions (*Rechtsgeschäfte*). A legal transaction consists of at least one declaration of will and often of several other additional elements. Thus, a contract is a legal transaction which comes into existence

---

2   BGHZ 29, 352/354; 87, 337/343 ff.

by way of several declarations of will. The transfer of ownership in moveable property is a legal transaction consisting of agreement that ownership should pass plus the physical handing over of the thing in question.

The declaration of will is an expression of will which is aimed at the achievement of some legal consequence. This requires firstly an outer act of expression, in other words, an externally perceivable act such as speaking, nodding, or writing. A declaration of will can also take place implicitly (*konkludent*), that is, by behaviour which justifies the reasonable conclusion that there is such a will. An example is the act of placing a newspaper on a newsagent's counter by the customer. This is generally understood to mean: "I wish to buy this newspaper". A particular form of declaration, e.g. in written form, is only necessary when expressly required by statute. In addition to this external element, a particular internal state is required. In this respect a distinction is made between the desire to act (*Handlungswillen*), consciousness of the declaration (*Erklärungsbewusstsein*) and the desire to enter a specific legal transaction (*Geschäftswillen*). The first of these, the desire to act, involves a conscious and deliberate act. Therefore, a person who speaks in his or her sleep or in a state of hypnosis does not make a declaration of will. A person has consciousness of the declaration when he or she is aware that by doing the act in question he or she is making a declaration with legal consequences. The courts seem increasingly inclined to leave out this element of a declaration of will.[3] The lack of consciousness of the declaration will not, however, prevent a declaration of will from coming into existence if the following requirements are met: Firstly, the person making the declaration ought to have realised that a person acting in good faith and interpreting his or her utterance in accord with the ordinary meaning of the words would have thought that a declaration of will was being made; secondly, the person could have taken steps to prevent this from happening had he or she applied the degree of care necessary when entering transactions; thirdly, the other party actually did believe that a declaration of will was being made. However, if a declaration of will comes into existence in this way it can be voided at the instance of the person who made it[4] in terms of §§ 119, 121, 143 BGB and its legal effect can thus be avoided. A simple example of this is provided by the "Trier Wine Auction" situation. A stranger visiting a wine auction, who is ignorant of the customs applicable at auction sales, raises his or her hand to greet a friend. The auctioneer takes this as an offer and knocks the lot down to that person. The visitor has made a declaration of will even although he or she had no consciousness of the declaration, and a contract of sale has come into existence. The visitor can, however, escape the contract by challenging the declaration. Finally, there must be the will to enter the specific legal transaction (*Geschäftswille*). If this is lacking then there is once again a declaration of will, but in terms of § 119 para. 1 BGB it can be challenged on the grounds of mistake and be declared voided.

594

Generally speaking silence will not constitute a declaration of will. However, in certain circumstances the Code attaches legal consequences to silence. It is then usually interpreted as a refusal (§§ 108 para. 2 sentence 2; 177 para. 2 sentence 2; 415 para. 2 sentence 2; 451 para. 2 sentence 2 BGB) but it is taken to be consent in certain circumstances (§§ 416 para. 1 sentence 2; 455 sentence 2; 516 para. 2 sentence 2 BGB; and 362 para. 1 HGB). Of considerable commercial significance in this context is the so-

595

---

3 BGHZ 91, 324; 109, 171.
4 *Anfechtung.*

called businessman's confirmation (*kaufmännisches Bestätigungsschreiben*) which the courts developed on the basis of § 362 HGB. If one businessperson writes a letter to another confirming in writing the result reached in prior negotiations, then if the other responds with silence he or she is taken as accepting the written statement of the position.

596   The distinction between declarations of will requiring receipt by another party before taking effect (*empfangsbedürftige Willenserklärungen*) and those which do not need to be received (*nicht empfangsbedürftig*) is important. A declaration of will which does not need to be received, such as a will, becomes effective as soon as the intention to make the declaration has been manifested (*Abgabe der Willenserklärung*). In contrast, declarations of will requiring receipt become effective only once they have been made and delivered to the addressee (*Zugang der Willenserklärung*). They can be recalled at any time prior to delivery, and if this is done they are without legal effect (§ 130 para. 1 sentence 2 BGB). A declaration of will made to a person who is not present is delivered (*zugegangen*) when is has been placed in the sphere of control of the addressee in such a way that in normal circumstances the addressee would be in a position to take cognizance of it and, according to common practice, this can also be expected of him or her. A typical example would be when the letter containing the declaration is placed in the addressee's letter box.

597   The declaration of will, which is directed toward a particular legal effect, is to be distinguished from the *Realakt*, which is any act to which the legal system attaches legal consequences without reference to the will of the person doing the act. For example, the duty to pay damages is attached to an act which amounts to a tort. A *geschäftsähnliche Handlung* is once again something different. It is a statement or declaration of will to which the law attaches legal consequences irrespective of whether these are desired by the person making the statement. Examples of this are the letter of demand (*Mahnung*), or the notice of termination (*Kündigung*). The rules concerning declarations of will are often applicable to such statements where appropriate.

5. Void and Voidable Declarations

598   The basic principle is that a person making a declaration must expect to be bound by the meaning which would be attributed to it by a reasonable person acting in good faith (*nach Treu und Glauben,* §§ 116 ff. BGB). This is necessary in the interests of commercial certainty. However, in some cases the law places less emphasis on commercial certainty and instead concentrates on the subjective intention of the person making the declaration. If the declaration of will suffers from certain defects then it is void (*nichtig*) or, at any rate, voidable (*anfechtbar*). Declarations of will which are void are without effect from the very beginning. Voidable declarations of will are indeed initially valid, but once their validity is challenged, they are treated as if they had been of no effect from the very beginning, i.e., with retrospective effect. This last rule does not apply to labour law and the law of corporations (*Gesellschaftsrecht*). In these fields the successful challenge of a declaration only makes the declaration invalid *ex nunc*, i.e. from the moment when it is challenged. The reason is that in these fields many different benefits may have been exchanged making restitution (*Rückabwicklung*) impracticable or – in the case of work already performed – impossible. Generally speaking, the person who succeeds in getting the declaration of will voided is liable to make good any loss suffered by someone who acted in reliance on the declaration (§ 122 BGB).

Generally, if someone makes a declaration of will without seriously meaning it, that person will nevertheless be bound by it (§ 116 sentence 1 BGB). However, if the person to whom the declaration was made knew that it was not seriously meant (§§ 116 sentence 2, 117 BGB), or if a declaration is not seriously meant and is made in the expectation that this will be recognised, then the declaration is void. The latter situation is called a declaration in jest (*Scherzerklärung*). However, even in such a case the person making the declaration will be liable for damages if the other party nevertheless relied on the validity of the declaration (§§ 118, 122 BGB). 599

If the person making the declaration is mistaken as to its objective meaning the declaration will nevertheless be valid. He or she can, however, challenge the declaration. This must be done as soon as possible (*unverzüglich*), i.e. without culpable delay (§§ 119, 121, 122 BGB). A declaration can be challenged successfully in various circumstances, for example, where the person making the declaration made a mistake relating to the subject matter of the transaction because he or she was not familiar with certain weights and measures. This is called a "declaration error" (*Verlautbarungsirrtum*). The person can also challenge it if he or she has confused the actual subject matter of the transaction or the actual person with whom the person is dealing with some other. This is called a "mistake of individualisation" (*Individualisierungsfehler*). If the person making the declaration mistakenly says, writes or does something other than what he or she actually intended there is a "mistake of expression" (*Erklärungsirrtum*) and once again the declaration of will can be challenged. If the person's declaration of will is communicated inaccurately, it can be challenged as an "error in communication" (*Übermittlungsfehler*, § 120 BGB). 600

Significant defects of will can also arise in the formation of the will itself. General errors of motive or errors in calculation are irrelevant. An example of an irrelevant error of motive is when the father of the bride buys a wedding dress for his daughter because he believes that she is about to marry, and then the couple decide not to marry after all. An example of an error in calculation is when a building constructor sets a fixed price for the finished job and in doing so forgets to take into account the cost of building certain walls. However, if the person making the declaration of will is mistaken as to a commercially significant characteristic (*verkehrswesentliche Eigenschaft*) of a person or thing he or she can once again challenge the declaration and get it voided (§ 119 para. 2 BGB). 601

Unlawful threats (duress, *widerrechtliche Drohung*) also entitle the person who made the declaration to challenge its validity, and fraudulent misrepresentation (*arglistige Täuschung*) usually does so too. In these cases the victim of the threat or misrepresentation does not have to pay damages when his or her declaration is voided (§§ 123, 122 BGB). 602

6. Legal Transactions

The legal transaction (*Rechtsgeschäft*) is one of the key concepts of German civil-law dogma. It contains basic premises of the system as a whole and its philosophical background. The legal transaction is the most important tool which the legal system defines for the individual to structure his or her private affairs of his or her own initiative. It is thus an expression of the idea of private autonomy and individual freedom. 603

A declaration of will (*Willenserklärung*) forms the core of a legal transaction. In addition, it often has further elements. For example, in concluding a marriage there is the 604 additional requirement that the declaration of the will to marry must be made before a marriage officer. Finally, it is necessary that the legal system should attach the desired legal consequence to the declaration of will.

605 There are unilateral legal transactions such as, for example, the drawing up of a will. They contain the declaration of will of only one person. Multilateral legal transactions such as a contract or the taking of a resolution by a general meeting require declarations of will by at least two persons.

606 Of crucial importance for an understanding of the German system of private law is the distinction between the obligation transaction (*Verpflichtungsgeschäft*) which creates rights *in personam*, and the disposition transaction (*Verfügungsgeschäft*) which creates rights *in rem*. This distinction, which is unknown in most other legal systems, is an expression of the principle of abstraction (*Abstraktionsprinzip*) which does not exist in some legal systems. The obligation transaction *(Verpflichtungsgeschäft)* is a legal transaction by which (only) an obligation to do something is created. These transactions are usually contracts, for example, a contract of sale. They do no more than to create the obligation to perform. The legal rights surrounding the object of the transaction, for example, the question of who has ownership of the thing sold, are not directly influenced in the least by this transaction. Disposition transactions (*Verfügungsgeschäfte)*, on the other hand, are legal transactions which, with direct effect, transfer, burden, alter or terminate rights in a thing. A disposition transaction usually also takes the form of a contract (agreement). An example is the agreement to the transfer of ownership of a thing in terms of § 929 sentence 1 BGB.

607 The above is the expression of two principles which are unknown in many other legal systems, or which are at least not known in conjunction. These two principles are the principle of separation (*Trennungsprinzip*) and the principle of abstraction (*Abstraktionsprinzip*). In terms of the principle of separation a strict distinction is drawn between the obligation transaction and the disposition transaction. Ownership of the thing bought does not pass on completion of the obligation transaction, for example, the contract of sale. Only an obligation to transfer ownership is created by the obligation transaction. Ownership only passes to the buyer on completion of the disposition transaction. According to the principle of abstraction the disposition transaction is abstracted from the obligation transaction, in other words, the validity of the transfer of ownership is not dependent on the validity of the contract creating the obligation to transfer ownership.

608 The obligation transaction is generally the legal cause for the disposition transaction. On the other hand, the validity of the disposition transaction is in principle independent of the validity of the obligation transaction. However, if the obligation transaction is invalid, an obligation to reverse the disposition transaction by making restitution may arise. For example, the obligation may arise to transfer ownership in the object of the invalid contract of sale back to the original owner. This possibility is governed by the provisions on unjustified enrichment (restitution, §§ 812 ff. BGB). For example, the seller of a sports car has concluded a contract of sale with the buyer and has transferred ownership to him or her. The buyer then successfully challenges the contract of sale on the basis of mistake. The contract of sale is then indeed void, but the transfer of ownership remains valid. However, the seller gains a right to re-transfer of the car which is enforceable against the buyer on the basis of unjustified enrichment.

The validity of a disposition (*Verfügungsgeschäft*) presupposes a particular power on the part of the person claiming to make the disposition. This power is usually in the hands of the person whose rights are being disposed of. This would be, for example, the owner of a thing when ownership is being transferred. Exceptionally, the power of disposition (*Verfügungsbefugnis*) may lie in the hands of some other person such as the executor of a will or an insolvency administrator. In contrast to this, the validity of the obligation transaction (*Verpflichtungsgeschäft*) does not depend on a power of disposition. If the person who has undertaken the obligation is unable to perform due to the lack of the power of disposition he or she will generally be liable in damages. 609

It is thus possible for a seller to sell the same thing several times over and thus enter several valid obligation transactions. The seller can conclude a contract to sell a painting to someone and then contract to sell the same painting to someone else two days later, perhaps for a higher price. If the seller then transfers ownership in the painting to the second buyer by way of a disposition transaction he or she becomes incapable of fulfilling the obligation transaction entered into with the first buyer. The first buyer will have to resort to a claim for damages. 610

7. Contract

One of the most important legal transactions (*Rechtsgeschäfte*) is the contract (*Vertrag*, §§ 145 ff. BGB). It is involved in such varied situations as the buying of a sandwich or an agreement to build a nuclear power station. The starting premise is that there is complete freedom to contract, this being an important expression of the private autonomy which is protected in the constitutional guarantee of the free development of the personality (article 2 para. 1 GG). Every person should be able to structure his or her life and relationships in cooperation with others according to his or her own inclination. 611

A contract consists of declarations of will made with respect to one another by at least two persons. The declarations of will must agree in content. The first of these declarations of will is called the offer (*Angebot*) and the second the acceptance (*Annahme*). The offer is a declaration of will which must be received by another person before it has legal effect. By means of the offer one person proposes the conclusion of a contract to another person in such a way that all that is required for the contract to come into existence is the assent of the other party. The acceptance is also a declaration of will which must be received by another person before it becomes effective (German law has no postal rule). By means of the acceptance the person to whom the offer is made assents to the proposal made by the offeror. This means that both the offeror and the person accepting can freely recall their declarations of will so long as the offer or the acceptance has not yet reached the other party. 612

Once the offer has been received, it is binding on the offeror i.e., it cannot be withdrawn at will. He or she can, however, reserve the right to recall the offer at any time by a provision to this effect in the offer (§ 145 BGB). The offer only ceases to be valid if the other party does not accept in good time. If the offer is made *inter praesentes* it must be accepted at once. If the offer is not made face to face then it ceases to be valid if the offeror does not receive an answer within the period in which, under normal circumstances, he or she would be entitled to expect an answer. The offeror can also expressly stipulate when the offer is to expire. A further way in which the offer may be extinguished is if the offeree rejects it. If the offer is accepted after it has expired, then 613 the purported acceptance is regarded as a counteroffer. The same applies if the offeree purports to accept with modifications to the original offer (§§ 146-149 BGB).

614 The offer and acceptance must correspond for a contract to come into existence. In case of doubt, whether there is in fact such consensus must be determined by interpretation (*Auslegung*). If there was in fact a true consensus between the parties there will be a contract, even if the statements made do not correspond objectively. In contrast to this, there will be no contract if there is no true consensus. However, if the lack of consensus relates only to secondary aspects of the contract such as the exact time or place of delivery and in all other respects the parties are in agreement, then there may still be a valid contract. This will depend on how much importance the parties attached to the secondary point in question and whether they wish to make the whole transaction dependent on agreement on this point (§ 155 BGB). If the process of interpretation cannot exclude doubt as to the parties' intentions, then the contract does not come into existence.

8. Standard Form Contracts

615 The practice of including standard terms in a contract has arisen primarily from the need to make it easier to deal with routine transactions which recur on a regular basis. Such terms are often referred to in lay terms as "the fine print" because they are often included in the contract in smaller print, which in itself makes no difference to their legal validity. Standard terms are all contractual terms which are formulated in advance for use in a large number of contracts and which one party – the user – imposes on the other party when the contract is concluded. They become part of the contract by the agreement of the parties. If the circumstances make other measures impractical, it is sufficient that the standard terms are prominently displayed at the place of business of the user. It is essential that the other party should have had a reasonable opportunity to take notice of the standard terms, and he or she must accept them.

616 Standard form contracts have often been abused by users who use them to impose unreasonable, surprising, or highly disadvantageous terms on inexperienced customers who have either not had the terms truly drawn to their attention at all, or who have no choice but to accept because the user enjoys a monopolistic dominance. To ensure a fair balance of interests between the parties, §§ 305-310 BGB regulate standard terms.

617 This provides that surprising terms do not become part of the contract. Terms are invalid if they impose unreasonable disadvantages on the other party contrary to good faith (*Treu und Glauben,* §§ 305 c, 307 BGB). Terms which have been held to fall foul of this provision include terms which place the risk of unauthorised use of a credit card on the client irrespective of whether he or she was at fault or not,[5] or a pre-formulated consent to make the patient's body available for research purposes if he or she should die in the course of an operation in the hospital.[6] Certain typical terms are expressly declared to be invalid by the act. If specific terms are invalid, then general statutory provisions take their place.

618 In accordance with the general trend in the law, which can also be seen in the public interest action in environmental protection law and in competition law, it is not only the specific person who has entered the contract who can take legal action against ille-

---

5 BGH NJW 1991, p. 1886.
6 BGH NJW 1990, p. 2313.

gal standard terms in a contract. Consumer organisations and chambers of commerce and industry also have a legally enforceable right to demand that someone who is using illegal standard terms cease to do so or that he or she should recall them in terms of the *Injunction Applications Act* (§ 3 *Unterlassungsklagengesetz*).

9. Form

Generally speaking legal transactions and declarations of will are legally binding without fulfilling any requirements of form. An oral agreement or even mere behaviour may suffice. However, in some special cases certain forms must be complied with (§§ 125-129 BGB). The main purpose of such formal requirements is to act as a warning. The parties should be quite clear as to the content of their declarations. Formal requirements also serve the interest of the parties and the general public in legal certainty. If the formal requirements are not complied with, then the declaration of will and the legal transaction are void. Only in exceptional cases can the defect of form be cured by performance, confirmation or re-interpretation. A person who has made fraudulent misrepresentations to the other party concerning the formal requirements of a transaction will also be estopped from relying on the defect in form.

619

There are various different types of obligatory form which the law may require. The most important of these are that a transaction may be required to be in writing or that it should be publicly attested to or that it should be executed in a notarial deed. Further formal requirements may be established by agreement between the parties. The requirement that a transaction must be in writing means that a document must be drawn up and personally signed by the parties. If the person making the declaration cannot write, a notarially attested personal mark must take the place of the signature (§ 126 BGB). In certain special cases, such as a will not made before a notary, the entire document must be personally written by hand and signed (§ 2247 BGB).

620

Public attestation (*öffentliche Beglaubigung*) means that the declaration must be reduced to writing and the signature of the person making the declaration must be attested to by a notary (§ 129 BGB). What the notary is attesting to is that the signature is that of a person who has produced proof that he or she is the person whose name has been signed.

621

Execution in a notarial deed (*notarielle Beurkundung*) is the strictest of all formal requirements. It means that the declaration has been made before the notary after its significance has been explained by the notary, that the notary has written the declaration down and read it back to the person making the declaration, that this person has confirmed the correctness of the written text and signed it, and that the declaration has then been signed by the notary as well. The detailed requirements are contained in § 128 BGB and in the Notarial Deeds Act (*Beurkundungsgesetz*). Execution of a notarial deed is prescribed for those legal transactions which the legislator regards as being particularly important: contracts for the sale of land, contracts appointing heirs *inter vivos*, contracts renouncing rights to an inheritance, pre-nuptial (ante-nuptial) contracts and contracts of donation (without consideration). The execution of a notarial deed, being the stricter requirement, supersedes any requirement that a declaration must be in writing or that it must be publicly attested to.

622

10. Agency

623   One of the practically and theoretically important subjects regulated in the Book of General Provisions of the Civil Code is the law concerning agency (*Vertretung* or *Stellvertretung*, §§ 164-181 BGB). Minors, insofar as they have limited capacity to enter legal transaction must be represented by their legal guardian (person with parental responsibility). Generally speaking this will be the parents (§§ 1626, 1629 BGB). Other persons who lack full legal capacity must also be represented by their guardians. Legal persons act through their organs. Here, once again, the rules on agency are applicable. The same applies to the acts of other types of association. Details can be found in the specific statutes relating to the law of corporations (§ 35 para. 1 GmbHG, § 78 para. 1 AktG and numerous provisions of the HGB). Agency can be created not only by statute, but also by means of a legal transaction (*Rechtsgeschäft*). In this case one speaks of a power of attorney (*Vollmacht*). A power of attorney can be cancelled at any time.

624   The basic requirements for agency are that the agent must have authorisation (*Vertretungsmacht*) and must act in the name of the person being represented. Agency only exists in the context of action in legal transactions. If the agent concludes a contract with a third party for his or her principal then the contract has immediate effect between the principal and the third party. If the agent acts under the impression of a material mistake, or fraudulent misrepresentation, or illegal threats (duress) the principal can rescind the contract (*Anfechtung*). On the other hand, knowledge of facts of which the agent was aware of or which the agent ought to have been aware will be attributed to the principal (§ 166 para. 1, 2nd alternative BGB). An agent must be distinguished from a person acting as a mere messenger. The agent makes a declaration of his or her own will on behalf of the principal; the messenger merely transmits the principal's declaration of will. Two important limitations on the agent's power aimed at avoiding conflicts of interest are contained in § 181 BGB: In principle the agent may not conclude a contract with him- or herself on behalf of the principal. The agent may also not simultaneously represent two different parties who are to contract with one another. However, in many cases the agent can be authorised to ignore these rules.

625   A person authorised to act as an agent who does not make it sufficiently clear that he or she is acting as an agent for someone else will bind him- or herself rather than the principal by his or her declaration of will (§ 164 para. 2 BGB). If a person without authority to act as an agent purports to conclude a contract with a third party on behalf of a putative principal, then the putative principal may ratify the contract, which then acquires binding force between him or her and the third party. This situation is known as representation without authority (*Vertretung ohne Vertretungsmacht*, §§ 177-179 BGB). If the putative principal refuses to ratify the transaction, then the third party can choose between holding the agent to the contract and suing for damages.

11. Public Policy

626   Statutory provisions often involve legally binding evaluations of competing social interests. The law thus lays down rules for ordering life in a way which the law considers to be good and just. However, the legislator cannot foresee all possible constellations and know and take account of all possible interests and relationships. To make a just solution possible in such situations the positive law regularly contains provisions

which act as general clauses referring to external bases for value judgements such as morality, custom or public policy in a particular field.

The private law has such a general clause in § 138 para. 1 BGB. This provides that a legal transaction which is contrary to public policy is void. What exactly is meant by public policy can only be determined by an evaluative concretisation of the concept. The case authority takes as its starting point "the legal and moral instincts of all just and reasonable citizens[7]". It is thus a standard based on the social morality actually observed at the relevant time, not some pre-ordained moral code. However, of particular significance in this respect are the value judgements contained in the fundamental rights provisions of the constitution.

627

One the basis of § 138 para. 1 BGB various groups of cases have identified types of legal transactions which will, generally speaking, be contrary to public policy and thus void. Legal transactions will be contrary to public policy if the law disapproves of their content, for example, a contract in which one person promises another a reward for committing a crime. Surrogacy agreements, in terms of which one woman is to bear the child of another after implantation of a fertilised ovum from the first woman, are also considered to be contrary to public policy. The reasoning is that such an agreement reduces the child to being the object of a legal transaction, a mere commercial object. Unreasonable restraints of trade (*Knebelungsvertrag*) are also contrary to public policy. These are contracts in which the one party accepts severe restraints on his or her personal or economic freedom, for example, where a restaurant or pub obtains a loan from a brewer in exchange for a promise to sell only that brewer's products for the next thirty years.

628

§ 138 para. 2 BGB takes particular aim at transactions which involve undue exploitation of inequality of bargaining power (usury, undue influence, economic duress), referred to in German as *Wucher*. Specifically, this provision operates wherever the following requirements are fulfilled: 1) Somebody obtains a benefit, or the promise of some benefit, for him- or herself or for a third party, which is totally disproportionate to the consideration provided, and 2) The benefit or promise was obtained by exploiting the desperate situation, inexperience, lack of judgement or significant weakness of will of the other party. The courts have found that this provision is applicable, for example, in cases where the interest charged on a loan is 100 % higher than the current market rate. The current standard interest rates are published in monthly reports issued by the *Bundesbank*.

629

The first step in determining whether a legal transaction is contrary to public policy is to consider the values which underlie the entire legal system. For this reason too one must first check whether the transaction in question is expressly illegal in terms of some statutory provision. That in itself will suffice to make the transaction void in terms of § 134 BGB (See §§ 135, 136 BGB). Statutory prohibitions may be contained in any type of legal rule, including by-laws and subordinate legislation (*Verordnungen und Satzungen*). Examples are transactions involving the bribery of an official or illegal forms of gambling (§§ 334 para. 1, 284 para. 1 StGB). However, the aim of the provision must be to prevent the transaction from taking place at all. Mere irregularities in the way in which an otherwise legal transaction is carried out, for example,

630

---

7 BGHZ 52, 17/20; 69, 295/297; 141, 357/361.

where alcohol is served after closing time, will not be sufficient to make the transaction void.

12. Limitation of Actions (Prescription)

631   Rights of action, in other words, the right to demand something from another person, are generally subject to periods of limitation (§§ 194-218 BGB). Once the limitation period has elapsed the claim loses its force. This means that the person who previously had a legal obligation is still in principle under an obligation to perform, but can refuse performance indefinitely. The aim of these rules is to preserve legal certainty and avoid unnecessary disputes. Litigants must be barred from raising old claims whose genuineness has become difficult to test due to the passing of long periods of time so that everyone can rely on the existing factual situation as also representing the true legal situation.

632   In principle time begins to run at the end of the year in which the claim arose and the claimant became aware of the defendant's identity and the facts establishing the claim. Time will begin to run in the absence of such knowledge if the claimant would have discovered the relevant facts but for gross negligence (§ 199 para. 1 BGB). There are a number of exceptions to these rules. The standard period of limitation is three years (§ 195 BGB). Some types of claim only become time-barred after a period of thirty years. For example, the longer period applies in the case of claims for the return of property to its rightful owner, claims relating to inheritance and family law, and claims arising out of a court judgement (§§ 197, 199 para. 2 BGB). There are also other claims, such as for the transfer of ownership of a piece of land, to which a limitation period of ten years applies (§§ 196, 199 para. 3 and 4 BGB).

633   Once the period of limitation has elapsed, the person originally under an obligation can no longer be forced to perform (§ 214 BGB). However, if the person does perform, the person cannot claim his or her performance back later. Furthermore, the court will only take notice of the fact that the period of limitation has expired if the defendant specifically raises the point.

Literature:

Reinhard Bork, Allgemeiner Teil des Bürgerlichen Gesetzbuchs, 4. ed. 2016
Hans Brox/Wolf-Dietrich Walker, Allgemeiner Teil des Bürgerlichen Gesetzbuches, 42. ed. 2018
Christoph Hirsch, Der Allgemeine Teil des BGB, 11. ed. 2018
Helmut Köhler, BGB Allgemeiner Teil, 42. ed. 2018
Manfred Wolf/Jörg Neuner, Allgemeiner Teil des Bürgerlichen Rechts, 11. ed. 2016
Dieter Medicus/Jens Petersen, Allgemeiner Teil des BGB, 11. ed. 2016

III. The Law of Obligations

1. General Provisions of the Law of Obligations

a) Fundamental Principles

634   The law of obligations (*Schuldrecht*), as its name implies, regulates obligations, that is, debtor – creditor relationships. An obligation is a legal relationship in terms of which one person is entitled to demand some performance or some benefit (*Leistung*) from another person (§ 241 BGB). The person who owes performance is called the debtor (*Schuldner*). The person to whom performance is owed is called the creditor (*Gläubiger*). Legal obligations must be distinguished from mere social agreements.

These do not aim at the creation of legal rights: Someone who out of friendliness invites acquaintances to dinner is not legally obliged to provide them with a meal.

The basic provisions of the law of obligations are contained in the second book of the **635** Civil Code. Although it is not formally divided into two sections, for practical purposes this second book can be seen as consisting of a general part and a special part. The general part contains provisions which in principle apply to all obligations. The special part contains special rules for various particularly important types of obligation. Additional rules relating to legal obligations can be found scattered throughout the Civil Code. Furthermore, other statutes, such as the Product Liability Act (*Produkthaftungsgesetz*) contain specialised rules which are often aimed at regulating situations in which inequality of bargaining power is a problem. Some legislation, such as the Standard Form Contracts Act (*Gesetz zur Regelung des Rechts der allgemeinen Geschäftsbedingungen,* abbreviated AGBG) and the Consumer Credit Act (*Verbraucherkreditgesetz*) have been integrated into the Civil Code. The Commercial Code (*Handelsgesetzbuch,* abbreviated HGB) provides special rules regulating obligations between business people.

The very underlying presumptions of the law of obligations are a particularly clear in- **636** stance of the dynamic character of legal development in the private sphere. The rules of the law of obligations are generally optional (*dispositiv*), in other words, they only apply insofar as the parties to the obligation do not of their own free will stipulate otherwise. The parties can develop quite atypical contracts and conclude new types of agreement. This is an expression of the constitutionally guaranteed freedom of contract and of private autonomy. This legally approved factual flexibility of relationships has, amongst other things, had the consequence that many contracts which are of central commercial importance receive no mention in the law of obligations of the Civil Code. Examples are leasing, factoring, and franchising agreements. Nevertheless, the structural principles of the law of obligations in the Civil Code remain of decisive theoretical importance.

The law of obligations is distinguished from the law of things (property) (*Sachenrecht*) **637** which is regulated in the third book of the Civil Code. The law of things regulates the relationships between persons and things, in other words relationships such as ownership, possession and liens. Such rights in things are generally enforceable against the whole world. They are therefore called absolute rights. In contrast, the law of obligations involves relative rights. They are always only enforceable between specific individuals.

b) How Obligations Come Into Existence

Obligations may arise by way of a legal transaction (*Rechtsgeschäft*). This will usually **638** be a contract, but may also take the form of a unilateral legal transaction such as a legacy in a will.

Obligations also often have the law as their immediate source. The most important of **639** these statutory obligations are those arising out of tort (*unerlaubte Handlung, Delikt,* see especially §§ 823 ff. BGB). A person who wrongfully and culpably causes another person harm is generally obliged to pay damages as compensation for the resulting harm. A further statutory obligation is necessitated by the Abstraction Principle. This is the claim based on unjustified enrichment (§§ 812 ff. BGB): A person who has been enriched at the expense of another person without legal justification generally has an obligation to make restitution.

c) How Obligations End

640 An obligation is generally terminated by fulfilment. In terms of § 362 para. 1 BGB this is defined as the carrying out of the performance owed. However, some form of performance other than that which is owed may also extinguish the obligation if the creditor accepts it in lieu of the actual performance owed (*Leistung an Erfüllungs statt,* § 364 para. 1 BGB). Less dramatic in its effect is alternative performance directed towards the extinction of the obligation which, however, does not in itself terminate the obligation (*Leistung erfüllungshalber,* § 397 para. 2 BGB). In this case the intention is that the alternative performance should give the creditor the means to satisfy his or her claim, for example by selling goods which have been handed over when the obligation consists of a monetary debt. Until the creditor actually receives the money, the obligation and any rights of security remain in existence.

641 Occasionally the creditor refuses to accept performance of the obligation, although he or she has a duty to do so. This is known as *Gläubigerverzug* (*mora creditoris*). In such a case the debtor can fulfil his or her obligation by payment into court (*Hinterlegung*). This is achieved by payment to the appointed government officer. Its effect is to release the debtor from the duty to perform so long as the debtor does not reserve the right to reclaim the payment. Only certain objects such as money and negotiable instruments are capable of payment into court. Other objects of debt can be sold by public auction according to a special procedure and the sum raised can then be paid into court. Payment into court can only be used to discharge the debt if the debtor's inability to perform has in some way been caused by the creditor, for example, where the creditor has refused to co-operate in the debtor's attempts to perform, or where the debtor is not able to determine the identity of the creditor despite reasonable attempts to do so (§§ 372 ff. BGB).

642 Sometimes the debt can also be extinguished by set-off (*Aufrechnung*). For this to be possible there must be two claims which are capable of being set off against one another. Each party must be both the creditor and the debtor of the other. If one of them then declares that he or she is setting the two claims off against one another, then the two claims are extinguished to the extent that they are for the same amount (§§ 387 ff. BGB). Thus, if the one party has a claim for € 1 000 arising from the fact that he or she has sold a stereo system to the other, and the other in turn has a claim of € 500 arising from the fact that the stereo seller has broken the other party's window negligently, then the two claims can be set off against one another to the extent of € 500 and to that extent the two claims are extinguished.

643 If the creditor makes a contract with the debtor in which he or she agrees that his or her alleged claim is unfounded, or if the creditor discharges him or her from the debt by contract, then the debt is once again extinguished (§ 397 BGB).

644 The duty to perform an obligation may also be extinguished by rescission (*Rücktritt*, §§ 346-359 BGB). Rescission is the nullification of a debtor-creditor relationship by means of a declaration of will. The right of rescission is exercised by means of a declaration of will requiring receipt. The right to terminate an obligation in this way may arise from contract or from statutory provisions. Contractual obligations which have not yet been fulfilled need no longer be fulfilled in the case of justified rescission.

Restitution must be made insofar as the parties have already performed. The original obligation is transformed into an obligation to undo the transaction by making restitution (*Rückgewährschuldverhältnis*). In the event that something which has already been delivered in terms of the contract cannot be returned, for example, because it has been destroyed or has deteriorated, the issue of who bears the loss is regulated in detail in §§ 346, 347 BGB.

d) The Content of Obligations

aa) Good faith

The content of an obligation can, to a large extent, be determined by contract. However, since it is never possible to provide for all eventualities, and since one party often attempts to take unfair advantage of the other, § 242 BGB contains an extremely important provision: "The debtor is obliged to perform the obligation in accordance with good faith, with due regard to normal business practice." It is particularly this general provision, together with others such as § 138 BGB (which provides that transactions which are contrary to public policy are void) which opens the private law to the influence of the Fundamental Rights as fundamental value judgements (*wertentscheidende Grundsatznormen*). With due regard to the structures and rules of the private law, it is the Fundamental Rights which determine what good faith involves and what can be accorded recognition as normal business practice when the various affected legal interests are being weighed up and evaluated against each other.   645

The principle of good faith acts as a guideline in determining how an obligation is to be performed, in other words, what the main obligations arising from the contract should be considered to be. Furthermore, § 242 BGB also creates auxiliary duties. This means that the parties may be obliged to provide certain information, give warning of dangers, or act with due care. The main duty to perform may also undergo change in terms of § 242 if the basis of the transaction has been destroyed by a radical change in circumstances (*Wegfall der Geschäftsgrundlage*).   646

bb) Place of Performance

The debtor is obliged to perform at the right place; otherwise the debtor will not be discharged from his or her obligation. Which place is the right place depends on what the parties agreed in their contract. If there is no explicit agreement it will be determined from the circumstances of the legal relationship. Three different categories of obligation are distinguished on the basis of where performance is due. These are: Debts to be discharged at the debtor's address (*Holschuld*), debts to be discharged at the creditor's address (*Bringschuld*) and debt's to be discharged by sending the thing owed on its way to the creditor (*Schickschuld*). The significance of the distinction is that in each case the incidence of the risk is different and the debtor's obligations are discharged at a different point in time. In the case of the *Holschuld* the creditor is required to fetch the thing owed from the debtor. The debtor's duty is to stand ready to hand the goods over. The Code provides that this is the general rule (§ 269 BGB). In the case of the *Bringschuld* the debtor is obliged to bring the thing owed to the creditor. In the case of the *Schickschuld* the obligation is discharged by performance once the debtor has sent the thing owed to the creditor. The debtor is discharged from his or her obligation to perform as soon as the debtor has given the thing owed into the   647 hands of the person who is to deliver it, for example, the post office or the freighting company. Unless otherwise stipulated, debts in money are a *Schickschuld*, but the risk of loss remains with the debtor (§ 270 BGB). This means that if the money is lost under way the debtor must pay a second time. However, if the debtor has made payment in good time, for example, by paying the money into a bank account, and has made allowance for the time usually required for the completion of an electronic transfer, then the creditor must bear any loss which results from late arrival of the performance.

cc) Obligations to supply ascertained goods and obligations to supply unascertained goods

648 The law distinguishes between an obligation to supply ascertained goods (*Stückschuld*) and an obligation to supply unascertained goods identified by generic description (*Gattungsschuld*, see for both § 243 para. 1 BGB). *Stückschuld* thus describes the situation in which a specific, identified object is owed. In the case of *Gattungschuld* the debtor's obligation is to deliver objects belonging to a generically defined class, for example, potatoes. In such a case the goods actually delivered must be of at least average quality (merchantable quality, *mittlerer Art und Güte*). The so-called "own stock" obligation (*Vorratsschuld*) is an obligation to deliver goods by description (*Gattungsschuld*) but from a specific stock of such goods, for example, potatoes from the debtor's own stock. Once the debtor concretises the obligation by setting aside goods from his or her stock or from the generic class (*Konkretisierung, Aussonderung*), then from that point on the obligation only relates to the specific objects set aside (§ 243 para. 2 BGB).

dd) Liability for the actions of third parties (Vicarious liability)

649 Often the debtor does not perform the obligation in person, but instead makes use of a third person to perform the obligation for him or her. This option is open to the debtor so long as there is no express agreement to the contrary and so long as the surrounding circumstances do not give rise to an implied term to the contrary (§ 267 BGB). This third person is called an *Erfüllungsgehilfe*, that is, someone charged with the performance of an existing obligation. If the debtor chooses to make use of an *Erfüllungsgehilfe* then the debtor is liable for the wrongful acts of the *Erfüllungsgehilfe* just as if they were his or her own (§ 278 BGB). The relationship of the *Erfüllungsgehilfe* to the debtor is not necessarily one of social dependency. For example, he or she need not be an employee of the debtor. Thus, another firm acting as a sub-contractor may be the *Erfüllungsgehilfe*.

650 In contrast to this, the relationship of social dependency is a characteristic of the so-called *Verrichtungsgehilfe* described in § 831 BGB, that is, an employee acting in the course and scope of his or her duty. A debtor who employs somebody to discharge some function in this way will be liable in damages for any harm caused by the employee in breach of a duty of care while acting in the course and scope of his or her duties. This is an instance of pure tortious (delictual) liability which, in contrast to liability for the *Erfüllungsgehilfe*, is not dependent on the existence of a contractual relationship with the injured third party. On the other hand, the fact that there is some sort of contractual relationship between the injured party and the employer does not exclude the possibility of liability on the basis of tort. Both forms of liability may exist

side by side and may simultaneously give rise to two possible causes of action. However, there is a significant difference between liability for the *Erfüllungsgehilfe* under § 278 BGB and liability for the *Verrichtungsgehilfe* under § 831 BGB. In the case of liability in tort for the actions of the *Verrichtungsgehilfe,* the employer may raise as a defence the fact that the employee was chosen with due care and was subject to proper supervision. This defence is not available if a claim is based on (contractual) liability for the acts of the *Erfüllungsgehilfe* under § 278 BGB.

ee) Contracts for the Benefit of a Third Party

Third parties may also be involved in obligations in other ways. In some circumstances the creditor may wish performance to be made not to him- or herself, but to a third party. If the intention is that the third party should have a directly enforceable claim to performance against the debtor, then one speaks of a contract for the benefit of a third party (*Vertrag zugunsten Dritter,* §§ 328-335 BGB).   651

A contract with protective effect for third parties (*Vertrag mit Schutzwirkung für Dritte*) is a special case. In such contracts the primary contractual obligations are between the parties privy to the contract, but certain secondary obligations of one of the parties also operate in favour of third parties not privy to the contract. Examples are the duties of the landlord to act carefully and to provide information and warnings of danger to members of the tenant's family. Although they are not themselves parties to the contract, these persons have an independent right based on the lease to sue the landlord for damages if, for example, they suffer harm due to a negligent failure to maintain the staircase.   652

ff) Plurality of Creditors and Debtors

Often it is not merely one person but several who have a duty to perform a particular obligation. The position is relatively simple if several persons owe a divisible obligation (§ 420 BGB). In cases of doubt the debtors are then considered to be jointly liable to the creditor, that is, each is liable only for an equal proportion of the debt. Similarly, where there are joint creditors each can only sue for a share of the debt equal to the share of each of the others.   653

On the other hand, the debtors are said to be jointly and severally liable where several persons owe performance in such a way that each of them has accepted liability to perform the whole obligation but the creditor is only entitled to demand performance once (*Gesamtschuld,* § 421 BGB). In such a case the creditor has a free discretion in deciding against which debtor he or she wishes to enforce the claim. Whichever of the debtors he or she chooses is obliged to perform the whole obligation. Once this debtor has performed all the other debtors are also freed of their obligations to the creditor. However, unless otherwise provided, the debtor who discharged the obligation will then have a right of recourse against all the other debtors, i.e., the debtor who performed the joint and several obligation can demand reimbursement of their shares of the debt (§ 426 BGB).   654

gg) Assignment and novation

Unless otherwise provided, the debtor has a duty to perform in person, that is, the debtor must bear the responsibility for the discharge of the obligation him- or herself.   655

Substituting someone else for the original debtor is only permissible with the permission of the creditor because the creditworthiness of the particular debtor is usually material to the creditor (*Gesamtschuld*, § 415 BGB). In contrast to this, a substitution of one creditor with another is possible without further ado (§ 414 BGB): all that is required is a contract between the old and the new creditor in terms of which the claim is transferred to the new creditor (*Abtretung*, § 398 BGB). However, if the debtor makes performance to the original creditor because the debtor has not been notified of the cession the debtor will also be discharged from any obligation to the new creditor (§ 407 BGB). The new creditor must then recover the debt from the original creditor.

hh) Damages

656 A person liable in damages (*Schadensersatz*) must restore the state of affairs which would have existed had the circumstances giving rise to the obligation to make compensation not come about (§ 249 BGB). The essential idea is thus that there should be restitution in kind (*Naturalrestitution*) so as to restore the prior situation. If this is not possible, or if the debtor does not perform in good time, then appropriate compensation in money takes its place. The damage which is to be made good includes any loss of profits which might have been suffered.

657 According to the Code, compensation in money can only be demanded for pecuniary loss, in other words for material damage. Immaterial harm such as damage to reputation or loss of enjoyment of life cannot usually be replaced by an award of money in terms of § 253 BGB. The injured party is essentially limited to restitution in kind. For example, in the case of defamatory statements the proper remedy is a retraction by the offender. Only in the case of liability in tort under § 847 BGB does the Code provide for damages for pain and suffering in the event of infringements of physical integrity, health and freedom. However, contrary to the wording of § 253 BGB, the courts have also allowed damages in money for certain types of immaterial damage, particularly damage to reputation and loss of enjoyment of life in a significant range of cases.[8]

658 The aim of this is to provide the injured party with reasonable compensation in money for the loss of well-being which he or she has suffered. These damages for pain and suffering (*Schmerzensgeld*) form an independent cause of action alongside the claim for damages for pecuniary loss. Tables giving an overview of amounts awarded on previous occasions provide assistance in the calculation of the amount which should be awarded. For example, a lump sum of € 375 000 plus a monthly pension of € 750 was considered an appropriate amount of compensation for the pain and suffering of a forty-eight year old man who was so severely injured in an accident that he was reduced to the most primitive forms of existence. In another case € 250 000 plus a monthly pension of € 200 was considered an appropriate award where someone had completely lost the sight of both eyes as well as his senses of smell and taste and suffered from a walking impairment due to a car accident. From these examples it can be seen that the damages awarded by German courts do not come anywhere near the amounts often awarded in the United States of America.

659 The Code makes no mention of damages for the infringement of general rights of personality (*Allgemeines Persönlichkeitsrecht*). The legislature of 1896 felt it improper to compensate injuries to a person's honour with sums of money. In more recent times

---

8 See BGHZ 26, 349; 35, 363; 39, 124; BVerfGE 34, 269.

the courts have come to the conclusion that the guarantee of the general rights of personality in articles 1 and 2 of the constitution (*Grundgesetz*) require the award of damages for pain and suffering in such cases too, and such awards are therefore made, contrary to the express wording of § 253 BGB. A famous case on this point is the Soraya judgement of the Federal Constitutional Court. A tabloid published a fictitious interview with the Persian Empress Soraya in which various scandalous admissions concerning her private life were freely invented. She succeeded in a claim for damages against the publishers.[9]

The injured party is often insured against the harm in question or, as an employee, profits from the right to continued full payment of wages in case of illness. The injured person him- or herself has then in fact suffered no harm. On the one hand it would be unjust if the wrongdoer were to escape the consequences of his or her act. On the other hand the injured party should not receive double compensation by claiming both from the wrongdoer and his or her insurance. In such cases there is said to be normative damage; generally speaking the claim to damages will then pass to the insurer or the employer (subrogation).   660

ii) Causation

The wrongdoer is only liable to provide compensation for such harm as was caused by his or her behaviour. There must therefore be a causal connection between the wrongdoer's act and the harm which has occurred. To prevent the imposition of liability even for consequences which were completely unforeseeable, a test of remoteness of damage (legal causation) is applied in private law (*Adäquanztheorie*). This means that there must be an adequate causal connection between the infringement of the right and the harm. The wrongdoer is not liable for highly unusual consequences of his or her act. The following test was already formulated by the *Reichsgericht*, the forerunner of the *Bundesgerichtshof*: The wrongdoer will only be held liable for harm if the situation created by him or her would in the normal course of events be conducive to the occurrence of such harm. The wrongdoer will not be held liable for harm if it was only likely to arise from his or her acts in particularly unusual or highly unlikely circumstances which in the normal course of things need not be taken into account.[10] To give a standard text-book example, if a defendant has injured the claimant in a motor accident in breach of a duty of care he or she will be liable for the medical expenses arising from the primary injuries as well as the expenses arising from an infection to which the claimant succumbs while in hospital. However, the wrongdoer will not be liable for the loss of the claimant's wallet if it is stolen by a hospital employee during the hospital stay.   661

jj) Contributory Negligence

Normally the wrongdoer must make good all the damage which his or her act has caused. However, the claimant him- or herself often does something to aggravate the damage. For example, the injured person does not go promptly to the doctor after an accident and as a result the injury becomes more severe than it otherwise would have been; or the claimant fails to warn the wrongdoer of a hidden danger of unusually se-   662

---

9 BVerfGE 34, 296; see also BGHZ 26, 349, (Gentleman-rider case); BGHZ 35, 363, (Ginseng roots case); BGHZ 131, 332 (Caroline of Monaco).
10 RGZ 133, 126.

vere harm. In such a case the injured party must bear some of the harm him- or herself since by his or her contributory negligence the injured party helped to cause it (§ 254 BGB).

e) Irregularities in the Performance of a Contract (Mistake, Breach and Frustration)

663   One speaks of irregularities in the performance of a contract (*Leistungsstörungen*) when for some reason the contract is not performed in accordance with its terms. If the debtor fails to meet an obligation (*Pflichtverletzung*) then the creditor can claim compensation for the resulting loss on the basis of § 280 BGB.

664   The term *Pflichtverletzung* used in § 280 para. 1 BGB therefore is the generic term for all irregularities in the performance of contracts. § 280 para. 1 BGB sets common pre-requisites for damages stemming from all forms of irregularity caused by a *Pflichtverletzung*. Additional conditions for damages arise from the references in § 280 para. 2 and 3 BGB depending on the *Pflichtverletzung* in the particular case.

aa) Impossibility of Performance (Frustration, and Certain Forms of Mistake and Breach)

665   The German concept of impossibility (*Unmöglichkeit*) cuts across various categories of English thinking such as mistake, frustration and breach. Impossibility covers those situations in which the debtor is unable to perform his or her obligations. In this category various groups of cases must be distinguished, since they sometimes lead to different legal consequences. The situation is described as one of objective impossibility (*objektive Unmöglichkeit*) if it would be impossible for anyone at all to make performance. Subjective impossibility (*subjektive Unmöglichkeit*) means that the particular debtor is not in a position to perform, although performance is objectively possible, a situation which often occurs in the context of contracts to supply unascertained goods which have been defined generically. Initial impossibility (*anfängliche Unmöglichkeit*, mistake, breach) is the situation where performance was already impossible at the time when the obligation arose. If performance only becomes impossible after conclusion of the contract, then one speaks of subsequent impossibility (*nachträgliche Unmöglichkeit*, frustration, breach).

666   If the performance owed is impossible from the beginning (*objektive anfängliche Unmöglichkeit*) then the contract remains valid (§ 311 a para. 1 BGB). However, neither party can claim performance of the contract. The creditor can claim one of the following remedies: damages in place of performance (expectation loss), or the creditor can claim compensation for any expenses which he or she has incurred (reliance loss, §§ 311 a para. 2, 284 BGB). The consequences of subsequent impossibility (*nachträgliche Unmöglichkeit*) are determined by considering whose fault it was that performance became impossible. It is irrelevant whether the inability to perform is subjective or objective (§§ 275 para. 1, 280 BGB). If the subsequent impossibility is not due to the fault of the debtor then the debtor is discharged from his or her obligation to perform (§ 275 para. 1 BGB). On the other hand, if it is the debtor's fault that the contract has become impossible to perform subsequent to its conclusion then the debtor will be liable to pay damages to the creditor in lieu of performance.

667   Additional provisions applying only to those contracts which impose obligations on both parties are contained in §§ 323-326 BGB. Such contracts oblige both parties to

fulfil primary obligations, in other words to performance and counter performance, as is the case in most contracts (but not all, since German law has no requirement of consideration). In these cases both parties are both creditor and debtor. This means that in the case of impossibility it is necessary not only to regulate the fate of the performance (this is already done in §§ 275, 311 a BGB) but also that of the counter-performance (§ 326 BGB).

In the case of initial impossibility (*anfängliche Unmöglichkeit*) the solution is once again simply provided by § 311 a BGB in terms of which the contract remains valid. The debtor is, however, discharged from his or her obligation to perform, and also loses his or her right to claim counter-performance (§§ 275 para. 1, 326 para. 1 BGB). In the case of subsequent impossibility (*nachträgliche Unmöglichkeit*) which is not the fault of either of the parties the debtor once again loses his or her claim to counter-performance (§ 326 para. 1 BGB). The reason for this rule is obvious: in terms of § 275 BGB the debtor has also been discharged from his or her duty to perform. However, if the debtor has received some substitute or some claim to a substitute for the thing owed, the creditor can demand delivery of the substitute in place of the performance which was originally owed subject to the condition that the creditor then remains bound to perform (§ 326 para. 3 BGB).

668

If the impossibility is due to the fault of the creditor, then the debtor is discharged from his or her obligations but is still entitled to demand performance from the creditor (§ 326 para. 2 BGB). However, any expense which the debtor saved by his or her discharge, or which the debtor would have saved had he or she not acted maliciously, will be deducted from the damages. For example, if the debtor could have used the time saved to conclude and perform some other contract, the profits the debtor did or could have made in that way will be deducted from his or her claim.

669

If the impossibility is the fault of the debtor the creditor has several courses of action open to him or her (§§ 275 para. 4, 283, 326 para. 5 BGB). The debtor can withdraw from the contract or claim damages in lieu of performance, or, if the debtor has received a substitute for the object of the transaction, the creditor can instead choose to demand that any substitute be delivered or that any claim to a substitute be ceded to him or her.

670

bb) Failure to Perform Within the Prescribed Time (Mora)

The debtor is liable not only to perform, but to perform in good time, that is, within the time limits defined in the contract or by other means. If the debtor does not do this he commits a *Pflichtverletzung*; he is in breach (*Schuldnerverzug, mora debitoris*). The requirements for this sort of breach are satisfied if performance is due and it has not been made due to the fault of the debtor. Furthermore, to put the debtor in default (*mora*), the creditor must have given the debtor a letter of demand (*Mahnung*) demanding performance, unless the date for performance had been fixed from the beginning (§§ 286 ff. BGB). In the case of claims for a sum of money, the requirement that a formal demand be made falls away. In such a case the debtor is automatically in default if thirty days have passed since the debt became due and payable and an account or similar demand for payment has been delivered (§ 286 para. 3). As a rule the debtor will then be liable for any loss incurred by the creditor due to the delay. Once the date for performance has passed the liability of the debtor for any loss becomes wider. The debtor is liable then not only for any loss caused by even the slightest negligence on his

671

or her part, but also for loss resulting from the frustration of the contract due to the fault of neither party. An exception to this is that the debtor will not be liable for loss arising from frustration if that loss would have occurred even if the debtor had performed in due time. If the debt owed was a money debt, then the debtor is liable for interest on the amount owed at a rate of at least 5 % above the basic rate of interest which is fixed by the Deutsche Bundesbank. If the debtor's failure to pay compelled the creditor to take out a loan, then the debtor will be liable instead for any such higher interest rate as may have been charged for that loan (§ 288 BGB).

672 The creditor may also be in *mora* (*Verzug*), that is the creditor may be guilty of failing to co-operate (§§ 293 ff. BGB). If the debtor tenders performance as owed, the creditor is obliged to accept it. If the creditor refuses to accept performance, for example, because the creditor has received a more favourable offer in the interim, the creditor will be in breach (*Annahmeverzug, mora creditoris*). The same applies if the debtor tenders performance and the creditor does not make counter-performance. During *mora creditoris* the liability of the debtor for any loss which occurs is reduced. The debtor is then only liable for loss caused by his or her deliberate or grossly negligent conduct.

cc) Pre-Contractual Liability (Culpa in Contrahendo)

673 Even before a contract is concluded, the parties have obligations, a violation of which can lead to damages. The violation of these statutorily created pre-contractual legal obligations stemming from §§ 311 para. 2, 241 para. 2 BGB leads to liability. It is still known as *culpa in contrahendo*.

Literature:

Hans Brox/Wolf-Dietrich Walker, Allgemeines Schuldrecht, 43. ed. 2019
Christoph Hirsch, Allgemeines Schuldrecht, 11. ed. 2018
Dirk Looschelders, Schuldrecht Allgemeiner Teil, 16. ed. 2018
Dieter Medicus/Stephan Lorenz, Schuldrecht I. Allgemeiner Teil, 21. ed. 2015
Hans Peter Westermann/Peter Bydlinski/Ralph Weber, BGB Schuldrecht, Allgemeiner Teil, 8. ed. 2014
Rainer Wörlen/Karin Metzler-Müller, Schuldrecht AT, 13. ed. 2018

2. The Law of Obligations – Special Obligations

a) Contracts Expressly Regulated by the Code

aa) Fundamental Principles

674 The Civil Code has provided special rules for certain typical types of contract. These rules were formulated on the basis of value judgements which, in the view of the lawgiver, would be most likely to produce a just balance between the legitimate interests of both parties. To a very large extent these rules are at the disposition of the parties (*dispositives Recht*), that is, they apply only insofar as the parties to the contract do not make provision to the contrary. This means that in practice one often encounters hybrid contracts which combine elements of various different standard contracts, such as a contract which combines elements of sale and lease, or of sale and employment. In addition, many new types of contract have been invented since the Civil Code came into force in 1900. As yet the rules relating to such contracts have not been subjected to comprehensive codification. Here too the whole of the law of contract is subject to the principle of private autonomy entrenched in the constitution.

Nevertheless, one of the distinguishing characteristics of the more recent legal develop- 675
ments in Germany is that the principle of private autonomy is limited to an ever increasing extent in the interest of society as a whole. By now there are a large number
of mandatory provisions which have as their aim the protection of weaker elements in
the population. Generally speaking, divergences from these rules are only allowed insofar as they provide even stronger protection to the weaker party. Agreements to the
contrary are void even if both parties consented. The Civil Code itself was originally
based on a liberal, *laissez faire* approach to legal transactions. This approach starts
from the assumption that all legal subjects are equal, not only in law, but also in social
power and legal skills. Every person was seen as being sufficiently capable, competent
and responsible to watch out for his or her own interests when entering legal transactions. The Civil Code only recognised an exceptional need for protection in the case of
minors and mentally incapacitated persons.

Today the private law takes a different view. Numerous special statutes and individual 676
provisions modify the general provisions of the Civil Code so as to protect those who,
in the opinion of the legislature, are in particular need of legal protection. Examples
are the provisions for the protection of tenants, the protection of employees against
termination of employment, special rules relating to consumer credit agreements, provision for a period of reflection and a right of cancellation applying to door-to-door
salesmen who apply high-pressure sales tactics, and the law on standard-form contracts, which outlaws certain unfair terms. Further protection is afforded by the courts
using general clauses in the Code. For example, in cases where a business has a dominant market share and is of importance for everyday life the courts will impose on it
an obligation to contract with anyone who wishes to do so because of its monopolistic
position (§ 826 BGB). However, these modifications can only be properly understood
against the background of the basic original contracts.

bb) Special Rules Protecting Private Consumers

There are many different rules that can be summarised as protecting private con- 677
sumers. They serve an important overall function.

They are among the many new provisions which have departed from the original *lais-* 678
sez faire attitude of the Civil Code and replaced it with a different concept of the individual and society. In this view equality of ability among individuals is no longer assumed to be the norm. Instead it is considered necessary to make some attempt to
equalise the uneven power relationships in society, protecting the weaker members of
society against exploitation by the stronger. This approach does not assume social
equality, it sets out to create it.

These rules modify the general rules in those statutorily defined circumstances, in 679
which a consumer and an entrepreneur (§§ 13, 14 BGB) contract. They serve the special protection of the consumer, who is usually less experienced in commercial matters
and therefore needs to be strengthened in order to ensure parity of contracts.

§ 13 BGB defines a consumer as every natural person who enters into a legal transac- 680
tion for a purpose that is outside his or her trade, business or profession.

According to § 14 BGB an entrepreneur is a natural or legal person or a partnership 681
with legal personality who or which, when entering into a legal transaction, acts in exercise of his, her or its trade, business or profession.

682 Important rules realted to consumer contracts (§ 310 para. 3 BGB), which usually result from European Union regulations in the field of consumer protection, can, for example, be found in §§ 312-312 k, 355 BGB (*außerhalb von Geschäftsräumen abgeschlossene Verträge und Fernabsatzverträge*, so-called contracts concluded away from business premises and distance contracts), §§ 358, 491-515 BGB (*Verbraucherkredit- und ähnliche Geschäfte*, consumer loans and similar transactions), §§ 474 ff. BGB (*Verbrauchsgüterkauf*, purchase of consumer goods), but also in the rules governing the validity of standard contracts, which contain special reasons for invalidation (§§ 308 ff. BGB).

683 The rules often obligate the entrepreneur to provide the consumer with all relevant information (§§ 312 d para. 1, 477 para. 1, 491 a para. 1, 493 para. 1 BGB) and give the consumer special rights of revocation and return (§§ 312, 312 g, 485, 495 BGB).

684 For example, one well-known right of revocation is contained in the rules governing the revocation of contracts negotiated away from business premises (§§ 312b ff. BGB). In practice, this is particularly relevant to the sale of household appliances and subscriptions to publications on a door-to-door basis. However, the act also affects so-called free-lunch joyrides, that is, organised trips, usually aimed at elderly people, during which the organiser attempts to sell something to the participants.

685 Within the last couple of years distance contracts, especially the online trade, have gained considerable economic importance. A distance contract is a contract about the delivery of goods or about services which has been concluded between a business and a consumer exclusively using means of distant communication unless this happens outside of a selling or service system established for the purpose of distance transactions. The consumer who has concluded such a contract usually has a right of revocation (§ 312g para. 1, 355 BGB).

686 These and similar modifications to the general contractual rules always apply when an entrepreneur and a consumer contract.

cc) The Contract of Sale

687 The Civil Code places the contract of sale (*Kaufvertrag*) at the start of its catalogue of specially regulated contracts (§§ 433-507 BGB). This is also practically the most important contract in modern commercial society. The objects of a contract of sale may be either things or rights, insofar as these are susceptible to being transferred. But other transferable goods can also be bought and sold even if they are neither rights nor things, for example, electricity, or a business as a going concern. The seller must deliver the thing bought to the buyer free of physical or legal defects, and also transfer ownership of it to him or her. In the event that a right is being bought and sold the seller must transfer the right to the buyer (§ 453 BGB), and if the right entitles the holder to possession of a thing, the seller must hand that thing over. The buyer, in turn, has a duty to pay the purchase price on which they have agreed and receive delivery of the object of the sale (§ 433 para. 2 BGB).

688 A sale is thus in essence the exchange of a thing or a right for money. If one thing is exchanged for another, or if a right is exchanged for a right, then it is a case of barter (*Tauschvertrag*). § 480 BGB provides that the rules for contracts of sale are to be applied, where appropriate, to contracts of barter as well.

The statutory definition also gives clear expression to the principle of abstraction (*Abstraktionsprinzip*) and of separation (*Trennungsprinzip*). The conclusion of a valid contract of sale does not cause ownership to pass. There is no automatic change in position from the point of view of the law of property. The contract of sale is merely the causal transaction. It does no more than create an obligation to transfer ownership in the property. Vice versa, if ownership has already been transferred pursuant to a contract of sale which proves to be void, then an obligation exists to re-transfer ownership to the original owner in terms of the law of unjustified enrichment (restitution, §§ 812 ff. BGB). In other words, there is no necessary relationship between the passing of ownership and the validity of the contract of sale. 689

As a general rule a contract of sale is valid without complying with any formal requirements. Only in a limited number of cases is execution by notarial deed (*Notarielle Beurkundung*) necessary. These are: the purchase and sale of land (§ 311 b para. 1 BGB); the purchase of an inheritance (§ 2371 BGB); and contracts between future statutory heirs concerning the statutory right of inheritance by intestate succession or the monetary compensation owed to disinherited heirs (§ 311 b para. 5 sentence 2 BGB). 690

The seller has the obligation to transfer the object of the sale to the buyer free of any claims of third parties. The seller of a right guarantees the existence of the right, but does not bear responsibility if it in fact cannot be enforced (§§ 435, 453, 433 BGB). If the seller does not fulfil these obligations then the buyer has the right to resort to the general remedies applicable to bilateral transactions set out in §§ 320-326 BGB. 691

The seller is liable for any defects (*Mängel*) in the thing sold, i.e., for the fact that it is not of merchantable quality, if these defects were present at the time of the passing of the risk and if they are not completely insignificant. There is a defect if the quality of the thing sold deviates to the disadvantage of the buyer from the quality agreed upon. The seller is also liable in principle for any publicly proclaimed qualities of the thing. These are cases of strict liability (§ 434 BGB). Determining when the risk passes is thus particularly important. § 446 BGB provides that as a general rule the risk passes when the object of the transaction is handed over to the buyer. The buyer then has no further rights against the seller if by chance the object of the transaction should perish or deteriorate and in such a case he or she will nevertheless be liable to the seller for the purchase price. Until the goods are delivered the seller bears this risk. If the parties have agreed that the seller is to send the goods to the buyer at some place other than where the performance of the contract would usually be completed (*Erfüllungsort*) then the risk passes as soon as the seller has handed the goods over to the carrier (§ 447 BGB). However, sales of consumer goods are not governed by § 474 para 2 BGB. A sale is a sale of consumer goods if a consumer (§ 13 BGB) buys moveable goods from an entrepreneur (§ 14 BGB). In this case the risk only passes once the goods have been delivered to the buyer. 692

Insofar as the seller is liable for the fact that the goods are defective (not of merchantable quality), the buyer has a number of possible remedies. The buyer first has to continue to insist on performance after the breach has occurred (*Nacherfüllung*) by demanding that the thing be repaired or that an alternative be delivered. The buyer can rescind the contract if his or her second demand for performance has been without effect (§§ 440, 323, 326 BGB). Alternatively the buyer can also demand that the price for which the goods were sold be reduced to the extent that the defects in the goods 693 diminish their value (*Minderung*, § 441 BGB). Where a defect is due to the fault of the seller the buyer will also have a claim for damages on the basis of §§ 280, 281, 283, 284, 311 a BGB. General claims about the goods such as is regularly found in catalogues and prospectuses, in other words in advertisements, will in principle also give rise to liability on the part of the seller (§ 434 para 1 sentence 3 BGB).

694   Of the numerous forms which the contract of sale may take, the agreement to sell, that is, a conditional sale under reservation of ownership (*Kauf unter Eigentumsvorbehalt*, § 449 BGB), is a particularly common form. Usually both parties must be prepared to perform simultaneously (*Zug um Zug*). However, in sales involving large amounts of money the buyer is often unable to pay the whole amount at once, and instead receives the goods from the seller on credit. They often agree that the purchase price is to be paid off in instalments. A frequent term of such contracts is that ownership of the goods in question should only pass on the payment of the last instalment even although the buyer has been given possession of the goods beforehand. The buyer then has a transferable contingent right to the goods (*Anwartschaftsrecht*). On payment of the last instalment the buyer automatically becomes the owner of the goods. If the buyer does not make the payments in accordance with the terms of the agreement then the seller may rescind the contract and demand the return of the subject matter.

dd) Contract of Donation

695   A donation (*Schenkung*) is also a bilateral contract. In such a contract the one party binds him- or herself to enrich the other party out of his or her estate without receiving any consideration in return (§ 516 para. 1 BGB) (Consideration is not a requirement for a valid contract in German law). Things may be donated, as may claims or other rights. Releasing a debtor from an unpaid debt is thus also classified as a donation.

696   To be enforceable, the offer (in contrast to the acceptance of it) must be made by way of notarial deed (*notarielle Beurkundung*). However, even if the promise was not made in this form it will become binding as soon as it has been performed, i.e., performance heals the formal defect (§ 518 BGB). A promise of donation which is made subject to the condition that the donee outlive the donor is called a donation in contemplation of death (donation *causa mortis, Schenkung von Todes wegen*, § 2301 BGB). Such donations are subject to the formal requirements of the law of succession.

697   Generally speaking the donor is not liable for any defect in the thing donated or his or her legal title to it. However, if the donor has maliciously concealed such a defect, with the result that the donee suffers some loss, then the donor will be liable to pay damages (§§ 523, 524 BGB).

698   The donation can be rescinded on the basis that the donee has shown gross ingratitude by committing some grave wrong against the donor or a close relative of the donor (§ 530 BGB). If the donor becomes unable to support herself, she is generally released from her promise and may demand the return of the thing given (§§ 528, 529 BGB).

699   Since donations are defined by the fact that no consideration is given in return for them, neither the Christmas bonus given by an employer nor the tip given to a waiter are donations. Both of these are given in consideration of services rendered.

ee) Contracts of Lease, Hire, Loan and Loan for Consumption

Lease and hire (both *Miete* in German) involve giving the use of a thing in exchange   700
for payment. The contract of *Pacht*, in contrast, includes not only the right to use a
thing, but also the right to appropriate its fruits. For example, the *Pacht* of a farm will
also include the right to sell the pigs once they have been fattened for market or to sell
timber cut in the farm's plantation. In contrast to a lease (*Miete*), *Pacht* can also apply
to a right or to a whole business as a going concern.

The conferment of a right to use a thing without payment or other consideration con-   701
stitutes a contract of loan (*Leihe*, §§ 598 ff. BGB). The colloquial use of the word *lei-*
hen for a "loan" of money or vehicles on a commercial basis is usually technically incorrect. Such a contract will be a *Darlehen* (§§ 488 ff., see also §§ 607 ff. BGB; explained below) in the case of money or other fungibles, or a contract of lease or hire
(*Miete*) in the case of things such as cars or boats to the extent that a payment is made
in consideration for the use of the thing. In determining the legal consequences of a
particular agreement it is the actual content of the contract, not the name given to it,
which is decisive.

The *Darlehen* contract, like *Miete*, *Pacht* and *Leihe*, involves giving the use of some-   702
thing. Here the receiver of the *Darlehen* receives money or other fungibles for his or
her use and consumption. At the end of the contract period the receiver's obligation is
not to give back exactly what the receiver received. It is to give back articles of the
same type, quality and quantity as he or she received. The *Darlehen* for consideration,
that is, a loan of money in exchange for the payment of interest, is of supreme importance in commercial life. Such contracts are the main field of application for the provisions against unconscionable or usurious contracts *(Wucher)*, in particular § 138 BGB.

Returning to the contract of lease or hire *(Miete)*, the obligation of the lessor is to give   703
the lessee the use of the thing rented for the duration of the contract. The lessee's obligation is to pay the agreed rent (§ 535 BGB). Generally speaking there are no formal
requirements.

The lessor has an obligation to keep the rented property in good repair (*gebrauchs-*   704
fähiger Zustand). If the lessor fails to do so, then the lessee is entitled to make a pro-
portionate deduction from the rent (§§ 536, 537 BGB). In cases involving residential
property the courts have declared substantial deductions of this sort to be legitimate. If
the lessor does not take steps to repair defects within a reasonable time the lessee will
have a claim for damages. In some cases the lessee even has the right to terminate the
lease without notice. In practice the parties often agree that the lessee is to undertake
so-called cosmetic renovations at his or her own expense, for example, painting the
walls and doors on a regular basis. However, in recent years court practice has limited
these duties considerably in favour of the lessee.

Particularly where the lease is for residential property the law gives comprehensive   705
protection to the tenant. Since the demand for cheap accommodation exceeds the supply and since the great majority of people in Germany live in rented accommodation,
the legislature deemed it necessary to intervene heavily in the parties' freedom of contract in this field. This is justified by reference to the principle that Germany is a social
state (*Sozialstaat*), which is entrenched in the constitution. The frequency with which
the rent may be increased is regulated and the amount of increase can be limited. The
length of the period of notice which must be given by the landlord is essentially deter-

mined by the length of time for which the lease has run; for the lessee it always is three months (§ 573 c BGB). The landlord may also only terminate the lease for a limited number of reasons set out in the Code (§§ 573 ff. BGB). An example of an acceptable reason for termination by the landlord is if the tenant is guilty of serious breaches of the lease, for example, repeatedly paying the rent late or not at all, or giving the use of the property to some third person contrary to the terms of the contract. The landlord may also terminate the lease on the grounds that the residence is needed for his or her own use or that of a family member or other member of the landlord's household. The court must be convinced that this justification is well substantiated. In terms of the social clause of § 574 BGB, a tenant can reject the termination of the lease in cases where it would cause special hardship and can demand that the lease be continued for a reasonable period, having due regard to all the circumstances including the justifiable interests of the landlord. However, a case is already accepted as being one of special hardship if suitable alternative accommodation providing reasonable conditions cannot be obtained.

706   The sale of the unit of accommodation or of the land also does not terminate an existing lease. Instead the new owner steps into the shoes of the old landlord. The basic principle is: lease takes precedence over sale (§ 566 BGB). When the object of the contract of lease or hire is moveable property the lessee will be entitled to raise all defences against the new owner which he or she could have raised against the old owner, particularly defences arising from the contract of hire. This means that generally speaking it will not be possible to force the lessee to return the hired property.

707   A particular form of lease (*Miete*) which is not regulated in the Civil Code is a leasing agreement (also called *Leasing* in German). Here the lessor (*Leasinggeber*) places goods at the disposal of the lessee (*Leasingnehmer*) for his or her use in exchange for rental (*Leasingraten*). The lessee obtains all rights against third parties which the lessor has with respect to the thing leased. The lessee is liable for servicing and repairs and bears the risk if the thing leased is destroyed or damaged. Often the parties agree on a special payment at the start of the leasing agreement, and at the end of the leasing agreement the lessee has the option to buy the object of the agreement by making a further payment. This type of arrangement is often entered for tax reasons. The lessee has the advantage that the object leased is not taxed as capital of his or her business, and the payments are often deductible expenses. The lessee avoids the necessity of taking out a loan to buy expensive equipment. Finally, the lessee has the advantage of being able to react more quickly to new technological advances, not having committed a large sum of money to the old technology, in other words, the leasing agreement frees the lessee from some of the risk of predicting new innovations.

ff) The Contract of Service and the Contract for Specific Services

708   In a contract of service (*Dienstvertrag*) the employer promises to pay the employee and the employee promises to work for the employer (§ 611 BGB). The employee does not promise that his or her work will lead to the successful attainment of any particular goal, merely that he or she will work. The social significance of the contract of employment lies primarily in labour law (*Arbeitsrecht*) where it has been subjected to numerous modifications and been divided into different forms by specialised rules. The legal relationships between doctor and patient, legal adviser and client, occasional ba-

by-sitter and parents as well as between management level employees and a company also often fall under the heading of a contract of service.

To use its now outdated terminology, the service relationship required that the master should protect the interests of the servant (*Fürsorgepflicht*) and that the servant should be faithful to his or her master (§§ 617-619 BGB). The exact content of these duties varies according to how close the relationship between the parties is. The preferred approach today is to use more general terminology and to speak of a mutual duty of respect for the other parties' interests. These duties are of considerable significance in labour law and find expression, for example, in the prohibition on competing with one's employer. The violation of such duties can be a ground for the termination of employment and an action for damages.

709

While in a contract of service (*Dienstvertrag*) it is only service as such which is owed, in a contract for specific services (*Werkvertrag*) the aim of the contract is the performance of a particular job of work, in other words, the contract is directed toward the successful attainment of a particular objective. Examples are the restoration of a piece of antique furniture, the writing of an expert opinion, or the carrying of a passenger to a particular place. The contractor (*Werkvertragsunternehmer*) undertaking a contract for specific services may make use of the services of a third person (subcontractor) in performing his or her obligations. As in the case of the contract of sale, there is liability on the basis of an implied warranty for any defects in the work. As in the law of sale the person for whom the work is done has the additional remedy of being able to demand that the defect be improved subsequently (*Nachbesserungsanspruch*, §§ 633 ff. BGB).

710

If the contractor undertakes to produce a movable thing with materials to be provided by him- or herself, then the contract is a contract for the supply of goods and services (*Werklieferungsvertrag*, § 651 BGB). Here the transaction is essentially governed by the rules of the contract of sale because in practice the predominant element of the contract is the sale of the modified materials.

711

A practically important application of the contract for the provision of specific services is in the building industry. The person commissioning the project and the building contractor often agree to incorporate the Standard Building Contract terms (*Vergabe- und Vertragsordnung für Bauleistungen*, abbreviated VOB) in their agreement. This is a privately developed set of terms worked out and updated by a committee comprised of representatives of industrial and trade associations, government departments and other administrative officials.[11] It contains detailed rules for how a building operation should be carried out, the basis for calculating payment and the management of the legal relations between the parties.

712

gg) Other Types of Contract

Numerous other types of contract are expressly regulated by the Civil Code. These include mandates to act on someone's behalf without payment (*Auftrag*, §§ 662 ff. BGB), contracts to act as a managing agent (*Geschäftsbesorgung*, §§ 675 ff. BGB), deposit or bailment (*Verwahrung*, §§ 688 ff. BGB), brokerage agreement (*Maklervertrag*, §§ 652 ff. BGB), contract with a tour operator (*Reisevertrag*, §§ 651 a ff. BGB), composition agreement with creditors (*Vergleich*, § 779 BGB), admission of debt (*Schul-*

713

---

11 See *Ingenstau / Korbion / Leupertz / Wietersheim (Hrsg.)*, VOB Teile A und B, Kommentar, 19. Aufl. 2015.

danerkenntnis) and promissory note (*Schuldversprechen,* see for both §§ 780 ff. BGB), gaming and wagering (*Spiel und Wette,* §§ 762 ff. BGB), and *Auslobung,* a unilateral legal transaction which in German law is not classified as a contract but which in English law would be seen as a contract (§§ 657 ff. BGB). (Example: putting up a reward notice for the return of a lost dog. This is a completed legal transaction even if no-one responds to the notice.) All of these are of practical significance. In some cases they form the foundation for whole new fields of law. For example, the order to a third party to pay money or deliver fungible goods to the other contracting party (*Anweisung,* §§ 783 ff. BGB) and the provisions governing the issue of negotiable instruments (*Schuldverschreibung,* §§ 793 ff. BGB), which are the basis of the law of negotiable instruments (*Wertpapierrecht*).

714   In credit transactions the contract of suretyship (*Bürgschaft,* §§ 765 ff. BGB) plays an important role. Here the surety (guarantor) enters a contractual undertaking in which he or she makes a promise to the creditor of a third party to accept liability if the third party does not fulfil his or her obligations (§ 765 para. 1 BGB). The creditor can then sue the surety if the third party does not perform his or her obligations. A necessary precondition is that the obligation of the third party should in fact exist. The suretyship agreement must be in writing (§ 766 BGB). The aim of this provision is to protect the surety against making hasty promises. Generally speaking the surety will be able to raise all defences which would be available to the debtor him- or herself, for example, the defence that the creditor's claim is statute-barred by the statutory rules on periods of limitation (*Verjährung*). If the surety performs the obligation in place of the debtor, then the creditor's rights against the debtor pass to the surety by operation of law and the surety can then attempt to recover the amount from the debtor (§ 774 BGB).

b) Necessitous Intervention (Negotiorum Gestio)

715   Often one person acts on behalf of another despite the fact that there is no contractual relationship between them. For example, the good neighbour calls a plumber to repair a burst water pipe in the house of someone who is away on holiday, or an observant person walking on the beach rescues someone who is in danger of drowning. Such cases generally fall under the heading of necessitous intervention (*Geschäftsführung ohne Auftrag*). The issue here is: who has to pay the plumber, and who is liable to replace the ruined clothing of the rescuer?

716   Necessitous intervention gives rise to an obligation imposed by law. Its requirements and effects are set out in §§ 677 ff. BGB. A person who conducts business on behalf of another without having been authorised by the other person to do so and without having any other basis of authority (this person is called the *Geschäftsführer*) is obliged to conduct that business in accordance with the interests of the person on behalf of whom he or she is acting (called the *Geschäftsherr*) and with due regard to that persons actual or presumed wishes.

717   The basic requirement is that the conduct of the other person's business must be justified. This is the case if the conduct of the business in question is in the interests of the person assisted, with due regard to his or her actual or presumed wishes. The intervention may, however, be justified even if it is in fact not in accordance with the wishes of the person assisted. This is the case if an obligation of the person assisted, the fulfilment of which is in the public interest, would not have been carried out on time but for the intervention. The same applies if the intervention ensured that a duty of sup-

port which the law imposes on the person assisted was properly fulfilled (§ 679 BGB). Furthermore, the predominant view is that the intervention will also be justified if the contrary intention of the person assisted constitutes a violation of a statutory rule or is grossly immoral (i.e., is contrary to public policy). Finally, an intervention which in itself was not necessitous may be justified by the subsequent approval of the person in whose interests it was undertaken (§ 684 sentence 2 BGB).

If the situation in question constitutes a necessitous intervention, then the person intervening has certain obligations. He or she must conduct the business in accordance with the actual or presumed will of the person on behalf of whom he or she is acting. The person intervening must inform that person as possible of the steps he or she has taken, provide any relevant information and account for expenses incurred. The person intervening must render up any profits which he or she has derived from the conduct of the business. If the person intervening causes loss by his or her intervention he or she will be liable in accordance with the ordinary rules of the law of torts (delict). However, if the intervention was undertaken to save the other person from some imminent and serious danger then the person intervening will only be liable for harm caused by his or her deliberate or grossly negligent conduct (§ 680 BGB).   718

The other aspect of necessitous intervention is that the person on behalf of whom the intervention was undertaken must compensate the person intervening for the expenses she has incurred in the process. This includes compensation for harm which the person intervening has suffered as a consequence of the intervention.   719

Generally speaking the intervention will not be considered justifiable if it was contrary to the actual or presumed wishes of the person on behalf of whom it was undertaken and person intervening was in a position to have known this. In such a case the person intervening will be liable to the person on behalf of whom the intervention was undertaken for any harm resulting even if the harm was not due to any further fault on his or her part (§ 678 BGB). Anything which has been derived from the transaction must be restored on the basis of the provisions regulating unjustified enrichment (restitution, § 684 sentence 1 read with §§ 812 ff. BGB).   720

The person intervening may have had no intention whatsoever of acting on behalf of someone else. For example, this would be the case if the person intervening repairs a bicycle under the erroneous impression that it belongs to him or her, or when the person intervening knows perfectly well that it does not belong to him or her but sells it on his or her own account after stealing it. The person intervening then lacks the intention to intervene on behalf of another person (§ 687 BGB). These cases are not genuine instances of necessitous intervention. On the one hand such cases may involve the conduct of business on the actor's own behalf when he or she believes that the business is in fact his or her own. If so, the actor is liable to the person on behalf of whom the person intervening is in fact acting according to general principles of liability in tort (delict) and unjustified enrichment (restitution). On the other hand, if the person intervening is so presumptuous as to deliberately conduct the business of someone else as if it were his or her own, then the person on behalf of whom he or she is in fact acting will not only be able to sue on the basis of tort or restitution, but will have the additional option of claiming compensation from the person intervening as if it were a genuine case of necessitous intervention, that is, he or she will be able to claim damages as well as restitution of any benefits derived from the transaction. However, if he or she chooses this remedy he or she will be obliged to compensate the person inter-   721 vening for any expenses incurred, to the extent that these do not exceed the enrichment (§§ 687 para. 2 sentence 2, 684, 683 BGB).

c) Unjustified Enrichment (Restitution)

722   Because of the principle of separation (*Trennungsprinzip*) and the principle of abstraction (*Abstraktionsprinzip*) which is applied in German private law there is no necessary connection between an obligation entered with the intention of altering rights in a thing and the actual alteration of such rights. It is possible to obtain ownership of a thing although the underlying contract of sale is void. Another situation which may arise is that a person acting under a misapprehension may discharge a debt owed by somebody else, with the result that the actual debtor is discharged from his or her obligation to the creditor. It is necessary for the law to provide some mechanism to undo such unjustified transfers of wealth.

723   This purpose is served by the law on unjustified enrichment (restitution, *Bereicherungsrecht*). Its provisions are set out in §§ 812 ff. BGB. The idea underlying these provisions is that a person who obtains something in the absence of legal justification must return that thing to the person who is actually entitled to it. (Contrast the English concept of unjust enrichment, which requires a positive reason why the enrichment should be returned.) The claim of the person entitled to the thing is called a condiction (*Kondiktion*). There are two main types of condiction, the condiction applicable where a benefit has been obtained by the performance of the other party of an obligation which he or she erroneously believes is owed to the person enriched (*Leistungskondiktion*), and the condiction "by other means" (*Kondiktion in sonstiger Weise*). The basic principle of the law of unjustified enrichment is contained in § 812 para. 1 sentence 1 BGB: Any person who gains something from another, whether by some act of the other person or by any other means, without legal justification, and to the detriment of the other person, has an obligation to render up to the other person whatever he or she has gained.

724   The performance condiction (*Leistungskondiktion*) applies in essence when an unjustified transfer of wealth has taken place due to the performance of a putative obligation. Someone must have gained something without legal justification from the actions of another. For example, this is the case if someone pays the account for a book by electronic transfer, not knowing that his or her spouse has paid the debt in cash at the book shop a short while before. This second payment took place without legal justification, because the claim has been discharged by payment. The shop owner must therefore return the second payment. The requirement that the defendant must have gained something is satisfied whenever there has been any transfer of wealth which results in an increase in the defendant's wealth. For example, this may take the form of gaining some right, or gaining possession or the use of a thing, or obtaining the discharge of some obligation.

725   The requirement of some act of performance (*Leistung*) by the claimant is satisfied whenever the claimant has deliberately increased the wealth of some other person with a specific purpose in mind. This may take the form of the payment of a purchase price, or the transfer of ownership in property, or the cession of a claim, or simply the performance of some beneficial act, such as painting a house. However, in each case the claimant must be acting deliberately with the intention of transferring wealth to another person.

Finally, the act of performance must lack legal justification. This is the case if there is 726
no legal ground for the transfer of wealth, in other words, when the obligation which
the act of performance was intended to discharge in fact did not exist. One can thus
say that the act of performance was without legal justification if the person receiving
the performance had no legal right to do so. For example, this would be the case if,
after ownership in property has been transferred, it is discovered that the contract of
sale is void.

The enrichment action can, however, not be brought if the person making perfor- 727
mance knew at the time that he or she was not legally obliged to do so, or if the performance was in accordance with some moral obligation or with principles of public
policy (§ 814 BGB). An example of this sort is where someone contributes to the
maintenance of a relative whom he or she is not legally obliged to support.

Three other instances of the performance condition are treated in the same way as the 728
performance of a putative obligation. If the object, as defined in the legal transaction,
of making performance is not achieved, then once again the return of the wealth transferred can be demanded (§ 812 para. 1 sentence 2). An example of this is if someone
pays a sum of money to another person on the understanding that the other will then
make him or her his or her heir. Although a promise of this sort is not legally enforceable (§ 2302 BGB), the parties may nevertheless be in agreement that this is the object
to be achieved by the payment. If the person receiving the money then fails to make
the other his or her heir, the person who has made the payment is entitled to recover
it. However, according to § 815 BGB the enrichment action is not available in such circumstances if it was impossible from the very beginning to achieve the object of the
transaction and the person making the payment knew this. The same applies if the person making the payment frustrates the object of the transaction in bad faith.

A further instance of the performance condition is the subsequent invalidation of the 729
legal basis (*causa*) of the transaction. The Code provides (§ 812 para. 2 sentence 2, 1st
alternative BGB) that the obligation to retransfer whatever has been gained also exists
when the originally valid legal basis of an obligation falls away after the obligation has
been performed. A common example of this is the situation where an insurer compen-
sates the insured for the theft of his or her property and the insured subsequently recovers the stolen property. In such a case the insured has an obligation to return the
payments which the insurer has made to him or her.

Finally, the person enriched must give back what he or she has received if his or her 730
acceptance of the performance was illegal or contrary to public policy (*gute Sitten*,
§ 817 sentence 1 BGB). However, this action can only be brought if the person making
performance was not him- or herself acting illegally or contrary to public policy (§ 817
sentence 2 BGB).

The performance condition cannot be invoked if the claimant has not made any per- 731
formance. In such a case the condiction "by other means" (*Kondiktion in sonstiger
Weise*) may, however, be applicable (§ 812 para. 1 sentence 1, 2nd alternative BGB).[12]
This enrichment action takes three different forms. These are the "interference condiction", the "recourse condition" and the condiction for expenditure on improvements.

The interference condiction (*Eingriffskondiktion*) applies to those situations where the 732
enrichment occurs due to some intervening cause. This may take the form of interfer-

---

12   § 812 para. 1 sentence 1, second alternative BGB.

ence by a third party, but it may also be caused by a non-human agency. An example of this is when the person enriched has appropriated the property of someone else for his or her own use: A builder uses the bags of cement which have been delivered under the misapprehension that the cement used is that which he or she had ordered recently. Later it is discovered that the cement was actually the property of the person's neighbour who is also engaged in building operations.

733   The recourse condiction (*Rückgriffskondiktion*) is applicable when a third party performs the obligations of a debtor with the result that the debtor is discharged from his or her obligations to the creditor.

734   Finally, the condiction for expenditure on improvements (*Verwendungskondiktion*) is applicable when money has been spent on improving property belonging to another person: for example, if somebody repairs a chair in the erroneous belief that it belongs to him or her. Such claims are, however, often the subject of special rules, for example, §§ 994 ff. BGB which regulate such problems in the relationship between owner and possessor, and § 951 BGB in cases where two things have been united or mixed together (*Verbindung, Vermischung*) or where work has been invested in specification (*Verarbeitung*).

735   A further variant of the enrichment action based on the condiction "by other means" is relevant in the situation where someone disposes of property without having a right to do so. If the act of the unauthorised person in disposing of the property is legally effective against the person actually entitled to it, then the person disposing of the property must hand over to the person actually entitled any benefit which he or she gains from the transaction (§ 816 para. 1 sentence 1 BGB). This is generally the case where there is a *bona fide* purchase, which is an institution recognised by the law of things. If a yacht owner loans his or her vessel to someone else, and that person then sells it for his or her own account to a third party to whom the lessee has represented that he or she is the owner, then the third party does in fact become the owner of the yacht. The buyer cannot be compelled to return it to the original owner. The original owner can, however, demand that the dishonest seller who has sold the boat without authorisation, hand over any proceeds of the sale. If no consideration was given for the transfer of the property, then the person receiving it will be liable to return it to the owner (§ 816 para. 1 sentence 2 BGB). Thus, if the person who borrows the yacht gives it to a third party rather than selling it, the third party will be obliged to return it to the owner. Here the reliance of the third party on the validity of the transaction does not merit protection and return of the yacht is the owner's only remedy, since the dishonest borrower was not enriched by the transaction. The owner can therefore demand his or her boat back from the person to whom it was given.

736   Finally, § 816 para. 2 BGB regulates the situation where performance is made to someone who is not entitled to receive it. If performance is made to a person who is not entitled to it, with the result that the true creditor loses his or her claim, then the person who actually received performance has an obligation to account for any benefit which he or she has derived to the true creditor. This situation may arise, for example, where an assignment takes place without the knowledge of the debtor. If the debtor then makes performance to the original creditor the debtor will also be discharged from his or her obligation to the new creditor in terms of § 407 BGB. The new creditor will, however, have an enrichment action against the former creditor.

The claim for restitution relates to whatever the person enriched has gained from the transaction. In the first place this will include whatever the debtor actually received, whether it is the ownership of a thing, possession, or the assigned right. However, the claim to restitution goes further, also including the benefits which the debtor has gained from having the use of the thing or from its fruits (§§ 818 para. 1, first alternative, 100 BGB). Furthermore, the claim to restitution extends to anything which has been substituted for the thing originally received, such as a claim for damages if the thing has been destroyed by the fault of a third party acting in breach of a duty of care (§ 818 para. 1, 2nd instance BGB). If the nature of the benefit obtained makes its return impossible, for example, if it consisted of the performance of work, or if the person who received it is for some other reason not in a position to make restitution, then he or she must repay the value of the enrichment (§ 818 para. 2 BGB). 737

The enrichment action is aimed at reversing certain transfers of wealth which, in the judgement of the lawgiver, are unjustified. It does not attempt to regulate claims to damages. For this reason the enrichment action can only be brought if the defendant was in fact enriched. It aims to achieve restitution of the thing gained, or its substitute, or the use had, but the main focus is not on the restoration of the economic position of the enrichment creditor to what it was before the enrichment took place. He or she will only succeed if the enrichment has not been lost. § 818 para. 3 BGB provides that the duty to make restitution is excluded insofar as the person who received the benefit is no longer enriched. To return to the earlier example, if the yacht borrowed from A by B, and then donated by B to C, sinks in a storm, the person who received it will have no obligation to make any restitution to the former owner. 738

If consideration was provided by both parties to an enrichment action then the so-called balance theory (*Saldotheorie*) is applied. If both parties to a contract of sale have performed before discovering it to be void then the seller has a right to the re-transfer of ownership of the goods sold and delivered and the buyer has a claim to have the purchase price returned to him or her. Generally speaking, only the party who can prove that a remainder (balance) in his or her favour remains after the performance of each party has been set off against that of the other, i.e., the person who would have got the worst of the bargain had it been valid, will be able to bring an enrichment action. For example, a painting is bought and sold for € 1 000. Its actual market value is € 500. The sale is void. Before restitution can take place, the painting is destroyed by fire through no fault of the buyer. Only the buyer will have the option of bringing an enrichment action against the seller and his or her claim will be for the amount of € 500. 739

To prevent unjust results, the Code contains provisions for a stricter degree of liability in certain cases (§§ 818 para. 4; 819 and 820 BGB). These apply, inter alia, where the enrichment debtor became aware of the fact that he or she was not legally entitled to the enrichment before it is dissipated. In such circumstances it will be no defence to plead that he or she is no longer enriched, because the enrichment debtor knew of his or her obligation to make restitution before the enrichment was disposed of and had the opportunity to arrange his or her affairs accordingly. The same applies if, in accepting the enrichment in the first place, the enrichment debtor was acting illegally or contrary to public policy. Finally, the loss of the enrichment while proceedings are pending will also be no defence since by that stage the debtor knows that there is a possibility that he or she has an obligation to make restitution. 740

d) Law of Torts (Delict) and Strict Liability

aa) Basic Principles

741   The law of torts (*Deliktsrecht/Recht der unerlaubten Handlungen*) is regulated in §§ 823 ff. BGB. Someone who commits a wrongful act, in other words, an act contrary to law, and thereby causes damage to the protected legal interests of another person, will generally be liable to compensate the injured party for the resulting harm. This obligation is not penal in nature. Ethical reproach, penance for the deed and attempts to reform the perpetrator are left to the criminal law. In private law the issue is simply compensation for the harm suffered.

742   Generally speaking it must be proved that the tortfeasor acted culpably, that is deliberately (or recklessly) or negligently before he or she will be held liable to pay damages. Only then can the tortfeasor be said to be responsible for the harm. If the defendant did not act culpably (*schuldhaft*) then he or she cannot be held liable in tort. The tortfeasor may, however, be liable on the basis of a type of strict, no-fault liability called *Gefährdungshaftung*. The basic idea here is that a person who undertakes some essentially dangerous activity must take responsibility for any damage arising from it irrespective of whether he or she acted culpably (negligently or deliberately) in causing the harm and irrespective of whether the activity in question was legal or not. Compare (§ 7 para 1 StVG.)

bb) The Main Basis of Liability in Tort

743   The main basis for claims in tort is provided by § 823 para. 1 BGB: Anyone who, contrary to law, deliberately or negligently causes harm to the life, person, health, liberty, property or other rights of another person has an obligation to compensate that person for the resulting damage.

744   A claim for damages thus depends on proof of damage to one of various specific rights of another person. The act causing the harm may be a positive act, but an omission will also suffice if the defendant had a legal duty to act. Such duties to act may arise from statute, from prior conduct creating a potentially dangerous situation, or from a duty of care owed to persons who stand in a close social relationship to the person causing the harm. The duty of care (*Garantenpflicht*) may also arise from the encouragement of traffic: The person responsible for a building has a duty to keep the publicly accessible entrance of his or her building in a safe condition.

745   The infringement of rights and the resulting damage must be attributable to some culpable act on the part of the defendant. To make a determination on this point the private law applies the "adequacy theory" (*Adäquanztheorie*), a test for remoteness. According to this theory, only those causes which, according to everyday experience, may lead to the damage in question are adequately causal and therefore attributable to the defendant. Highly improbable and unusual chains of events generally will not form an adequate basis for imposing liability. However, this statement must be qualified by reference to the interests which this provision aims to protect. Even if it is, for example, highly unlikely that an attempt at arson will succeed, because unsuitable materials are being used to start the fire, the wrongdoer will nevertheless be held liable for any resulting damage because such damage falls in the centre of the problem which § 823 BGB is aimed at, namely, the provision of compensation for wrongful acts.

In cases where the rights expressly named in § 823 para. 1 BGB are infringed there is a **746** rebuttable presumption that the act causing the harm was wrongful, i.e., it is rebuttably presumed that the defendant owed the claimant a duty of care. It is then up to the defendant to raise some ground of justification such as self defence (*Notwehr*) or use of force in defence of property (*Selbsthilfe*) or consent of the claimant, i.e., the defence of *volenti non fit iniuria* (*Einwilligung des Verletzten*).

A claim for damages based on § 823 para. 1 BGB will only succeed if it can be shown **747** that one of the rights or groups of rights which it specifically mentions has been infringed. The provision deals exclusively with absolute rights, that is, rights which can be enforced against anyone. § 823 para. 1 BGB first expressly names life, person, health, liberty and property as protected rights. In addition this provision provides protection against the violation of "other rights"(*ein sonstiges Recht*). The courts have recognised the following as falling into this group of other absolute rights: the right of possession (*Besitz*), real rights such as the inchoate right to property which exists during the process of transfer (*Anwartschaft*), rights of security such as lien, pledge, mortgage etc. (*Pfandrechte*), and usufructs (*Nießbrauch*). It also includes immaterial property rights such as patents (*Patente*), utility model patents (*Gebrauchsmuster*), trademarks (*Warenzeichen*) and copyrights (*Urheberrechte*).

A right which is particularly important from a commercial point of view is the right to **748** a business as a going concern (*eingerichteter und ausgeübter Gewerbebetrieb*). A person who sets up and runs a shop, legal practice or other business has a claim to damages in terms of § 823 para. 1 BGB if some other person wrongfully and culpably (in breach of a duty of care) causes harm to the business. The protected interest is, however, restricted to narrow limits, the underlying idea being that in private enterprise opportunities to earn profits, turnover, clients and market share must constantly be re-earned. The protection of the business as a going concern includes the protection of business activity itself. It is the value of the business, which is made up of many factors such as the client base, goodwill, the name and reputation of the business, its accounts receivable and its field of activity, which is protected. These interests cannot be defined as property – they are merely aspects of wealth as a whole. However, wealth as such is not one of the interests protected by § 823 para. 1 BGB. It can only be protected if it takes on the concrete form of an absolute right in order to be protected under this provision. For this reason the objective basis provided by the business as a going concern is particularly important. A claim for damages on this basis also requires direct damage to the business. The act complained of must thus relate specifically to the business. If a business is brought temporarily to a halt due to negligent interruption of the water supply in the entire area by workers building a road this requirement of a specific relation to the business will not be satisfied.

A matter which has especially aroused public interest in this respect is the comparative **749** evaluation of products which is undertaken by many consumer publications. Such comparative evaluations can indeed be damaging to a business and can thus be the tort of damaging the business as a going concern. However, when such comparisons are based on careful and objective analysis, for example, taking into account differences in price and avoiding sensationalist presentation of the facts, then the act of damaging the going concern will not be wrongful and an action for damages will fail. In this way a balance is reached between the competing interests represented by the comparative evaluation (based on article 5 para. 1 GG, which guarantees freedom of opinion and of the press), and the interests of the business owner (based on articles 12 and 14 GG).

750 The general right to protection of the personality (*allgemeines Persönlichkeitsrecht*) also falls under "other rights" in the sense of § 823 para. 1 BGB. This right has a constitutional basis in articles 1 para. 1 and 2 para. 1 GG. This means that a person who has been defamed or otherwise been injured by attacks on his or her honour (*Verletzung der Ehre*), for example, by being the object of insults, vilification or exaggerated public criticism, can claim damages on the basis of § 823 para. 1 BGB. The same applies where a person's name or image has been misused, particularly for advertising purposes. Finally, this right can give a claim to damages where there has been an invasion of privacy, for example, when secret tape recordings have been made and used wrongfully.

cc) Other Forms of Tort

751 Since § 823 para. 1 BGB only provides for damages in the case of the infringement of an absolute right, it can leave important interests unprotected. This problem is of considerable practical importance due to the fact that there is no general provision in German law allowing a claim for damages on the basis of tort wherever it would be appropriate. There are thus numerous additional provisions complementing the rather narrow basic provision in § 823 para. 1 BGB. However, these additional provisions each relate to a specific problem.

752 An important provision is § 823 para. 2 BGB. This imposes an obligation to pay damages on anyone who wrongfully (in breach of a duty of care) infringes against any law which has as its purpose the protection of other persons. Thus, while § 823 para. 1 BGB provides generally for the protection of the various rights which it lists, § 823 para. 2 BGB refers to specific protective statutes (*Schutzgesetze*). This creates the possibility of a claim for damages even where none of the absolute rights in § 823 para. 1 BGB have been infringed, and is particularly relevant to the protection of wealth which does not take the form of one of the absolute rights in § 823 para. 1 BGB.

753 The main issue in dealing with this provision is to determine whether a particular statute is a protective statute (*Schutzgesetz*) in the sense of § 823 para. 2 BGB. The courts have repeatedly taken the position that a statute will be a protective statute in the sense of § 823 para. 2 BGB if at least one of the objects of the statute is to protect a claimant such as the claimant in the particular case before the court against the infringement of his or her rights. An example of the practical importance of § 823 para. 2 BGB is provided by the problem of fraud. The swindler merely damages the wealth of the victim, not his or her property, and thus, the swindler cannot be said to have infringed any of the rights specifically mentioned in § 823 para. 1 BGB. The swindler has, however, infringed § 263 StGB, which is considered to be a protective statute, and he or she is thus liable in damages.

754 § 826 BGB also provides a general basis for the protection of wealth. A person who deliberately causes harm to another in an immoral manner (*in einer gegen die guten Sitten verstoßenden Weise*) will be liable to that person in damages. This is thus once again a general rule which founds a claim to damages with respect to the protected rights and legal interests. Its reach is, however, at once subjected to the drastic limit that it only applies when the harm is caused in a particularly reprehensible way, that is, immorally or contrary to public policy. Another key requirement for a successful

claim on this basis is an intentional act, and, in contrast to § 823 BGB, in this case the intention must extend to the causing of the damage. Mere negligence is not sufficient. An act will be immoral in the sense of this provision if the behaviour in question offends against the sense of propriety of all just and reasonable people (*alle billig und gerecht Denkenden*).

§ 826 BGB has proved to be particularly relevant to actions in a commercial setting. Thus, reprehensible behaviour such as fraudulent misrepresentation (*arglistige Täuschung*) inducing the conclusion of a contract will generally give rise to a duty to pay compensation for the resulting damage. Unfair competition, the abuse of monopolistic dominance of a market, unjustified calls to boycott a product, and inducing someone to breach a contract will also give rise to an obligation to pay damages.

755

§ 831 BGB imposes liability for the actions of a subordinate acting in the course and scope of his or her duty (*Verrichtungsgehilfe*). Anyone who employs another person is liable for any damage caused by the employee to third parties while acting in the course and scope of his or her duty. Examples of such a relationship are where a garage entrusts the repair of a motor car to a mechanic in its employ, or where a medical doctor allows her assistant to administer medicine to a patient. § 831 BGB only applies where there is a relationship of social dependency between the person causing the damage and the person for whom the work is being performed in that the employee is subject to his or her instructions. The provision applies to all such relationships of social dependency irrespective of whether the relationship is long-term or short-term, paid or unpaid. The damage must have been caused by the subordinate while acting in the course and scope of his or her duties. For example: the plumber's assistant breaks the bathroom mirror while attempting to fix the bath. This requirement excludes damage caused by the subordinate which the subordinate happens to cause while working but which has no connection to the performance of his or her duties. For example, if the plumber's assistant takes advantage of his or her presence in the house to steal money out of a bedroom cupboard this is done during work (*bei Gelegenheit der Verrichtung*) but not in the course and scope of his or her duty. There must therefore be some direct inherent relationship between the harmful act and the performance of the duty which has been entrusted to the subordinate. The liability for harm caused by subordinates is strict, in other words it is sufficient that the causing of the harm is wrongful, and it is not necessary that it should also be culpable in that the subordinate acted negligently or intentionally. There must, however, be a certain degree of fault on the part of the master, particularly in relation to the appointment or supervision of the subordinate. Otherwise the master will be able to rely on the defence set out in § 831 para. 1 sentence 2 BGB. This says that the master will not be liable in damages if he or she exercised due care (*die im Verkehr erforderliche Sorgfalt*) in choosing the subordinate to do the job in question and also showed due care in supervising the performance of the job or in providing the equipment necessary insofar as supervision or provision of equipment could reasonably be required. The defence also applies if reasonable precautions would not have prevented the harm in question from occurring.

756

Making an employer liable for the acts of his or her subordinates in the interests of protecting third parties is reasonable (*angemessen*) because the subordinate will often not have the means to pay an appropriate amount of compensation him- or herself. However, the employee will also be liable, alongside his or her employer, if the em-

757

ployee acted culpably in causing the harm. The interests of the employer are adequately protected by the defences mentioned above.

758   Various other bases for claiming damages take specific factual situations as their starting point. By making specific exceptions to the rules in question they attempt to find a just solution in exceptional circumstances. § 824 BGB gives a claim for damages where the defendant has published false allegations about the claimant which the defendant knew or ought to have known to be false and which are likely (*geeignet*) to damage the claimant's ability to obtain credit or are likely to damage his or her career or his or her ability to earn a living.

759   Liability may also arise from a breach of a duty to provide supervision. This is particularly relevant in cases where the person directly causing the damage lacks the capacity to be held liable in tort. Anyone who has a contractual or statutory duty to supervise someone requiring supervision because of their youth or physical or mental condition will be liable in damages to any person who suffers harm at the hands of the person in his or her charge. However, the defendant will not be liable if the defendant has taken reasonable steps to supervise his or her charge or if the harm would have occurred even if the defendant had taken reasonable steps.

760   A claim based on tort generally requires proof of a culpable state of mind on the part of the defendant. A finding to this effect can only be made if the defendant has capacity to be liable in tort (*Deliktsfähigkeit*, §§ 827, 828 BGB). People who have not yet completed the seventh year of life are irrebuttably presumed to lack the capacity to be liable in tort. Young people under the age of eighteen lack capacity in tort if they lacked the degree of insight necessary to realise their responsibility when committing the deed.

761   A person also lacks capacity in tort if, at the time of causing the harm, the person was in a state of unconsciousness or was suffering from a pathological disturbance of his or her mental functions which excluded the free exercise of his or her will. These grounds for excluding liability do not apply if the person relying on them culpably induced his or her own incapacity, for example by voluntarily taking some form of drug. In such a case the person will be held liable in the same way as if he or she had acted negligently in causing the harm.

762   If a person lacks capacity in tort a duty to pay damages may nevertheless be imposed on grounds of fairness. If the person who has suffered harm cannot recover compensation from some person with a duty of supervision, then the person who would otherwise not be liable in terms of §§ 827, 828 BGB will be held liable to pay compensation to the extent that this is reasonable (*nach Billigkeit*). This is generally relevant where an underaged defendant is in possession of considerable wealth while the claimant is not. Under no circumstances may a person lacking capacity in tort be deprived of the means to support him- or herself or to fulfil some statutory duty of support on the basis of this exception.

dd) Extent of Liability

763   The extent of the liability to pay damages arising from an action in tort is determined essentially by reference to §§ 249 ff. BGB. However, in terms of §§ 842 ff. BGB various special provisions are applicable.

Occasionally a person who has suffered only indirect harm will also be able to succeed in an action for damages. § 844 BGB forms the basis of a dependant's action. If a person who has a duty to support someone else is killed, then the person with a right to support has a claim for damages against the person causing the death to the extent of the lost support. The payment takes the form of a pension (see also § 845 BGB). 764

If several persons were involved in causing the harm, for example, if they have participated by inciting the perpetration of the tort, or if they were an accessory to its commission or joint perpetrators, then they will be jointly and severally liable for the resulting harm (§§ 830, 840 BGB). The same applies if it is not possible to establish which of several persons involved in the commission of the tort caused the harm. For example, if an innocent passer-by is injured in a mass brawl but it proves impossible to prove who threw the punch which injured him or her, then all the participants in the brawl will be liable. However, it is open to each of the participants to prove that he or she was not the one who caused the damage. If this can be proved, then that particular participant will be freed from liability. 765

ee) Mandatory and Prohibitory Injunctions

The causes of action for tort set out in the Code are all directed at the provision of damages as compensation for harm already suffered. Often this will be an unsatisfactory remedy for the person affected, for example, when harm has not yet occurred but is imminent. His or her interest is then in demanding that the other party desist from the potentially harmful course of action so that the harm does not occur in the first place. For example, if one person is making untrue defamatory statements about another the aggrieved party will not only want damages for the harm already done, but also some way of preventing the continued spread of the defamatory statements. The appropriate remedy is then a prohibitory injunction (*Unterlassungsanspruch*). The Code makes express provision for prohibitory injunctions in certain special cases. Thus, in § 12 sentence 2 BGB provision is made for the protection of a person's name, § 862 para. 1 sentence 2 BGB allows an injunction to protect possession, and § 1004 para. 1 sentence 2 BGB protects ownership. By analogy the courts have also recognised the general possibility of granting an injunction to protect the absolute rights dealt with in §§ 823 ff. BGB, for example, liberty, life, health, the general personality right or the rights in a business as a going concern. An injunction will be granted if there is an serious danger of harm from a wrongful act on the part of the respondent. It is not necessary to establish culpability (negligence or intention) on the part of the respondent. Similarly, the removal of a continuing nuisance can be ordered by a mandatory injunction (*Beseitigungsanspruch*). 766

ff) Strict Liability

Generally speaking a defendant will only be held liable for harm which he or she has caused if the defendant acted culpably, i.e., negligently or intentionally, in causing it. This is the basic position adopted by the Code. However, in some cases this would lead to unsatisfactory results. 767

The Civil Code initially made provision for strict liability in the context of the keeping of dangerous animals, a problem which is less prominent in modern times. § 833 sentence 1 BGB provides as follows: If a human being is killed by an animal, or if the health of a person is impaired or goods are damaged, then the person responsible for 768

193

the animal has an obligation to compensate the victim for the resulting harm. This is an instance of strict (no-fault) liability (*Gefährdungshaftung*). It holds the keeper of the animal responsible even if the keeper has taken reasonable care in supervising it and even if his or her behaviour in all other respects is blameless. This is so even although the keeping of an animal is perfectly compatible with the law as a whole.

769   The basic idea underlying strict liability is that a person who creates a source of danger must take the responsibility for any harm which does in fact arise from it. An instance of strict liability outside of the Civil Code which is of the greatest practical importance is contained in §§ 7 ff. of the Road Traffic Act (*Straßenverkehrsgesetz,* abbreviated *StVG*). If, in the course of operating a motor vehicle, a person is killed, or damaged in his or her health, or deprived of the amenities of life, then the person responsible for the vehicle will generally have an obligation to compensate the injured party for the resulting harm (§ 7 para. 1 StVG). However, the liability of the person responsible for the vehicle is excluded if the accident was caused by force majeure . Apart from this, and a few additional exceptions which are of lesser practical significance, the strict liability means that when an accident between two vehicles takes place, the person responsible for the one vehicle will have to bear part of the loss even if the fault was entirely on the part of the other driver. However, in saying this one must bear in mind that in the majority of cases it is the insurers of the parties who bear the loss and that the insurers set off their various claims against one another.

770   There is generally an upper limit to the amount which can be awarded if a claim is based on strict liability. As far as the liability of persons in charge of motor vehicles is concerned, the maximum liability, which arises when one or several people have been killed, is a lump sum of € 5 000 000. If the damages are paid in the form of a pension, then the same amount forms the maximum of its capital value (§ 12 para. 1 number 2 StVG).

771   Instead of taking the drastic step of imposing strict liability, the law often attempts to achieve an appropriate apportionment of the risk by simply reversing the burden of proof (*Umkehrung der Beweislast*). Generally speaking the person making a claim must prove all the elements required for his or her cause of action. This is a general principle of procedural law and of the law for determining the incidence of liability. However, sometimes it is difficult or impossible for the claimant to prove all the elements of a tort even if all the requirements are in fact satisfied. If the difficulty arises from the fact that the origin of the danger is not within his or her sphere of knowledge, then a possible solution is to reverse the burden of proof. This legal construction can be seen in the case of the defence available to the master who is being sued for acts done by his or her servant in the course and scope of his or her duties.

772   A situation in which it is often particularly difficult for the injured party to prove the requirements of the tort is where the harm is caused by the use of the defendant's product. If, for example, the construction of the product is defective and the consumer suffers harm as a result, it will be difficult for the consumer to prove that the producer acted in a blameworthy manner, because the consumer has no knowledge of the production process used. Numerous examples are provided by past decisions: The brakes of a particular model of motor car are defective, a plant spray is ineffective against

parasites,[13] or a dangerous product gives no warning of the danger involved in its use.[14]

Here, once again, it has long since been established that the courts will come to the assistance of the claimant by reversing the onus of proof: If an industrial product is used in accordance with its instructions and harm to person or property nevertheless results because the product was in some way defective, then the onus is on the producer to prove that the defect was not due to any culpable act on his or her part. If the producer is unable to prove this, then the producer will be liable for damages in tort.[15]

773

Apart from the possibility of liability in tort with a reversal of the onus of proof, there is also the Product Liability Act (*Produkthaftungsgesetz*), which implements a corresponding directive of the European Union. This legislation also provides for strict liability, but does not allow for damages for pain and suffering and limits liability to a certain maximum amount, which is why the claim in tort based on the provisions of the Civil Code remains practically significant. If a defect in a product causes someone's death or bodily injury or impairment of health, then the producer has an obligation to make good the resulting damage. However, there are a number of situations in which liability is excluded. For example, the producer will not be held liable if the defect in his or her product was due to legal guidelines compelling the producer to make it that way, or if the defect in question was not reasonably recognisable, measured by the standards of knowledge and technology available at the time that the product was brought onto the market. When the damage resulting from the defect involves damage to property, the liability of the producer in terms of the legislation extends only to damage caused to property other than the defective product itself. Furthermore, the defective product must be of such a nature that it is primarily intended for private use or consumption and the claimant must have been using it primarily for such private purposes. Alternatively, the supplier of the product is held liable if the identity of the producer cannot be established and the supplier does not identify the producer or the person who delivered it to him or her within a period of one month. Liability under the act cannot be excluded in advance by contract. The onus is on the producer of the product to show that one of the defences set out in the act is applicable. On the other hand, the onus is on the consumer to prove that the product was defective, that the consumer suffered harm, and that there is a causal connection between the harm and the defect.

774

Literature:

Hans Brox/Wolf-Dietrich Walker, Besonderes Schuldrecht, 43. ed. 2019
Volker Emmerich, BGB-Schuldrecht, Besonderer Teil, 15. ed. 2018
Dieter Medicus/Stephan Lorenz, Schuldrecht II: Besonderer Teil, 18. ed. 2018

IV. The Law of Things (Law of Property)

1. Basic Principles

In the law of property English and German law diverge significantly at the fundamental theoretical level, although the practical results achieved by both systems are often the same. In particular, the English concept of equitable interests and the original feu-

775

---

13 BGHZ 80, 186.
14 BGH NJW 1999, 2815.
15 BGHZ 51, 91.

dal thinking of English land law are alien to German law, which is derived from the Roman tradition.

776 While the law of obligations (*Schuldrecht*) regulates the legal relationships between persons, the law of property, or, to put it in German terms, the law of things (*Sachenrecht*) deals with real rights (*dingliche Rechte*). Real rights are the rights which persons have over things. A distinction is made between possession (*Besitz*), ownership (*Eigentum*) and the so-called limited real rights (*beschränkte dingliche Rechte*) which confer specific rights of use, consumption, or security in relation to a thing. The basic provisions of the law of things are contained in the third book of the Civil Code (BGB). In addition, certain basic provisions of general application are to be found in §§ 90-103 BGB. The distinction between the law of obligations and the law of things is yet another expression of the principle of abstraction (*Abstraktionsprinzip*) and that of separation (*Trennungsprinzip*).

777 Real rights are enforceable against all the world: as a general rule the owner of land can expel anyone who trespasses, irrespective of who it is. These rights are absolute, in contrast to the relative rights regulated by the law of obligations which in principle only have legal consequences for the immediate parties to the particular legal relationship. For example, a contract only creates obligations for the parties to the contract. Because of the absolute nature of the real rights the German law applies a principle of publicity (*Publizitätsprinzip*) to them. This means that the existence of the right must be clear to everyone who cares to know. In the case of personal property, or, in German terms, moveable property (*bewegliche Sachen*) the publicity function is served by the fact of possession. In the case of land the requirement of publicity is fulfilled by the existence of the land register (*Grundbuch*) which is usually to be found at the local *Amtsgericht*, that is, the local court. All rights in land should be entered in the land register.

778 Furthermore, there is the socalled specialty or certainty principle (*Spezialitäts- oder Bestimmtheitsprinzip*) which requires that there should be clarity as to who is the owner of a thing and what the extent and content of the right is. Rights on an aggregate of things can therefore only be transferred when it is clear to which specific objects the will of both parties to transfer relates. This means, it is only possible to have real rights in specific, individual things, not in aggregates of things.

779 Finally, it should be noted that as a result of the various principles mentioned above the law of things imposes a closed catalogue of rights (*Typenzwang*). This means that strict limits are imposed on freedom of contract in the interests of clarity and legal certainty. It is not possible to create by contract real rights other than those provided for in statute law. The provisions of the law of things also cannot be excluded by agreement. The law of things is thus characterised by a significant degree of rigidity. It aims at a static ideal, in contrast to the law of obligations, which is strongly dynamic.

2. Possession

780 Possession (*Besitz*) is an important real right (§§ 854 ff. BGB). In colloquial German a person is often said to "possess" (*besitzen*) something when the speaker means to say that the person owns it, but these concepts are quite distinct from a legal point of view. It is quite possible to have possession of a thing without owning it, and vice versa. For example, the owner of a thing may lose it, thus losing possession. Any person finding it will gain possession, but not ownership. As used in the Civil Code the term

"possession" means the factual control of a person over a thing. Control is the key requirement. Even a person who controls a thing illegitimately, such as a thief, will nevertheless be in possession of it from a legal point of view. In such circumstances an owner who wishes to assert that he or she has a superior right to possess the thing must generally invoke the assistance of the courts rather than resorting to self help. This is in the interests of preserving law and order.

The law distinguishes various categories of possession (§§ 865 ff. BGB). Direct possession (*unmittelbarer Besitz*) is used to describe the situation where a person exercises actual control over a thing. An indirect possessor (*mittelbarer Besitzer*) is someone whose possession of a thing is exercised indirectly through another person holding the thing on his or her behalf. Such a relationship is called a *Besitzmittlungsverhältnis*. For example, the tenant under a lease is the direct possessor of the property while the landlord is a mere indirect possessor (§ 868 BGB). There are also various degrees of indirect possession, so that a single thing may not only have a direct possessor, but also several indirect possessors. For example, if the lessee loans the thing in question to somebody else, then both the lessor and the lessee are indirect possessors and the borrower is the direct possessor. A further distinction is made between possessing a thing with the intention of holding it for oneself (*Eigenbesitz*) and possessing a thing with the intention of holding it for some other person (*Fremdbesitz*). Co-possession (*Mitbesitz*, § 866 BGB) describes the situation in which several people possess a thing simultaneously. If only one person possesses the thing then that person is said to be sole possessor (*Alleinbesitzer*). | 781

An essential requirement for acquiring possession is the obtaining of actual control over the thing (§ 854 BGB). In addition, there must be a subjective intention to possess the thing on the part of the person in control of it, otherwise he or she will, despite his or her factual control, not be the possessor. If actual control is lost more than temporarily, then possession will also be lost. For the loss of possession it is irrelevant whether the loss of actual control was voluntary or involuntary. | 782

The possessor of a thing has significant rights. The law protects that person against unlawful interference with his or her possession, which is the case when the person is disturbed in his or her possession, or deprived of it, without justification and against his or her will. The possessor is entitled to use force to ward off unlawful interference with his or her possession (§ 859 BGB). If the possessor is deprived of possession he or she may use force to regain it if he or she was acting in hot pursuit of the person responsible, that is, if he or she reacts as soon as he or she is deprived of possession. If he or she does not regain possession at once, then he or she will have to resort to the assistance of the courts to regain possession (§§ 858-861 BGB). The law also offers the possessor the option of seeking an injunction (interdict) if the possessor fears that the disturbance of his or her possession will be repeated in the future. | 783

3. Ownership

Ownership is the central concept of the law of property. Ownership is generally defined as meaning not only the factual, but also the legal *dominium* of a person over a thing. § 903 BGB proclaims that the owner of a thing can do as she pleases with it, and can forbid all other people from doing anything with it, insofar as her right is not qualified by the law or the rights of others. This limitation has its constitutional basis in article 14 para. 2 GG which states that property (ownership) implies obligations | 784

(*Eigentum verpflichtet*). The use of property should simultaneously serve the common good. Thus, the guarantee of property rights in the constitution gives the concept of ownership in the Civil Code, which was developed in the laissez-faire 19th century, a new and more strongly social structure. At the same time, for the purposes of the constitution the concept *Eigentum* is wider than in the Civil Code. It applies to all the private rights which make up wealth, in other words the term *Eigentum* in the constitution includes rightful possession, which for purposes of private law is a distinct concept. The practical significance of this wider constitutional definition is that if, for example, the state expropriates rented property without sufficient justification it will also be violating the property rights of the lessee. Various subjective public rights such as accrued future pension rights against the social security system are included in the concept of *Eigentum* for purposes of constitutional law but not for the purposes of private law.

785   There are various different categories of private law ownership. Sole ownership (*Alleineigentum*) is the situation where something is owned by a single person alone (§ 903 BGB). If a thing is owned by several persons jointly then one speaks of co-ownership (*Miteigentum*, §§ 1008 ff. BGB). This can take the form of owning fractions of a thing. For example, in the case of a married couple living in a house each party owns a half share of the matrimonial home. Another possibility is the joint ownership of a thing in undivided shares (*Gesamthandseigentum*). In such a case the community of joint owners is the owner of the thing. The community may take the form of, for example, a partnership (§§ 718, 719 BGB), the subparticipation in community of heirs by the heirs of a deceased member (*Erbengemeinschaft*, § 2032 para. 1 BGB) or a couple married in community of property (§ 1416 para. 1 BGB). If the co-ownership takes the form of the ownership of defined shares, then each co-owner can deal with his or her share as he or she pleases. In the case of joint ownership in undivided shares the property can only be dealt with if all the co-owners consent. *Wohnungseigentum*, that is, property in a freehold flat (condominium/sectional title) in terms of the Condominium Act (*Wohnungseigentumsgesetz*), allows for the co-ownership of the land on which the building stands while each individual dwelling is separately owned.

786   Ownership can be gained by means of a legal transaction, but also by operation of law. For ownership of moveable property (personal property, specifically, choses in possession) to be transferred by legal transaction there are two requirements: The buyer and seller must be in agreement as to the passing of ownership (*dingliche Einigung*), and the thing in question must be handed over (*Übergabe*). The latter requirement falls away if the person to whom ownership is to pass is already in possession of the thing, or if the parties agree that the old owner is to remain in possession but is to hold the thing for the new owner in the future (*Besitzmittlungsverhältnis*) or if the right of the owner to reclaim possession of the thing from a third party possessor (*Herausgabeanspruch*) is ceded to the buyer (vindication/replevin, §§ 929-931 BGB).

787   Although German law does not distinguish ownership of personal property and rights relating to land as sharply as the English common law historically does, the process for transferring ownership of land (§§ 925 ff. BGB) is nevertheless more complicated than the process for transferring movables. Ownership of land corresponds to the fee simple absolute in possession (freehold) of English law. For ownership to pass, the first requirement is once again a common understanding between the parties that ownership is to pass. However, to this is added the requirement that the alteration of the le-

gal position must be registered in the Land Register (*Grundbuch*). This additional requirement is unknown in many other legal systems, for example, that of France. The agreement concerning the passing of ownership over land is called the *Auflassung*. It must be declared before an authorised official in the presence of both the parties concerned. The officials empowered to carry out this function are notaries, German consular officials abroad, and, in the case of settlements reached in court, the courts.

Since ownership in land only passes once the name of the new owner is entered in the land register, and since a significant period of time can pass between the declaration of agreement before a notary and the making of the entry in the register, the passing of ownership is endangered. After the formal declaration of agreement and before the entry into the register the owner-to-be has a future interest (*Anwartschaft*) in obtaining the land. This right could be jeopardised by the entry of the name of a second buyer into the register, or by the registering of a mortgage or some other right. To guard against such eventualities the owner to be can therefore arrange for a preliminary entry (§§ 883 ff. BGB) to be made in the land register. This can be done at short notice and prevents the possibility of someone else acquiring rights over the land, since third parties then have notice of his or her future interest. If in fact an attempt is made to register some other right after the preliminary entry has been made, then the claim of the first person to transfer of land free of burdens will take precedence over all conflicting claims.   788

The public is entitled to rely on the entries in the land register, in other words the entries in the land register are irrebuttably presumed (§ 892 BGB) to be an accurate reflection of the legal position, subject to one exception. That is that a person who can be proved to have known that an entry was inaccurate will be precluded from relying on that entry.   789

Generally speaking ownership will be passed by the owner or some other person authorised to deal with the property. However, it is possible that ownership may be obtained from a person who has no actual authority to deal with the property. This is the case if the person obtaining ownership did so in good faith (*gutgläubig*, §§ 932 ff. BGB) and without notice. For example, if the owner of a thing has leant it to a borrower, and the borrower then proceeds to sell it to a third party contrary to the intentions of the owner, the third-party buyer will become the new owner of the goods unless he or she knew or ought to have known that the seller was not entitled to sell the goods. The reason why the buyer acting in good faith is protected in this way is because the impression is created that the person selling the goods is the owner. It is the reliance of the buyer on this appearance which is protected, which means, of course, that the buyer will not be able to obtain ownership from a non-owner if the buyer acted in bad faith. Thus, obtaining ownership from a non-owner is not possible if the buyer knew or ought to have known that the person purporting to transfer title was not entitled to do so. The person obtaining transfer will already be excluded from claiming that he or she had acted in good faith if that person's ignorance of the true legal position was due to gross negligence. If the owner's loss of possession was involuntary, for example, if his or her property was lost or stolen, then, once again, he or she cannot lose ownership to someone acting in good faith and without notice. In such circumstances the law gives the claims of the owner precedence over the claims of the person attempting in good faith to obtain ownership. Since the contents of the land register are presumed to be an accurate reflection of the legal position, it is also possi-   790 ble to acquire in good faith an absolute title to land if other persons who have rights over the land have failed to have them entered in the register. However, this possibility is excluded if a note has been made in the land register challenging the correctness of an entry.

791 The transfer of ownership is often used to provide security for other types of claim. When moveable (personal) property is transferred, the transfer of ownership can be made subject to a condition (in contrast to the transfer of ownership in land which must be unconditional). To provide security in cases where the price is only to be paid in the future it is common practice to make a contract of sale subject to retention of title (*Eigentumsvorbehalt*). Based on the contract of sale, the agreement concerning the passing of ownership is then reached subject to the suspensive condition that the full purchase price is to be paid before ownership will pass. Only once the buyer has paid the last instalment of the purchase price will he or she then become owner of the thing bought.

792 *Sicherungsübereignung*, the mortgage of goods by security bill of sale is a somewhat different transaction. Here ownership of a thing is transferred unconditionally, usually to a creditor who requires security from the person making the transfer. The debtor, however, remains in direct possession of the thing and can use it. The creditor who is acquiring ownership merely obtains indirect possession (*mittelbarer Besitz*). At the same time the parties usually agree that ownership is to pass back to the debtor as soon as the debtor has completely repaid the capital and interest on the loan together with all incidental expenses.

793 Ownership may also be acquired by operation of law if two things have been mixed or united together (*Vermischung, Verbindung*; *commixtio et confusio*) or if work has been invested in specification (*Verarbeitung*, see §§ 937 ff., 946 ff. BGB). The finder of a thing becomes its owner by operation of law if it is not reclaimed within six months of his or her reporting the find to the lost property office (§ 973 BGB). Ownership can also be gained by a possessor in good faith if the property in question is not claimed by the original owner before the elapse of the ten-year period of limitation which applies in such cases (*Ersitzung*). To acquire ownership in this way the person claiming to have acquired ownership must show that he or she was acting in good faith at the time of acquiring possession and at all times thereafter until the period of limitation elapses (§ 937 BGB).

794 The Code contains very detailed rules for regulating the relationship between the owner and the possessor of a thing (§§ 985 ff. BGB). The owner can demand that the possessor deliver up the thing if the possessor does not have some right as against the owner to be in possession (§§ 985, 986 BGB). This claim is called the *Herausgabeanspruch* (cf. The Roman-law *rei vindicatio*). For example, the owner of a thing will not be able to demand its return from a possessor who holds it under a lease which has not yet terminated, but can do so as soon as the lease comes to an end (see also § 546 para. 1 BGB; if the owner is also the lessor of the thing, he can choose whether to demand it according to § 985 BGB or § 546 BGB); the owner will be able to claim the return of his or her property from a thief. Under certain prerequisites, the owner may demand emoluments or damages from the possessor. The extent of a particular claim is determined, above all, by whether the possessor has legitimate grounds for relying on his or her right of possession or not. If it is foreseeable for the possessor that someone will bring an action against him or her, because the possessor knows or

ought to know that his or her right to possession is defective or because the owner has already started proceedings to recover the property, then his or her liability will be stricter than it would be if he or she were acting in good faith in reliance on the validity of his or her right. Such a person is called a mala fide possessor (§ 990 BGB). Thus, in certain circumstances, the owner will be able to recover from the possessor any fruits and advantages derived from the thing and may also be able to recover damages. Anyone who has obtained possession by means of a criminal act or of unjustified self-help (*verbotene Eigenmacht*) is liable to the owner in damages according to the provisions of the law of tort. Such a person is called a tortious possessor (*deliktischer Besitzer*) (§ 992 BGB).

On the other hand, if the possessor has behaved reasonably, that is, if the possessor is entitled to believe that his or her right of possession is valid, then the possessor is only liable to render up the fruits and advantages gained from his or her possession of the thing in accordance with the provisions on unjustified enrichment. This might be the rent derived from a house or the crop from a field. However, insofar as the fruits and advantages derived are merely a result of the ordinary use of the thing (as opposed to its excessive exploitation) the possessor may keep them and will also not be liable in damages. The owner must recompense the possessor for any necessary expenses incurred for the upkeep of the property in question. However, insofar as the possessor is entitled to keep the advantages from the use of the thing, the possessor will be liable to bear the normal costs of its upkeep him- or herself. On the other hand, if the expenses incurred by the possessor were merely for useful improvements rather than for necessary improvements (for example, if the possessor replaces the existing windows of a house with larger windows which let in more light) then the possessor is only entitled to compensation if the improvements were made in good faith and before the owner brought his or her action for recovery, and even then the possessor may only recover his or her expenses if they still increase the value of the property at the time when the owner recovers it (§ 996 BGB). 795

§ 985 BGB gives the owner a basic right to demand that he or she be given possession of his or her property. However, deprivation of possession is not the only way in which the owner's rights may be infringed. This would be the case if, for example, someone commits what in English law would be a trespass or nuisance by depositing stones on the owner's land without permission or causing excessive noise or noxious emissions. The solution to unauthorised interference of this sort is provided by § 1004 BGB. This provides that if there is an imminent danger that rights of ownership will be infringed on, the owner is entitled to a prohibitory injunction (*Unterlassungsanspruch*), and if the infringement has already taken place or is ongoing the owner has a right to a prohibitory or mandatory injunction for the cessation or removal of the cause of offence (*Beseitigungsanspruch*). 796

4. Limited Real Rights

The limited real rights relate to various isolated possibilities for deriving some advantage from particular things. The following rights are distinguished: rights of use, (*Nutzungsrechte*), rights of security (*Sicherungsrechte*), and rights of administration and realisation (*Verwertungsrechte*). 797

A usufruct (*Nießbrauch*), comparable to the English idea of *profits à prendre*, is the right to make all forms of use of someone else's property (§§ 1030 ff. BGB). The object 798 of the usufruct can be land or moveable (personal) property, but it could also be immaterial property rights (choses in action). A usufruct is not transferable, whether be cession *inter vivos or mortis causa.*

799   An easement or servitude (*Grunddienstbarkeit*) exists in the context of the relationship of two landowners to each other (§§ 1018 ff. BGB). A piece of land, the servient tenement, can be burdened in favour of the successive owners of another piece of land, called the dominant tenement, in such a way that the owners of the dominant tenement are accorded a right to use the servient tenement in a particular way. For example, the owner of the dominant tenement might be accorded a right of way (*Wegerecht*) over the servient tenement. The easement may also take the form of a prohibition on certain activities on the servient tenement. For example, the owner of the servient tenement may be prohibited from building above a certain height so as to preserve the view of the beautiful valley enjoyed by the owner of the dominant tenement.

800   §§ 1090 ff. BGB provide for the possibility of creating a limited personal servitude (*beschränkte persönliche Dienstbarkeit*). This is a life interest in someone else's property. Such an interest is granted to a particular person and cannot be transferred, whether *inter vivos* or *mortis causa.* In other respects the rules governing such a right are the same as those applicable to easements (servitudes).

801   Another of the rights of use in land is the building lease, a heritable building right (*Erbbaurecht*). The purpose of this right is to make it possible to build on land without owning it. The building lease serves particularly to give the less wealthy elements of the population an opportunity to obtain residential property. The right is usually granted by local government bodies or the owners of large estates. The subject is regulated in detail by the Building Leases Act (*Erbbaurechtsverordnung*). The holder of the building lease must pay rent at regular intervals for the use of the land. The building lease is always for a fixed term of years, usually 99 years, after which the right extinguishes and ownership of the building passes to the landowner. This is, however, subject to the proviso that the owner of the land must pay compensation to the former house owner.

802   The rights of security include the pledge (pawning of goods) and possessory lien (both translated as *Pfandrecht*). The purpose of security rights is to provide security for the creditor in the event that the debtor does not fulfil his or her obligations. If the claims of the person to whom goods are pledged (the pledgee) are not satisfied by the debtor, the creditor can instead realise the pledged asset, generally by selling it by public auction. If the pledged asset is worth more than the amount of the debt then the pledgee must pay the balance over to the pledgor after deducting the costs of realisation. To create a pledge over moveable (personal) property the parties must agree to the creation of such a right and the thing which is to be the object of the pledge must be given into the possession of the pledgee (§§ 1204 ff. BGB). Rights of security can also be created by operation of law. Here the English equivalent of the *Pfandrecht* would be the possessory lien. For example, the lessor of a piece of land on which residential property stands has a lien over such property of the tenant which the tenant brings onto the lessor's land (§§ 562 ff. BGB). In the contract to perform specific work (*Werkvertrag*) the person performing the work has a possessory lien conferred by statute (§ 647 BGB). This means that, so long as that person is still in possession of the moveable property which he or she has created or improved, the person performing

the work is entitled to retain it until the owner settles his or her debts. Rights of security may also exist in respect of choses in action (intangible rights, §§ 1273 ff. BGB). A right of security may be created without the consent of the person affected by way of civil action (§§ 828 ff., 803 ff. ZPO).

There are also detailed provisions regulating rights of security and realisation relating to land (mortgages). As in the case of rights of ownership and real rights of use, these rights are recorded in the land register (*Grundbuch*).   803

Another type of right is a land charge (*Reallast*). This is a charge over land giving the holder the right to receive recurring payments derived from the land (§§ 1105 ff. BGB).   804

The most common right of security over land today is a type of mortgage called a *Grundschuld* (§§ 1191 ff. BGB). The land is burdened in such a way that the beneficiary is entitled to the payment of a sum of money out of the land. This means that the creditor can sell the land to satisfy his or her claim if the debtor does not fulfil his or her obligations, or, in the case of lesser debts, have it placed under compulsory administration until the debt is satisfied from the profits from the land (*Verwertung*). The *Grundschuld* is not dependent on the existence of the claim which it is intended to secure. It continues in existence and the amount agreed upon remains unchanged even if the debt which is was to secure has been partly or wholly discharged. However, if the debt has been discharged, then a claim for the retransfer of the *Grundschuld* arises.   805

In contrast, the type of mortgage called the *Hypothek*, which the drafters of the Code treated as being the most important form of security over land, exists only so long as the claim which it was intended to secure exists (§§ 1113 ff. BGB).   806

If a *Grundschuld* is formulated in such a way that a specific sum of money derived from the land is to be paid to the creditor at regularly recurring intervals, then one speaks of an annuity land charge (*Rentenschuld,* §§ 1199 ff. BGB).   807

The realisation of the land in the event that the debtor fails to pay as agreed (*Verwertung*) takes place in accordance with a strictly regulated procedure set out in the Act on Sales in Execution and Compulsory Administration (*Gesetz über Zwangsversteigerung und Zwangsverwaltung*). The first possibility in terms of this act is to place the land under the administration of a sequestrator (*Sequester*) who uses the land and satisfies the creditor's claim out of the profits (for example, rents received). The second possibility is for the land to be sold by public auction. After the costs of the auction have been recovered the remaining money derived in this way is used to satisfy the creditor.   808

Literature:

Wolfgang Brehm/Christian Berger, Sachenrecht, 3. ed. 2014
Hanns Prütting, Sachenrecht, 36. ed. 2017
Harm P. Westermann/ANsgar Staudinger, BGB-Sachenrecht, 13. ed. 2017
Marina Wellenhofer/Manfred Wolf, Sachenrecht, 33. ed. 2018

V. Family Law

1. Basic Principles

Family law is made up of the legal rules which regulate relationships within the family, in other words, the law of marriage (*Ehe*) and engagement (*Verlöbnis*), the law on relationship by consanguinity (*Verwandtschaft*) or affinity, the law on adoption (*Adop-*   809 *tion*) and on parental responsibility (*Vormundschaft,* guardianship). Family law is based primarily on the fourth book of the Civil Code (*Bürgerliches Gesetzbuch*). Since 2001 the Partner in Life Act (*Lebenspartnerschaftsgesetz*) has been in force. It made it possible to register a partnership between two people of the same sex who intend to spend the rest of their lives together. In many aspects such a partnership has the same legal effects as marriage.

The procedural rules for family matters and actions for maintenance are contained in the Act on Procedures in Family Matters and Miscellaneous Matters (*Gesetz über das Verfahren in Familiensachen und in den Angelegenheiten der freiwilligen Gerichtsbarkeit,* abbreviated FamFG). Marital status, births, gender, marriages, deaths and degrees of relationship are recorded in the Registers of Births, Deaths and Marriages (*Personenstandsregister*), an administrative service provided by the state in the form of the registry office (*Standesamt*). The gender 'divers' can be registered if neither the gender female nor the gender male applies.

810   The constitutional foundation of family law is provided by article 6 GG. It provides that the family and the institution of marriage are to enjoy the special protection of the state (article 6 para. 1 GG). Bringing up and caring for children is a natural right and also a duty which rests primarily on the parents (article 6 para. 2 GG). Society as represented by the state has a supervisory duty with respect to the way in which this parental responsibility is exercised. However, children may only be removed from the family against the will of the persons exercising parental authority in accordance with express rules of law, or when the persons with parental responsibility fail to fulfil their duties, or where there is a danger that the children will suffer from moral neglect. Alongside the parents' right to bring up their children there is an independent right to educate exercised by the state especially through the schools in terms of article 7 para. 1 GG.

811   The imperative to treat all people equally contained in article 3 para. 2 and 3 GG also applies in family law. Every mother has a right to the protection and support of the community (article 6 para. 4 GG). The law must create the same conditions for the physical and spiritual development for children born outside marriage and for their position in society as for children born within marriage (article 6 para. 5 GG). In today's society this goal has been realised in most respects.

812   In the constitution the term "marriage" has the meaning of a relationship subject to the forms previously established in the private law. This means that it is a relationship between two persons which is entered into with the intention that it should last for life. Since 2017, marriage between two people of the same sex is possible. However, the increasing incidence of people living together without getting married is placing the institution of marriage in question. In some legal situations, for example, in the law of landlord and tenant, the parties to an extramarital relationship are increasingly treated as if they were married.

813   The concept of "family" is less clearly defined than that of "marriage". It encompasses at very least the global community of life of parents and their children insofar as these are still subject to parental care. This includes the relationship with step-children, adoptive children and foster children. A mother and her child born outside of marriage are also a family from the point of view of the constitution. It is an open question whether the relationships between grandparents and their grandchildren and between siblings fall under the constitutional protection of the family.

2. Engagement to Marry

An engagement to marry (*Verlöbnis*) may be a preliminary step towards marriage. However, in social reality it has lost a great deal of its significance. An engagement is the mutual promise of a man and a woman that they intend to marry one another at some stage in the future. This promise also creates a legal relationship which is also called "Engagement".   814

An engagement does not found a legal right to demand that the other party go through with the marriage (§ 1297 BGB). However, the parties to the engagement have a special legal status with respect to one another. For example, the close relationship between the partners which it indicates provides the justification for the rule that the parties cannot be compelled to give evidence against one another whether in court or before administrative bodies, and the relationship is also the basis for various privileges in criminal law. On the other hand, the relationship can give rise to various obligations, for example, the parties are to some extent responsible for one another, which in some situations can give rise to criminal liability for an omission if the partner commits a crime. Breach of the engagement without adequate reason also gives rise to a claim for damages in terms of § 1298 BGB.   815

3. Marriage

a) Entering a Marriage

The constitution guarantees the complete freedom of the parties to choose whom they wish to marry. The possibility of some third party, particularly the parents, determining to whom someone should be married is not recognised in German law. Matrimonial law is laid down essentially in §§ 1303 ff. BGB.   816

Civil marriage is an obligatory requirement for a valid marriage in Germany. A marriage only comes into existence if the parties declare their will to be married before a state registry official. Otherwise, whatever the intention of the parties, the marriage will be void and without effect. From the point of view of the law marriages in church or by some other legal ceremony are usually without effect. Whether the parties enter a religious marriage in addition to their civil marriage is of no importance from the point of view of the law. An exception to the rule that a marriage will not be recognised unless it takes place before the civil authorities is made in the case where neither party is a German citizen.   817

According to article 13 para. 3 EGBGB it is sufficient if they enter the marriage before an institution authorised by either one of the countries of origin, this may take place according to the laws of this country of origin. There are only a few essential requirements for marriage in German law (§§ 1303, 1304 BGB). Thus, persons lacking legal capacity cannot enter a valid marriage, nor can someone who is in a state of unconsciousness or who is suffering from a temporary disturbance of their mental functions. In the case of marriage between minors or other persons with limited capacity the consent of the person with parental responsibility (guardian) is required. The consent of the family court can take the place of the consent of the person with parental responsibility.   818

There is an absolute bar to marriage between blood relations in the direct line, in other words, between parents and their children, between grandparents and their grandchildren, and between brothers and sisters. Polygamy is not permitted in German law.   819

Any marriage entered into contrary to these rules is invalid. This means that the marriage can be nullified by order of court with the same consequences as if the parties were being divorced (§§ 1306 ff. BGB).

820 In certain circumstances defects of will (*Willensmängel*) on the part of the parties will also affect the validity of the marriage. These defects of will include mistake as to the fact that a marriage is being concluded, mistake as to the identity of the other party, or inducement of marriage by duress or fraud (§ 1314 BGB). The consequences are essentially the same as in the case of divorce.

b) Rights and Duties Arising From Marriage

821 The parties to the marriage have a duty of *consortium* (*eheliche Lebensgemeinschaft*, § 1353 para. 1 sentence 2 BGB) and they bear responsibility for one another. This means, above all, the duty to live together in the same home and to have sexual contact with one another, to be faithful to one another, to take care of matters of common interest to them, to support one another and to behave in a considerate manner. It is possible to sue for the enforcement of these rights, but such judgements are not enforceable (§ 120 para. 3 FamFG) because the state should not intervene forcibly in such highly personal, often intimate relationships. The partners to the marriage have a reciprocal duty of support (§ 1360 BGB) which can, if necessary, be enforced by obtaining a judgement. The right to co-possession of household goods and the family home and the integrity of the physical environment of the marriage can be protected by suing in tort: for example, the offended spouse can take legal action to prevent his or her partner from introducing a different partner from outside the marriage into the marital home.

822 The spouses are equal partners in the marriage. They are both equally responsible for the running of the household and both equally entitled to go out and find employment, having due consideration to the interests of the family (§ 1356 para. 2 BGB). How exactly they run the marriage on an everyday basis must depend on what they agree between themselves. Both have the right to buy goods necessary for the everyday needs of the family (§ 1357 BGB). This means that transactions entered by the one spouse to provide for the daily needs of the family also create rights and obligations for the other spouse.

823 The spouses are required to choose a name. This is usually the surname of the man or the surname of the woman. Alternately each spouse may choose to keep the name she or he had before marrying, or add it to the shared name (§ 1355 BGB). If they make such an agreement, then they must also reach some agreement as to what name their children are to bear.

c) Matrimonial Property

824 The financial relationship between the spouses is, to a large extent, determined by the rules on matrimonial property (§§ 1363 ff. BGB). These rules determine to what extent the community of life represented by the marriage also extends to a community of property. However, the rules of matrimonial property law do not provide binding rules for all aspects of the financial relationship between the partners. Rules on the duty of support, employment contracts and partnership agreements may all be relevant in this respect.

The Civil Code recognises three different matrimonial property regimes (*Güterstände*). **825** The standard statutory regime, is called the *Zugewinngemeinschaft* (sharing of accruals). If the parties do not want this, they can enter a special agreement in terms of which they are to be married in community of property (*Gütergemeinschaft*) or out of community of property (*Gütertrennung*). To what extent additional types of matrimonial property regime may be instituted by marriage agreements is not clear. The notaries, before whom such a contract must be concluded, adopt a cautious attitude to new forms. The parties to the marriage can apply to have their matrimonial property regime recorded in a register of marriage agreements which is kept by the local *Amtsgericht* (the lowest level of courts, §§ 1558 ff. BGB). This register serves to give constructive notice of the agreement. In other words, the parties to the marriage cannot invoke the terms of their marriage agreement against third parties if the agreement was capable of being entered in the register but they failed to have it entered and the third party had no actual knowledge of the agreement.

The statutory matrimonial property regime, which provides for the sharing of accruals, comes into operation automatically if two people marry and make no alternative arrangement for their matrimonial property regime (§§ 1363 ff. BGB). It is also possible to make an agreement regulating the matrimonial property regime after the marriage has been concluded (§§ 1408 ff. BGB). The basic idea of the accrual system is that all wealth gained by the couple during the marriage should belong to both of them equally. It was formerly often the case that the wife attends to running the common home while the husband earns money. The Code takes the view that the husband was only able to earn as much money as he did because the wife relieved him of various household tasks which he would otherwise have had to perform.

The fact that the parties are married subject to the system for sharing accruals does **827** not mean that a common estate comes into existence. Each spouse remains the sole owner of any property which he or she had prior to the marriage. Each spouse also controls whatever wealth accrues to his or her estate during the subsistence of the marriage, since each spouse administers his or her own estate in terms of § 1364 BGB. The only restrictions on the ability of each spouse to dispose of his or her property at will are various rules aimed at protecting the other spouse. For example, the one that one may not dispose of his or her entire estate without the permission of the other (§ 1365 BGB).

The accrual to each estate only becomes available to the other spouse on dissolution of **828** the marriage. If one of the spouses dies leaving the other as heir then the surviving spouses statutory portion is increased by an additional quarter share of the entire estate of the deceased (§ 1371 para. 1 BGB). The surviving spouse will thus get ½ of the estate if the couple had children and ¾ of the estate if there were no children, the remainder going to the parents of the deceased.

If the marriage is terminated in some other way, for example, by divorce or an annulment, then a distribution of the accrual (*Zugewinnausgleich*) takes place (§§ 1373 ff. BGB). The accrual is that amount by which the value of the estate of a spouse at the time of dissolution exceeds the value of the estate at the time of entering the marriage. Negative accruals (in the event that he or she is poorer at the end of the marriage than at the beginning) are not taken into account, the accrual never being less than 0. The starting value on marriage is also presumed to be at least 0, in other words the fact that there were debts outstanding on the conclusion of the marriage which have been paid off in the interim is also not taken into account. Certain accruals, to the acquisition of which the other spouse has made no contribution, are also not considered in calculating the accrual. Examples of accruals which are not taken into account are inheritances or donations which were intended to be exclusively for the benefit of the one spouse. After calculating the accrual to each spouse's estate the smaller accrual is then subtracted from the larger accrual. Half the difference between the two amounts is then transferred to the spouse with the smaller accrual. The net effect of this operation is that the wealth which has accrued to the spouses during their marriage is shared equally between them.

830   If the parties wish to be married out of community of property (*Gütertrennung*, § 1414 BGB) they must enter a special agreement to this effect. If they do so their marriage essentially has no influence on the distribution of wealth between them. Both parties maintain absolute discretion in disposing of their property and no transfers take place. However, this does not absolve either party of the duty of support. It also does not prevent transfers ordered on divorce such as transfers to compensate for the loss of old age pensions and similar benefits.

831   Community of property (*Gütergemeinschaft*, §§ 1415-1518 BGB) creates a joint estate (*Gesamthandsvermögen*) which, depending on the exact terms of the agreement, is either administered jointly by both spouses, or by one of the spouses alone. In this case the property of the spouses belongs to both of them jointly. Certain items may be specially excluded from the joint estate by statute, other items of property may be expressly excluded from the joint estate by the agreement.

d) Divorce

832   The dissolution of marriage by divorce is only possible by order of court (§§ 1564 ff. BGB). The Family Courts (*Familiengerichte*), which are a division within each *Amtsgericht*, are responsible for divorces and the regulation of the relationship between the parties subsequent to the divorce as well as for family matters generally. Appeals (*Berufung*) go straight to the *Oberlandesgericht*, proceedings in error (*Revision*) go to the *Bundesgerichtshof*.

833   Divorce is based on the principle of irretrievable breakdown (*Zerrüttungsprinzip*). The failure of the marriage is the only basis on which divorce can be granted (§ 1565 BGB). The reasons for the failure are essentially irrelevant. This is indicative of the fact that the legal system does not attempt to use divorce law to enforce any particular moral view on marriage. Instead its aim is a relationship which is subjectively satisfactory to both partners. Thus, as far as the legal consequences are concerned, it is of no relevance which of the parties was guilty of causing the marriage to fail and, in any case, experience indicates that generally speaking both parties will be partly to blame. On the other hand the law makes little attempt to give the parties external assistance which might help them to continue with the marriage, even if in less than ideal circumstances. Currently about every third marriage in Germany eventually ends in divorce.

834   If the parties have been living separately for at least one year and both desire a divorce then divorce must be granted. Irretrievable breakdown, which can also be proved by other means, is then presumed (§ 1566 para. 1 BGB). For these purposes the parties may be regarded as living separately even if they are still both living in the matrimonial home. On the other hand, mere spatial separation, as in the case of long periods of absence for career reasons, or because one partner is serving a term of imprisonment,

does not in itself constitute separation, in other words the decisive factor is the subjective reason for the separation. If the parties have been living separately for three or more years then irretrievable breakdown must be presumed even if one of the parties objects to the granting of a divorce (§ 1566 para. 2 BGB). A rather weak hardship provision is contained in § 1568 BGB: In special circumstances a divorce shall be refused if, and so long as, this is in the interests of minor children of the marriage or in the interests of the party to the marriage who is defending the divorce action. The requirements for the application of this provision are very seldom met, with the result that it has little real impact.

The divorce, or even the indefinite separation of the parties to a marriage, produces complicated legal consequences. The ease with which a divorce may be obtained is thus subject to the catch of the legal consequences which it brings with it. These consequences may ensure that a marriage remains in fact a lifelong relationship even after it ceases to exist in law.   835

An allotment of custody of children of the marriage (*elterliche Sorge*) in case of divorce is decided on only on application of a parent, in doing so the best interest of the child serves as a basis (§ 1671 BGB). Otherwise the custody of children of the marriage remains with both parents. The parent with whom the children are living has the sole power of decision on matters of daily life (§ 1687 BGB).   836

As far as maintenance is concerned the law starts from the position that after dissolution of the marriage each of the spouses is responsible for his or her own support for the future (§ 1569 BGB). For less wealthy parties sharing of accruals during the marriage has often already taken place. Nevertheless, in cases of need the economically weaker of the parties will generally be awarded a right to maintenance from the economically stronger party which may last for many years or, indeed, for life. The claim for maintenance may, for example, last so long as he or she is caring for the children of the marriage. The amount awarded will depend on the standard of living to which the parties are accustomed and it aims to ensure that both parties will be able to support themselves. The award may take the form of payment of the costs of some sort of employment-related training and an appropriate old age and disability pension. A hardship clause provides for exceptions to the general duty to provide maintenance (§ 1579 BGB). Maintenance may be refused or granted at a reduced level, for example, if the marriage was of short duration, or if the person who would otherwise be entitled to maintenance has committed some serious crime against the other party or his or her family, or if the person requesting maintenance has deliberately rendered him- or herself destitute.   837

In determining what financial arrangements should be made on divorce the court will also consider other claims or potential claims to old-age and disability payments, in other words, it will take into account pensions. In carrying out this equalisation of pensions (*Versorgungsausgleich*) the basic idea is to divide equally the rights which have accrued during the marriage: The difference in value between the pension rights gained by each spouse is calculated, and then the spouse who has gained the greater pension rights during the marriage must generally transfer half of the difference between what he or she has gained and what the other spouse has gained to the other spouse (§§ 1587 ff. BGB). Finally, in the case of divorce or separation the household goods and the matrimonial home are apportioned to one or the other of the spouses largely without reference to the existing obligations and property rights. §§ 1568 a   838 and b BGB grant the spouses certain rights in case an understanding cannot be reached.

4. The Registered Partnership for Life

839   Between 2010 and 2017 it was possible for two people of the same sex to establish a partnership for life. They are then under an obligation to care for and support one another and plan their lives together. Details are contained in the Life Partnerships Act (*Lebenspartnerschaftsgesetz*). The life partners can take the same surname. Each is under a legal obligation to provide for the other's maintenance and they are entitled by law to inherit from one another. The life partnership can be terminated by court order on application of one or both partners if both partners declare that they no longer wish to continue in the partnership and 12 months have passed since the declaration was made. Since 1 October 2017 partners for life may convert their life partnership into marriage pursuant to the Act on Introduction of the Right to Marry for Persons of the Same Sex; entering into life partnership is no longer possible.

5. The Law on Children

840   Family law also regulates the relationships between parents and children (§§ 1589 ff. BGB). The former distinction between legitimate and illegitimate children has widely been abolished in the structure of legal regulations as well as in the terminology. Mother of the child is the woman who gave birth to the child. The father is either the husband of the mother at the time of birth, the one acknowledging paternity, or the one whose paternity is determined by court (§ 1592 BGB). Particularities evolving if the child is born within three hundred days after dissolution of the marriage by death of a partner are laid down in § 1593 BGB. Paternity may be challenged either by the child, the mother or in principle also by the supposed father (§ 1600 BGB).

841   A highly contentious issue on which the law has yet to establish satisfactory rules is the issue of modern reproductive medicine. Homologous insemination, in other words, the situation where the sperm donor is the husband of the woman who is to bear the child, presents no problems: here the father is the husband, the mother the wife. In the case of heterologous insemination the sperm donor is some other man. Even in such a case the husband of the mother cannot challenge the paternity, if he has agreed to the insemination. Furthermore, the dominant view is that the sperm donor is the father of the child and thus bares a duty of support if it proves impossible to obtain support from the apparent father. The insemination and the identity of the donor must be documented by the medical practitioner performing the operation and must be disclosed on demand. If the doctor refuses to disclose this information he or she will be liable to pay damages. The sperm donor may not remain anonymous because the child has a claim, based on his or her constitutional rights, to know his or her own origins.[16]

842   Children and parents have a mutual duty of support, insofar as the one party has need of support and the other has the ability to provide it (§§ 1601 ff. BGB). The extent of the support owed to a child is determined with reference to the standard of living of the parents and the overall needs of the child (§ 1610 BGB). The parents also have a legal duty to finance the training of the child for suitable employment.

---

16   BVerfG NJW 1989, p. 891.

Formerly so-called illegitimate children are today described by the law as children whose parents are not married to one another (§§ 1615 a ff. BGB). In principle, the same general regulations are applied to them as to children whose parents are married to one another. A minor child's minimum maintenance allowance (*Mindestunterhalt*) is determined in § 1612 a BGB. It is a percental calculation based on the tax-exempt living wage . In 2016 the amount is set at € 460 Euro per month for a child between the ages of 12 and 17. Apart from this amount, the determination of an appropriate amount of maintenance is often made with reference to the so-called "Düsseldorf Table".[17]   **843**

The parents have the duty and the right to care for the minor child (§§ 1626 ff. BGB). This parental care includes care for the person of the child (*Personensorge*) and care for the child's property (*Vermögensorge*). It is derived directly from article 6 para. 2 GG, in terms of which the caring for and bringing up of children is the right of the parents and is also a duty which rests primarily on them. This imposition of primary responsibility on the parents reflects the belief that, generally speaking, the interests of the child can best be realised by the parents even if their views and abilities are not what most people would consider appropriate for bringing up children. On all aspects of the law relating to children the best interests of the child have become the central point of reference. The presumption is that to realise the child's best interests both parents should have equal powers and should act in concert. However, there are certain exceptions in the case of children whose parents are not married to one another and in the case of children whose parents are separated. If the parents prove incapable of co-operating then the family court may transfer the decision-making authority to one parent alone (§ 1628 BGB).   **844**

Caring for the person of the child (*Personensorge*) includes in particular the right and duty to attend to the child's physical well-being and up-bringing, to supervise him or her and to determine where the child spends its time and with whom (§ 1631 BGB). All personal matters are included. The parents are the statutory representatives of the child. They must always take into consideration the steadily increasing perceptiveness and independence of the child as he or she grows older. Children have a right to be brought up without being subjected to violence. Corporal punishment, psychological abuse or other humiliating treatment are not permitted. In determining what career and what career training the child is to have the parents must take into account the inclinations of the child.   **845**

Caring for the property of the child (*Vermögenssorge*, §§ 1638 ff. BGB) involves essentially all wealth belonging to the child. However, in certain circumstances where there is a conflict of interests the power to act on the child's behalf is excluded (§§ 1629 para. 2, 1795 BGB). Certain important transactions, such as those involving the disposition of an interest in land, require the approval of the family court acting as upper guardian (§§ 1821, 1643 para. 2 BGB). The court of first instance in obtaining such approval is the *Amtsgericht*.   **846**

The family court can also order necessary steps to be taken if the well-being of the child is endangered and the parents are unable or unwilling to avert the danger. For this purpose the parental authority can be limited or terminated, always having strict   **847**

---

17 A current version can be found at: http://www.olg-duesseldorf.nrw.de/infos/Duesseldorfer_tabelle/Tabell e-2016/.

regard to the principle of proportionality (*Verhältnismäßigkeitsgrundsatz*, §§ 1666 ff. BGB). If neither parent is available to take care of the child then the parental responsibility may be conferred on some other person (*Pfleger*, § 1909 BGB). However, before the court resorts to such drastic measures there are many different types of help which can be made available to parents and child, for example, in terms of the Children and Young Persons Assistance Act (*Kinder- und Jugendhilfegesetz*). This help ranges from counselling to transferring the child to children's home or a foster family.

848 The parents are liable to the child for not carrying out their parental duties properly (§ 1664 BGB) if they fail to show the degree of care which they are accustomed to exercise in attending to their own business, and they will always be liable if their behaviour is grossly negligent (§ 1664 read with § 277 BGB).

849 If one of the parents has been deprived of parental responsibility he or she nevertheless will generally still have the right to personal access to the child (§ 1684 BGB). The Family Court may issue more specific instructions as to the extent of the contact. The Family Court also determines who is to care for the child in the event of divorce or separation if the parents prove unable to reach an agreement.

6. Relationship, Adoption, Guardianship and Similar Topics

a) Relationship by Consanguinity (Blood) and by Affinity (Marriage)

850 Relationship by consanguinity (relationship by blood, *Blutsverwandtschaft*) is determined by ancestry (§ 1589 BGB). If one person is descended from another then they are relations in the direct line (*in gerader Linie*), for example, in the relationship grandmother-mother-daughter. Relationship in the collateral line (*Seitenlinie*) exists when people share a common ancestor, for example, brothers and sisters, cousins, or uncle and nephew. The closeness of the relationship is measured in degrees. The number of degrees is calculated by counting the number of births intervening between the two people whose degree of relationship is to be determined. Parents and children are related in the 1st degree, brothers and sisters in the 2nd degree, an aunt and niece in the 3rd degree, and cousins in the 4th degree. A husband and wife are, as such, not related. Their relationship is regulated by special rules.

851 There are numerous legal consequences attached to blood relationship. These legal consequences are justified by the particular closeness between relations which is presumed by the law. Relationship is the basis for prohibitions on marriage (§ 1307 BGB), duties of support (§§ 1601 ff. BGB), and a *prima facie* right of inheritance (§§ 1924 ff. BGB). Relationship can be a mitigating circumstance in criminal law (§§ 247, 258 StGB), and can entitle a witness to refuse to give evidence (§§ 383, 408 ZPO, §§ 52, 55, 61, 72 StPO) and can impose on a judge a duty of recuse him- or herself (§§ 41, 49 ZPO, §§ 22, 31 StPO; § 6 FamFG, § 54 VwGO). In some cases these legal consequences depend on the degree of relationship.

852 Relationship by affinity, i.e., by marriage (*Schwägerschaft*) is somewhat less important (§ 1590 BGB). It describes the relationship between one spouse or life partner and the blood relations of the other spouse or life partner. Here too distinctions are made between relationship in the direct and collateral lines, and between degrees of relationship. The wife is related by affinity to the mother of her husband, in other words, her mother in law, in the first degree. The relationship by affinity creates neither a duty of

support nor a right to inherit by intestacy, but, as in the case of blood relations, certain relations by marriage can refuse to give evidence against one another.

b) Adoption

The parent-child relationship can also be established by adoption (§§ 1741 ff. BGB). Apart from the adoption of minors, it is also possible for people over the age of 18 to be adopted, although the requirements are stricter and the effects of the adoption more limited (§§ 1767 ff. BGB). The adoption of a minor gives the child a status equivalent to that of a child whose parents are married to one another. Essentially the relatives of the parents become the relatives of the child and the child's relationship to its former relatives is terminated.

853

The main requirements for adoption are that it should be in the best interests of the child and that there should be a reasonable chance that a parent-child relationship can develop between the persons wanting to adopt and the child to be adopted (§ 1741 para. 1 BGB). The finalisation of the adoption is preceded by a reasonable period of foster care by way of trial (§ 1744 BGB).

854

The adoptive parents or parent must be over the age of 25. An unmarried person can only adopt a child by him- or herself, whereas spouses can in principle only adopt a child together. In cases where one spouse is already parent of the child, the other spouse can also adopt the child by him- or herself. This holds true also if one spouse is not yet over the age of 21 or legally incapable, since in principle at least one of the parents adopting must be over the age of 25 and the other at least over the age of 21. Only in exceptional cases, specifically, when the well-being of the child is endangered, can an adoption be reversed (§§ 1759 f., 1763 BGB).

855

c) Guardianship, Custodianship, and Curatorship for Specific Matters

The purpose of guardianship (*Vormundschaft*) is to make provision for parental care in cases where the parents are unable to provide it themselves (§§ 1773 ff. BGB). This could be the case if the parents have died or if they have been judged unfit to care for the child. Guardianship is usually declared ex officio by the Family Court (*Familiengericht*, § 1774 sentence 1 BGB, § 151 number 4 FamFG). The guardian is the legal representative of the child who is his or her ward (*Mündel*). It is the guardian's duty to care for the person and property of the child. For certain transactions the guardian needs the consent of the Guardianship Court (§§ 1821 ff. BGB).

856

The possibility of guardianship over an adult who lacks legal capacity because he or she is, for example, mentally deficient, has been replaced by the concept of custodianship (*Betreuung*, §§ 1896 ff. BGB). This comes into operation by order of the Custodianship Court (*Betreuungsgericht*) and is appropriate when a person over the age of 18 is partially or wholly incapable of dealing with his or her own business. The cause may be mental illness or some physical, mental or psychological disability. In contrast to the earlier approach, which was to entirely deprive such a person of legal capacity, there are different degrees of custodianship, with the custodian's authority being limited to the specific matters which the specific disabled person is unable to attend to him- or herself. The custodianship may, however, also be comprehensive. The basic policy consideration underlying the institution of custodianship is that the disabled

857

person's legal capacity should be left intact insofar as this person is capable of acting for him- or herself.

858   Apart from guardianship and custodianship the Code also recognises the institution of curatorship (*Pflegschaft*, §§ 1909 ff. BGB). This is a type of partial guardianship. The curator does not attend to every aspect of his or her wards business, but only to certain specific aspects. The exact extent of the curator's authority is defined by statute or by his or her letters of appointment (*Bestellungsakt*). Thus, for example, an auxiliary curator (*Ergänzungspfleger*) is appointed for a minor child in situations where the parent or guardian of the child is prevented from representing the child by a conflict of interests (§§ 1795, 1796, 181 BGB). This could be the case where business is being transacted between the father or mother and the child. Similarly, when a child is given into the care of foster parents (*Pflegeeltern*) they can be given parental authority in certain limited fields to make it easier for them to care for the child. A curator in the form of a curator in absence can also be appointed for an adult, for example, when this person's whereabouts are unknown, or when for some reason the person is unable to return and attend to his or her affairs (§ 1911 BGB). Sometimes the identity of a party in a piece of business which must be attended to is unknown, for example, in the case of an inheritance where it has not yet been determined who is to inherit. Here, once again, a provisional administrator (*Nachlasspfleger*) can be appointed (§§ 1960 ff. BGB).

Literature:

Nina Dethloff, Familienrecht, 32. ed. 2018
Dieter Schwab, Familienrecht, 26. ed. 2018

VI. The Law of Succession

1. Basic Principles

859   The constitution guarantees the right of inheritance in article 14 para. 1 GG, which states that ownership and the right of inheritance are guaranteed and that the content and limits of these rights are determined by statute. The most important provisions on the law of succession are contained in the fifth book of the Civil Code (BGB). Numerous other relevant provisions are scattered throughout the law. For example, the inheritance of farms is regulated in different ways in the laws of each state of the Federation (*Land*). The important rules relating to the estate duty (*Erbschaftsteuer*), which must be paid to the state in the case of succession by death, are contained in the Estate Duty and Donations Tax Act (*Erbschaft- und Schenkungssteuergesetz*).

860   The German law of succession is guided by three basic principles, namely, the principle of universal succession (*Universalsukzession* or *Gesamtrechtsnachfolge*), the principle of testamentary freedom (*Testierfreiheit*), and the principle of inheritance by the family (*Familienerbfolge*). Freedom of testation (testamentary freedom) refers to the power of the testator (*Erblasser*) to freely determine the fate of his or her property after his or her death (§§ 1937 ff. BGB). This power is to some extent limited by the principle of inheritance by the family. The legislator's assumption is that the deceased was close to his or her family and that, in most cases, they have also contributed in some way to his or her accumulation of wealth. Freedom of testation does, however, as a general rule take precedence over the principle of inheritance by the family: Only insofar as the deceased has made no provision to the contrary does his or her property pass by

operation of law to his or her blood relatives and to his or her spouse. However, a certain minimum portion is reserved for the spouse and blood relatives even if the testator has provided otherwise. In such a case the excluded family members have a claim against the beneficiaries appointed by the testator under the will for a certain minimum share of the estate (*Pflichtteilsanspruch*, see § 2303 BGB).

An aspect in which German law differs from English law is that general speaking the person inheriting, whether by the rules of intestate succession or under a will, will act as the administrator or executor of the estate without the interposition of some third party as the deceased's personal representative. The principle of universal succession (§ 1922 para. 1 BGB) thus means that, immediately on the death of the deceased, the person inheriting steps into the shoes of the deceased, that is, he or she takes over all the assets and liabilities (*Aktiva und Passiva*) of the deceased. This takes place by operation of law and without any formal act of transfer. 861

A glance at the structure of the fifth book of the Civil Code (BGB) indicates the most important institutions of the law of succession. Firstly the hierarchy of beneficiaries on intestacy (*Erbfolge*) is set out, and then the legal position of persons benefiting is regulated. Next come the provisions on wills (*Testamente*), then the inheritance contract appointing heirs *inter vivos* (*Erbvertrag*), the claim of family members to a compulsory portion of the deceased's estate (*Pflichtteil*), grounds of disqualification from inheritance (*Erbunwürdigkeit*), renunciation of the inheritance (*Erbverzicht*), the inheritance certificate (*Erbschein*), which corresponds in part to letters of administration or a grant of probate, and lastly the purchase and sale of an inheritance as a whole (*Erbschaftskauf*). 862

2. Intestate Succession

The ability to inherit is dependent on having legal capacity. This means that both natural and legal persons can inherit, but an animal cannot. In some cases legal capacity is fictitious, for example, in the case of an unborn child after conception (*nasciturus*, § 1923 para. 2 BGB). The person whose property is in question (*Erblasser*) may determine who is to benefit on his or her death by a disposition in contemplation of death (*Verfügung von Todes wegen*), which would generally take the form of a will (§§ 1937 ff. BGB). If the deceased has failed to specifically appoint beneficiaries then the rules of intestate succession operate. Only when no appropriate beneficiaries can be found does the property pass to the state. 863

In terms of §§ 1924 ff. BGB the beneficiary on intestacy is the spouse. Which of the blood relations is to inherit beyond the spouse is determined in accordance with a complicated parentela system *per stirpes*. The law makes distinctions based on degrees (*Ordnungen*) of common ancestry. The decisive factor is whether the claimant is descended from the intestate deceased, or from his or her parents, or grandparents, and so forth. Beneficiaries by intestacy in the first degree are the descendants of the deceased and their descendants. Beneficiaries in the second degree are the deceased's parents and their descendants, in other words the parents, sisters, brothers, nephews and nieces of the deceased. Beneficiaries in the third degree are the grandparents and their descendants. 864

As long as any relations of one of the prior degrees can be located all those of the next degree are excluded from benefiting. Within a particular degree an existing beneficiary excludes all his or her descendants from benefiting. Thus, if the deceased has a child 865 and grandchildren, the child will inherit everything to the exclusion of the grandchildren. However, if the child does not inherit, for example, because the child has predeceased the intestate deceased, then the child's children will inherit his or her share of the intestate's estate. They will inherit that proportion of the estate which their parent would have inherited from the intestate had he or she still been alive. Thus, for example, if the intestate is survived by a son and two grandchildren who are the children of a predeceased daughter, then the son will get ½ of the estate and the two grandchildren will share the ½ share of the daughter, that is, they will each receive a ¼ share. This is called succession *nach Stämmen (per stirpes)*. If the intestate deceased has no descendants then the estate, insofar as it does not pass to a surviving spouse, passes upwards to his or her father or mother, who each are entitled to a ½ share. If either of them has predeceased the intestate, then his or her half share passes to his or her descendants. This is called the *Liniensystem* (passing in the line). After the 4th degree has been passed these two principles (*Stammessystem, Liniensystem*) are abandoned in favour of the *Gradualsystem* which provides that the person within a particular degree most closely related to the deceased is to inherit.

866 Children whose parents are not married to one another are with respect to the law of succession essentially treated in the same way as children whose parents are married to one another. The surviving spouse or life partner is also entitled to inherit under the rules on intestacy (§§ 1931 ff. BGB, § 10 LPartG). In the case of married person the exact proportion to which the surviving spouse is entitled depends on which matrimonial property regime is applicable and on the degree of relationship between the deceased and the other potential heirs. The marriage must still have subsisted at the time of the intestate's death. The most important exception to the right of the surviving spouse to inherit is if the circumstances were such as to justify the granting of a divorce and the deceased had initiated divorce proceedings or had assented to divorce proceedings initiated by the surviving spouse. If there are other heirs who stand in the first degree of relationship to the deceased, in other words children or their representatives, then the surviving spouse is entitled to ¼ of the estate, irrespective of how many children there are. If the other heirs are relations of the deceased in the second degree or are the grandparents of the deceased then the surviving spouse is entitled to ½ of the estate. In all other cases the surviving spouse is entitled to the whole of the estate. This means that descendants of the intestate's grandparents do not receive anything if competing with the intestate's surviving spouse for a share. If the surviving spouse was married to the deceased under the standard accrual regime (*Zugewinngemeinschaft*), then he or she is entitled to an additional ¼ of the estate on intestacy (§ 1371 BGB). By way of concrete example, this means that if the intestate deceased is being survived by a spouse and children, the spouse (assuming that they were married under the standard accrual regime) will receive half of the deceased's estate and the children will share the other half between them. The various other matrimonial property regimes provided for in the Civil Code will also produce differing results on intestacy if there is a surviving spouse.

3. Deliberate Regulation of Succession (Including Wills) and Specific Gifts

867 Deliberate regulation of succession (*gewillkürte Erbfolge*) can take the form of a will (*Testament*, § 1937 BGB), an inheritance contract (*Erbvertrag*, § 1941 BGB) or the joint will of a married couple (*gemeinschaftliches Testament*, §§ 2265 ff. BGB). By

means of these various instruments the *Erblasser*, that is, the person whose estate is being regulated (who will be referred to in the rest of this section as the testator for the sake of convenience) can make various stipulations regarding the succession. For example, he or she can determine who is to be a beneficiary (*Erbe*), state how the estate is to be divided and how it is to be used, and burden the estate in various ways.

Wills are subject to strict formal requirements (§§ 2064 ff. BGB). A distinction is made between a private will (*privates Testament*) and a public will (*öffentliches Testament*) which may only be drawn up by a notary or an authorised consular official. A private will must be entirely hand written by the testator him- or herself and signed by the testator (§ 2247 para. 1 BGB). If not, it is void. To create a public will the testator can orally declare his or her will to a notary, who will reduce it to writing, or the testator can hand over to the notary an open or sealed written declaration (§ 2232 BGB). If the circumstances make it impossible to comply with these formal requirements, for example, because the testator is on the point of death, then an emergency will (*Nottestament*), valid for a limited period of time, can be created. This should be done in the presence of the mayor and two witnesses, or, if that is also not possible, the testator can declare his or her will orally before three witnesses (§§ 2249 ff. BGB). 868

The capacity to create a will comes into existence with the celebration of a person's 16th birthday (§ 2229 para. 1 BGB). However, if a minor wishes to make a will he or she is bound by special formalities which are directed at assuring that the minor will have the advice of some official such as a notary (§ 2233 BGB). 869

A will can be cancelled at any time. No reasons need be given. A later will takes precedence over an earlier one insofar as the later will is incompatible with the validity of the earlier will. 870

A testator (in the broad sense) can also make arrangements for the inheritance of his or her property by means of an inheritance contract (*Erbvertrag*) entered into with another person (§§ 2274 ff. BGB). The beneficiary may be the other party to the contract or a third person, and all arrangements which can be made in a will can also be made in an inheritance contract. The "testator" is bound by the inheritance contract. This means that a subsequent will departing from the terms of the inheritance contract to the detriment of the beneficiary named in the contract will be invalid insofar as it is incompatible with the contract. The only way of unilaterally terminating an inheritance contract is on the basis of certain grounds of rescission or voidability which are specially regulated in the Code. The inheritance contract may, however, be terminated by a new agreement. Furthermore, the "testator" can still freely dispose of his or her property (for example, by selling or donating some of his or her property) during his or her life. However, if the "testator" makes donations which detrimentally affect the position of the beneficiary under the inheritance contract, then the beneficiary will have an enrichment action against the person who received the gift (§ 2287 para. 1 BGB). 871

A joint will (*gemeinschaftliches Testament*) describes the situation in which a husband and wife jointly draw up a single will (§§ 2265 ff. BGB). The declaration of each of the testators is mutually dependent on the declaration of the other. A common instance of the joint will is the so-called "Berlin Will" (*Berliner Testament*, § 2267 BGB). Here each spouse declares the other to be the sole beneficiary of the first dying, and some third party, usually the child or children of the couple, is declared to be the heir of the surviving spouse. 872

873   In a provision which in some ways resembles the creation of a testamentary trust the Code also allows for the possibility of determining a series of heirs who are to inherit in succession (*Nacherben*). Here the property is first inherited by a prior heir (the *Vorerbe*) and subsequently passes as specified by the testator to another person (the *Nacherbe*). This will generally occur on the death of the *Vorerbe*, but the testator can stipulate some other point in time for the property to pass if he or she chooses. The *Vorerbe* will be subject to numerous restrictions in his or her dealings with the property (§§ 2100 ff. BGB). The aim of providing for a series of heirs (*Nacherbschaft*) will often be to keep the property of the testator in the family for as long as possible.

874   Any regulation of succession *mortis causa* can be challenged by anyone who would stand to benefit from its invalidity. Errors of motive are a valid ground for challenging dispositions by the testator (§§ 2078 ff. BGB). However, particularly when challenging a will on the basis of error of motive, the challenger will face considerable difficulties of proof. Wherever possible the court will interpret the will in accordance with the intentions of the testator and avoid interpretations which make it necessary to set it aside (§ 2084 BGB).

875   The beneficiaries can be deprived of the inheritance with retrospective effect if grounds of disqualification (*Erbunwürdigkeit*) can be shown (§§ 2339 ff. BGB). This is only done in cases of a few particularly serious defects in the claim of the beneficiary. The withdrawal of benefits takes place by order of court when a person with some interest in the invalidity of the disposition challenges it successfully.

876   An executor or executors (*Testamentsvollstrecker*) can be appointed by the testator if he or she feels that such an appointment is necessary to protect the estate or to ensure that the wishes expressed in his or her will are carried out (§§ 2197 ff. BGB). This would once again serve a similar purpose to the creation of a testamentary trust in English law. If an executor is appointed he or she is generally empowered to administer the estate. The beneficiaries can then not dispose of those assets of the estate which are subject to the executor's authority without the permission of the executor. The testator is free to stipulate the extent and the duration of the executor's authority.

877   It is also possible for a testator to leave some part of his or her wealth to a particular person in his or her will without making that person a residuary beneficiary (*Erbe*). Such specific bequests or devises are called a *Vermächtnis* (§§ 2147 ff. BGB). The bequest burdens the deceased's estate and can operate against either a residuary beneficiary or against another specific beneficiary (*Vermächtnisnehmer*). On the death of the deceased the beneficiary of the *Vermächtnis* will then have a personal claim based on the law of obligations against the person who has been obliged to transfer the object of the *Vermächtnis*.

878   A statutory *Vermächtnis* is imposed in favour of the surviving spouse in respect of household goods of the common home and of wedding presents insofar as these are necessary for him or her to continue living in appropriate circumstances (*Recht auf den Voraus*, § 1932 BGB). A further imposition is the "thirty" (*das Dreißigste*). This is a right of the members of the deceased's household to maintenance for the thirty days immediately following his or her death (§ 1969 BGB).

4. Family Provision – The Minimum Claim of the Spouse and Blood Relatives

The basic principle of testamentary freedom also includes the right of the testator to exclude the spouse and blood relatives from benefiting under the will. No special reasons need to be given when disinheriting relatives in this way. As compensation, and to protect the principle of inheritance by the family (*Familienerbfolge*), family members have a right to a certain compulsory portion of the deceased's estate (*Pflichtteilsrecht*, §§ 2303 ff. BGB). The surviving spouse, the parents and the descendants can all base a claim on this right if they have been excluded from inheriting by the testator's will. The minimum provision to which they are entitled is one half of what they would have been entitled to had the deceased died intestate. The claim is a personal claim under the law of obligations enforceable against the beneficiaries under the will. However, the person bringing the claim does not have the status of a beneficiary under the will and has no claim to specific objects which form part of the deceased's estate. 879

This minimum provision for family members can only be excluded if the potential claimant has committed certain particularly grave offences against the testator (§§ 2333 ff. BGB). There are a variety of protective measures to prevent the testator from avoiding the minimum provision in other cases, for example, by making donations to third parties during his or her lifetime (§§ 2305 ff. BGB). 880

5. The Position of the Heir (Beneficiary)

The heirs acquire this status automatically on the death of the person to whose property they are succeeding (§ 1942 para. 1 BGB). It is thus possible for someone to be an heir without or even contrary to his or her wishes. Particularly because the heirs also assume responsibility for all the liabilities of the deceased's estate, it is possible for them to renounce the inheritance (*Ausschlagung*, §§ 1942 ff. BGB). In such a case the passing of the inheritance to the heir is voided with retrospective effect. Only in exceptional cases is it possible to renounce only a part of the inheritance while accepting the rest. 881

The heir is liable to the full extent of his or her own assets for the liabilities of the deceased's estate (§ 1967 BGB). The heir does, however, have the options of placing the estate under administration on behalf of the creditors (*Nachlassverwaltung*) or of having the estate declared bankrupt (*Nachlassinsolvenzverfahren*). In such a case the inheritance is kept separate and the liability of the heir with respect to the creditors of the deceased is limited to the extent of the assets inherited. There are also certain other cases in which liability is limited. One is where the assets in the estate would not cover the costs of bankruptcy administration. Another is where the residuary inheritance is insufficient to cover all the specific bequests (*Vermächtnisse*) and charges (*Auflagen*) on the estate (§§ 1990, 1992 BGB). 882

The heir can sell the estate as a whole (§§ 2371 ff. BGB). If the heir does so he or she bears no liability if the goods are not of merchantable quality (*Sachmängelhaftung*, liability for latent defects). 883

If several people are heirs to the same estate they are called joint heirs (*Miterben*, §§ 2032 ff. BGB). They then form a community of joint owners of the estate (*Erbengemeinschaft*). This is a form of *Gesamthandsgemeinschaft* (§ 2032 BGB). Each heir then has a share in the estate, which is separate from the rest of his or her property. Each heir can deal with this share as such, for example, by selling or donating all of part of 884 it. However, only the community of joint owners as a whole can make decisions as to what is to be done with specific assets in the deceased's estate.

885 The community of joint heirs continues in existence until the deceased's estate is divided between them. This involves bringing to an end all the legal obligations in which the deceased's estate is involved particularly its debts. The residue of the estate is then divided amongst the heirs according to their shares and then becomes part of their own private fortunes. In cases of disagreement between the heirs the division of the estate is decided by order of court. Until the estate has been divided up in this way each of the heirs is entitled to refuse to settle obligations of the deceased's estate out of his or her own personal property.

886 It is possible to renounce an inheritance even before the death of the person whose estate is in question (*Erbverzicht*, §§ 2346 ff. BGB). This is achieved by concluding a notarial contract with the testator. The person renouncing the inheritance is then treated as if they had predeceased the testator for purposes of the law of succession. A contract for the renunciation of inheritance rights (*Erbverzichtsvertrag*) is often concluded on marriage, for example, where one of the parties already has children by an earlier marriage. The contract renouncing rights of inheritance is then often combined with an inheritance contract, in other words the rights of inheritance are renounced in return for the promise of a specific legacy.

887 Sometimes the deceased has chosen to regulate the legal position after his or her death by various types of legal transactions between living persons. For example, the deceased can promise a gift (German law has no requirement of consideration) which is only to be handed over on his or her death. To prevent prejudice to the heirs and the creditors of the deceased's estate such gifts which remain unperfected during the deceased's lifetime are subjected to the same restrictions as inheritance contracts and wills (mainly § 2301 para. 1 BGB).

888 Evidence of the right to inherit is the inheritance certificate (*Erbschein*). To some extent this corresponds the grant of probate or of letters of administration, since the heirs administer the deceased's estate. The certificate is issued on application to the probate court (*Nachlassgericht*, § 2353 BGB). This function is carried out at first instance by the *Amtsgericht*. The probate court has the official duty to determine who the heirs are. Once an inheritance certificate has been issued there is a presumption that the holder is entitled to inherit. Any person who in good faith makes performance to the holder of the certificate will be discharged from his or her obligations to the deceased's estate. For example, a person who owed a debt to the testator will be discharged from the debt if he or she makes performance to the holder of the certificate, and cannot subsequently be sued by the true heirs if the certificate was issued in error.

889 Estate duties (*Erbschaftsteuer*) must be paid on any inheritance. On the other hand, an inheritance is not subject to income tax. Donations tax and estate duties are regulated in the same statute and essentially in the same way. The amount of estate duty payable depends on the degree of relationship between the beneficiary and the testator or intestate deceased (§ 15 ErbStG): Tax category I includes the surviving spouse and life partner, children and stepchildren, their descendants, as well as parents and the parents' ancestors when inheriting. Tax category II is for parents and parents' ancestors if they do not fall into category I, siblings, their descendants in the first degree, for step-parents, children in law and parents in law, and lastly for the divorced spouse or the life partner of a dissolved partnership in life. Tax category III applies to all other beneficia-

ries and earmarked gifts. Furthermore, within each category the amount payable gradually increases with the value of the inheritance. For category I the range is between 7 % and 30 %, for category III the range is between 30 % and a maximum of 50 % (§ 19 ErbStG). Certain sums are tax exempt. For example, in the case of spouses and life partners there is a tax-free allowance of € 500 000 and an additional tax-free amount of € 256 000 for retirement purposes. Children have a basic tax-free allowance of € 400 000 plus an additional amount of up to € 52 000 for their support, depending on their age (§§ 16, 17 ErbStG).

Literature:

Hans Brox/Wolf-Dietrich Walker, Erbrecht, 28. ed. 2018
Rainer Frank/Tobias Helms, Erbrecht, 7. ed. 2018
Dieter Leipold, Erbrecht, 21. ed. 2016
Lutz Michalski, BGB-Erbrecht, 5. ed. 2019

VII. Conflict of Laws (Private International Law)

Each country has its own rules on private international law. The purpose of private international law is to determine which country's law is to be applied to a legal problem with an international dimension. German private international law will often make reference to the rules of some foreign legal system which the German court must then apply in reaching a decision. The basic provisions of German private international law are contained in articles 3 to 48 of the Act on Introductory Provisions to the Civil Code (*Einführungsgesetz zum Bürgerlichen Gesetzbuch*, abbreviated *EGBGB*). In addition, there are numerous international treaties, special in statutes dealing with specific areas and a significant amount of case-law. | 890

The possibility of transferring cases in terms of German private international law is subject to the *ordre public* proviso set out in article 6 EGBGB. This states that if a legal rule of a foreign legal system, which ordinarily would be applicable, would lead to an outcome which is patently incompatible with basic principles of German law, then that rule may not be followed. This applies particularly to rules which are in conflict with the fundamental rights in the constitution. Similar principles apply to the recognition of foreign court decisions according to § 328 ZPO and article 45 European Regulation on Jurisdiction, recognition and enforcement of judgments in civil and commercial matters (EuGVVO) with some modifications as to the scope of such limitations. | 891

German private international law often directs that a foreign legal system should govern all aspects of a particular dispute. This is referred to as a global remission (*Gesamtverweisung*). Not infrequently the private international law of the country whose law is thus referred to in terms of German private international law will in turn refer the case for decision according to German law or according to the law of some other country. In such cases of renvoi or referral to some third state the parties are generally bound to follow the various referrals. This, however, does not apply where the parties have made a choice of law or when the case concerns contractual obligations (article 4 para. 2 EGBGB, article 20 Rome I-VO). | 892

With respect to the law of natural persons and legal transactions, the basic principle is that the law of nationality (*lex patriae* or *Heimatrecht*) of the parties is applicable in determining issues of capacity, a person's name, and when they can officially be declared dead (articles 7, 9 and 10 EGBGB). The formal validity of a legal transaction is determined either with reference to the law of the place where the transaction was en- | 893 tered into, or is treated as being governed by the rules of the legal system whose laws govern the substantive aspects of the transaction.

894 With respect to contracts the German law provides, in accordance with the principle of private autonomy, that a transaction is governed by the legal system chosen by the parties, whether expressly or implicitly (article 3 Rome I-VO). If the parties did not choose the applicable law in accordance with article 3 Rome I-VO, then the applicable law for the contract is generally determined by article 4 Rome I-VO. In the interests of consumers, carriers, insurance companies and employees the law makes special provision for contracts involving members of these groups (articles 5, 6, 7, 8 Rome I-VO). For damages claims arising out of tort the basic principle is that the law of the place where the tort occurred is applicable (article 40 EGBGB). This could either be the place where the harmful act was committed or the place where the harm was suffered. In private international law the term "tort" has a much wider meaning than in the German substantive law. It thus includes also strict liability, the claim to compensation against a public authority for impairment of health and claims based on breach of duty at the time of contracting where general duties of care are violated.

895 In Germany the international law of property is governed by the law of the country in which the thing is located (*lex rei sitae*). If a thing in respect of which rights are asserted ends up in a different state, then it is not possible to exercise the rights in question in a manner contrary to the laws of that state (article 43 para. 1, 2 EGBGB).

896 International family law is of considerable practical significance. The requirements for a valid marriage are generally determined according to the legal system of each of the parties to the marriage (article 13 para. 1 EGBGB). If the marriage was concluded in Germany then, generally speaking, its validity will be determined solely according to German law. For a number of questions in family law the basic rule is that the law of nationality (*lex patriae* or *Heimatrecht*) of the spouses is the starting point. Alternately, the law of their normal place of residence may apply if they are both resident in the same state. If neither of these rules provides a solution, then the law to be applied is the law of the state with which the spouses have the closest connections. These rules are applied in determining the matrimonial property regime and divorces (articles 14-17 EGBGB). Rules for partnerships in life can be found in article 17 b EGBGB. The parties have only a limited choice of law in these circumstances (articles 14 para. 2-4; 15 para. 2 EGBGB). The descent of the child is subject to the law of the normal place of residence (article 19 EGBGB).

897 For the protection of the interests of minors, for example in the case of custody proceedings following a divorce, the 1961 Hague Convention concerning the protection of minors is applicable. Whether a person is entitled to maintenance is determined according to the law of the normal place of residence of the person claiming maintenance (article 18 para. 1 EGBGB).

898 The international law of succession takes as its starting point the *lex patriae* of the testator or intestate deceased. For land within Germany the testator may provide in his or her will that German law is to govern the devolution to his or her heirs (article 25 EGBGB). Numerous special rules apply to wills in terms of article 26 EGBGB.

Literature:
Peter Hay/Hannes Rösler, Internationales Privat- und Zivilverfahrensrecht, 5. ed. 2016
Abbo Junker, Internationales Privatrecht, 3. ed. 2019
Gerhard Ring/Line Olsen-Ring, Internationales Privatrecht, 2. ed. 2017

VIII. Corporate and Commercial Law

1. Commercial Law

Commercial law (*Handelsrecht*) regulates the relationships between business people 899
(*Kaufmann*). It is a specialisation of the private law which aims to provide for the specific needs of commercial life, for example, taking into account that a business person needs less protection than an ordinary consumer, and greater freedom of contract. The field includes not only the buying and selling of goods, but also other areas of business life such as the transport, banking and insurance industries and manufacturing and craftsmanship. The German system of commercial law, in the narrow sense in which the phrase is often used in Germany, applies specifically to the "businessman" (*Kaufmann*). Who has this status, and what legal consequences follow from it, is defined by the law. It is thus in principle a subjective system of special rules applicable only to business people, in contrast to the objective system of France, which is applicable to all business transactions. Since commercial law regulates a sphere of life in which business enterprises play a major part and in which the individual business person often only plays a secondary role, commercial law is often also referred to as business enterprises law (*Recht der Unternehmen*).

The basic provisions of commercial law are contained in the Commercial Code (*Han-* 900
delsgesetzbuch, abbreviated *HGB*). The HGB was completed in 1897 but came into force simultaneously with the Civil Code (*BGB*) on the 1st of January 1900 and has been amended many times since then. In addition, there are numerous other relevant statutes, such as the Act for the Prevention of Restrictive Trade Practices (*Gesetz gegen Wettbewerbsbeschränkungen*), the Coal and Steel Co-Determination Act (*Montanmitbestimmungsgesetz*), the Co-Determination in Industry Act (*Mitbestimmungsgesetz*), the Employees' Representation Act (*Betriebsverfassungsgesetz*) and the statutes regulating the various types of corporation such as the Stock Corporation Act (*Aktiengesetz*) and the Act on Private Limited Companies (*GmbH-Gesetz*). Some of these specialisations have already attained the status of independent fields of law.

Commercial law is exposed to strong currents in favour of international harmonisa- 901
tion, particularly within the European Union. These attempts at harmonisation apply, amongst other areas, to protection of firm and brand names, carriage by air and sea, road and rail traffic, and the law of cheques and negotiable instruments. The Vienna UN Convention on Contracts for the International Sale of Goods is of particular significance for international trade.

The rapid pace of change in the commercial world has rendered many statutory provi- 902
sions obsolete. Judge-made law and commercial custom therefore play a significant role, and, indeed, the Code refers to commercial custom in various places. Many important forms of commerce, such as leasing, franchising, factoring (for all of which the English word is used in German) and distributorships (*Vertragshändler*) are almost entirely unregulated by statute in German law. Leasing is regarded as a special form of the German lease, in which especially maintenance and repairs are up to the lessee; franchising is the practice of the right to use a firm's business model and brand for a

prescribed period of time and often for a special region; factoring is a financial transaction in which a business sells its accounts receivable (e.g. invoices) to a third party (called a factor) at a discount . A further example is the contractual dealer, often found in automobile trade; these are independent traders who sell goods of certain providers in their own name and on their own account

903 The Commercial Code (*HGB*) consists of five books. It first defines the class of people governed by its provisions (*Handelsstand*). Thereafter it deals with the different types of business entity (of which numerous others are regulated in other statutes), books of account (*Handelsbücher*), commercial transactions between professional business people (*Handelsgeschäfte*), and shipping law (*Seehandelsrecht*).

904 Businesspeople (*Kaufleute*) are the class of people governed by the *HGB*. They are referred to collectively as the *Handelsstand*. A businessperson (*Kaufmann*) is defined as any person running a commercial enterprise (*Handelsgewerbe*, § 1 HGB). Legal certainty is particularly important for commerce, and the ideas that people should be held to their statements and that reliance on appearances should be protected are therefore given particular emphasis in commercial law. Thus, for example, the law of agency is specially regulated in the commercial context, with the special form of the *Prokura*. Here the agent (*Prokurist*) is vested with a very wide power of representation empowering him or her to run a business. The agent's powers are laid down in the Code and cannot be varied by agreement between the parties. The *Prokura* authority must be granted to the *Prokurist* either by the owner of the business or the owners representative (§§ 48 ff. HGB).

905 The commercial register (*Handelsregister*, §§ 8 ff. HGB) satisfies the need for publication of important commercial information. In this register, which is kept by the *Amtsgericht*, relationships such as authority to represent the firm, the place of business of the firm and its name are recorded. Third parties are entitled to assume that every entry in the register is correct and still valid until a change has been entered into the register and made public. This presumption of correctness can only be rebutted if it can be shown that the third party in question had actual knowledge of the true situation (§§ 15 HGB). The need for openness also necessitates the publication of financial statements and business reports.

906 Another important institution is a businessman's confirmation letter (*kaufmännische Bestätigung*). This is a letter from one businessman to another concerning the writer's understanding of an agreement. The terms set out in the letter will be binding on the person receiving it unless he or she raises objections as soon as reasonably possible (*unverzüglich*). If this is not done a contract is considered to have come into existence on the terms set out in the letter irrespective of what the person receiving it actually had in mind. This is one example of a businessman's duty to actively protest if he or she is not satisfied.

907 For transactions governed by the HGB periods of limitation are shortened, and numerous formal requirements and other protective measures, particularly with respect to standard form contracts, are not applicable. In this way the HGB respects the particular need for legal manoeuvrability and contractual freedom in the commercial world. Because of their basic and necessary profit-orientation, there is a presumption in favour of business people that any service performed by them was intended to be in exchange for payment and that any debt owed to them bears interest. There are accorded special liens and rights of retention. The need to limit risk is recognised in vari-

ous forms of limited liability. In particular, the law recognises the possibility of separating business capital from private assets by way of corporate entities with their own legal personality.

Literature:
Peter Bülow/Marcus Artz, Handelsrecht, 7. ed. 2015
Peter Jung, Handelsrecht, 11. ed. 2016
Eugen Klunzinger, Grundzüge des Handelsrechts, 14. ed. 2011
Karsten Schmidt, Handelsrecht, 6. ed. 2015

2. Corporations and Other Forms of Joint Undertaking

a) Basic Principles

German law recognises a greater variety of joint undertakings (corporations and unincorporated associations) than does Anglo-American law. One reason for this may be that German law does not have the trust. Since the forms of corporation and other joint undertakings often correspond only approximately to Anglo-American equivalents the German names will be used here to avoid misleading analogies.   **908**

The law on joint undertakings (*Gesellschaftsrecht*) includes and structures the law relating to private associations, large business structures and also various types of organisation outside of the commercial sphere. These include the *Gesellschaft bürgerlichen Rechts* on the one hand, and the *Verein* on the other (§§ 705 ff.; 21 ff. BGB). The *Verein* stands in the Roman tradition. The most important types of corporate entity which derive from it are the *Aktiengesellschaft (AG)*, which is the equivalent of English public limited company or the American public stock corporation; the *Gesellschaft mit beschränkter Haftung (GmbH)*, a type of private limited company; the *Kommanditgesellschaft auf Aktien (KGaA)*, which involves a mixture of limited and unlimited liability; the *Genossenschaft (Gen)*, a type of co-operative society; and the mutual insurance company (*Versicherungsverein auf Gegenseitigkeit – VVaG*).   **909**

The *Gesellschaft bürgerlichen Rechts*, which stands rather in the Germanic tradition, is a variety of partnership. It is the basic model for the *Offene Handelsgesellschaft (OHG)* which combines elements of a partnership and a sole trader; the *Kommanditgesellschaft (KG)*; and the *Stille Gesellschaft (StG)* and the *Partnerschaftsgesellschaft*.[18] In the following pages the social role played by each of these forms of joint undertaking will be explained.   **910**

Apart from the fact that German law on joint undertakings offers a far greater variety of forms than Anglo-American law, it is also characterised by the fact that persons setting up such an undertaking have an almost completely free choice as to which form they use. The idea is to allow the form which is most appropriate to the particular business to be chosen by the interested parties. Often tax considerations will play a major role in this choice. There are certain exceptions to the basic principle of free choice of form. The simple *Verein* is intended for non-profit activities (*ideale Zwecke*). With special permission it is indeed possible to use it for commercial purposes, but this permission is seldom granted (§ 22 BGB). Both the *OHG* and the *KG* must be engaged in a full-scale trading business (*vollkaufmännisches Gewerbe*), otherwise they are, by   **911**

---

18 The *Partnerschaftsgesellschaftsgesetz* (*PartGG*) enables members of so-called *"Freie Berufe"* such as doctors, architects and artists (§ 1 para. 2 PartGG), which according to German law are not considered as commercial enterprises, to form some sort of joint undertaking.

225

operation of law, a *Gesellschaft bürgerlichen Rechts*. Vice versa, the *Gesellschaft bürgerlichen Rechts* automatically becomes an *OHG* if it engages in full-scale trading business.

912 It is also possible to convert a joint undertaking from one form to another.[19] Many of the statutory rules governing the inner structure of a particular form of undertaking are also capable of being changed by an agreement between the persons contributing capital to it (*Gesellschafter*)[20] according to their needs. The forms and structures contained in the relevant statutes are therefore merely a guideline. On the other hand, certain rules which are essential to the protection of shareholders and third parties cannot be altered. This applies particularly to the *Aktiengesellschaft* (*AG*).

913 Joint undertakings are traditionally divided into *Kapitalgesellschaften*, analogous to a company, and *Personengesellschaften*, analogous to a partnership. In the case of the *Kapitalgesellschaften* the dominant feature is independent capital. This group includes the incorporated association (*eingetragener Verein*, abbreviated *e.V.*) and the various types of entity derived from the *Verein*. These entities are always legal persons from the point of view of the private law. They are independently liable for taxation. As a general principle their shareholders are not personally liable to cover the obligations of the corporation with their own private assets. Their shares (*Gesellschaftsanteile*) are transferable. The corporation has members and is organised as an independent unit. It acts through its own organs and is controlled by the shareholders according to the majority principle.

914 In contrast, the assets of the *Personengesellschaften* such as the *Gesellschaft bürgerlichen Rechts* are seen as the property of a community of joint owners (*Gesamthandsgemeinschaft*), in other words, the property is the private property of the owners, subject to joint control. The *Personengesellschaft* is also not an independent taxpayer. Its members are personally liable to pay its debts out of their own private assets. The act of joining together in such an entity is based on the personal relationship of trust between the members, and their shares in the joint undertaking are thus essentially not transferable. Because of the personal nature of the organisation decisions are taken unanimously. The partners themselves are personally involved in running the *Personengesellschaft*. However, in individual cases the details of the arrangement may be such that there is a convergence between *Personengesellschaft* and *Kapitalgesellschaft*. However, the rules relating to liability and ownership of assets are fundamental and cannot be changed.

915 All joint undertakings must be registered, either in the commercial register (*Handelsregister*), or the register of associations (*Vereinsregister*) or register of co-operative societies (*Genossenschaftsregister*). The only exceptions are the *Gesellschaft bürgerlichen Rechts* and the *stille Gesellschaft*, which do not have to be registered. The making of the entry must be publicised in the Federal Gazette (*Bundesanzeiger*) and a local newspaper. The *Verein* and the related forms of corporation only come into existence once the entry is made in the register. All changes to the articles of association (*Satzung*) must also be registered, as must the extent of its capital or the holdings of each limited partner in a *Kommanditgesellschaft*.

---

19 Particularly relevant to this subject are the Conversions Act (*Umwandlungsgesetz*).
20 Equivalent to shareholders or partners.

It frequently occurs that projects are conducted as a joint venture, especially when on an international scale. From a legal point of view a joint venture has several different components. Firstly, a contract is concluded between the parties who wish to establish the joint venture. This contract usually contains provisions setting out the aim, timetable, choice of law and choice of forum in the event of a dispute. In doing this the parties are forming a *Gesellschaft bürgerlichen Rechts*. This is to be distinguished from the yet to be formed *Aktiengesellschaft (AG)* through which the joint venture would usually be carried out.

916

In execution of various provisions in European Union Law the European Economic Interest Grouping (EEIG) has been formed to provide a formal basis for international co-operation.[21] At least two members of a project must belong to different member-states of the European Union to make use of the EEIG.

917

There also is the European Corporation called *Societas Europaea (SE)*. It is directly based on European Union Law and can act within the whole of the Union without having dependencies. The SE can be established by partners from at least two different Member States.

918

b) Aktiengesellschaft (AG)

One of the most legally successful forms of joint undertaking and one of the most commonly used by major businesses is the *Aktiengesellschaft (AG)*. This is the equivalent of the public limited company (plc) of English law or the stock corporation of American law, subject to certain differences. The law on this subject is regulated primarily in the German Stock Corporation Act (*Aktiengesetz*, abbreviated *AktG*) of 6 September 1965. Only a few provisions are subject to modification in the memorandum of association (*Satzung*).

919

The *Aktiengesellschaft* has independent legal personality. It is automatically classified as a commercial trading company for the purposes of the Commercial Code (*HGB*) irrespective of whether or not it is in fact commercially active, although it almost always is. The provisions of the Commercial Code for *Kaufleute* are therefore also applicable to an *Aktiengesellschaft (AG)*. The form of the *AG* is particularly useful for enterprises which require large amounts of capital. It is also useful for enterprises which involve high risks since the shareholder is only liable to the extent of the value of his or her shares. When an *AG* is founded its founding members undertake to contribute a specific amount of capital. They have no liability either to the *AG* or to its creditors beyond this amount which they have undertaken to contribute. The creditors of an *AG* have no recourse except against the assets of the *AG* itself. The membership of the participants in the *AG* is indicated by the issue of shares (*Aktien*) to them. Such shares are easily transferable. They generally also carry with them a right to share in any dividend that is to a proportion of the profit made by the *AG* which the appropriate organ of the *AG* has decided to distribute as a dividend. Generally the shares are traded on the stock exchange and the price for which they are being traded indicates the estimated total worth of the *AG*. The rights and powers of individual shareholders generally depend on how many shares they hold.

920

---

21 See the EEIG Implementation Act (Europäischer wirtschaftlicher Interessenverein Ausführungsgesetz) of 14 April1988.

921   A single natural or legal person is sufficient to form an *AG* (§§ 23 ff. AktG). The founding member or members make the initial capital contribution and lay down the memorandum and articles of association in a notarial deed (*notarielle Beurkundung*). Once the entry has been made in the commercial register (*Handelsregister*) the AG comes into existence as a legal person. The authorised minimum capital of an *AG* is at least € 50 000 which must be divided into shares with a nominal value of at least € 1 each (§§ 6 ff. AktG).

922   The *AG* has three organs. These are the executive board (*Vorstand*), the supervisory board (*Aufsichtsrat*) and the general meeting of shareholders (*Hauptversammlung*). The memorandum and articles of the *AG* cannot alter the powers allocated to each of these organs by statute. There is nevertheless a certain amount of leeway in that the memorandum and articles or the supervisory board itself can make certain types of transaction undertaken by the executive board subject to the approval of the supervisory board (§ 111 para. 4 AktG).

923   The executive board (*Vorstand*) manages the company (§ 76 AktG). It is theoretically not bound to follow the directions of the supervisory board or the general meeting of shareholders, but in practice it is often dependent on the supervisory board even in individual questions because of the role played by the supervisory board in determining the composition of the executive board. The executive board represents the company in dealings with the outside world. It generally has several members. They are appointed for a maximum of five years at a time by the supervisory board and may be re-appointed. They can be removed from office if there is a serious reason for doing so. For certain types of transaction such as those involving land or the acquisition of significant interests in other corporations the executive board regularly requires the consent of the supervisory board.

924   The supervisory board (*Aufsichtsrat*, §§ 95 ff. AktG) has various duties in addition to those already mentioned. Generally stated its function is to supervise and advise the executive board. It is the central control organ of the *AG*. A member of the supervisory board may not simultaneously be a member of the executive board or an employee of the *AG*. The executive board reports to the supervisory board.

925   The composition of the supervisory board is partly determined by the employees' right of co-determination and is rather complicated. In the case of family concerns with fewer than 500 employees and in the case of businesses with an ideological aspect (*Tendenzunternehmen*), such as the print and electronic media, the supervisory board is elected for a maximum of five years by the shareholders in general meeting. In those *AG*'s which are subject to the law on co-determination by employees between one third and one half of the supervisory board is chosen by the employees and the trade unions. Even under the most extreme situation foreseen by the Co-Determination in Industry Act (*Mitbestimmungsgesetz*) the shareholders will nevertheless have the upper hand because the chairman of the supervisory board, who is chosen by the shareholders, is able to cast a second, deciding vote in the case of a deadlock. The rights of co-determination of employees and trade unions in Germany's big firms are thus very strong. The justification offered for this approach is that the social existence of the employees is dependent on the employing company and they therefore also have an

interest in its running. The property rights of the shareholders are nevertheless sufficiently respected to satisfy the requirements of article 14 of the constitution.[22]

The shareholders gather periodically in the general meeting (§§ 118 ff. AktG). Each   926
shareholder is entitled to participate in person or by proxy. The shareholder's representative, for example, a bank, is bound by the shareholder's instructions. The shareholders have a right to vote and a right to information which may be excluded in the case of certain classes of shares. Improper decisions of the general meeting can be challenged by the shareholder, in court if necessary, and can be declared null and void. Specific minorities of shareholders can also demand that a general meeting be called, or that a special investigation take place or that claims for compensation be enforced.

The general meeting votes on proposed alterations to the memorandum and articles of   927
association, the alteration of share capital, the appointment of shareholders' representatives on the supervisory board, the winding up of the company, the conclusion of agreements with other companies for the transfer of assets, the formation of a group with other companies, the use of inappropriate retained earnings. Finally, it can also vote to approve the actions of the executive board and the supervisory board.

c) Gesellschaft mit beschränkter Haftung (GmbH)

The *Gesellschaft mit beschränkter Haftung* (GmbH) is a type of private limited com-   928
pany similar to the US close corporation. It is one of the most successful legal forms for conducting business in Germany. It was developed in Germany at the end of the 19th century[23] and has proved popular in most of the world. This type of corporation is characterised by the fact that its members are not personally liable for its debts. They contribute to the starting capital of the undertaking which, together which any other property which the GmbH may acquire, is the only capital against which creditors of the GmbH can enforce their claims. In many other respects the GmbH is more like a partnership (*Personengesellschaft*) than a public company. The members have a relatively wide discretion in determining the internal relationships in the GmbH.

The GmbH can be used for any legal purpose, including non-profit purposes (§ 1   929
GmbHG). It can be founded by natural or legal persons, or both. Although it is a corporation it can be founded by a single person in which case it is a so-called one-man GmbH. The GmbH must be founded by notarial deed (*notarielle Beurkundung*) and comes into existence once it has been registered by entry into the Commercial Register (*Handelsregister*) of the local *Amtsgericht*. It must have a nominal capital of at least € 25 000. Special rules apply to one legal version of the GmbH, the so-called entrepreneurial company (*Unternehmergesellschaft*). Deviating from the usual rule that makes a notarial deed necessary for founding, the *Unternehmergesellschaft* may be founded by a model protocol (§ 2 para. 1 a GmbHG). According to § 5 para. 1 a GmbHG, its nominal capital may be lower than the € 25 000 stipulated by § 5 para. 1 GmbHG. It is therefore theoretically possible for a single person to found an *Unternehmergesellschaft* with a nominal capital of € 1.

The GmbH is managed and represented by one or more executive directors (§§ 35 ff.   930
GmbHG). They are appointed and dismissed by the members' meeting (*Gesellschafterversammlung*, §§ 48 ff. GmbHG). The executive directors have a fiduciary duty not to

---

22   See BVerfGE 50, 290 ff.; 99, 367/391 f.
23   *GmbH Gesetz* – GmbH Act – of 20 April 1892.

compete with the GmbH. The members' meeting (§§ 40 ff. GmbHG) is the dominant organ of the GmbH; unless otherwise stipulated in the articles of association, its decisions are taken by a simple majority. For amendments to the memorandum and articles a ¾ majority is necessary and sufficient. In contrast to the supervisory board (*Aufsichtsrat*) of an *Aktiengesellschaft (AG)* the members meeting can pass resolutions on the running of the GmbH which are binding on the executive directors. GmbHs can appoint a supervisory board, and must do so insofar as this is required by the law on co-determination by employees. The law is unclear on the extent to which the members meeting can pass resolutions binding on the executive directors in a GmbH which is subject to the co-determination legislation. The Employees Representation Act (*Betriebsverfassungsgesetz*) prescribes that a GmbH with a regular workforce of over 500 must have a supervisory board. If the workforce is in excess of 2000 then the supervisory board must include employees' representatives in the same proportions as is prescribed for an *Aktiengesellschaft* in the Co-Determination in Industry Act (*Mitbestimmungsgesetz*).

931　The members of the GmbH can sell their shares, although this possibility can be excluded in the memorandum and articles of association. The members have a duty to promote the interests of the GmbH (§ 705 BGG). They also stand in a fiduciary relationship to one another; the intensity of the duty diminishing as the number of members increases.

d) Genossenschaft

932　The *Genossenschaft* is a type of co-operative society. In terms of the Co-operative Societies Act (*Genossenschaftsgesetz*) a *Genossenschaft* can be registered by way of an entry in Co-operative Societies Register kept at the local *Amtsgericht*. It is a type of society for the promotion of the commercial activities of its members (§ 1 para. 1 GenG). The individual members remain largely independent. They elect the board of directors and the supervisory board of the *Genossenschaft* in a general meeting. Farmers' Co-operatives for wholesale buying and selling are economically significant, as are co-operatives of small traders. Financial business is also conducted on a co-operative basis, for example, in farmers' credit co-operatives or banking co-operatives (*Volksbanken*).

e) Gesellschaft bürgerlichen Rechts

933　The basic model for the German version of a partnership (*Personengesellschaft*) is the *Gesellschaft bürgerlichen Rechts*. It is regulated by the Civil Code in § 705-740 BGB. Commercial forms of partnership are the *Offene Handelsgesellschaft*, the *Kommanditgesellschaft*, the *Stille Gesellschaft* and the *Partnerschaftsgesellschaft*.

934　Most of the statutory provisions can be excluded or altered by the partnership agreements (*Gesellschaftsvertrag*). A *Personengesellschaft* is also not required to subject itself to an independent audit or to publish its financial statements.

935　The *Gesellschaft bürgerlichen Rechts* is used to achieve a common purpose of its members. The purpose may be of any sort. The only type of activity which may not be conducted in this form is a full-scale trading business (*Vollkaufmännisches Gewerbe*) as defined by the Commercial Code (*HGB*). The *Gesellschaft bürgerlichen Rechts* is an often-used form. Examples are operations as big as a working group (*Arbeitsge-*

meinschaft, abbreviated *Arge*.) of several large concerns which are working on a communal project (such as the building of a dam or the opening of an oil field) or as small as a group of colleagues who have set up a betting pool to play lotto. Law firms and medical practitioners today are sometimes organised in this way, in case they do act in the form of the *Partnerschaftsgesellschaft*. This is a unit in which natural persons who exercise a free profession work together and into which a mere equity investment is not possible.

A partnership in the form of the *Gesellschaft bürgerlichen Rechts* is created by a part-   936
nership agreement. The property of the partnership is jointly owned (*Gesamthandsvermögen*) and consists of the contributions of the partners and of the profits made by the partnership. If the partnership incurs liabilities then not only the partnership as such but also each of the individual partners are liable. However, it is possible to limit the liability of a *Gesellschaft bürgerlichen Rechts* to the assets of the *Gesellschaft* itself. Every partner has the right and the duty to take part in directing the partnership and in representing it in dealings with the outside world. According to statute all partners are involved in decision making and the running of the business, but it is possible to enter agreements to the contrary. Although a *Gesellschaft bürgerlichen Rechts* has no independent legal personality, it can, according to the jurisprudence of the Federal Supreme Court, sue and be sued in its own name.

f) Offene Handelsgesellschaft

The *Offene Handelsgesellschaft* (*OHG*) is a type of partnership which always has un-   937
limited liability and can sue in its own name. This form is generally used for small middle-class family businesses. It is a joint undertaking which has as its object the pursuit of some commercial object (§§ 105 ff. HGB). All members have unlimited liability for the debts of the *OHG* to the full extent of their private assets. This liability cannot be excluded and may be the reason why this form has lost rapidly in popularity in the last few years. The unlimited liability does tend to make it easier to obtain credit, but brings with it considerable personal risks for the participants. The *OHG* must be registered by entry in the Commercial Register (*Handelsregister*) and is by definition a *Kaufmann*, in other words, the special rules of the Commercial Code (*HGB*) are applicable to it.

The *OHG* is administered by its members (§§ 114 ff. HGB). Unless the association   938
agreement provides otherwise each member is empowered to represent the *OHG* and act on its behalf in dealing with outsiders. Any departures from this general rule are only binding on outsiders if they are recorded by an entry in the Commercial Register. The members stand in a fiduciary relationship to one another. This involves, amongst other things, a duty not to compete with the *OHG* in its particular field.

In case of a member's death, he or she regularly retires from the OHG (§ 131 HGB),   939
but arrangements can be made that the OHG will continue with the heirs.

g) Kommanditgesellschaft and Related Forms

The *Kommanditgesellschaft* (*KG*) differs from the *OHG* primarily in that for some of   940
its members liability is limited to their contribution to the starting capital as soon as registration by entry into the Commercial Register (*Handelsregister*) has taken place (§§ 161 ff. HGB). Such a member with limited liability is called a *Kommanditist*. In

addition, there is a type of member called a *Komplementär* who is personally liable to the full extent of his or her assets in the same way as a member of an *OHG*. According to the statutory rules on the subject, a *Kommanditist* may not be involved in directing and representing the *KG*. They do, however, have powers of control and the right to raise an objection when extraordinary transactions are being contemplated. However, it is possible to provide in the founding agreement that *Kommanditist* members are also to have a part in the running of the business. However, they can only act as its representatives if granted a separate power of attorney.

941 A very popular combination of legal forms is the *GmbH & Co KG*. This is a *Kommanditgesellschaft* in which the member with personal liability is a GmbH. Since a GmbH is only liable to the extent of its own assets this creates in effect a *Kommanditgesellschaft* in which all the members have limited liability, thus avoiding the dangerous situation in which the person acting as the executive director of the *KG* is personally liable.

942 The *Kommanditgesellschaft auf Aktien* is a corporate entity with many similarities to an *Aktiengesellschaft (AG)*. Its similarity to a normal *Kommanditgesellschaft* lies in the fact that it also has members who are liable to the full extent of their personal assets (§§ 278 ff. AktG).

943 The *Stille Gesellschaft*, which is related to the *Kommanditgesellschaft*, is a type of silent partnership. Here one person makes an agreement with at least one other in terms of which the other person is to provide capital for the enterprise without his or her involvement being made public (§§ 230 ff. HGB). The silent partner is then not involved in the running of the business and is not responsible for its liabilities.

Literature:

Ulrich Eisenhardt/Ulrich Wackerbarth, Gesellschaftsrecht I. Recht der Personengesellschaften, 1. ed. 2015
Barbara Grunewald, Gesellschaftsrecht, 10. ed. 2017
Jens Koch, Gesellschaftsrecht, 11. ed. 2019
Marc-Philippe Weller/Jens Prütting, Handels- und Gesellschaftsrecht, 9. ed. 2016

IX. Negotiable Instruments and Securities

944 The German law on negotiable instruments and securities (*Wertpapierrecht*) is regulated in numerous statutes and the provisions on this matter are in many respects incomplete. The most important federal statutes on this subject are the Civil Code (*BGB*), the Commercial Code (*HGB*), the Bills of Exchange Act (*Wechselgesetz*), the Cheques Act (*Scheckgesetz*), the Stock Corporation Act (*Aktiengesetz*) and the Securities Deposit Act (*Depotgesetz*). In addition, each of the *Länder* has its own laws on this subject. There is also no general definition of *Wertpapier* in German law, in contrast to, for example, § 965 of the Swiss law of obligations. The dominant view is that an instrument of value may be defined as a document in which a private right has been confirmed in writing in such a way that it is necessary to be in possession of the document to be able to enforce the right.

945 Instruments of value serve to confirm claims in writing and thus to make them more easily transferable. However, by now the development has gone beyond that to the stage where instruments of value are often merely entries recorded by credit institutes, the actual written document being a mere fiction.

Important forms of *Wertpapier* are bills of exchange and promissory notes (*Wechsel*), the cheque (*Scheck*), debentures and bonds (*Schuldverschreibung*). All of these record the existence of a claim to money. Stocks and shares (*Aktien*) are documents indicating membership. Land charge certificates (*Grundschuldbriefe*), mortgage certificates issued by the land registry (*Hypothekenbriefe*), and investment fund unit certificates (*Investmentanteile*) are all assets falling under the law of property. Bank notes are not instruments of value as defined because, although they are official means of payment, they are not confirmation of any right lying outside of themselves.   946

A distinction is made between bearer instruments (*Inhaberpapiere*) and order instruments (*Orderpapiere*). Bearer instruments are made out to the bearer. Examples are bearer share certificates and bearer bonds. In accordance with the rules of the German law of property such instruments are transferred by agreement and delivery. Here the right evidenced by the instrument follows the right to the instrument.   947

Order instruments are made out to a particular named person. Here the right to the instrument follows the right evidenced by the instrument. To transfer such an instrument one needs not only agreement and delivery, but also a written declaration of the intent to transfer, that is, an endorsement (*Indossament*). Frequently a blank endorsement is given by merely signing the instrument. If this is done the order instrument becomes effectively a bearer instrument.   948

Shares are written proof of a right to participate in a company. This right of participation usually includes the right to vote, demand information, and participate in dividends. In Germany most shares are bearer shares.   949

Shares and similar instruments are frequently exposed to significant swings in value and therefore represent a risk for the owner. Such risk can be diminished by investing one's capital in a wide variety of shares, but this option is not open to a small investor acting alone. The solution is an investment fund (*Investmentfonds*) in the form of mutual funds or unit trusts (*Kapitalanlagegesellschaft*). The small investor can buy units in the unit trust, and the large amounts of capital which are assembled in this way are then invested in shares and other instruments by professional fund managers. The instruments in which the capital is invested are then jointly owned by the various investors. This subject is regulated in detail by the Investment Act (*Investmentgesetz* [*InvG*]).   950

Bonds (*Schuldverschreibungen* or *Obligationen*) give the holder a claim to the payment of interest and repayment of the nominal value at a specified date of maturity. Convertible debentures or bonds (*Wandelanleihen*) give the holder the additional option to convert the bonds into shares in the debtor company within a specified period. If this option is exercised then the debt of the company to the bondholder is extinguished. Bonds with warrants attached (*Optionsanleihen*) confer, apart from the right to interest and repayment of capital, the additional right to buy shares in the issuing company within a particular period at a fixed price. The share option is then not extinguished by the exercise of the claim for repayment.   951

The basic model for the cheque, which is very important in practice, and for a variety of other types of instrument, is the payment order (*Anweisung*) provided for in §§ 783 ff. BGB. The BGB payment order itself does not, however, occur very often in practice. A payment order is a document in which one person orders another to deliver money, instruments of value or fungible goods to another person. If the person issu-   952 ing the payment order hands it over to the payee then the payee can demand performance from the drawee and the drawee can discharge the order by making performance to the payee.

953 The same applies to a cheque (*Scheck*). In terms of article 3, 54 of the Cheques Act (*Scheckgesetz*, abbreviated *SchG*) a cheque may only be drawn on a credit institution at which the drawer has credit facilities. If this rule is not complied with, then the cheque is subject to stamp duty. The result is that in practice all cheques are drawn on credit institutions.

954 One of the basic forms of negotiable instrument is the bill of exchange or promissory note (*Wechsel*). It is of importance in the commercial sphere and, in contrast to the cheque, which serves as a means of payment, its main purpose it the provision of credit. If the instrument takes the form of a promise by the drawer to pay a fixed amount to a particular person then it is a promissory note (*Eigenwechsel*). If the instrument orders another person – the drawee (*Bezogener*) – to pay the sum then it is a bill of exchange (*gezogener Wechsel* or *Tratte*). If drawn in German it must be expressly stated in the instrument that it is a bill of exchange or promissory note and such instruments are also subject to various other strict formal requirements. Such instruments are easily negotiable, but any person negotiating the instrument will be liable on it if it is dishonoured by the drawee. Various defences which could be raised in an action on the transaction underlying the bill cannot be raised in an action on the bill itself. An additional advantage is that a claim on the negotiable instrument can be brought under a special, particularly speedy summary procedure for liquidated claims of this sort called a *Wechselprozess*. A bill of exchange is frequently discounted. This involves a bank's buying the bill and thus the right to sue on it. It pays the holder the face value of the bill minus a fee, the discount (*Diskont*), which serves to compensate the bank for the delay until the bill matures.

Literature:

Hans Brox/Martin Henssler, Handelsrecht, 22. ed. 2016

X. Competition Law and the Protection of Intellectual Property

955 In German thinking competition law and the protection of certain types of intellectual (industrial) property such as patents and trademarks are classified together under the concept *gewerblicher Rechtsschutz*.

1. Competition Law

956 Competition law (*Wettbewerbsrecht*) is a core element of this field of law. It is governed by the Unfair Competition Act (*Gesetz gegen den unlauteren Wettbewerb*, abbreviated *UWG*). The aim of this act is the preservation of a functioning market economy by combating forms of competition which are considered to be unfair. It thus aims simultaneously to protect business people against the unfair practices of competitors and to protect consumers against the possibility of being misled and overcharged. The overall goal is to ensure that the business providing the better service should prevail in the long run.

957 Any person who, in the course of commercial dealings (*geschäftliche Handlungen*), does acts which are contrary to public policy (*gute Sitten*) with the intent of gaining a competitive advantage can be prevented from doing so by way of injunction and may

also be liable for damages (§§ 3, 8 ff. UWG). This general provision gives competition law the flexibility to develop as social circumstances change. There is no statutory definition determining what is contrary to public policy. The test is to consider what is contrary to proper practice in trade, craft or independent business activities. In this context the term "commercial dealings" refers to any conduct which is intended to promote the commercial success of one's own business, or of some other person's business. Internal business arrangements of a purely private nature or official actions taken, for example, for the prevention of a public danger, do not fall within the sphere of competition law.

Viewed as a whole in comparison to some other legal systems, German competition law gives the impression of a rather restrictive system aimed at the preservation of the *status quo* and discouraging aggressive competition wherever possible. Several activities specially described in the UWG are regarded as being contrary to public policy such as the use of quality labels without the necessary permit or certain untrue statements, but also telephone calls without prior consent of the consumer.. Competitive activities are also considered to be unfair if they are directed at the destruction of a competitor, or the encouragement of illegal acts or breaches of contract by third parties, since such activities are essentially detrimental to free competition. Comparative advertising has been illegal, particularly if it criticises another producer's product or attempts to make use of the good reputation of another product. Because of European Union Law comparative advertising is now in principle allowed, as long as the comparison is not misleading or reviling and typical and verifiable characteristics of the various products are being compared. Competitive methods will also be unfair if they deceive consumers or create the danger of one product being mistaken for another (passing off). The consumers' powers of rational decision may not be impeded by exploiting feelings of sympathy or gratitude, or a weakness for gambling. Promotional gifts may not be used to give the consumer the impression that he or she is morally obliged to buy something. **958**

Various special cases concretising the general clause are set out. Misleading advertisements are forbidden, knowingly publishing false information in advertisements is an offence punishable by up to two years imprisonment (§ 16 para. 1 UWG). It is an offence both to bribe other people and to receive bribes (§§ 299 ff. StGB). Even making uncomplimentary factual allegations damaging to a competitor's business will give him or her a claim to damages if the allegations are not demonstrably true (§ 4 No. 8 UWG). Finally, the betrayal and unauthorised use of commercial secrets, industrial espionage and the unauthorised use of information are all punishable offences (§§ 17, 18 UWG). **959**

Intensive protection is accorded to various characteristics by means of which products are recognised and distinguished. Examples include names, registered trade names (*Firma*), business logos, certain commercially recognised shapes and colours, and the titles of publications. **960**

In the case of infringements of these rules it is generally possible to obtain an injunction to eliminate infringements or to prevent further infringements, and damages can also be claimed. In special cases it is also possible to obtain an injunction to hand over the profit made to the Federal budget (§ 10 UWG). An action can be brought by any person who has suffered as a result of the unfair competition. In addition, it is also possible to bring actions in the interest of the public at large. Such actions can be **961** brought by competitors, interest groups, consumer groups and chambers of trade, commerce and industry (§§ 8 para 3, 10 UWG).

2. Monopolies and Anti-Competitive Practices

962 The law on restrictive practices in restraint of trade (*Kartellrecht*) is also directed primarily at the protection of a competitive economy. Its chief instrument is the Act Against Restrictive Trade Practices (*Gesetz gegen Wettbewerbsbeschränkungen*, abbreviated *GWB*) and the provisions of European Union law on the subject of cartels.[24] A cartel is an agreement between businesses, a decision of a consolidation of businesses or coordinated activities for the purpose of restricting competition. Examples of this sort are price fixing agreements by firms tendering for public contracts or agreements to divide the market up so as not to compete against one another. In terms of the German law on this subject, which is rather strict, the basic approach is that cartels are illegal (§ 1 GWB). Exceptions are made where the cartel does not present any great threat to the free market or if it promotes the general progress. Cartels and agreements contrary to § 1 GWB, and which are not allowed by way of exception, are null. Sanctions can be applied to stop the violation. These sanctions can lead to a claim of injunction or damages (§§ 32 ff. GWB). The cartel authorities keep a particularly close watch on businesses which have a dominant share of the market to ensure that they do not abuse their dominant position (§§ 19 ff. GWB). Mergers which could lead to a single concern dominating a market require authorisation to proceed. A Monopolies Commission consisting of independent experts exists to monitor on a regular basis tendencies towards business concentration in Germany (§§ 44 ff. GWB).

963 Breaches of individual provisions of the Act Against Restrictive Trade Practices are offences punishable by fines of up to € 1 000 000 to skim off the additional profit made by resorting to the restrictive practice; in certain cases the fine can be even higher (§ 81 para. 4, 5 GWB). The authority primarily responsible for the enforcement of the act is the Federal Cartel Office (*Bundeskartellamt*). Other authorities with jurisdiction in this area are the cartel offices of the various *Länder* and the Federal Minister for the Economy.

3. Patents and Trade Marks

964 A patent provides special legal protection for technical inventions. In terms of the Patents Act (*Patentgesetz*) the German Patent Office (*Deutsches Patentamt*) in Munich will grant a patent for inventions which are novel, which are the result of an inventive step in research and which have industrial applications. This means that the invention for which a patent is being sought must go beyond the existing state of the art and must not be an application of existing knowledge which would appear obvious to someone with expertise in the field. A patent secures for its owner a right to be protected against the exploitation of the invention by other persons. The protection lasts for twenty years in Germany and involves the payment of fees. There are numerous international treaties which attempt to extend the protection of patents beyond national boundaries. To obtain Europe-wide protection for a patent an application must be made to the European Patent Office, which is also in Munich.

---

24 See articles 101 and 102 TFEU.

It is not possible to patent things which are discovered if they already exist. Examples   965
of this sort are molecular particles or laws of nature. The same applies to intellectual
procedures, plans, games, computer programmes, plants and animals. Biological
breeding methods for plants and animals can only be patented to a very limited extent.

In several of these instances other forms of intellectual property protection provide a   966
remedy. Some inventions do not fulfil the strict requirements for the granting of a
patent. If they do not qualify for a patent, inventions of useful articles are afforded a
lesser form of protection by registration as utility models (*Gebrauchsmuster*). This is
more or less the equivalent of a right in an unregistered design. Such recognition is
granted if the invention serves to make a thing more useful by rearrangement, reshap-
ing or inventing new attachments to make work easier. After a utility model has been
registered only the owner may produce it for commercial purposes and put it into cir-
culation, use it or market it.

Industrial designs and models (*gewerbliche Muster und Modelle*) are protected by the   967
Designs Act (*Geschmacksmustergesetz*) if they are new and original. Independent
recreations of the design cannot be acted against, but an injunction may be obtained
against copying.

Literature:
Volker Emmerich, Unlauterer Wettbewerb, 11. ed. 2019
Helmut Köhler/Joachim Bornkamm/Jörn Feddersen, Gesetz gegen den unlauteren Wettbewerb,
  37. ed. 2019
Jan Bernd Nordemann/Axel Nordemann/Anke Nordemann-Schiffel, Wettbewerbs- und Marken-
  recht, 11. ed. 2012

XI. Copyright

The Copyright Act (*Urheberrechtsgesetz*, abbreviated *UrhG*) protects intellectual   968
works in the cultural sphere. The protection of copyright is extended to the creators of
literary, academic and artistic works so long as these are personal intellectual creations. This includes, in particular, music, film, academic and technical treatises, oral
creations such as a speech, written works and computer programmes, pantomimic
works including dance, and the fine arts, including architecture. The reworking of intellectual property can also be protected by copyright, for example, a particular production of a play or the translation of a book. Official publications such as statutes or
law reports are expressly excluded from copyright protection.

Copyright arises as soon as a work is created – there is no requirement that the right   969
must be registered or granted by some authority to be enforceable. As a general rule a
work loses copyright protection seventy years after the death of the creator (§ 64
UrhG). The holder of the right has, amongst other things, the exclusive right to publish the work, and alterations to the work generally require his or her permission. The
holder of the right also has the exclusive right to use the work. This includes the exclusive right to produce works such as plays and the exclusive right to reproduce other
types of copyright work. If his or her work is put to any sort of commercial use he or
she is entitled to royalties. It the work is used on a large scale, for example, by broadcast on public radio or by being made available in public libraries, then the royalties
are often paid in the form of a lump sum arranged by performing rights societies or
copyright collecting societies such as the German Society for Musical Performance and
Mechanical Reproduction Rights (GEMA). Copyright in a work can be inherited, but

it cannot be ceded as a whole. Specific rights of use can, however, be ceded, for example, in a contract with a publisher. Infringements of copyright will generally give the owner the right to claim whatever profit has been derived from the illegitimate use of her work as well as damages. Certain specifically listed types of infringement are punishable offences (§§ 106 ff. UrhG).

970 In the interests of promoting access to information and cultural development, copyright is subject to certain limits (§§ 44 a ff. UrhG). With the exception of sheet music and computer programmes, it is permissible to make individual copies for private use. It is also permissible to make use of a work to a certain extent for academic purposes or for purposes of informing the public about issues of current interest. The copyright owner is, however, entitled to compensation which is provided, for example, by a special charge on large-scale copiers such as universities, schools and libraries. A special tax is also imposed on tape-, video- and other types of recorders. Such charges are regularly collected and distributed by copyright collecting societies.

Literature:

Hartmut Eisenmann/Ulrich Jautz, Grundriss Gewerblicher Rechtsschutz und Urheberrecht, 10. ed. 2015
Manfred Rehbinder/Alexander Peikert, Urheberrecht, 18. ed. 2018
Haimo Schack, Urheber- und Urhebervertragsrecht, 8. ed. 2017

XII. Labour Law

971 The relationship between employer and employee involves numerous special problems for which the law must provide solutions. A key consideration here is the personal and economic dependence of the employee. This is the justification for the principle of protection (*Schutzprinzip*) which is a guiding principle of the rules of labour law (*Arbeitsrecht*). Many of the provisions of labour law are binding, and can only be varied in favour of the employee. Labour law consists partly of private law, partly of public law, and provides a clear instance of the limited practical usefulness of such theoretical classification.

972 A distinction is generally made between employment law (*Individualarbeitsrecht*) and the law of industrial relations (*Kollektivarbeitsrecht*). Employment law governs the private law relationship between employer and employee. It also includes statutory rules on worker protection (*Arbeitsschutzrecht*) which have a strong public law element. Examples of the issues covered by *Arbeitsschutzrecht* are safety measures in the workplace, maximum hours of work, and the prohibition of child labour.

973 The law on industrial relations, on the other hand, is concerned with the types of association which are relevant in the employment sphere (unions and employers' associations). It also includes the law on industrial disputes (*Arbeitskampfrecht*), on collective agreements between the various associations, i.e. the agreements arising from industry-wide collective bargaining (*Tarifverträge*) and on employee's rights of representation (*Betriebsverfassungsrecht*) and co-determination.

974 Labour law is governed by numerous different statutes. There is no code on the subject. A particular characteristic of German labour law is that wide areas of it are not regulated by statute at all. The courts therefore regularly base their decisions directly on the constitution. In particular, the values set out in the fundamental rights are often drawn upon in forming and interpreting the rules of labour law. The courts, particu-

larly the Federal Labour Court (*Bundesarbeitsgericht*) have created a considerable body of judicial precedent which undergoes constant development. Finally, the collective bargaining agreements reached by the unions and employers' associations regulate many aspects of labour relations.

In these sources of law a distinction is still made between workers (*Arbeiter*) and white-collar employees (*Angestellte*), although differences in treatment are tending to vanish. A worker is any employee who is not an *Angestellter*. An *Angestellter* is an employee in a clerical position or higher.   975

The employment relationship comes into existence by contract. Occasionally it might arise from a *de facto* relationship where work is simply performed without prior agreement. Certain groups of the population may not be discriminated against (§§ 1 ff. *Allgemeines Gleichbehandlungsgesetz*, abbreviated AGG, i.e. General Act on Equal Treatment). However, there is no duty to employ quotas of groups such as young job-market entrants or minorities. Larger businesses are obliged to employ quotas of severely handicapped persons, but they can avoid doing so by paying a special tax instead. Since 2016 all supervisory boards of businesses which are listed on the stock market and which are subject to worker's participation in management must be staffed with at least 30% females. Some statutory provisions place limits on the freedom to enter contracts of employment, for example, foreigners who are not citizens of a Member State of the European Union can only be employed if they have a work permit (*Arbeitserlaubnis*). The aim of this provision is, in part, to prevent employers from creating "sweat-shops" by paying low wages and evading social security and tax payments, but, above all, to place restrictions on the labour market. Child labour is illegal, as is employing workers illicitly, that is, without deducting social security, tax and insurance from their pay (*Schwarzarbeit*).   976

The employment relationship imposes an obligation to work as agreed on the employee and an obligation to pay the agreed amount on the employer. The contract is a contract of service (employment, *Dienstvertrag*), in other words, the employee does not undertake to achieve any particular result, but merely to make him- or herself available for work and to follow whatever instructions are given by the employer. Maximum working hours are regulated both by statute and by numerous collective bargaining agreements, with a growing tendency to flexibility. The pay to which an employee is entitled is also regulated to a large extent by collective agreements, although individual agreements play a role in some cases. The same applies to the right to leave, which is the subject of much statutory regulation.   977

The employment relationship also creates mutual duties to respect the interests of the other party. Thus, the employee must refrain from competing with the employer and must keep confidential business information secret and the employer must take proper precautions to ensure the safety of the workplace. The employer is only liable for injuries suffered by the employee in the course of his or her duties if they were caused deliberately or by the gross negligence of the employer, on the other hand, the employer is essentially responsible for any damage caused to third parties by the employee.   978

Termination of the employment relationship by the employer is only allowed subject to periods of notice and only in certain sets of circumstances. These include misconduct by the employee, and also urgent business interests, particularly in cases where the business has insufficient work and the employee has become redundant. The dismissed employee has the option of bringing a case before the Labour Court (*Arbeits-*   979 *gericht*), the equivalent of an Industrial Tribunal, in terms of the Protection Against Dismissal Act (*Kündigungsschutzgesetz*).

980 The law on industrial relations (*kollektives Arbeitsrecht*) has as its basis article 9 para. 3 GG, which guarantees the freedom to form associations. This means that every person, irrespective of what career they are following, has a right to join together with others to form associations for the promotion and preservation of working and business conditions. Agreements which aim to limit this right or impede its exercise are void and steps taken with such an intent are illegal. On the basis of this constitutional guarantee relatively large, strong trade unions (*Gewerkschaften*) and employers associations (*Arbeitsgeberverbände*) have been created in Germany. These organisations, as parties to collective bargaining agreements (*Tarifverträge*), have considerable influence in forming the employment relationship. This has proved to be a factor for stability and prosperity. The freedom to associate may not be infringed, but the same applies to the negative freedom not to associate, in other words, the right not to be a member of such associations.

981 It is a rule of industrial relations law that only such associations as are willing and able to apply pressure to their opponents are capable of taking part in collective bargaining rounds. The participants in collective bargaining negotiate agreements setting out the terms which are to be included in individual contracts of employment, such as pay levels, working hours, entitlement to leave, and the conditions under which the employment relationship may be terminated. The agreements also contain general provisions dealing with the way businesses are run, for example, with respect to worker representation. Such an agreement is, firstly, binding on the parties who took part in the negotiations, but can be declared to be binding on the whole of a particular sector of the economy by the responsible minister.

982 The most important instrument in collective bargaining is industrial action (*Arbeitskampf*). The right to strike is guaranteed, as is the right to lock out, that is, the right of the employer to refuse to accept the services of the employee, the point being that the obligation to pay the employee then also falls away. The only legitimate reason for resorting to such measures is to influence negotiations on conditions of employment. A right to strike in support of general political objectives is not guaranteed by article 9 para. 3 of the *Grundgesetz*. Strikes may only be called by parties to collective bargaining. Wildcat strikes (*wilde Streiks*) are an illegal breach of the employment contract. The Federal Labour Court (*Bundesarbeitsgericht*, equivalent of the Employment Appeal Tribunal in Britain) has developed the principle that industrial action must satisfy a test of proportionality (*Verhältnismäßigkeit*). This means, inter alia, that industrial action may only be resorted to after all other means of reaching an agreement have been attempted. This will also require an attempt at mediation by an independent mediator appointed by the negotiating parties. The constitutions of the unions require a strike ballot (*Urabstimmung*) before strike action can be resorted to. Warning strikes are already allowed at an early stage in negotiations.

983 The law of industrial relations also includes the issue of employee representation (*Mitbestimmungsrecht*) which is regulated primarily in the Co-Determination in Industry Act (*Mitbestimmungsgesetz*) and the Employees' Representation Act (*Betriebsverfassungsgesetz*). Co-determination within a business involves, in particular, the creation of works councils (*Betriebsräte*) which have a considerable say in the employment, transfer and dismissal of employees and in social matters such as working

hours. They must be set up even in smaller businesses. They also have a right to participate in business decisions such as changes to the business or to its production and distribution plans. The rights of co-determination are enforced particularly through the right of employees with respect to the composition of company organs such as the supervisory board (*Aufsichtsrat*) and the executive board (*Vorstand*).

Literature:
Wolfgang Däubler, Arbeitsrecht. 17. ed. 2017
Wilhelm Dütz/Gregor Thüsing, Arbeitsrecht, 23. ed. 2018
Manfred Löwisch/Gregor Caspers/Steffen Klumpp, Arbeitsrecht, 11. ed. 2017
Raimund Waltermann, Arbeitsrecht, 19. ed. 2018
Rainer Wörlen/Axel Kokemoor, Arbeitsrecht, 12. ed. 2017

XIII. The Law of Insolvency

If a debtor is unable to pay his or her debts or is on the point of becoming unable to pay, then it is possible to make an application to start insolvency proceedings against his or her estate. In the case of legal persons an excess of liabilities over assets (*Überschuldung*) is also a basis for commencing proceedings. The aim of insolvency proceedings is to satisfy the creditor of the insolvent debtor and at the same time to save the business if at all possible and make it possible for the debtor to survive in economic terms. For this purpose an insolvency plan may be drawn up which can derogate from the statutory regime. An insolvency plan regulates the settlement of claims of the secured and unsecured creditors, the realisation and distribution of the insolvent estate, and the debtor's liability after completion of the insolvency procedure. The aim of allowing derogation from the statutory regime is to make more flexible measures suited to the facts of the case possible. | 984

If the Insolvency Regulations (*Insolvenzordnung*, abbreviated InsO) are applied, an administrator (*Insolvenzverwalter*) will usually be appointed to conduct the insolvency proceedings (§ 56 InsO). The administrator's primary duty is to secure the debtor's assets. To this end he or she is empowered to administer and deal with the estate in the debtor's place (§ 80 InsO). The *Amtsgericht* in its capacity as insolvency court can leave the debtor with the power to deal with his or her assets (§§ 270 ff. InsO), in which case the debtor is placed under the supervision of an officer of the court. | 985

The entire estate of the debtor at the time at which proceedings are commenced as well as any property which the debtor acquires during proceedings forms the insolvent estate (*Insolvenzmasse*, §§ 35 ff. InsO). Only such objects on which execution cannot be levied are excepted. Certain rights such as a pledge (charge) entitle a creditor to have his or her claim satisfied independently of the general mass of creditors (§§ 49 ff. InsO). | 986

The insolvency court will summon a meeting of creditors (*Gläubigerversammlung*). The meeting of creditors must decide, on the basis of a report by the administrator, whether the business should be wound up, or whether it should be kept as a going concern with the aim of restructuring its debt. The guiding principle of the insolvency procedure is that the existing estate and business should, if at all possible, not be dismembered. Instead it should be restructured so as to also make it easier for the debtor to continue its economic existence. | 987

988   Discharge from remaining bad debts (*Restschuldbefreiung*, §§ 286 ff. InsO) can be granted to natural persons to make it possible for them to resume economic activity. Discharge allows the insolvent debtor to be released from any remaining debt after seven years if the debtor has made every effort required by the law to pay off his or her debts during that period.

989   A simplified insolvency procedure is applicable to persons engaged in a small business and consumers (§§ 304 ff. InsO). The aim is to promote a settlement out of court.

Literature:
Reinhard Bork, Einführung in das Insolvenzrecht, 7. ed. 2014

XIV. Procedure in Civil Litigation and Special Procedures in Miscellaneous Matters

1. Basic Principles

990   The procedure in civil litigation is regulated primarily in the Civil Procedure Act (*Zivilprozessordnung*, abbreviated ZPO). It contains provisions on the conduct of contentious proceedings before a court and the execution (*Vollstreckung*) of judgements. The Court Fees Act (*Gerichtskostengesetz*), the Judiciary Remuneration and Compensation Act (*Justizvergütungs- und Entschädigungsgesetz*, abbreviated JVEG) and the Legal Advisors Remuneration Act (*Rechtsanwaltsvergütungsgesetz*, abbreviated RVG) provide information on the costs involved in a civil trial and also on the costs involved in bringing cases before other courts. The ZPO came into effect in 1877 and has undergone frequent and far-reaching amendments since then.

991   It is a principle of German civil litigation that the decision to bring a matter to court is entirely at the discretion of the individual involved (*Dispositionsmaxime*). It is a facet of private autonomy that the individual has a free choice as to whether to enforce his or her rights or not. With the issue of the writ of summons (*Klageerhebung*) the claimant (*Kläger*) simultaneously determines what the action is to be about. Without a specific statement of claim (*Klageantrag*) the court will not hear the matter. The court is bound by the statement of claim. It cannot consider matters which have not been dealt with in the statement of claim and it cannot award the claimant more than what he or she has claimed. The parties to the action also have a wide discretion as to how to pursue the matter once legal proceedings have commenced. They thus have the option to settle the matter (*einen Vergleich schließen*), or the defendant (*Beklagter*) can acknowledge the claimant's claim. The parties can claim the remedies offered by the law or refrain from doing so: an action can be withdrawn and a judgement need not be enforced. The defendant is also not obliged to appear in the course of oral proceedings or to obtain legal representation or to even defend the matter. However, if the defendant takes this attitude he or she runs the risk that a default judgement (*Versäumnisurteil*, §§ 330 ff. ZPO) might be entered against him or her, which means that the defendant loses the case without any consideration having been given to possible defences which the defendant might have raised since the matter is decided purely on the basis of the evidence which the claimant adduces in support of his or her alleged right.

992   There are only limited exceptions to the principle that the parties are free to decide whether to proceed with a matter or not. These exceptions are always based on the principles of the substantive law at issue in each case. For example, in matters relating to marriage, the parties cannot settle the case or concede to the other side's demands without the approval of the court.

Another basic principle is the adversary system (*Verhandlungsmaxime*). While the assessment of which legal provisions are relevant to deciding the case is a matter for the court (*iura novit curia*), the parties are responsible for providing the factual basis for the decision. There is thus no independent inquisitorial investigation of the factual background by the court. The parties decide on which points evidence should be led. It is only necessary to lead evidence on those matters which are disputed. The court must assume the truth of all allegations which are not disputed or which are admitted to be true. In isolated cases the court can, however, follow a more inquisitorial procedure, for example in matrimonial cases. Furthermore, it can take account of obvious facts concerning which the parties have not given evidence. These include facts of which the court is aware, for example, because they also arose in an earlier case, and facts which are public knowledge. Evidence is always officially led at the behest of the court. Thus, for example, witnesses are summoned to give evidence by the court, not by the parties to the case.

993

If the evidence adduced by the claimant does not support the legal conclusion for which he or she is arguing, then the action may be dismissed on the basis that it does not disclose a cause of action (*die Klage ist unschlüssig*). If, on the other hand, the claimant has made out a *prima facie* case, then it is up to the defendant to seriously raise a defence, otherwise the court will find for the claimant.

994

A limit is placed on the principle that it is for the parties to raise whatever evidence is relevant to their case by § 139 ZPO. This imposes on the court a judicial duty to ask questions and clarify the situation (*richterliche Frage- und Aufklärungspflicht*). This means that the judge has a duty to encourage the parties to make a full statement of the facts and to submit all appropriate prayers for relief. This is particularly of relevance in the case of a litigant in person who lacks legal expertise. On the other hand, the court may not act as the advocate of one of the parties and provide legal advice in a one-sided way. The line between encouraging each party to present his or her case properly and showing bias is a difficult one to draw and is highly contentious. For example, the dominant view is that the judge may not point out to one of the parties the possibility of raising the defence that a claim is time barred, and the court may not consider this defence unless it is raised by the parties. The parties have a duty to state the case truthfully and fully. However, they are fully entitled to put allegations to the court if they do not know whether they are true or not.

995

2. The Course of Civil Proceedings

The course of proceedings before a civil court is divided into different stages. The aim is to give proper consideration to the sometimes conflicting aims of, on the one hand, investigating the truth as thoroughly as possible so as to ensure that the court reaches the correct decision and, on the other hand, settling the matter as quickly as possible. Generally speaking, proceedings before a civil court will be oral unless the parties have consented to having the case decided on the basis of written submissions only. In some situations the court is entitled to order that the case is to be decided on the basis of written submissions only. Ideally, the case should be decided in a single, thoroughly prepared oral hearing called the main hearing (*Haupttermin*). Two types of preliminary proceedings may be followed, the choice being at the discretion of the court. The one possibility is to order a preliminary oral hearing. At this hearing it may be possible to decide the matter by a settlement agreement between the parties, or the court may

996

be able to give judgement at once. If not, then the preliminary hearing serves as preparation for the main hearing. The alternative is for the preliminary proceedings to take the form of purely written pleadings. At the main hearing argument is heard, the necessary evidence is presented to the court, and sometimes judgement is given *ex tempore*. However, the usual practice is to reserve judgement.

997   In the interests of ensuring a speedy procedure the court has the power to preclude one or other of the parties from further presenting his or her case by dismissing the case for undue delay on the part of the claimant or by granting default judgement if the defendant is the offending party (*Präklusion*). The defendant must deliver his or her defence within a particular time of having had the summons served on him or her. If the defendant does not do so within the prescribed period then the defendant will be barred from raising a defence irrespective of how relevant and correct his or her argument may be. The court must warn the defendant of this possibility. Similarly, the court can set deadlines for the submission of pleadings throughout the proceedings. If any of these deadlines are not observed, the offending party will be precluded from submitting further pleadings in the interests of avoiding undue delay unless that party can show good cause for the delay (§§ 275 para. 1 and 3; 276 para. 1 sentence 2; 277 para. 1-3; 296 para. 1 ZPO). It is not always easy to see how the numerous and occasionally very rigid provisions for the preclusion of the one or the other party are to be reconciled with the right to be heard before a court which is guaranteed by article 103 para. 1 GG.

998   A legal remedy is often only effective when it is granted quickly. However, legal proceedings often take a very long time. A solution is provided in the form of interim (interlocutory) protection (*einstweiliger Rechtsschutz*). A court can grant an interlocutory injunction (*einstweilige Verfügung*) if this is necessary to prevent a change in the existing state of affairs which would make it much more difficult or even pointless for one of the parties to the dispute to enforce his or her rights. It can also make a temporary ruling to put end a conflict for the time being. The court has a discretion to decide what orders are necessary to achieve this aim (§§ 935, 940, 938 ZPO). A basic rule is that such a remedy may only constitute a temporary solution. Execution of a claim for a sum of money can be effected by means of arrest and attachment (*Arrest,* §§ 916 ff. ZPO). In terms of the law on execution of judgements the property of the debtor can be attached temporarily or the debtor him- or herself can be arrested.

999   A normal action is filed in writing with the court of first instance. If the court of first instance is the *Amtsgericht* proceedings can also be initiated by an oral declaration which is recorded by the clerk of the court. If the case is being brought before the *Landgericht* the statement of claim must be drafted and filed by a lawyer who is admitted to the bar. In civil courts of the level of the *Landgericht* and above the parties must be represented by a lawyer. The officials of the court then serve the summons on the defendant.

1000   The territorial jurisdiction of the court (*Gerichtsstand*) is generally determined with reference to the normal place of residence of the defendant (§§ 12, 13 ZPO). In addition to the possibility of suing the defendant at his or her place of residence, there are several other possible venues, for example, the place where the tort was committed or the place where the defendant is accustomed to spend long periods of time (§§ 15 ff. ZPO).

The court of first instance will always be either the *Amtsgericht* or the *Landgericht*. **1001**
Deciding on which court is appropriate depends on the amount claimed, unless the
subject matter jurisdiction is expressly assigned to one court (§§ 23, 71 GVG). For example, the *Amtsgericht* is court of first instance in family matters according to § 23 a
GVG.

In cases of a pecuniary nature the amount claimed determines which court should hear **1002**
the case at first instance. The general rule is that claims for up to € 5 000 come before
the *Amtsgericht*, thereafter the *Landgericht* is the court of first instance. The most important of the exceptions to this rule is constituted by cases involving a dispute between the landlord and tenant of residential property. In such cases the *Amtsgericht* is
always the court of first instance irrespective of the amount involved. Another exception is that the *Landgericht* is automatically the court of first instance for claims arising out of breaches of official duty irrespective of the amount of the claim (§ 71 para.
2 number 2 GVG).

The right of resort to a higher court (*Rechtsmittel*) only exists if the case has gone **1003**
against the person wishing to take the matter further. In civil cases it can take one of
three forms, namely *Berufung*, *Beschwerde* or *Revision*.

An appeal (*Berufung*, §§ 511 ff. ZPO) from a decision on a pecuniary claim is general- **1004**
ly only permissible if the additional amount claimed or the amount felt to have been
wrongly awarded is higher than € 600, but the court has the discretion to hear a matter under this amount (§ 511 para. 2 number 1 ZPO). The appeal must be lodged by
delivering a notice of intent to appeal (*Berufungsschrift*) to the appellate court (*Beru-*
fungsgericht). This must be done within one month of having received a copy of the
judgement by registered mail (*Zustellung*) and, at the latest, five months after the decision has been made public by the court (*Verkündung*, § 517 ZPO). (This often takes
place in chambers, often without the attendance of the parties, and some time may
pass before the judgement is then officially sent to the parties by mail.) Appeals from
the *Amtsgericht* are generally heard by the *Landgericht*, appeals from the *Landgericht*
go to the *Oberlandesgericht*.

Revision (§§ 542 ff. ZPO) is the procedure used to take the case further after final **1005**
judgement has been given in an appeal. It can also be invoked against a judgement of a
court of first instance, as an alternative to the ordinary appeal procedure – the so-
called *leap-frog Revision* (§ 566 ZPO). *Revision* brings the case before the *Bundes-*
gerichtshof, the highest civil court in Germany. As a general rule *Revision* is only possible with the leave of the court. This leave is given in the judgement of the court
against whose judgement the *Revision* is being made. In the case of a leap-frog *Revi-*
sion permission is required from the court to which the revision is being brought.
Leave will be granted if the point in issue is of fundamental importance or if it is required for the development of the law or if a decision of the highest court is required
for the purpose of preserving a common approach by all courts (§ 543 ZPO).

If the court against whose decision *Revision* is sought refuses leave for *Revision* then it **1006**
is possible to seek review by the higher court of the decision not to allow an appeal
(*Nichtzulassungsbeschwerde*, § 544 ZPO). If the higher court decides that the matter
should be allowed to proceed then it will proceed as a *Revision* rather than as a
Beschwerde. The period within which revision must be brought is the same as that for
appeal by *Berufung* (§ 548 ZPO).

1007   The *sofortige Beschwerde* (§§ 567 ff. ZPO) procedure is an interlocutory appeal used primarily against intermediate rulings (*Beschlüsse*) and directions, i.e., it is not used against the final judgement of the court at the end of the trial. It can be used if expressly provided for by statute, and generally against decisions which do not involve oral proceedings and which refuse an interlocutory application. It is generally brought before the court against whose decision the appeal is directed. The *sofortige Beschwerde* must be brought within two weeks of official notification of the decision which is being challenged (§ 577 ZPO). The court can either rule on the *Beschwerde* itself or refer the matter to a higher court. If the court rejects a *Beschwerde* it is possible to launch a further *Beschwerde* in the *Bundesgerichtshof* (§ 574 ZPO).

1008   Proceedings before the civil courts involve the payment of court fees (*Gerichtskosten*). The amount payable is determined with reference to the Court Fees Act and is progressive, depending on the value of the dispute, which is determined by the court. Court fees also cover expenses incurred by the court. The debtor responsible for these fees is the person who initiated proceedings in the particular court, although he or she in turn is entitled to recover the court fees from any other party against whom the court has awarded costs.

1009   Generally speaking the party who loses the case will have to pay the legal costs of both sides. This includes all expenses incurred by the other side insofar as these were necessary for the proper prosecution of the claim and thus includes lawyer's fees. The fees due to the lawyers who deal with the case are calculated from the Legal Advisers Remunerations Act (*RVG*). These fees are, once again, on a progressive scale depending on the amount in dispute and the extent of the lawyer's effort. A contingency fee agreement, in terms of which the client is only to pay the lawyer if the case is won, is unusual and admissible on a case-by-case basis only if the client would be deterred from pursuing a claim in court because of his economic situation without the agreement (§ 4 a para.1 sentence 1 RVG).

1010   Legal costs can often be very extensive. By the time a case has been taken on appeal the costs may exceed the amount in dispute and the situation is even worse if the case is taken through three instances. However, the legal aid provided by the state (*Prozesskostenhilfe*) generally ensures that the poorer members of society also have access to justice (§§ 114 ff. ZPO). Legal aid is paid by the state and covers all the costs of taking a matter to trial. A claim to legal aid arises if the planned course of action has sufficient prospects of success and is not merely vexatious. Furthermore, the income of the applicant may not exceed a certain net amount which is calculated by means of a complicated formula. If the applicant is granted legal aid he or she will nevertheless be expected to contribute as much as can reasonably be expected from the applicant to the costs of litigation. Not only German citizens but also any foreigner litigating in Germany has a right to legal aid if he or she fulfils these requirements.

1011   To avoid the difficulties and expenses of the state-run court system the parties to disputes often resort to arbitration. This involves the parties agreeing that their dispute should be decided by a private arbitrator. In terms of §§ 1025 ff. ZPO the decision of the arbitrator are given state recognition.

3. Summary Proceedings for the Recovery of Liquidated Claims

1012   Summary proceedings for the recovery of liquidated claims (*Mahnverfahren*, §§ 688 ff. ZPO) are of great practical importance. The purpose of this procedure is to avoid putting simple matters through the complicated procedures of a full trial, thus providing quick remedies with the minimum of expense. This procedure is essentially available to enforce any claim for the payment of a specific sum of money which is due and payable. However, the procedure cannot be used if the claim is dependent on a not yet performed counter-performance by the claimant. Thus, for example, it can be used by the seller to enforce payment of the purchase price after having delivered the goods. This procedure is initiated by applying to the *Amtsgericht* for the issue of a default summons giving the other party summary notice to pay (*Mahnbescheid*). The amount of the claim is irrelevant to the procedure. The court issues the default summons without hearing the other party. There is not oral argument and no evidence is led. Once the debtor receives the default summons the debtor can object to the default proceedings (§§ 694 ff. ZPO). If the debtor does so the summary default proceedings are converted into a normal contested matter. If the debtor does not raise an objection within two weeks the creditor can apply for default judgement (*Vollstreckungsbescheid*). An objection can still be raised at any time before default judgement is granted. Thereafter the debtor, against whom default judgement has been granted, has the possibility of lodging a notice of objection to default judgement (*Einspruch*), which necessitates further legal proceedings. If this is not done, the creditor can execute the judgement against the debtor.

4. Model Declaratory Action

The model declaratory action (*Musterfeststellungsklage*) is a civil law action which can be brought by qualified associations pursuant to § 606 ff. ZPO. On this basis,qualified associations can demand that certain factual or legal prerequisites exist or do not exist for claims or legal relationships between consumers and a company. An example is the determination that certain technical measures for regulating exhaust gases of cars are illegal. Qualified associations are in particular defined by § 4 UKlaG, e. g. consumer protection bodies. Courts of first instance are exclusively the Higher Regional Courts.

The action requires a group of at least ten consumers. If the action is admitted, affected consumers can register in a litigation register at the Federal Justice Office. At least 50 consumers seeking compensation for damage are required to register within two months. Registration suspends limitation for the individual consumer (§ 204 para. 1 no. 1a BGB). There is no risk of legal costs for the consumer.

The court decides on the model declaratory action only whether there is a legal situation which in principle entitles the consumer to compensation by the defendant. If the court rules in favour of the association, each consumer registered in the litigation register has as a matter of principle to enforce his or her claims individually before court. The model declaratory action has no legal effect for consumers not registered in the litigation register.

5. Execution of Judgement

The actual satisfaction of the claim of the creditor, who has no more than a piece of paper in his or her hand once the creditor has obtained judgement against the debtor, is achieved by way of involuntary execution (*Zwangsvollstreckung*) if the debtor still does not co-operate. Judgements are executed exclusively by state institutions. The subject is regulated in detail in §§ 704 ff. ZPO. Insolvency proceedings under the Insolvency Regulations (*Insolvenzordnung*) also amount to a form of involuntary execu-

1013

tion, but, since they are forms of global execution, they follow different rules from the execution of individual claims under the Civil Procedure Act (*ZPO*).

1014 Involuntary execution generally takes place on the basis of a judgement or other instrument entitling the creditor to obtain execution (*Vollstreckungstitel*). Apart from ordinary judgements, other grounds for execution are a summary default judgement for a liquidated claim (*Vollstreckungsbescheid*) or composition agreements which have been formalised before a court. The procedure for execution differs depending of the nature of the claim to be enforced.

1015 Claims sounding in money can be executed against physical property. Execution is carried out by the bailiff (sheriff's officer), called in German the *Gerichtsvollzieher*, as representative of the state. If it proves necessary to use force the bailiff can summon the police to his or her assistance.

1016 The execution of judgement against moveable (personal) property takes place by levying attachment (*Pfändung*, §§ 803 ff. ZPO). Money, instruments of value such as share certificates (*Wertpapiere*) and other valuables are seized by the bailiff. The bailiff hands money over to the creditor whereas share certificates are sold by the bailiff. Other objects, such as television sets and motor cars may be attached for execution by attaching the bailiff's seal (*Pfandsiegel*, known colloquially as a *Kuckuck*) to them. If the debtor takes steps to make the goods unavailable to the creditor once the seal has been placed on them (for example, by selling them) the debtor will be criminally liable for pound breach, i.e., the unlawful recovery of goods (*Pfandkehr*, § 289 StGB). The attached goods are sold by public auction and the proceeds are used to cover the costs of attachment and to pay the creditor whatever he or she is still owed by the debtor.

1017 Often the judgement debtor is him- or herself the creditor of some other person (§§ 828 ff. ZPO) and it is then possible to order that his or her debtor should pay the amount owed directly to the creditor who has obtained the judgement. This situation might arise, for example, if the debtor is owed wages by his or her employer. This is done by way of a garnishee order or an order for the attachment of earnings (*Pfändungs- und Überweisungsbeschluss*) which is issued by the *Amtsgericht* in its capacity as court for the execution of judgements. The court order is communicated to the third party (for example, the debtor's employer) who is then freed from his or her obligation to make performance to his or her original creditor (his employee, the judgement debtor) and becomes obliged to make performance instead to the judgement creditor.

1018 A judgement is executed against immovable property (land) by a charging order on land ordering the Land Registry (*Grundbuchamt*) to make an entry recording a charge (the equivalent of a mortgage) over the land as security for the payment of the judgement debt. A further possibility is for the *Amtsgericht* in its capacity as court for the enforcement of judgements to sell the land by public auction. Finally, the court may issue a writ of sequestration, placing the land under compulsory administration until the creditor's claim has been satisfied out of the profits from the land (§§ 864 ff. ZPO and the provisions of the Act on Sales in Execution of Judgement, *Zwangsversteigerungsgesetz*).

1019 Execution of judgement with respect to things essentially involves the bailiff's taking a thing away from the debtor and giving it to the creditor (§§ 883 ff. ZPO). Execution of judgement can, however, also involve the doing of acts (injunctions). In the case of acts which can be performed equally well by anybody the court may authorise the creditor to perform the act, any expenses incurred in doing so being for the account of the debtor (§ 887 para. 1 ZPO). An example would be the replacement of a window pane which the debtor has broken. The court which may give such authorisation is the court of first instance which tried the case. In the case of acts which cannot be performed by anyone other than the debtor, for example, the communication of information, the court will put pressure on the debtor by fining him or her (*Zwangsgeld*) or committing the debtor to prison (*Zwangshaft*) if he or she does not comply voluntarily. The same applies to prohibitory injunctions (§§ 888 para. 1; 890 ZPO). A declaration of will (*Willenserklärung*) which the debtor is liable to make, for example, the declaration of agreement to the passing of ownership is presumed to have been made as soon as the judgement takes effect (§§ 894 ff. ZPO).

There are various legal remedies available to the debtor to prevent execution of the judgement against his or her will. By a procedure called *Erinnerung* (§ 766 ZPO) the debtor can raise the objection that provisions setting out the preconditions for execution have been violated, for example by execution taking place without a valid judgement or other instrument entitling the creditor to execution. Similarly, this course of action can be followed if the procedure followed in executing the debt was improper. The action to oppose execution (*Vollstreckungsgegenklage*, § 767 ZPO) can be used by raising allegations which could not be made at the time when the court granted the original order, for example, that the creditor's claims have been satisfied subsequent to the passing of judgement. Third parties can take steps to prevent the execution of the judgement against their property by means of the third-party action against execution (*Drittwiderspruchsklage*, § 771 ZPO), for example, where the debtor has borrowed the third-party's bicycle and the bailiff attaches it as it appears to belong to the debtor. Sometimes the third party is a secured creditor whose claim takes priority over the execution of the judgement, for example, in the case of the landlord's lien. Such rights may be defended by means of the secured creditor's action for preferential satisfaction (*Klage auf vorzugsweise Befriedigung*, § 805 ZPO). The creditor who originally obtained the judgement against the debtor will then only receive that part of the value of the attached object which is left over once the claims of the secured creditor have been satisfied. **1020**

Certain items which the debtor must be allowed to keep so as not to violate his or her constitutional right to dignity may not be attached by the bailiff (see §§ 811, 850 a ff. ZPO). These include various basic household goods such as clothing and necessary accommodation, and certain tools of his or her trade. It has also been held that a simple radio falls under the head of basic household goods. Limits are also placed on the extent to which the debtor's earnings may be attached for the same reason. The amount of his or her earnings which will be protected will be whatever the debtor needs for ordinary living expenses. The exact amount will vary according to how many dependants the debtor has to support. **1021**

If the bailiff is unable to find sufficient assets to satisfy the creditor, then the debtor can be compelled to make complete disclosure of his or her financial position. This will generally involve a sworn declaration of bankruptcy (§ 807 ZPO). If this proves to be untrue the debtor will be liable for various penalties. A refusal to make such a statement will lead to imprisonment for contempt of court for a period of up to 6 months. The sworn statement is registered in a Debtors Register for a fixed period, **1022** with the effect that the debtor will be unable to obtain credit in the future (§§ 899 ff. ZPO).

6. Special Procedures In Family and Miscellaneous Matters (Freiwillige Gerichtsbarkeit)

1023 A very significant part of legal business is subject to the rules on *freiwillige Gerichtsbarkeit* (literally: "voluntary jurisdiction"). They are contained in the Act on Procedure in Family Matters and *freiwillige Gerichtsbarkeit* (*Gesetz über das Verfahren in Familiensachen und in den Angelegenheiten der freiwilligen Gerichtsbarkeit*, FamFG). The rather misleading name complicates attempts to explain what is meant by this. It involves specific procedures for dealing with various types of legal business. This business is, however, scattered throughout the legal system, and so it is not possible to be more precise than to say that the rules of *freiwillige Gerichtsbarkeit* are applicable whenever they are expressed by statute to be applicable. It consists predominantly, but not exclusively, of non-contentious proceedings.

1024 The most important types of business governed by the rules of *freiwillige Gerichtsbarkeit* are the procedures of the Land Registries and the keeping of public registers such as the Register of Associations (*Vereinsregister*) and the Matrimonial Property Register. Various elements of the law of succession also form an important part of this sort of legal business: the granting and withdrawal of certificates of inheritance (*Erbscheine*), the proving of a will, or the supervision of the administration of (potentially) insolvent estates and provisional administration. Areas of family law which are governed by its rules include inter alia orders relating to matters of relations between parents and children (*Kindschaftssachen*, §§ 151 ff. FamFG), lineage (*Abstammungssachen*, §§ 169 ff. FamFG), adoption (§ 186 FamFG), protection from violence (*Gewaltschutzsachen*, §§ 210 ff. FamFG), pension equalisation in divorce cases (*Versorgungsausgleichsachen*, §§ 217 ff. FamFG), and curatorship (*Betreuungssachen*, §§ 271 ff. FamFG). § 113 FamFG provides an exception for marital and family matters regarding financial support or claims (so-called *Ehe- und Familienstreitsachen*, translatable to "marital and family matters in dispute"), which it refers in principle to the general rules of Civil Procedure contained in the ZPO. They are therefore matters of general civil procedure, not the FamFG.

1025 Procedures in the area of the FamFG are characterised by wide-ranging official involvement in the matters dealt with, such as official enquiries as to the relevant facts. Further characteristics are the wide discretion left to the instance deciding the matter, and by the fact that rulings can easily be altered if this is justified by changes of circumstance or further information coming to the attention of the court or official responsible.

Literature:

Adolf Baumbach/Wolfgang Lauterbach/Jan Albers/Peter Hartmann, Zivilprozessordnung, 77. ed. 2019

Ursula Bumiller/Dirk Haders/Werner Schwamb, FamFG Freiwillige Gerichtsbarkeit, 12. ed. 2019

Wolfgang Grunsky/Florian Jacoby, Zivilprozessrecht, 14. ed. 2014

Martin Haußleiter, FamFG, 2. ed. 2017

Wolfgang Lüke, Zivilprozessrecht, 11. ed. 2019
Hans-Joachim Musielak/Wolfgang Voit, Grundkurs ZPO, 14. ed. 2018
Leo Rosenberg/Karl-Heinz Schwab/Peter Gottwald, Zivilprozessrecht, 18. ed. 2018
Kurt Schellhammer, Zivilprozess, 15. ed. 2016
Friedrich Stein/Martin Jonas, Kommentar zur Zivilprozessordnung, 23. ed. since 2014
Heinz Thomas/Hans Putzo, Zivilprozessordnung, 40. ed. 2019
Richard Zöller, Zivilprozessordnung, 32. ed. 2018

Glossary

Abgabenordnung (AO)	Fiscal Ordinance
Abgeordneter	delegate, equivalent to a Member of Parliament or Congressman
Abitur	equivalent of A-levels, after a total of thirteen years of school
Abschiebung	deportation
Abschnitt	chapter
Absatz	paragraph; subsection (The term „paragraph" is used in this translation)
Absicht	see *Vorsatz*
Absonderungsrecht	claim of a secured creditor to preferential settlement before the assets of the bankrupt's estate are distributed to the ordinary creditors.
Abstraktionsprinzip	the principle of abstraction which distinguishes between legal transactions affecting rights *in personam* and transactions affecting rights *in rem* (obligation transactions and disposition transactions). The effect of the principle is that the validity of the one transaction is independent of the validity of the other. For example, there is no necessary connection between the passing of ownership in property and the validity of the relevant contract of sale, and vice versa. See *Trennungsprinzip, Verpflichtungsgeschäft*, and *Verfügungsgeschäft*.
Abwehrfunktion	defensive function
Abwehrrecht	defensive right
Adequanztheorie	test for remoteness of damage in German law of torts – is there an adequate causal link between the wrongful act (breach of duty of care) and the resulting harm?
Adoption	adoption
Äquivalenzprinzip	equivalence principle
Äquivalenztheorie	equivalence theory
Aktien	shares (in a company)/stocks
Aktiengesetz (AktG)	Stock Corporation Act
Aktiengesellschaft (AG)	the approximate equivalent of the public limited company (plc) of English law or the stock corporation of American law
Aktiva	assets, often in the phrase *Aktiva und Passiva*, that is, assets and liabilities
Alimentationsgrundsatz	principle of financial support
Alleineigentum	sole ownership, the situation in which a thing is owned by a single person alone. See *Miteigentum*
Allgemeine Geschäftsbedingungen (AGB)	standard form contract
Gesetz zur Regelung des Rechts der allgemeinen Geschäftsbedingungen (AGBG)	Standard Form Contracts Act
Allgemeine Leistungsklage	general action for relief
Allgemeines Gleichbehandlungsgesetz (AGG)	General Act on Equal Treatment

Allgemeines Landrecht (ALR)	the Prussian codification of 1794, the first German codification
Allgemeinverfügung	general order or ruling; this is a specific kind of *Verwaltungsakt* in which the scope of affected persons is only determined or determinable by general characteristica
Amtsermittlungsgrundsatz	principle of official investigation
Amtsgericht (AG)	the lowest level of court, equivalent to the Magistrates' Court or County Court, which also fulfils a range of administrative functions such as keeping the land register and the commercial register (register of companies)
Amtshaftung	official liability, also called *Staatshaftung*
Analogieverbot	prohibition of the *ad hoc* creation of new crimes by analogy with existing crimes
Anfechtbar	voidable
Anfechtungsklage	action to set aside
Angebot	offer
Angemessen	reasonable, proportional, appropriate
Angemessenheit	reasonableness, proportionality in the narrower sense
Angestellte und Arbeiter	two kinds of employees, white-collar and blue-collar workers
Anklageerhebung	stage of charging of the accused with the crime
Annahme	acceptance of an offer
Annahmeverzug	culpable refusal by the creditor to accept performance tendered in accordance with the debtor's obligation, mora creditoris
Anstalt	a quasi-administrative body with both material resources and personnel dedicated to the fulfilment of a particular objective. Examples are the various public broadcasters
Anstalt des öffentlichen Rechts	incorporated public-law institution
Anstifter	instigator of a crime
Antragsdelikt	crime which is only prosecuted on application
Anwartschaft	expectation, future interest. For example, in the situation where parties have formally agreed to transfer ownership of land but the new owner's name has not yet been entered in the land register, or where an employee will become entitled to pension payments at some time in the future.
Anweisung	1. order to a third party to pay to the other contracting party money or other fungibles. The basis of the law on bills of exchange 2. in the field of public law: directive
Arbeitsgemeinschaft der öffentlich-rechtlichen Rundfunkanstalten der Bundesrepublik Deutschland (ARD)	union of various different broadcasters financed by the *Länder*, „The First Channel"
Arbeitsgericht (ArbG)	Labour Court, Industrial Tribunal
Arbeitskampfrecht	the law on industrial disputes
Arbeitslosengeld	unemployment insurance payment

Arbeitslosengeld II	Formerly unemployment assistance, granted only after unemployment insurance payment has expired and significantly lower, colloquially called „Hartz IV"
Arbeitsrecht	labour law. See also *Individualarbeitsrecht* and *Kollektivarbeitsrecht*
Art und Güte, mittlerer	(goods of) at least average quality; goods of merchantable quality
Asylverfahrensgesetz (AsyVfG)	Asylum Procedure Act
Aufenthaltserlaubnis	residence permit
Aufenthaltsgenehmigung	permit to enter and spend time in the Federal Republic
Aufenthaltsgesetz (AufenthG)	Residence Act
Auflage	condition
Auflassung	the agreement concerning the passing of ownership in land
Aufopferung	sacrifice, concept of compensation for expropriation; also used in cases of infringements against non-pecuniary interests
Aufrechnen	to set one claim off against another
Aufrechnung	set-off
Aufsichtsrat	the supervisory board of an *Aktiengesellschaft* company, comprised of members elected by the general meeting of shareholders and, in bigger companies, of employees representatives. See also *Vorstand*. Some *GmbHs* are also required to have an *Aufsichtsrat*.
Aufstacheln zum Rassenhass	incitement to racial hatred
Auftrag	mandate to act on behalf of someone else without payment
Auftragsverwaltung	administrative acts performed on a commission basis by the *Länder* on behalf of the Federation
Aufwandsteuer	tax on luxury goods, tax on consumption
Augenscheinseinnahme	inspection of the scene of an alleged crime
Ausländerbehörde	Foreigners Office
Ausländergesetz (AuslG)	Aliens Act, in 2005 replaced by the *Aufenthaltsgesetz*
Ausländerrecht	law relating to foreigners and asylum
Auslieferung	extradition
Auslobung	a unilateral legal transaction which in English law would by analysed as a contract. Example: the act of putting up a notice offering a reward for the return of a lost dog
Auslegung	interpretation
Ausschließung aus der Rechtsanwaltschaft	striking the offender off the roll (of lawyers)/disbarment
Außenbereich	outlying areas (public construction law)
Außergewöhnliche Belastungen	extraordinary expenses
Aussonderungsrecht	a claim by the owner for separation and recovery of property which is in the possession of a debtor in bankruptcy so as to prevent its distribution to the ordinary creditors
Ausweisung	order to leave the country

Barscheck	an uncrossed cheque (literally „cash cheque"), entitling the bank to pay the amount in cash over the counter
Baubehörde	authority responsible for regulating construction
Baugesetzbuch (BauGB)	Federal Construction Code
Baunutzungsverordnung (BauNVO)	Building Purposes Act
Bauordnungsrecht	building regulations law
Bauplanungsrecht	zoning law
Baurecht	construction law
Bayrischer Rundfunk (BR)	Channel Bavaria
Beamtengesetz (BG)	Civil Servants Act
Beamtenrechtsrahmengesetz (BRRG)	Act on the Basic Principles of the Law Relating to Civil Servants
Beamtenstatusgesetz (BeamtStG)	Federal Act on the Status of Civil Servants
Beamtenverhältnis	literally „*Beamten* relationship"; term for the employment of a civil servant
Beamter	official; in the strict sense: career civil servant
Bebauungsplan	building plan
Bedingungstheorie	condition theory, a test of factual causation
Befugnis zur Klage	locus standi
Begehungsdelikt	crime consisting of an act. Contrast *Unterlassungsdelikt*
Beglaubigung, öffentliche	public attestation
Begriffsjurisprudenz	analytical jurisprudence of legal terms. The theory that legal problems can be solved with almost mathematical precision by the application of rules.
Behörde	public authority/office, institutional unit within the public administration
Beklagter	defendant
Beleidigung	criminal defamation
Bereicherungsrecht	the law of restitution (unjustified enrichment) §§ 812 ff. BGB
Bereitschaftspolizei	emergency reserve force
Berufsbeamtentum	professional civil service
Berufung	appeal on points of fact or of law or both
Berufsgenossenschaften	employer's liability insurance associations
Berufungsgericht	appellate court
Berufungsschrift	notice of intent to appeal
Beschwerde	request for relief from an administrative act; interlocutory appeal in civil proceedings
Beseitigungsanspruch	owners right to a mandatory or prohibitory injunction if his rights of ownership are being or have been infringed upon
Besitz	possession
■ mittelbarer	the situation in which the legal possessor of a thing exercises control through another person – for example, where the landlord exercises possession of his property through the tenant, who holds it for him.
■ unmittelbarer	the direct exercise of control over a thing, for example, where the owner of property holds it for himself.

Besitzmittlungsverhältnis	the relationship between two persons in which the one person (the *unmittelbarer Besitzer*) holds something on behalf of the other (the *mittelbarer Besitzer*)
Besonderer Teil (des StGB)	book of specific offences (of the Criminal Code)
Bestätigung, kaufmännische	a letter from one businessman to another confirming in writing the writer's understanding of an (oral) agreement. According to the HGB the terms in such a letter will bind the other party unless he objects as soon as reasonably possible.
Bestechlichkeit	taking of bribes
Bestimmtheitsgrundsatz/-gebot	principle of legal certainty
Betäubungsmittelgesetz (BtMG)	Narcotics Act
Betreuung	custodianship, a type of guardianship for adults who lack full legal capacity. In contrast to guardianship over a child, the authority of the *Betreuer* (custodian) is limited to those aspects of life which the specific *Betreuter* is in fact unable to manage himself.
Betriebsausgaben	operating expenses
Betriebsrat	works council
Betriebsverfassungsgesetz (BetrVG)	Employee's Representation Act
Betrug	fraud
Beurkundung, notarielle	execution of a transaction by notarial deed. This is the strictest of all formal requirements. It means that the declaration of will involved has been made before a notary after its significance has been explained by the notary, that the notary has written the declaration down and read it back to the person making the declaration, and that this person has confirmed the correctness of the written text and signed it.
Beurkundungsgesetz (BeurkG)	Notarial Deeds Act
Beurteilungsspielraum	see *Ermessen*
Bewährungszeit	period for which a sentence is suspended
Beweggründe	motives
Beweiserhebungsverbot	prohibition on the gathering of evidence
Beweislast	burden of proof
-, Umkehrung der	reversing the burden of proof
Beweisverwertungsverbot	prohibition on the use of illegally obtained evidence
Bezirk	administrative district, the largest administrative unit within some *Länder*
Billigend in Kauf nehmen	to take deliberately into the bargain, see also *Vorsatz, bedingter*
Bote	messenger (not authorised to act as an agent). See also *Stellvertreter, Erfüllungsgehilfe, Verrichtungsgehilfe.*
Bringschuld	debt which is discharged only once the thing owed is delivered to the creditor's premises
Brandgefahr, Herbeiführen einer	creation of a fire hazard, arson
Bürgermeister	mayor

Bund	federation, federal level of government
Bundesagentur für Arbeit	Federal Employment Agency
Bundesarbeitsgericht (BAG)	Federal Labour Court, equivalent of the British Employment Appeal Tribunal
Bundesfinanzhof (BFH)	Federal Fiscal Court
Bundesgerichtshof (BGH)	the highest court in Germany for all matters not dealt with by the constitutional, administrative, labour or social courts, that is mainly private and criminal law
Bundeskanzler	Chancellor, Head of Government of the Federal Republic of Germany, corresponding approximately to the British Prime Minister or the President of the United States in his capacity as head of government
Bundeskartellamt	Federal Cartel Office, responsible for the implementation of the Act Against Restrictive Trade Practices
Bundeskriminalamt (BKA)	Federal Criminal Police Office
Bundesmeldegesetz (BMG)	General Provisions on Residence Registration Act
Bundesnachrichtendienst (BND)	Federal Intelligence Service
Bundesnaturschutzgesetz (BNatSchG)	Federal Nature Protection Act
Bundesoberbehörde	higher federal authority
Bundespolizei	Federal Police
Bundespolizeigesetz (BPolG)	Federal Police Act
Bundespräsident	President of the Federal Republic, Head of State of Germany, who plays a role similar to that of the Queen in Britain with some more substantial tasks in politics
Bundesrat (BR)	second house of parliament consisting of representatives of the States. See *Bundestag*
Bundesrechnungshof	Federal Court of Auditors
Bundesrechtsanwaltsordnung (BRAO)	Federal Legal Practitioners Ordinance
Bundesregierung	Federal Government
Bundesstaat	federal state, one of the five structural principles of the Basic Law
Bundessteuerblatt	Federal Taxation Gazette
Bundestag (BT)	main house of parliament elected directly by the voters
Bundesunmittelbare Körperschaft	federal public-law corporation
Bundesverfassungsgericht (BVerfG)	Federal Constitutional Court
Bundesverfassungsgerichtsgesetz (BVerfGG)	Federal Constitutional Court Act
Bundesverfassungsschutz	Federal Office for the Protection of the Constitution
Bundesverfassungsschutzgesetz (BVerfSchG)	Federal Act for the Protection of the Constitution
Bundesversammlung	Federal Assembly or Federal Convention, body that elects the *Bundespräsident*
Bundesversorgungsgesetz (BVG)	Federal War Victims Relief Act
Bundesverwaltungsgericht (BVerwG)	Federal Administrative Court

Bundeszentralregister	Federal Central Register – register of various types of official decisions such as criminal sentencing and the pardoning of a crime or an order for an alien to leave the country
Bürge	surety, guarantor
Bürgerliches Gesetzbuch (BGB)	Civil Code
Bürgschaft	contract of suretyship
Chemikaliengesetz	Chemicals Act
Culpa in Contrahendo	a type of tortious (delictual) liability in which the duty of care arises from the fact that the parties have initiated an attempt to conclude a contract
Constitutio Criminalis Carolina	the criminal code of Emperor Charles V (1532)
Darf (dürfen)	may; used in a statute when a discretion regarding the legal consequences is possible. See *Ermessen*
Darlehen	the loan of a fungible (e.g. money), whether with or without consideration
Daseinsvorsorge	duty of the state to provide the basic necessities of life
Datenschutz	data protection, protection of information
Datenschutzbeauftragter	data ombudsman
Datenschutzgesetz (DSG)	Federal Data Protection Act
Datenschutzrecht	law on data protection
Datenverarbeitung	processing of (private) data
Deliktsfähigkeit	capacity to be liable in tort/delict
Deliktsrecht	the law of torts (delict). See also *unerlaubte Handlung*. Note that to some extent *Deliktsrecht* covers different ground from the law of torts. Certain actions which in English law would be regarded as being part of the law of torts are viewed differently in German law. Examples: *culpa in contrahendo, Beseitigungs- und Unterlassungsanspruch* § 1004 BGB (*Sachenrecht*)
Deliktstatbestand	the elements of a crime (actus reus)
Demokratie	democracy, one of the five structural principles of the Basic Law
Depotgesetz (DepotG)	Securities Deposit Act
Deutschenrechte	Rights (see *Grundrechte*; *Menschenrechte*) available to German citizens only; note that in order not to discriminate, these rights are made available to European Union citizens as well
Diebstahl	theft
Dienst	service, in the field of Public Service Law
■ einfacher	lower service, e.g. an official messenger
■ mittlerer	middle service
■ gehobener	higher service
■ höherer	high service, a university degree is needed to enter
Dienstbarkeit, beschränkte persönliche	limited personal servitude; a life interest in someone else's property
Dienstvertrag	contract of service (employment) defined by the object of the contract rather than the degree of control exercised by the employer. The object of the *Dienstvertrag* is

	the provision of work, as opposed to a *Werkvertrag* which is directed towards the achievement of some specific goal.
Dingliche Einigung	the agreement that ownership in a thing should pass. This is conceptually separate from the contract of sale, which merely creates a personal obligation to transfer ownership. In terms of the *Abstraktionsprinzip* there is no necessary connection between the validity of the two agreements.
Dingliches Recht	ius in rem, a real right in a thing, enforceable against all the world
Dispositionsmaxime	the principle that the decision to bring a civil case to court and how to argue it is entirely at the discretion of the party affected.
Dispositives Recht	legal rules which apply unless the person or persons affected stipulate otherwise.
Divergenzvorlage	„divergence referral", i.e., referring a case to a higher court for a decision on a point of law where the trial court feels that previous decisions by higher courts should not be followed
Dringender Tatverdacht	the strong suspicion that a person is guilty, necessary requirement for an arrest warrant
Drittwiderspruchsklage	third-party action to prevent execution of a judgment (where the debtor is in possession of things which are owned by the third party)
Drogenhandel	trading in forbidden drugs
Duldung	toleration
Ehe	marriage
Eigenschaft	characteristic
-, zugesicherte	warranted quality or characteristic
Eigentum	this word is ambiguous, combining the senses of „ownership" and „property"
Eigentumsvorbehalt	agreement to sell, i.e., sale subject to reservation of ownership by the seller. This construction is used to keep ownership of the goods even after the buyer has been given possession. Ownership is then usually passed once the buyer has paid the entire purchase price.
Eigenwechsel	promissory note
Eilversammlung	Urgent demonstration, where less than 48 hours lie between preparation and demonstration
Einführungsgesetz zum BGB (EGBGB)	Act on Introductory Provisions to the Civil Code
Einführungsgesetz zum GVG (EGGVG)	Act on Introductory Provisions to the Constitution of Courts Act
Einkommensteuer	personal income tax on natural persons
Einwilligung des Verletzten	(the defence of) volenti non fit iniuria
Einspruch	notice of objection to default judgement
Einstweilige Anordnung	interlocutory order
Enteignender Eingriff	expropriatory infringement
Entscheidung	decision of a court or an administrative body, see also *Verwaltungsakt*

Entschuldigungsgrund	ground of exemption, a defence to a criminal charge which excludes a guilty state of mind (mens rea)
Erbbaurecht	heritable building lease, giving the holder the right to build on someone else's land and use the building, usually for 99 years, with a right to compensation for improvements once the term ends.
Erbe	the person inheriting; the beneficiary
Erbfolge, gewillkürte	deliberate determination of succession. This is a wider concept than testate succession because it includes not only the will (*Testament*) but also the inheritance contract (*Erbvertrag*)
Erblasser	deceased person whose property is being distributed according to the law of succession; the testator
Erbengemeinschaft	community of heirs who are joint owners of the deceased's estate before it has been divided up
Erbrecht	1) the law of succession *or* 2) the right to inherit
Erbschaftskauf	the purchase and sale of an inheritance as a whole
Erbschaftssteuer	inheritance tax, estate duty
Erbschaft- und Schenkungs- teuergesetz (ErbStG)	Estate Duty and Donations Tax Act
Erbschein	inheritance certificate granted upon application by the probate court (*Amtsgericht*), corresponding to some extent to letters of administration or a grant of probate, since the heirs administer the estate
Erbunwürdigkeit	disqualification from inheritance
Erbvertrag	inheritance contract (deed of succession) appointing heirs inter vivos
Erbverzicht	renunciation of an inheritance (important due to the fact that the person inheriting also assumes the liabilities of the deceased)
Erfolgsdelikt	result crime
Erforderlichkeit	necessity (see *Verhältnismäßigkeit*)
Erfüllungsgehilfe	person charged with the performance of a specific obligation. Contrast *Stellvertreter, Bote* and *Verrichtungsgehilfe.*
Erlass	decree
Erlaubnisirrtum	mistake as to the permissibility of the deed
Ermessen	discretion as to whether or how to act
■ Beurteilungsspielraum	situation in which there is uncertainty as to whether the prerequisites for the exercise of a legal power have been fulfilled, and in such situations the deciding authority must make a decision itself, e.g. in the case of the value of an essay
■ Ermessensfehlgebrauch	the authority has based its decision on irrelevant considerations
■ Ermessensnichtgebrauch	the authority must consciously exercise its discretion, otherwise there is said to be *Ermessensnichtgebrauch*
■ Ermessensreduzierung auf Null	case in which there is only one proper result to be reached even though the authority in principle has a discretion
■ Ermessensüberschreitung	takes place if the authority exceeds the limits of its discretion

■ Ermessensunterschreitung	takes place if the authority does not make full use of the discretion which has been granted to it
■ Rechtsfolgeermessen	the discretion only relates to the drawing of a legal conclusion from a given set of facts
Ermittlungsrichter	investigation judge
Erpressung	extortion
Erschließungsbeitrag	contribution to the costs of opening the land for use by the creation of roads as well as electricity and water connections (construction law)
Ersitzung	the acquisition of ownership by possessing a thing in good faith until the appropriate period of limitation (prescription) has elapsed
Erziehungsgeld	child-raising benefits
Erziehungsmaßregeln	educational measures for juvenile delinquents
Ewigkeitsgarantie	„guarantee of eternity" in article 79 para. 3 GG forbidding absolutely the amendment of certain fundamental provisions of the constitution
Fachaufsicht	power to issue substantive directions, compare with *Rechtsaufsicht*
Fachbereich	faculty
Fachhochschule	technical college
Fahrlässige Körperverletzung	see *Körperverletzung*
Fahrlässige Tötung	negligent homicide
Fahrlässigkeit	negligence
-, bewusste	conscious negligence, perpetrator hopes that he will be able to avoid the possibility that his act will have a criminal result although he is aware that he is acting in breach of a duty of care
-, grobe	gross negligence
-, unbewusste	unconscious negligence, perpetrator does not foresee the criminal consequence and acts carelessly despite the fact that objectively from the point of view of a neutral observer, and subjectively, in his own particular circumstances, he should have been able to foresee and avoid the result
Fahrerflucht	hit-and-run driving
Fahrverbot	suspension of a person's driving licence
Fahrzeugführer	driver
Fahrzeughalter	person responsible for a vehicle
Fakultät	see *Fachbereich*
Familienerbfolge	the principle that, unless the deceased has stipulated otherwise, his or her family should inherit his property
Familienstiftung	family foundation (fulfilling a function similar to that of a trust)
Feststellungsklage	action for a declaratory order
Firma	registered trade name
Flächennutzungsplan	zoning plan
Folgenbeseitigungsanspruch	a claim to remedial action aimed at reversing the consequences of illegal administrative action
Forderungsverletzung, positive (pFV)	positive malperformance of a contract, previously a liability of customary law, now part of § 280 para. 1 BGB

Formelles Recht	law contained in an act of parliament
Fraktion	a group of *Bundestag* delegates consisting of at least 5% of the total number of delegates, usually members of the same political party, who are officially recognised as a unit in terms of the parliamentary rules of the *Bundestag*, thus gaining certain powers
Freibeträge	tax-exempt amounts, tax free allowances
Freie Entfaltung der Persönlichkeit	free development of the personality. The general right to freedom guaranteed in art. 2 para. 1 Basic Law.
Freiheitsberaubung	unlawful deprivation of liberty
Freiheitsstrafe	imprisonment
Freiheit von Wissenschaft und Kunst, Forschung und Lehre, Artikel 5 Abs. 3 GG	constitutional right to freedom of academic activity, the arts, research and teaching in art. 5 para. 3 Basic Law
Freiwillige Erziehungshilfe	voluntary assistance with bringing up children
Freiwillige Gerichtsbarkeit	special procedures followed in miscellaneous matters specified by statute. The procedures of *freiwillige Gerichtsbarkeit* are characterised by greater official involvement, greater discretion and more flexibility than the ordinary rules of civil procedure. These procedures are followed, for example, in regulating the parental responsibility of divorced persons.
Friedensverrat	endangering international peace
Führungsaufsicht	ongoing supervision
Fürsorgeerziehung	correctional education
Fürsorgepflicht	duty to take care, e.g. of the state to take care of its citizen or the employer of his or her employees
Garantenpflicht/-stellung	1) duty of care (in tort), 2) guarantee obligation (in criminal law) which may arise from a variety of situations and which imposes on the person affected to take steps to prevent a crime from occurring. If the person with the obligation fails to prevent the crime he can be charged with it himself as if he had actively committed it.
Gattungsschuld	obligation to supply unascertained goods identified by generic description
Gebrauchsmuster	utility model, a classification which gives a lesser form of recognition to inventions which do not satisfy the strict requirements for a patent, similar to an unregistered design.
Gebühr	fee
Geeignetheit	objective suitability (see *Verhältnismäßigkeit*)
Gefährdung des demokratischen Rechtsstaates	endangering democracy and the *Rechtsstaat*
Gefährdung des Kindeswohl	case where a child's well-being is threatened
Gefährdung des Straßenverkehrs	endangering road traffic
Gefährdungsdelikt	risk crime
Gefährdungshaftung	strict, no-fault liability in tort

Gefahr	the risk, relating to the question of who should bear the loss if the object of a transaction should perish fortuitously (civil law).
-, Übergang der	the passing of the risk
Gefahrenbegriff	concept of danger (police law)
Gegenwärtig	immediate
Gehilfe	accessory
Geiselnahme	hostage-taking
Geldstrafe	fine
Geldwäsche	money laundering
Gemeinde	commune (proper), basic unit of local government comparable to a parish. Largely synonymous with *Kommune*
Gemeindeordnungen	Communal Ordinances
Gemeinderäte	counsellors of which the *Gemeinderat* consists
Gemeinderat	communal council, primary organ of the commune
Gemeinsames Extremismus- und Terrorismusab-wehrzentrum (GETZ)	Joint Centre for Countering Extremism and Terrorism
Gemeinsames Terrorismusab-wehrzentrum (GTAZ)	Joint Counter-Terrorism Centre
Gemeinsamer Senat der obersten Gerichtshöfe des Bundes	Common Senate of the Supreme Federal Courts. A court made up of judges from the various supreme courts (*Bundesgerichtshof, Bundesarbeitsgericht* etc.) to iron out inconsistencies arising from the division of the legal system into different spheres of jurisdiction.
Gemeinschuldner	debtor in bankruptcy, undischarged bankrupt
Generalbundesanwalt	Federal Attorney General
Generalprävention	general deterrence
Genossenschaft	a type of co-operative society, for example, for selling agricultural products
Genossenschaftsgesetz (GenG)	Co-operative Societies Act
Genossenschaftsregister	register of co-operative societies
Gerichte	Courts: *Amtsgericht, Landgericht, Oberlandesgericht, Bundesgerichtshof* and all other courts
Gerichtsbarkeit, ordentliche	regular jurisdiction (civil and criminal courts as opposed to administrative, constitutional, labour, finance and social courts)
Gerichtskosten	court fees
Gerichtsstand	the issue of which court has territorial jurisdiction over a dispute
Gerichtsverfassungsgesetz (GVG)	Law on the Constitution of the Courts, Constitution of Courts Act
Gerichtsvollzieher	Bailiff, sheriff's officer
Gesamthandseigentum	joint ownership of property in undivided shares; the property which is the object of such a legal relationship
Gesamthandsgemeinschaft	community of joint owners (as in the assets of a partnership)
Gesamthandsvermögen	joint assets, e.g. joint estate in a marriage in community of property (*Gütergemeinschaft*)

Gesamtrechtsnachfolge	universal succession to all rights and duties of another person. See *Universalsukzession*
Gesamtschuld	debt for which all the debtors are jointly and severally liable
Gesamtschule	combined school which combines all different types of school into a single school system for everyone
Geschäftliche Handlungen	commercial dealings, term stemming from competition law: any conduct which is intended to promote the commercial success of one's own business, or of some other person's business
Geschäftsähnliche Handlung	a statement or declaration of will to which the law attaches legal consequences irrespective of whether these are desired by the person making the statement
Geschäftsbesorgung	contract to act as a managing/executive agent
Geschäftsfähigkeit	capacity to perform legal acts
-, beschränkte	limited capacity to perform legal acts, applying to minors over the age of seven
Geschäftsführung ohne Auftrag	necessitous intervention, negotiorum gestio (literally, conduct of business without authorisation). A basis for a statutory obligation imposed on the person assisted to compensate the person assisting
Geschmacksmustergesetz (GeschmMG)	Designs Act
Gesellschaft bürgerlichen Rechts (GbR)	a type of partnership
Gesellschaft mit beschränkter Haftung (GmbH)	a type of private limited company
Gesellschafter	person contributing capital, shareholder, partner
Gesellschafterversammlung	meeting of members of a GmbH
Gesellschaftsanteile	shares (in a company)
Gesellschaftsrecht	company law
Gesetz	
■ im formellen Sinn	parliamentary statute
■ im materiellen Sinn	statutory instrument, ordinance, regulation, executive order, by law
Gesetz über das Verfahren in Familiensachen und in den Angelegenheiten der freiwilligen Gerichtsbarkeit (FamFG)	Act on Procedures in Family Matters and Miscellaneous Matters, see also *freiwillige Gerichtsbarkeit*
Gesetzesvorbehalt	requirement of the specific enactment of a statute
Gesetzlichkeitsprinzip	a concept corresponding in part to the concept of the rule of law and incorporating the principle nullum crimen, nulla poena sine lege
Gewährleistung	guarantee, warranty
■ für Sachmängel	implied warranty that goods are of merchantable quality i.e., that the goods are free of latent defects and are fit for the purpose for which they have been bought. Compare the Aedilitian remedies of Roman law.
Gewahrsam	custody
Gewaltenteilung	separation of powers
Gewerbeordnung (GewO)	trade Regulations
Gewerbesteuer	trade tax

Gewerbesteuergesetz (GewStG)	trade Tax Act
Gewerbliche Muster und Modelle	industrial designs and models
Gewerblicher Rechtsschutz	competition law and the protection of industrial property such as patents
Gewerkschaft	trade union
Gläubiger	creditor
Gläubigerverzug	delay in accepting performance of an obligation, refusal to accept performance, mora creditoris
GmbH	See *Gesellschaft mit beschränkter Haftung*
GmbH-Gesetz (GmbHG)	Act on Private Limited Companies
GmbH & Co KG	a type of *Kommanditgesellschaft* (q.v.) in which the partner with unlimited liability is a GmbH, thus in effect creating a situation where none of the participants have unlimited liability
Große Kreisstadt	large sub-district town, such a town is allowed to exercise some of the powers of a sub-district
Grundbuch	Land Register
Grundbuchamt	Land Registry Office
Grunddienstbarkeit	an easement, a servitude, involving a dominant and a servient tenement. See *Dienstbarkeit.*
Grundgesetz (GG)	Basic Law, the German constitution, so called because it was originally seen as a provisional arrangement for the Western zone until a final constitution for a reunited Germany could be drawn up
Grundrecht	fundamental right
Grundrechtsgleiche Rechte	quasi-fundamental rights. These are rights guaranteed in the Basic Law, but not in the chapter dealing specifically with fundamental rights.
Grundschuld	a type of mortgage entitling the beneficiary to the payment of a sum of money out of the land, i.e., entitling him to sell the land or place it under administration if the debtor does not fulfil his obligations. Its existence is independent of whether the primary obligation which it was intended to secure has been discharged. See *Hypothek.*
Grundschuldbrief	land charge or mortgage certificate
Grundschule	primary school
Grundsteuergesetz (GrStG)	Land Tax Act
Gütergemeinschaft	marriage in which the matrimonial property regime is regulated by a special agreement providing that there is to be community of property between the spouses
Güterstand	matrimonial property regime
Gütertrennung	marriage in which the matrimonial property regime is regulated by a special agreement providing that the marriage is to be out of community of property, in other words, that the parties are not to share any property, whether gained before or during marriage
Gute Sitten	public policy, public standards of morality
Gymnasium	academic high school, school leaving diploma (*Abitur*) allows to attend university

Haftpflichtversicherung	insurance against liability for injuries to third parties
Handelsgesetzbuch (HGB)	Commercial Code
Handelsgewerbe	commercial enterprise, attracting the application of the special rules of *Handelsrecht*
Handelsrecht	commercial law, the special set of rules in the HGB applicable only to business people (see *Kaufmann*) which supplement and, to some extent, supplant the provisions of the BGB
Handelsregister	the commercial register, recording, for example, who has the authority to represent particular firms and serving also as the register of companies
Handelsstand	the class of persons to whom the provisions of the Commercial Code (HGB) are applicable
Handwerksordnung (HWO)	Trade and Crafts Regulations
Hauptschulabschluss	elementary school leaving certificate
Hauptschule	senior primary school
Hauptverfahren	main proceedings
Hauptversammlung	general meeting of shareholders
Hausfriedensbruch	criminal trespass
Haushaltsgesetz	Budget Act approving the budget for a particular period
Haushaltsplan	budget
Heranwachsender	youth between 18 and 20
Herausgabeanspruch	the right of the owner to reclaim possession of his property from a third party who is in possession (*rei vindicatio*)
Herstellungsanspruch	claim to restoration of the proper position
Hinreichender Tatverdacht	case in which there are sufficient reasonable grounds for believing that the suspect is guilty, requirement for submitting a bill of indictment to the competent court, see also *dringender Tatverdacht*
Hinterlegung	payment into court, depositing goods with the court in the event that the creditor refuses to accept due performance of an obligation. See *Gläubigerverzug*.
Hochverrat	high treason
Hoheitliche Maßnahme	sovereign act, which means an administrative action in general in the field of public law with all its relevant powers and limits
Holschuld	debt which is discharged by holding the goods ready at the debtors premises
Homogenitätsgebot	principle of homogeneity
Hypothek	a type of mortgage which exists only so long as the claim which it is intended to secure exists. See *Grundschuld*.
Hypothekenbrief	mortgage certificate issued by the land registry
Immunität	parliamentary privilege, immunity
Im Zusammenhang bebaute Ortsteile	coherently developed areas
Individualarbeitsrecht	employment law
Industrie- und Handelskammergesetz (IHKG)	Chambers of Commerce and Industry Act
Inhaberpapier	bearer instrument (see also *Orderpapier*)

Insolvenz	if a debtor is unable to pay his or her debts, insolvency, bankruptcy
Insolvenzgeld	claim against the Federal Employment Agency for loss of wages due to bankruptcy
Insolvenzgläubiger	creditor in insolvency
Insolvenzmasse	the entire estate of the debtor at the time at which proceedings are commenced as well as any property which the debtor acquires during proceedings, "insolvent estate"
Insolvenzordnung (InsO)	Insolvency Act
Insolvenzverwalter	administrator in bankrupty, insolvency
Institutsgarantie	institutional guarantee – the objective aspect of the Fundamental Rights
Investmentanteile	investment fund unit certificates
Investmentgesetz	Investment Act
Jugendamt	Youth Welfare Office, Youth Office
Jugendarrest	arrest for youthful offenders
Jugendgerichte (JG)	juvenile courts, juvenile offenders are tried by special juvenile courts in the first two levels of courts
Jugendgerichtsgesetz (JGG)	Juvenile Courts Act
Jugendgerichtshilfe	juvenile court assistants
Jugendhilfe, Vereinigungen für	Associations for Youth Support
Jugendstrafe	juvenile detention
Jugendstrafrecht	Law on Juvenile Offenders
Kammer	a subdivision of a court, a subdivision of one of the two senates of the Federal Constitutional Court consisting of a bench of three judges
Kann (können)	can; used in a statute when a discretion regarding the legal consequences is possible. See *Ermessen*
Kapitalgesellschaft (KG)	a corporate entity analogous to a company
Kartell	restrictive practices in restraint of trade, monopoly
Kaufmann	a businessman, a person who runs a commercial enterprise (*Handelsgewerbe*). This is a word with a specific legal meaning in German law. Any person who falls within the definition of *Kaufmann* is subject to the special rules of *Handelsrecht*.
Kaufvertrag	contract of sale
Kausalität	causation
Kavaliersdelikt	a crime which is considered by certain sectors of the population an amusing display of high spirits rather than a criminal act, e.g.: shoplifting
Kinderentziehung	child abduction
Kindschaftsrecht	the law relating to children
Kirchensteuer	church tax
Kläger	plaintiff
Klage	a lawsuit, specifically, the statement of claim
Klageantrag	prayer for relief, heads of claim
Klagearten	forms of action
Klageerhebung	issue of writ of summons
Knebelungsvertrag	adhesion contract, unreasonable restraint of trade.

Körperschaft des öffentlichen Rechts (KöR)	corporation at public law, statutory body, e.g. *Rechtsanwaltskammer*, a *Körperschaft* is characterised by the fact that it has members.
Körperschaftsteuer	corporate income tax
Körperschaftsteuergesetz (KStG)	Corporate Income Tax Act
Körperverletzung	assault and battery
-, fahrlässige	negligently causing bodily harm
-, mit Todesfolge	battery with fatal consequences
Kollektivarbeitsrecht	the law of industrial relations
Kommanditgesellschaft (KG)	a type of partnership in which the managing partners have unlimited liability and the other partners have a liability limited by shares
Kommunale Selbstverwaltung	communal self-administration
Kommunalrecht	law of communal administration
Kommune	commune, local government structure, generally synonymous with *Gemeinde*
Konstruktives Mißtrauensvotum	constructive vote of no-confidence – a Chancellor who has lost the confidence of the *Bundestag* cannot be toppled unless the opposition elects a new Chancellor
Kontaktsperre	complete isolation of an accused if special dangers are involved
Kostendeckungsprinzip	cost-price principle
Krankenversicherung	health insurance
Kreis	sub-district, comparable to a county. A sub-unit of a *Bezirk*
Kreisfreie Stadt	a town or city which is large enough to form a *Kreis* all by itself and which thus exercises the functions of the *Kreis*; "sub-district independent" town
Kreislaufwirtschaftsgesetz (KrWG)	Recycling Products Act
Kreisordnungen (KO)	Sub-district Ordinances
Kreistag	sub-district parliament
Kriminalpolizei	criminal investigation unit
Kuckuck	colloquial term for the bailiff's seal attached to goods which are to be sold in execution (*Pfandsiegel*)
Kündigung	notice of termination; e.g. termination of employment
Kündigungsschutzgesetz (KSchG)	Protection Against Dismissal Act
Kulturverwaltungsrecht	law relating to Cultural Administration
Kurzarbeitergeld	subsidies to firms which are suffering from temporary, abnormal loss of demand to prevent short-term problems from resulting in layoffs
Ländersache	a matter for the states
Lagerschein	negotiable warehouse receipt
Land, Länder	state, states
Landesbauordnung (LBauO)	State Building Regulation
Landesmedienanstalt	broadcasting authority of each *Land*
Landesoberbehörde	independent government department (or agency) – government structure at the level of the *Land* reporting to a particular minister but organisationally inde-

	pendent of the rest of that minister's ministry. Example: *Landesversicherungsanstalt*
Landespressegesetz	Printed Media Act
Landesregierung	state government
Landesverrat	treason
Landesversicherungsanstalt	regional insurance institution, see *Landesoberbehörde*
Landfriedensbruch	crime of civil disorder, rioting
Landgericht (LG)	middle court level within a *Land*, see *Gerichte*
Landrat	chief executive in the *Landkreis*
Landtag	state parliament
Lauschangriff	„bugging"
Lebenspartner	partner in a state registered homosexual relationship, life partner
Lebenspartnerschaftsgesetz (LPartG)	Partner in Life Act
Lebensunterhalt	basic living expenses
Lebenszeitprinzip	principle of life-long employment
Legalitätsprinzip	the principle that the state prosecution service is bound to uphold the rule of law
Lehre der unmittelbaren Verursachung	doctrine of proximate causes
Leibesstrafe	corporal punishment
Leihe	contract whereby the right to use a thing is given for no consideration
Leistungsdimension der Grundrechte	positive aspect of a fundamental right entitling the holder to some sort of service from the state
Leistungsstörung	any situation in which a contract is not performed as agreed (mistake, frustration and breach)
Leitsatz	a type of official headnote containing the ratio decidendi of a case
Lohnsteuer	income tax on wages and salaries, PAYE
Magistratsverfassung	magisterial system
Mahnbescheid	default summons giving the other party summary notice to pay
Mahnung	letter of demand, warning to a debtor that legal action will be taken if he does not perform his obligations
Mahnverfahren	summary proceedings for the recovery of a liquidated claim
Medienrecht	media law
Mehrheitswahl	winner-takes-all election decided by majority vote
Mehrwertsteuer (MwSt)	Value Added Tax (VAT)
Meineid	perjury
Melde- und Passrecht	law on identity documents and residence registration
Menschenhandel	human trafficking, slave trading
Menschenraub	kidnapping
Menschenrechte	Fundamental Rights (see *Deutschenrechte*; *Grundrechte*) which apply to every human being
Menschenwürde	human dignity
Minderung	a remedy available to the buyer in a contract of sale if the goods are defective (not of merchantable quality). The buyer may then claim a reduction in the selling price equal to the diminution in the value of the goods

	caused by the defect. Compare the aedilitian actio quanti minoris of Roman law. See also *Wandelung*.
Ministerialdirektor	director general, civil servant
Mitbesitz	the situation in which several persons are co-possessors of a thing simultaneously
Mitbestimmungsgesetz (MitbestG)	Co-Determination in Industry Act
Mitbestimmungsrecht	law on employee representation
Miteigentum	co-ownership
Mittäter	co-perpetrators, several people act to carry out a common purpose
Mittelbare Drittwirkung	indirect horizontal application, theory of the
Mittelbare Staatsverwaltung	indirect administration; can be organised as a *Körperschaft, Anstalt* or *Stiftung.*
Mittlere Verwaltungsbehörde	intermediate administrative authority
Mord	murder
Nachbesserungsanspruch	right to have defective work performed under a *Werkvertrag* redone properly. Analogous to the strict liability for latent defects in the contract of sale
Nacherben	a series of heirs who are to inherit in succession. A provision of this sort in a will binds the property and is in effect similar to a testamentary trust
Nachlass	deceased's estate
Nachlassgericht	probate court
Nachlassinsolvenz	declaring bankruptcy of a deceased's estate
Nachlassverwaltung	placing a deceased person's estate under administration on behalf of creditors
Namensaktie	registered share, registered in the name of a particular shareholder
Nebenfolge	a further consequence of being sentenced to a period of imprisonment of a year or more, e.g.: loss of capacity to hold public office within the next five years
Nebenstrafe	auxilary form of punishment, such as a *Fahrverbot*
Nichtig	void
Niederlassungserlaubnis	establishment permit, allowing foreigners to settle in Germany to open a business
Nießbrauch	usufruct, comparable to the English idea of profits à prendre
Nötigung	compulsion
Nötigung von Verfassungsorganen	intimidation of constitutional organs
Norddeutscher Rundfunk (NDR)	Northern Channel
Normenkontrolle	Constitutional Review Proceedings; action for the striking down of a legal rule before the administrative or constitutional courts
Normenkontrolle, abstrakte	Abstract Constitutional Review – procedure before the Federal Constitutional Court to test the constitutionality of a statute in the abstract
Normenkontrolle, konkrete	Specific Constitutional Review – procedure before the Federal Constitutional Court to test a question of con-

	stitutionality arising from a referral from a lower court for the purposes of deciding a specific dispute
Nothilfe	emergency assistance, which is a ground of justification where the defender acts to protect the interests of another person, see also *Notwehr*
Notstand	necesssity
-, entschuldigender	exculpating necessity, defence excluding culpability
-, rechtfertigender	necessity as ground of justification, defence excluding illegality
Nottestament	emergency will, valid without compliance with the usual formalities because of extreme circumstances
Notwehr	Self-defence, which can be raised as a ground of justification (defence) when charged with a crime
Notwehrexzess	the force used in self-defence is in excess of what is necessary, also a defence excluding culpability
Notwehrüberschreitung	see *Notwehrexzess*
Notwendige	necessary, self-defence is only justified insofar it is necessary
Notwendige Verteidigung	mandatory legal representation
Nutzungsrechte	rights of use, a type of limited real right
Oberste Landesbehörde	supreme state authority
Öffentliche Sicherheit	public safety
Offene Handelsgesellschaft	a type of partnership which always has unlimited liability and the capacity to sue in its own name.
Offizialprinzip	principle of official action
Opportunitätsprinzip	principle of discretionary prosecution
Orderpapier	instrument payable to order
Ordnung	Act, code, ordinance
Ordnungsstrafe	fine for contempt of court imposed for disorderly behaviour or refusal by witnesses to answer questions
Ordnungswidrigkeit	lesser or summary offence
Ordnungswidrigkeitengesetz (OWiG)	Lesser Offences Act
Organstreitverfahren	Internal Dispute Procedure – a type of proceeding before the Federal Constitutional Court to resolve disputes between two constitutional organs, for example, between the *Bundestag* and the *Bundespräsident*
Pacht	contract of lease or hire with the additional right to appropriate the fruits of the rented property
Paragraphzeichen (§)	section
Partnerschaftsgesellschaft	partnership
Passiva	liabilities. See *Aktiva*
Passive Sterbehilfe	passive euthanasia
Patentgesetz (PatG)	Patents Act
Personengesellschaft	the German equivalent of a partnership. See *Gesellschaft bürgerlichen Rechts, Offene Handelsgesellschaft, Kommanditgesellschaft* and *Stille Gesellschaft* for variations of this.
Personenstandsregister	Register of Births, Deaths and Marriages
Persönlichkeitsrecht, allgemeines	general personality rights, based on article 1 para. 1 read in conjunction with article 2 para. 1 GG. This

	right, which in essence provides protection against defamation and invasion of privacy can be the basis for an action for damages in tort.
Pfandkehr	the unlawful recovery of goods which have been attached for sale in execution or which have been pledged
Pfandrecht	lien, mortgage, pledge
Pfandsiegel	bailiff's seal, attached to goods which are being attached for execution
Pfändung	levy of attachment of a judgement debtor's moveable (personal) property by the bailiff or other competent officer of the court
Pfändungs- und Überweisungsbeschluss	garnishee order or order for the attachment of earnings
Pflegeversicherung	special care insurance
Pflegschaft	curatorship, partial guardianship
Pflichtenkollision	collision of duties, extra-legislative defence excluding culpability if the accused finds himself confronted by an unusual, almost insoluble collision of duties
Pflichtteilsanspruch	statutory right of the spouse and blood relatives of the testator to a certain minimum share of his estate which can be enforced against the beneficiaries under the will (family provision)
Pflichtverletzung	generic term for all irregularities in the performance of contracts, § 280 para. 1 BGB
Pflichtverteidiger	court-appointed counsel
Polizeiliche Verantwortung	responsibilities to the police
Polizeirecht	police law
Popularklage	public interest or taxpayer's action
Präklusion	the preclusion of one or other of the parties to litigation from further presenting his case because of undue delay
Präsident des Deutschen Bundestages	President of the *Bundestag*, the speaker of the house
Preußisches Allgemeines Landrecht (PrALR)	Prussian General Code 1794
Produkthaftungsgesetz (ProdHaftG)	Product Liability Act
Produktsicherheitsgesetz (ProdSG)	Product Safety Act
Prokura	a special, particularly wide form of agency specially regulated in the Commercial Code (HGB)
Prozesskostenhilfe	legal aid
Publizitätsprinzip	the principle that information as to the existence of real rights should be readily accessible to all members of the public since such rights are enforceable against all members of the public
Raub	robbery
Realakt	factual activity of a public body, see also *schlichtes Verwaltungshandeln*
Reallast	land charge giving the holder the right to receive recurring payments derived from the land

Realschule	technical school
Realsteuer	tax on land
Recht	law, justice, right
■ dispositives	rules of law which apply to the relationship between the parties to an obligation only insofar as they do not make special provision to the contrary
Rechtfertigungsgrund	ground of justification, defence excluding unlawfulness in a criminal trial, e.g. *Notwehr*
Rechtfertigender Notstand	see *Notstand*
Rechtsanwalt	legal practitioner (attorney/advocate/barrister/solicitor)
Rechtsanwaltskammer	Law Society, Bar Association, see *Körperschaft*
Rechtsaufsicht	power to issue procedural directions only, compare with *Fachaufsicht*
Rechtsbehelf	legal remedy
Rechtsfähigkeit	capacity to have legal rights and duties
Rechtsfolgeermessen	see *Ermessen*
Rechtsgeschäft	legal transaction
■ einseitiges	unilateral legal transaction
Rechtshängig	pending (litigation)
Rechtskreistheorie	„legal sphere" theory
Rechtsmittel	resort to a higher court
Rechtsstaat	constitutional state under the rule of law, one of the five structural principles of the Basic Law
Rechtsstaatsprinzip	principle of constitutional government under the rule of law
Rechtsverordnung (RVO)	delegated legislation made by an administrative body in terms of its statutory powers, regulations
Rechtswidrig	unlawful
Regierungspräsident	head of intermediate level of government
Regierungspräsidium	local government; depending on the individual State the government at this level is called *Regierung*, *Regierungspräsident* or *Bezirksregierung*
Reichspolizeiordnung	Imperial Police Ordinance
Rentenschuld	annuity land charge
Rentenversicherung	state pension system
Republik	republic, one of the five structural principles of the Basic Law
Ressortprinzip	doctrine of ministerial responsibility
Revision	judicial review, proceedings in error similar to certiorari, appeal on points of law
Rücktritt	rescission
Rückwirkendes Gesetz	retrospective legislation
Rückwirkung	retrospectivity
■ echte	genuine retrospective measures
■ unechte	quasi-retrospective measures; intervention in an ongoing situation
Rückwirkungsverbot	prohibition of retrospective creation of criminal offences
Sachbeschädigung	unlawful damage to property

Sache	a thingt
■ bewegliche Sache	moveable property; personal property, specifically, choses in possession (chattels personal)
Sachenrecht	the law of things, the law of property, in contradistinction to the law of obligations
Sachmängelhaftung	liability for the fact that goods are not of merchantable quality, liability for latent defects
Satzung	by-law, memorandum and articles of association of a corporation; a *Satzung* governs the internal business of self-regulating bodies; local regulation
Schadensersatz	damages
Scheck	cheque
Scheckgesetz (ScheckG)	Cheques Act
Schickschuld	debt which is discharged once the debtor has placed the thing owed in the hands of the prescribed intermediary who is to deliver it to the creditor
Schranke	(*Grundrechte*) limitation clause
Scheidung (Ehescheidung)	divorce
Schenkung	contract of donation
Schlichtes Verwaltungshandeln	factual activity of a public body, see *Realakt*
Schmerzensgeld	damages for pain and suffering
Schöffe	lay assessor
Schöffengericht	court of professional judges and lay assessors
Schuldanerkenntnis	admission of debt
Schuldfähigkeit	criminal capacity
Schuldhaft	culpable, culpably – referring to an act committed with a culpable state of mind, i.e. negligently, recklessly or intentionally
Schuldner	debtor
Schuldnerverzug	mora debitoris, failure of the debtor to discharge an obligation within the prescribed time
Schuldprinzip	the principal of criminal law that the accused may only be punished if he has a guilty state of mind
Schuldverschreibung	issue of negotiable instruments, debentures, bonds
Schuldversprechen	promissory note
Schutzbereich	(*Grundrechte*) sphere of protection
Schutzpolizei	see *Vollzugspolizei*
Schutzprinzip	principle of protection -1) a guiding assumption of German labour law, namely, that the employee requires protection because he is economically and personally dependent on the employer; 2) principle of criminal law that acts committed outside Germany which infringe on interests inside Germany are punishable under German law.
Schwarzarbeit	an employment relationship in which the employer is not deducting income tax, social security and insurance payments from the employee's salary as required by law
Selbstmord	suicide
Senat, großer	grand senate, body within the supreme courts of justice to ensure uniform application of the respective court

§	the symbol for *Paragraph*, the equivalent of a section in an English statute
Sicherung	detention of offenders, see also *Verbesserung*
Sicherungsrechte	rights of security, a type of limited real right
Sicherungsübereignung	mortgage of goods (bill of sale) in terms of which a debtor remains in possession of goods while transferring ownership to his creditor by way of security, usually subject to the condition that ownership is to be re-transferred once the debt has been repaid
Sicherungsverwahrung	detention for repeat offenders for reasons of public safety
Soll (sollen)	shall; general obligation to act in a certain way, in exceptional cases a departure from the rule is admissable. See *Ermessen*
Sonderabgaben	special levy
Sonderausgaben	deductable expenses
Soziale Marktwirtschaft	social market economy
Sozialgesetzbuch (SGB)	Social Security Code
Sozialhilfe	social welfare benefits
Sozialrecht	social security law
Sozialstaat	social state, one of the five structural principles of the Basic Law
Spezialprävention	specific prevention and deterrence, see also *Generalprävention*
Spiel und Wette	gaming and wagering agreements
Spontanversammlung	Spontaneous demonstration in which participants take part without any preparation
Staatsangehörigkeit	citizenship
Staatsangehörigkeitsgesetz (StAG)	Citizenship Act
Staatsanwaltschaft	state prosecution service
Staatshaftung	see *Amtshaftung*
Staatskirchenrecht	law regulating the relationship between state and church/religion
Staatsschutzdelikt	offences against the security of the state
Staatssekretär	under-secretary of state
Standesamt	registry office (for births, deaths and marriages)
Stellvertreter	agent, see also *Bote, Erfüllungsgehilfe, Verrichtungsgehilfe*
Stellvertretung	agency. This can be based on statute (*gesetzliche Vertretung*) or contract (*Vollmacht*).
Steuerklasse	tax bracket
Stiftung	foundation, a fund of money which has been appropriated to a particular purpose
Strafbefehl	simplified summary procedure
Strafgesetzbuch (StGB)	Criminal Code
Strafprozessordnung (StPO)	Criminal Procedure Act
Strafprozessrecht	law of criminal procedure
Strafvollstreckungsordnung (StVollStrO)	Execution of Criminal Sentences Act
Straßenblockade	obstruction of public ways
Straßenverkehrsgesetz (StVG)	Road Traffic Act

Straßenverkehrsordnung (StVO)	Road Traffic Regulations
Straßenverkehrszulassung-sordnung	Vehicle Licensing Regulations
Streik	strike (in the course of an industrial dispute)
▪ wilder Streik	wildcat strike
▪ Warnstreik	warning strike
Stückschuld	obligation to supply ascertained goods
Stufentheorie	analysing a situation into a number of different levels of control (media law)
Süddeutsche Ratsverfassung	South German council system
Täter	perpetrator
Täterschaft	liability as a principal perpetrator
-, mittelbare	commission of a crime through the agency of another person, see also *Tatmittler*
Tätigkeitsdelikt	state of affairs crime
Tagessatz, Tagessätze	daily earning rate
TA-Luft und TA-Lärm	Technical Regulations – Air, Technical Regulations – Noise
Tarifvertrag	agreement between employers' associations and trade unions arising from industry-wide collective bargaining
Taschengeldparagraf	Literally pocket money provision, § 110 BGB: contracts with minors are binding if the minor is able to perform his or her side of the bargain with resources which the minor's guardian has consented to dispose of freely
Tatbestandsirrtum	mistake of fact, see also *Verbotsirrtum*
Tatbestandsverwirklichung	the commission of an act corresponding to the elements of a crime
Tatentschluss, gemeinsamer	the common purpose co-perpetrators carry out
Tatmittler	person used as an instrument to commit a crime
Tauschvertrag	contract of barter
Teil, allgemeiner (des BGB)	Book of General Provisions (of the Civil Code)
Teilgeschäftsfähigkeit	partial legal capacity, legal guardian of a minor consents for him or her to enter a contract of employment or, subject to ratification by the Guardianship Court (*Vormundschaftsgericht*) give permission for the minor to set up as a self-employed business person
Teilnahme	participation (in a crime as an accessory)
Teilnehmer	participant, person guilty of aiding and abetting a crime, see *Anstifter* and *Gehilfe*
Territorialitätsprinzip	the principle that the criminal law applies to all crimes committed within the national territory
Testament	will
-, gemeinschaftliches	joint will (of husband and wife)
-, öffentliches	public will, drawn up by a notary and fulfilling various formalities
-, privates	private will, hand written and signed by the testator
Testierfreiheit	testamentary freedom, freedom of testation
Tierschutzgesetz (TierSchG)	Animal Protection Act
Todesstrafe	death penalty

Tötung auf Verlangen	the killing of a person with his consent
Tötungsdelikt	homicide
Totschlag	manslaughter (US: second degree murder)
Tratte	bill of exchange
Trennungsprinzip	the principle of abstraction which distinguishes between legal transactions affecting rights *in personam* and transactions affecting rights *in rem* (obligation transactions and disposition transactions). See *Abstraktonsprinzip*
Überbringer	bearer, in the phrase "*oder Überbringer*" – "or bearer" on a cheque.
Übergabe	the physical handing over of a thing. This, together with the *dingliche Einigung,* is a requirement for the passing of ownership in moveable property.
Überschuldung	balance-sheet insolvency, the situation in which the debtors liabilities exceed his assets. See also *Zahlungsunfähigkeit.*
Umsatzsteuer (USt)	tax on turnover, indirect turnover tax
Umweltrecht	environmental law
Unbestimmter Rechtsbegriff	undefined legal term, courts exert full judicial review over an administrative body's interpretation of such terms. See *Beurteilungsspielraum*
Unfallversicherung	accident insurance
Ungerechtfertigte Bereicherung	unjustified enrichment, the law of restitution
Unerlaubte Handlung	tort, delict. See also *Deliktsrecht.*
Universalsukzession	universal succession. See *Gesamtrechtsnachfolge.*
Unmöglichkeit	impossibility, various situations in which the debtor is unable to perform his obligations under a contract (frustration and certain forms of breach and mistake)
Unschlüssig	in the phrase *die Klage ist unschlüssig* – the plaintiff's argument does not disclose a cause of action
Unterlassungsanspruch	prohibitory injunction (interdict) available to the owner if there is an imminent danger of interference with his rights of ownership
Unterlassungsdelikt	crime consisting of an omission. Contrast *Begehungsdelikt.*
Unternehmergesellschaft	entrepreneurial company, version of the GmbH, that is easier to found
Unterschlagung	fraudulent misappropriation of property
Untersuchungshaft	investigative detention
Unverhältnismäßig	disproportional, see also *Verhältnismäßigkeitsgrundsatz*
Unverzüglich	without delay
Unzumutbar	unreasonable
Urabstimmung	strike ballot
Urheberrecht	copyright law
Urheberrechtsgesetz (UrhG)	Copyright Act
Urkundenbeweis	documentary evidence

Verarbeitung	the acquisition of ownership in raw materials belonging to someone else by virtue of the fact of having made something new out of them
Verbandsklage	an exception to the general prohibition of public interest actions in administrative court proceedings, the *Verbandsklage* allows associations that have been recognised as active in a particular field to bring actions in court, e.g. environmental associations in the field of environmental law
Verbesserung	reformation of offenders, see also *Sicherung*
Verbindung	see *Vermischung*
Verbotsirrtum	error as to the prohibited nature of an act, mistake of law (criminal law), see also *Tatbestandsirrtum*
Verbraucher	consumer, § 13 BGB
Verbraucherkreditgesetz (VerbrKrG)	Consumer Credit Act
Verbraucherschutz	protection of private consumers; rules modifying the general rules in those statutorily defined circumstances, in which a consumer and an entrepreneur contract, in order to protect the consumer
Verbrauchssteuer	tax on consumption
Verbrechen	serious offence, felony, compare with *Vergehen*
Verein	association, the archetype of various forms of joint undertaking
Vereinsregister	register of associations
Verfassungsbeschwerde	Constitutional Complaint – a type of action before the Federal Constitutional Court, brought when the petitioner alleges that his fundamental rights have been infringed by the state
Verfassungskonforme Auslegung	„constitutional conformity" approach to interpretation
Verfassungsstruktur-prinzipien	fundamental constitutional principles
Verfügung	(administrative law) the decision, direction or order of a public authority
Verfügungsbefugnis	the power to enter a valid *Verfügungsgeschäft* (see below)
Verfügungsgeschäft	disposition transaction, legal transaction creating rights *in rem*. See *Abstraktionsprinzip, Trennungsprinzip*.
Verfügungsgewalt	Someone has *Verfügungsgewalt* if he has the vehicle in use for his own purpose and has the necessary power to use it as he pleases
Vergabe und Vertragsordnung für Bauleistungen (VOB)	Standard Building Contract Terms
Vergehen	less serious crime, misdemeanour, compare with *Verbrechen*
Verhältnismäßig	reasonable
Verhältnismäßigkeit, ■ Grundsatz der -, ■ Verhältnismäßigkeitsgrundsatz	Principle of Proportionality, a central concept particularly in German constitutional law, but also in other areas such as labour and administrative law, where it is used to determine the legitimacy of industrial action.

It involves determining whether the means (*Mittel*) and the ends (*Zweck*) are legitimate in themselves and then considering whether they satisfy the following requirements: *Geeignetheit* – objective suitability of the means for reaching the defined end, *Erforderlichkeit* – necessity (the solution chosen must be the least burdensome of all those possible), *Angemessenheit* – reasonableness, or "proportionality in the narrower sense".

Verhältniswahl	election on the basis of proportional representation
Verjährung	becoming time barred, the prescription of a claim
Verhaltensverantwortlichkeit	responsibility to the police for acts
Verkehrspolizei	traffic police
Verletzungsdelikt	injury crime
Verletzung vermögenswerter Güter	damage of a pecuniary nature to property
Vermächtnis	a specific bequest in a will imposing on the residuary beneficiaries an obligation to transfer some part of the deceased's wealth to some other person
Vermischung und Verbindung	the acquisition of ownership by the mixing or joining together of two things (commixtio et confusio)
Vermittlungsausschuss	mediation committee (between *Bundestag* and *Bundesrat*)
Vermögensmasse	funds
Verordnung (VO)	ordinance, executive order, subordinate legislation, official regulations
Verordnung über die gerichtliche Zuständigkeit und die Anerkennung und Vollstreckung von Entscheidungen in Zivil- und Handelssachen (EuGVVO)	Regulation on jurisdiction and the recognition and enforcement of judgments in civil and commercial matters
Verpflichtungsgeschäft	obligation transaction, legal transaction creating rights in personam. See *Abstraktionsprinzip*.
Verrichtungsgehilfe	employee acting in the course and scope of his duty. See also *Erfüllungsgehilfe*.
Verpflichtungsklage	action for the issue of an administrative act
Versammlung	assembly
Versäumnisurteil	default judgement entered against the defendant if he does not defend the matter
Verschulden	fault
-, mitwirkendes	contributory negligence
Versuch	attempt (criminal law)
-, untauglicher	futile attempt
Vertrag	contract
■ zugunsten Dritter	contract for the benefit of a third party, i.e. a contract by which performance is to be made to a person who is not privy to the contract
■ mit Schutzwirkung für Dritte	contract which involves secondary obligations to persons not party to the contract while the primary obligations are between the contracting parties themselves

Vertragsstrafe	penalty payable in terms of a penalty clause in a contract
Vertragsverletzung, positive	see *Forderungsverletzung, positive*
Vertrauensschutz	protection of legitimate expectations
Vertreter, gesetzlicher	statutory agent, legal guardian, person with parental responsibility
Verwahrung	contract of deposit/bailment
Verwaltung	the civil service, administrative structures, public administration
Verwaltungsakt (VA)	administrative act, i.e. an administrative direction/order, decision or action of some sort which regulates with immediate effect the legal position of a specific citizen, a *VA* is defined in § 35 VwVfG
Verwaltungsakt mit Drittwirkung	*VA* with impact on third parties
Verwaltungsgerichtsordnung (VwGO)	Administrative Courts Act
Verwaltungsrechtlicher Vertrag	public law contract between a public authority with a person instead of *VA*
Verwaltungsverfahrensgesetz (VwVfG)	Administrative Procedure Act
Verwaltungsvorschriften (VV)	general directions for the conduct of business by which public authorities regulate their internal business
Verwandtschaft	relationship, specifically, relationship by consanguinity
Verwarnung	warning
Verwarnung mit Strafvorbehalt	warning and reserve sentencing isssued by the court
Verweisung	remission of a case to another court
Verwertungsrechte	rights of realisation or administration, a type of limited real right
Verzug	breach of contract by failing to perform within the prescribed time, mora
Völkermord	genocide
Völkerrecht	public international law
Volkshochschule	adult education centre
Volksverhetzung	stirring up hatred against minorities
Vollendung	the consummation of a crime
Vollkaufmann	full-scale trader/entrepreneur, a status which attracts certain consequences in terms of the *HGB*
Vollkaufmännisches Gewerbe	full-scale trading business, a criterion which determines to some extent what forms a corporation may take
Vollmacht	power of attorney, legal transaction (as opposed to a statutory rule) authorising someone to act as an agent
Vollstreckung	execution (of a judgement)
Vollstreckungsbescheid	default judgement in summary proceedings on a liquidated claim
Vollstreckungsgegenklage	action to oppose execution of a judgement
Vollstreckungsgericht	the *Amtsgericht* in its capacity as the court for the execution of civil judgements
Vollstreckungstitel	a general term for any instrument entitling a creditor to execution against his debtor

Vollzugspolizei	ordinary uniformed police forces, also called *Schutzpolizei*
Voraus, Recht auf den	right of the surviving spouse to take household goods and wedding presents before the deceased's estate is divided up between the beneficiaries
Vormundschaft	guardianship, parental authority and responsibility
Vormundschaftsgericht	Guardianship Court, the court in its capacity as upper guardian of a minor
Vorsatz	intent
■ direkter Vorsatz	direct intent, perpetrator sees the criminal consequence as an inevitable result of his acts
■ Absicht	direct intent where the perpetrator is motivated by the desire to cause the criminal consequence
■ bedingter Vorsatz	contingent intent, perpetrator regrets the criminal consequence but takes it nevertheless into the bargain
Vorstand	the executive board of directors of an *Aktiengesellschaft* company. See also *Aufsichtsrat*
Vorzugsweise Befriedigung	preferential satisfaction of secured creditors
V-Leute	informants
Wahlfälschung	electoral fraud
Wahlfeststellung	if it is certain that the accused has committed one or the other of two crimes but it cannot be established which, then the accused can be convicted of the lesser of the two crimes
Wahlkreis	constituency
Wahndelikt	an imaginary crime
Wandelung	the undoing of a transaction. This is a remedy open to the buyer if the goods prove to be defective (not of merchantable quality). The buyer may then rescind the contract and claim restitution. Compare the aedilitian actio redhibitoria of Roman law. See also *Minderung*
Warenzeichen	trade mark
Wasserhaushaltsgesetz (WHG)	Water Resources Act
Wasserpolizei	water police
Wechsel	bill of exchange (*gezogener Wechsel* or *Tratte*) or promissory note (*Eigenwechsel*)
Wechselgesetz (WG)	Bills of Exchange Act
Wechselprozess	a special, summary procedure for claims based on bills of exchange
Wegerecht	right of way
Wegfall der Geschäftsgrundlage	radical change in circumstances, frustration of a contract. This is derived from § 242 BGB in German law.
Weimarer Reichsverfassung (WRV)	Weimar Constitution – the republican democratic constitution of 1919
Weisung	direction
Werklieferungsvertrag	contract for the supply of goods and services
Werkvertrag	contract to perform some specific task. Contrast *Dienstvertrag*.
Weltrechtsprinzip	principle that certain crimes, such as genocide or slave trading, are punishable under German law irrespective of where they were committed

Wertentscheidende Grundsatznorm	norms containing a fundamental value principle which determine the basic values upon which a system is based
Wertpapier	negotiable instrument, securities or other instruments of value
Wesensgehalt	essential content
Westdeutscher Rundfunk (WDR)	Western Channel
Wettbewerb	competition
■ unlauterer Wettbewerb	unfair competition
Wettbewerbsbeschränkungen	restrictive trade practices
Wettbewerbsrecht	competition law
Widerspruch	objection, remedy in administrative proceedings
Widerspruchsbehörde	authority which rules on objections
Widerspruchsbescheid	final decision of the public authority on the objection
Widerspruchsverfahren	objection procedure, obligatory in order to bring an *Anfechtungsklage* or *Verpflichtungsklage*
Widmung	dedication, the allocation of public property for a particular purpose
Willenserklärung	declaration of will (with legal consequences)
■ empfangsbedürftig	a declaration of will of a sort which only takes effect once delivered to the addressee
■ nicht empfangsbedürftig	a declaration of will of a sort which takes effect as soon as the will to make the declaration is manifested, i.e., without delivery to another person.
Wirtschaftsprüferkammer	Association of Accountants
Wirtschaftsrecht	business law
Wohngeld	accomodation payments
Wohnungseigentumsgesetz (WoEigG)	Condominium Act, which provides for co-ownership of the land on which a building stands while allowing separate freehold ownership of each of the residential units in the building
Wucher	unconscionable bargain, overlapping with ideas such as usury, economic duress, exploitation of undue influence, undue exploitation of inequality of bargaining power
Zahlungsunfähigkeit	insolvency, ongoing inability to pay one's debts as they fall due. See also *Überschuldung*
Zerrüttungsprinzip	the principle that divorce is granted on the basis of irretrievable breakdown
Zivilprozessordnung (ZPO)	Civil Procedure Act
Zuchtmittel	disciplinary measures
Zugewinngemeinschaft	the standard matrimonial property regime which applies if the parties do not agree otherwise. It provides for a system whereby property which accrues during the marriage is essentially to be shared equally between the parties on dissolution of the marriage
Zulässigkeitsvoraussetzung	prerequisite for admissability
Zuständigkeit, sachliche	the issue of jurisdiction with respect to the subject matter and the amount of the claim
Zustandsverantwortlichkeit	responsibility to the police which arises from a state of affairs

Zustellung (eines Urteils)	official delivery of a copy of the judgement to the parties by mail. Once this has taken place the parties have one month to lodge an appeal
Zwangsgeld	fine for contempt of court aimed at compelling compliance with a judgement
Zwangshaft	imprisonment for contempt of court
Zwangsversteigerungsgesetz (ZVG)	Act on Sales in Execution of Judgement
Zwangsvollstreckung	execution of judgement against an uncooperative debtor
Zwecklehre	purposive approach, emphasises various different purposes of imposing penalties
Zweckmäßig	appropriate
Zweckveranlasser	person liable to the police, when he or she deliberately set in motion an earlier, initially neutral, causal event which then led others to behave in a certain dangerous manner
Zweites Deutsches Fernsehen (ZDF)	„Channel Two Germany"
Zwischenverfahren	interim proceedings

Index

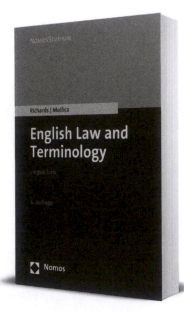